BY PETER VIERTEL

DANGEROUS FRIENDS

N.L. Terteling Library

THE COLLEGE
of IDAHO

At Large
with Hemingway
and Huston
in the Fifties

PETER VIERTEL

Dangerous

Friends

NAN A. TALESE

DOUBLEDAY

New York   London   Toronto   Sydney   Auckland

Published by Nan A. Talese, an imprint of Doubleday,
a division of Bantam Doubleday Dell Publishing Group, Inc.
666 Fifth Avenue, New York, New York 10103

DOUBLEDAY and the portrayal of an anchor with a dolphin
are trademarks of Doubleday,
a division of Bantam Doubleday Dell Publishing Group, Inc.

Unless otherwise credited, all photographs
are from the author's collection.

Library of Congress Cataloging-in-Publication Data

Viertel, Peter.
Dangerous friends : at large with Huston and Hemingway in the fifties/Peter Viertel.
—1st ed.
     p.   cm.
Includes index.
1. Viertel, Peter—Friends and associates. 2. Hemingway, Ernest, 1899–1961—Friends
and associates. 3. Huston, John, 1906–1991—Friends and associates. 4. Novelists,
American—20th century—Biography. 5. Motion picture producers and directors—
United States—Biography. I. Title.
PS3543.I326Z467   1992
813'.52—dc20   92-6960
[B]
CIP

ISBN 0-385-26046-6
Copyright © 1992 by Peter Viertel
All rights reserved
Printed in the United States of America
August 1992
First Edition

10   9   8   7   6   5   4   3   2   1

To Nan,
with unlimited admiration

And to Irving,
the most dangerous friend of all

The job of a writer is to betray . . .
　　　　　　　—GRAHAM GREENE

Part One

AT FIRST GLANCE the main street of Ketchum looked like an abandoned movie set for a western. Its one short block consisted of a row of flat-roofed buildings fronting on a rickety wooden sidewalk. Beyond their rooftops the view of the Sawtooth Mountains was almost equally unimpressive. "They're hills, not mountains," Jigee, my wife, said in a low voice so as not to be overheard by the driver of the taxi we had hired at the train station in Shoshone that morning in early January 1948.

But the man had sharp ears. "They're mountains all right," he said, ever loyal to his native Idaho. "Wait until you kids start sliding down them."

We were hardly kids anymore. I had just turned twenty-seven, and Jigee was five years my senior, although she looked younger than I did with her gleaming brown hair worn shoulder length and her pretty, heart-shaped face favored by a smooth skin which required little rouge or powder. My own closely cropped hair was already sprinkled with gray, a subtle warning of what might lie ahead. To the casual observer we probably did appear young and untroubled, although we had been through a great deal together in the last six years: the war and its anxieties of long separations, as well as the death of our first child, stillborn, less than a year ago. We were finally starting out on our first vacation since my transfer to the inactive reserve of the U.S. Marine Corps on the 15th of December 1945, a date not easily forgotten.

During the forty-five-minute drive through the flat Idaho countryside we had exchanged worried glances, alarmed by the sparse covering of snow on the stubble fields that lined the road, and now that we had arrived at our destination we were even more dubious about our choice of Sun Valley as a winter resort so early in the season. We had become fanatic skiers the previous year in Switzerland, where I had gone to write a screenplay for a Swiss movie producer of Polish origins, my services having been recommended by director Fred Zinnemann, whom I had known since early boyhood. Lazar Wechsler was the producer's name, and he had turned out to be somewhat less of a despot than his Hollywood counterparts, only at a lower pay scale.

It was 1946 then and Wechsler had met us at the airport; during the drive into Zurich he had informed us that he had reserved rooms for Jigee and myself in Davos-Dorf, a mountain village where he had decided I should work. The temptations of the big city were too dangerous for a young man, he had announced, and would impede my progress on the story I was to write, a surprising declaration, as Zurich in those days was known to be a town that rolled up the sidewalks at nine o'clock in the evening. Somewhat intimidated by his autocratic manner, I agreed to his plan, only to discover that being dispatched to Davos in November was akin to being sent to Siberia. The weather was cold and unfriendly, and a large number of the other foreign residents were there to recover from tuberculosis, a disease that was prevalent in Central Europe after the war.

But after we had spent four long weeks in a freezing rooming house, the first snow had fallen, and Jigee and I had decided that as we were being detained in the mountains against our will, we might as well learn to ski. We both learned to master the stem-Christiana, the basic maneuver of the sport to which we had soon become addicted and which was responsible for our presence in Ketchum, Idaho, twelve months later.

Now having shown us all there was to see of the town, our driver and guide made a U-turn and took us to the motel called MacDonald's Cabins where we had made our reservations. A friendly room clerk asked us to sign the register in the office of this rustic establishment, and once the formalities had been completed, our taxi driver helped us deposit our skis and luggage inside our cabin. Joining us in the relative warmth of the cabin's living room, he explained that a yellow bus made a stop every twenty minutes at the street corner less than fifty yards from the motel. It would take us free of charge to Mount Baldy, the main skiing area, or on to Dollar Mountain if we were beginners.

It was a clear, cold day, and the recently lit electric stove standing in the unused fireplace made the temperature indoors barely livable. Jigee declared that she would put on her parka and ski pants to unpack and, once she had become acclimatized, might venture out of doors. I was much too eager to try out my recently acquired Swiss technique, and after unpacking my one suitcase I set off alone to the corner bus stop. The yellow bus arrived on schedule, and I was borne away in solitary splendor to the bottom of the main chair lift, which turned out to be only a five-minute ride away.

With hindsight I have come to realize that the only small profit a writer can derive from the sport of downhill skiing is that it occasionally provides him or her with time to reflect while being transported up the mountain. So while taking in the scenery that December day, I found myself reviewing my more recent past. Only a week earlier I had been in Manhattan as a guest in the Central Park South apartment of Arlene Francis, the wife of Martin Gabel, the director and producer of a play I had written in collaboration with my closest friend, Irwin Shaw. The purpose of the small gathering after the opening of *The Survivors* was to await the reviews that would be transmitted to us by telephone from the city rooms of the principal New York morning newspapers.

Neither Irwin nor I had expected the notices to be very good, for despite an all-star cast, our play had not really come to life on the stage of the 48th Street Playhouse. Amazingly enough, Brooks Atkinson's article in the *New York Times* was an unqualified rave, and for a moment we thought our play might survive. But after a brief moment of euphoria, the remaining reviews all turned out to be bad, and our producers predicted with long faces that we would be forced to close in a very few days, as a serious play would not be able to withstand the unified assault of the gentlemen of the press. Woolcott Gibbs, writing for *The New Yorker*, had cast the only other positive vote, but coming as it did at the end of the week, it was cold comfort.

Yet all in all, it had been an honorable defeat. Financially the damage had been negligible, as Irwin and I had made a preproduction deal with a movie company, the down payment of which Irwin had turned over to me, for it had been at his insistence that we had shaped my original idea into a play instead of a movie script, for which we had had a much larger offer. Irwin had always held that the only reason a writer should work as a salaried employee in Hollywood was to make enough money to do his own work, and his intention had been to liberate me from the profession to which I had turned early in life to support myself and help my family after the two novels I had published in 1940 and 1947 had not met with any kind of popular success. Irwin was already an accomplished short-story writer at the time, and his work in that field limited his need to hire out as a screenwriter.

5

His love affair with the theater came to an abrupt halt that evening. He had already written half a dozen plays, and two of them, *Bury the Dead* and *The Gentle People*, had been mildly successful. But he had taken enough punishment, he declared, and would henceforth try his hand at writing novels. "For you, Pete," he said, "this is merely a baptism of fire, the first wounding. It doesn't hurt you quite as much as it hurts me."

There was a good deal of truth in this friendly midnight declaration. For a young screenwriter to have had a play produced on Broadway at all was an accomplishment. Obviously I would have preferred our play to run, but I was far from devastated because it had failed. Even a week before the threatening clouds of disaster had begun to gather over 48th Street I had written to the motel in Ketchum to make our reservations. After two months in the city Jigee and I were longing to get away; we had had enough of living in a hotel and eating in restaurants, not to mention the tedious hours spent seated in a cold, empty theater during rehearsals, made all the more tedious as Irwin and I seemed to be incapable of any helpful intervention in the labors of our director, who to complicate matters was an old friend of the Shaws.

I had escaped in the nick of time, I realized, and even if the snow was sparse and the mountains less majestic than the Alps, I was delighted to be there. Furthermore, my first descent through the woods of Mount Baldy had proved to be quite satisfactory and taxing enough for my skill. Carried away by enthusiasm, however, on my last run down into the valley I tripped over a hidden rock and crashed in a heap of skis and poles. As a result an undeniable stiffness set in once I was safely seated in the yellow bus again and on my way home.

My injury made walking the last fifty yards in ski boots even more difficult, and as I arrived nearer our cabin I saw that a muddy Buick convertible was parked in front of our neighbors' front door. A broad-shouldered man in a plaid hunting shirt and a sheepskin vest was unloading the trunk of the Buick. On his head he wore a knitted khaki cap, the kind that was issued to U.S. Army personnel during the war. He turned, and I saw that he had been examining the open breech of a twelve-gauge shotgun. As he slipped the weapon back into its leather case, I recognized him to be Ernest Hemingway, the writer I had hero-worshipped in my early youth.

. . . .

6

WHILE IN NEW YORK I had heard from Robert Capa, the famous war photographer, that Hemingway often went bird shooting in Idaho during the fall, but Capa had added that it was unlikely "the old bastard" would still be "hanging around Sun Valley" that late in the season. It was Bob who had recommended we stay at MacDonald's Cabins, and in spite of his disrespectful, vaguely affectionate remarks, I was amazed to see Hemingway so close at hand.

By the time I was sixteen years old I had read every published word Hemingway had written, including *The Torrents of Spring*, which I had taken at face value with no notion that it was meant to be a parody of Sherwood Anderson. His writing had made a lasting impression on me and had influenced me not only to want to be a writer, but to yearn for a life of adventure, including going to war.

I stepped inside the front door of our cabin and deposited my skis. Then I crossed to one of the living room windows. Hemingway was still busy rearranging the gear in the back of his car, and I recalled the first time I had seen him—it was almost ten years ago—when he had addressed a large meeting in the Shrine Auditorium in Los Angeles gathered to raise funds to buy ambulances for the armies of Republican Spain. André Malraux spoke at the same rally, but for me Hemingway had been the star of the evening. Malraux, who had addressed a smaller, select group of Hollywood notables at my parents' house a few evenings earlier, made the same kind of impassioned political speech to his larger audience, ending with a closed-fist salute that shocked most of the listeners, the minority of whom belonged to the far left.

Then Joris Ivens had shown his film *The Spanish Earth*, for which Hemingway had written the narration, and once the documentary with the author's factual voice on the sound track had ended, Hemingway was called to the stage. He had been seated only a few rows behind us during the showing of the movie, and before he got to his feet I noticed that he took a long drink from a bottle in a brown paper bag, which he slipped into the side pocket of his tweed jacket as he made his way to the rostrum. In contrast to Malraux's long harangue, given in French and translated by Haakon Chevalier, Hemingway's speech was brief and rendered in an almost sarcastic tone. The Spanish people will go on fighting and dying whether you support them with your money or not, he stated bluntly without making any reference to politics. And the response of the audience was overwhelming once they recovered from the shock of his direct message.

7

Now as I watched him I was surprised to see how much he had changed in the interim. His hair, partially hidden by the GI cap, had turned gray, and he looked thicker around the waist. I called Jigee over to the window. It would never have occurred to either of us to go out and speak to our famous neighbor, although we could easily have mentioned that we were friends of Capa and that he had urged us to say hello in case we did happen to "bump into Papa." But I had learned early in life to respect the privacy of literary celebrities, having met quite a few at my mother's house in years past.

I went into the bedroom to rest my back and Jigee put on her boots to go to the local market to shop for dinner. She returned half an hour later, flushed and excited. Hemingway had stopped her on her way out and had introduced himself. She had told him that I had had a bad fall, and he had been both friendly and sympathetic. It was a shame that there wasn't much snow, he had told her. He could no longer ski because of the various injuries he had collected in the war and was about to return to Cuba, as the partridge and duck hunting season in Idaho had ended.

A few minutes later there was a knock on our door, and there Hemingway stood. He mumbled that he had found a can of "lion fat" in the kit he always traveled with and offered to rub some of it on my back, as it was a most effective cure for muscular aches and pains, one frequently used by the Masai tribe of Kenya. I jumped to my feet, cured almost instantly, and we shook hands. My injury was not a serious one, I told him, no more than a temporary stiffness. Well, would I like to join him in a walk? he asked; if I dressed warmly the mild exercise would be beneficial. Then after I had taken a warm bath he would give me the promised massage.

I agreed, although I had no desire to have lion fat rubbed on my back. I put on a woolen cap and parka and followed him outside. Jigee elected to stay behind to prepare dinner. Despite the subzero temperature, Hemingway wore only the hunting shirt and sheepskin vest. His rather prominent stomach bulged over the waist of his khaki trousers, which were held in place by a Wehrmacht belt with the familiar *"Gott Mit Uns"* buckle. When I commented on the belt he explained somewhat sheepishly that it was "a prize of war," a souvenir of the fighting in the Hurtgen Forest. We stopped off at his cabin to collect his dog, a black mongrel that he said had adopted him. It was one of the strays that hung around Ketchum, he added, fastening an old piece of string to the dog's collar before we started off in the direction of the town.

We passed the first saloon, and Hemingway declared that it would be a good idea for us to have a drink but that he preferred to go on to a better place, as this first bar was frequented by members of the local branch of the American Legion, an organization he didn't particularly admire. A small boy was standing on the wooden sidewalk watching us. "What's your dog's name?" he called out to us.

"Blackie," Hemingway replied.

"And what's your name?"

"Ernie," Hemingway called out over his shoulder. "It's a name I never much cared for," he said to me. "Earnest," he muttered disparagingly and shook his head.

"What do you want me to call you?" I asked him.

"Papa," he said. "Okay if I call you Pete?"

"Everybody else does," I told him.

He chuckled. "Your back any better, Pete?" he asked.

I assured him that it was. We continued on and then turned off the main road until we arrived at an establishment called the Tram. "This joint is where all the Basque sheepherders go," Papa explained. After asking politely if he could bring his dog inside, he led me to the far end of the crowded bar. Hemingway ordered a tequila, complete with a mound of salt and a slice of lime, and I asked for a Coca-Cola.

"You don't drink, Pete?" he asked, sounding surprised.

"Not much," I admitted. "Not out of any conviction. I just don't like the taste."

"Alcohol's our worst enemy and our best friend," he said with a self-mocking laugh. "*Salud!*" He tossed off the thimble of tequila, licked the salt he had sprinkled on the back of his massive fist, and chewed the slice of lime. "Before I forget," he added, "would you guys like to join us for an early dinner at the Lodge tomorrow night. It's an all right place to go before the season starts. Pick us up at our joint and we'll go from there." He paid for our drinks, pulled the dog to his feet with a gentle tug on the makeshift leash, and we continued our walk in the gathering darkness.

THERE WERE PILES of books and discarded newspapers on the floor of the living room of the Hemingways' cabin, and an old phonograph on a corner table was playing a Marlene Dietrich record when Jigee and I arrived the next evening. Papa was sitting in an armchair listening intently to the husky voice of the singer. He rose as we entered and introduced us to a slight young man my own age who had blond hair and seemed to be the guardian of the victrola. *"Johnny . . . wenn Du Geburtstag hast . . . bleib ich bei Dir zu Gast . . . die ganze Nacht!"* The sentimental old German song sounded strangely out of place in the dark room, with the old hunter and his somewhat effeminate guest, as enthralled as if they were seated in a prewar Berlin nightclub.

Dietrich had often come to my parents' house in Santa Monica Canyon during the thirties, and I was surprised to learn she was a close friend of Papa's, as to me she was part of another world. My mother had been friendly with her, and both she and my father admired Dietrich's early anti-Nazi stand, although my mother thought her something of a *poseuse*, playing Mother Earth off the screen. I said nothing about having met Marlene, and we all listened politely to the other side of the record the young man insisted on playing.

Then Mary Hemingway appeared. Slight, with closely cropped blond hair, she was friendly and offered us drinks. Once we began talking, I noticed that she had a tendency to compete with her husband, correct his account of the day's shooting, and interrupt his stories about their life in Cuba. Mary had apparently not adjusted to living in the shadow of a great man, although Papa treated her affectionately and seemed to disregard her competitive efforts as a storyteller.

Soon the young man gathered up his collection of Dietrich records and departed. Mary slipped on her mink coat, a recent acquisition, she explained, that she would not be wearing in Cuba, and the four of us got into the Buick and drove to the Sun Valley Lodge. Gary Cooper and his wife would be joining us for dinner, Papa said; sitting beside me in the back of the car, Jigee turned to me and made a face. Cooper was reputed to be a reactionary, the son of a right-wing Montana judge whose political views the actor had inherited. Papa, who was driving, must have seen her face in the rearview mirror, for he said: "Coop's an all right guy and a fine shot with a rifle."

Along with his handsome wife, Rocky, Cooper was waiting for us in the bar of the Lodge, and he was indeed both friendly and charming, and clearly a good friend of Papa's. I sensed a certain reserve in his wife in regard to Hemingway and on the way home Papa remarked rather sardonically that Rocky was trying to convert "Coop" to Catholicism. That way Coop could have "all that money *and* God."

Jigee made some reference to Cooper's politics, to which Hemingway replied that most of his friends, on both the left and the right, disagreed with him. He mentioned Milt Wolfe, who had fought with the International Brigades in Spain and was having trouble making a living. Wolfe had attacked *For Whom the Bell Tolls* when it was published, but Hemingway had nevertheless sent him a check for ten thousand dollars to help him out. Wolfe had wired back his thanks, adding that in his opinion it was still a lousy book, which seemed to amuse Papa greatly. He also mentioned Eddie Rolfe, the poet, another friend who had served in Spain and who did not agree with Papa's politics. I told him that I had met Rolfe, as he had often been present at my mother's Sunday tea parties.

"Eddie's one of the kindest, sweetest guys in the world," Papa declared. "Never met your mother, Pete, but by all accounts she's quite a woman." By that time we had arrived back at the motel for a nightcap, a last glass of red wine for Papa and Mary and a couple of Cokes for Jigee and me.

Mary mentioned that my mother was known to host "a literary salon" out on the Coast. It wasn't really a "salon," I replied. She liked to cook for the people she admired and gave tea parties on Sundays, and that was about all there was to it. Papa said that he preferred "a saloon to a salon," a veiled rebuke to Mary. His good mood seemed to have left him. He asked me about my recent collaborator, Shaw, and I told him that our friendship had survived despite the failure of the play. Hemingway said that he had had a bad experience in the theater, too, "with a character called Jed Harris." I remarked that I had met Harris in California, and Papa growled that I seemed to "have met just about everybody out there."

I said: "Well, I've lived there most of my life."

He apologized, said he wasn't being sarcastic. Irwin was a damn good short-story writer, he admitted grudgingly; they had met in London during the blitz. Mary interrupted to say that she "adored Shaw" and that if I saw him again to be sure to give him a big kiss, a remark which did nothing to improve Papa's mood. He recalled that Shaw had been a member of George Stevens's photographic unit, and they had run into each other again in Normandy. "Walking into their encampment was a lot like reading Proust," he muttered, "the part where he describes all of the fairies."

"Shaw's no fairy," Mary chirped, to her husband's greater annoyance.

"My brother Leicester was in that outfit," Hemingway said. "Also a character I met named Ivan Moffat."

"He's not a fairy either," I said. Hemingway's attitude toward homosexuals surprised me, all the more so as he had been noticeably kind to the blond young man who had brought the Marlene Dietrich records earlier that evening.

"How much of the war did you see?" Papa asked me, his eyes narrowing.

I told him that I'd been a Marine and had served a year in the South Pacific as an enlisted man, then in Europe as a second lieutenant in the O.S.S. I had been fortunate, I added, and had missed the worst part of the fighting in both theaters. "Shot at and missed, shit on and hit all over," I added, shamelessly repeating one of the Corps' saltier sayings.

Papa laughed. His son Bumby had served with the O.S.S. in France, he said, had parachuted into the Vosges mountains with a fly-rod on some sort of crazy mission. I explained that I had been in the same unit but had arrived in Saverne a month or so after Bumby had been captured while trying to infiltrate an agent through the German lines and that I had done the same kind of work as his son. This provoked a somewhat rambling account of how he, Papa, had tried to avenge Bumby, believing the Germans had shot him for spying. As it turned out Bumby had been well treated by his captors, had been sent to a hospital to have the wound he had received looked after, and had ultimately escaped from the prisoner-of-war camp in which he was interned. I had heard the story, I told Hemingway, and knew that Bumby had been recaptured after his escape, which had occurred when Patton attempted to liberate the POW camp where his own son-in-law was being held, a reckless and shameful operation that had gone wrong.

"Well, at least you know what it was like to serve in a line outfit," Papa said. "I envy you that."

Jigee and Mary commented that it was too late for all the reminiscing about "foxhole time," and we thanked our hosts for dinner and returned to our cabin. Hemingway was friendly and paternal again as the evening ended. He warned us to look out for the rocks on Mount Baldy, and bade us good night.

Jigee and I had both felt the tension of being in Hemingway's presence. There seemed to be an element of testing in his remarks and questions. It was obvious that he lived in a special world of his own. His language was limited to a telegraphic style that dispensed with the rules of grammar and sounded like an affectation until you got used to it. His sudden change of mood was disquieting. "Miss Mary," as he referred to his wife, didn't help matters when she corrected his memory, although she invariably addressed him as "Lamb," an odd noun for her to choose. To us he appeared to be more like an aging lion, although there *was* something gentle about him, too: his shyness, his hesitant speech, the apologies that nearly always followed one of his sarcastic, or even slightly disagreeable, comments. All of that made him so different from the myth that surrounded him. His self-inflicted nickname was disturbing, too: he insisted we call him Papa, although the hated adjective *earnest* described his manner best.

HE WAS STANDING outside the front door of his cabin the following morning as we set out on our short hike to the bus stop. "Come by after skiing," he called out, and I felt flattered to be invited again so soon. "We don't have to go if you don't want to," I told Jigee.

"I know I don't have to," she replied, somewhat testily. "But I enjoy listening to him." Before we were married we had often argued about Hemingway, for Jigee objected to the various attitudes his person and his writings represented. She was a feminist, and Papa's alleged statement that "women had their brains between their thighs" had outraged her. But now he had charmed her and treated her quite differently than he treated Rocky Cooper or even Mary. He seemed a little in awe of her, probably because she was very pretty and intelligent to boot. He also must have realized that she would never flatter him or treat him with anything approaching fawning reverence.

Jigee had been married to Budd Schulberg before the war and had belonged to the group of young leftists of which Budd was a prominent member. After the Russo-German nonaggression treaty and during the early months of World War II, the Communist party line had condemned the Allied cause as being imperialist, had even accused the British and French leaders of being no different than Hitler and Mussolini, a doctrine Jigee had defended for quite a while, causing innumerable bitter arguments to erupt between us. Like Milt Wolfe and many of the other "fellow travelers," Jigee had considered Hemingway a traitor to the cause of Republican Spain. But in the years that followed she had altered her opinions, and once we were married she had left her political group, although she had maintained her friendship with many of the writers who belonged to the extreme left, such as Dalton Trumbo and Ring Lardner.

Our four-year-old marriage had survived the long separations that the war years had imposed, although not without mutual infidelities that we had both ultimately owned up to, rather foolishly I think now. Having been alone together for the first time during the brief run of my play in New York (we had had to live with my mother after my discharge from the service two years earlier, and then Jigee's mother had come to stay when we built our small house north of Malibu), we were now a lot happier together than we had been at any time during the last two years. Jigee was a good skier and, in spite of her dislike of the Idaho cold, she began to enjoy her initial encounter with the slopes of Mount Baldy.

Many of the ski teachers were Austrians, and we soon discovered that they enforced a rather Teutonic discipline not only on their classes but on other skiers using the same trails. Jigee was outraged by the rude reprimands of one of the red-jacketed guides, and when we later joined the Hemingways in their living room she complained to Papa about being shouted at in guttural English.

Hemingway agreed with her about the lack of manners shown by some of the guides. He had had a run-in with one of them in a bar only recently, a man named Sepp Froelich, who had taunted him about having given up skiing, insinuating that Papa had lost his nerve. Hemingway described how he had taken Froelich aside and had threatened to cut out his liver with his hunting knife, and I became aware that he was capable of sudden, extreme rages that reminded me of my father's quick temper.

Mary was obviously embarrassed by the anecdote and made reference to her husband's high blood pressure, which did little to calm Papa's anger. He went on to talk about the recent visit of Lillian Ross, the *New Yorker* writer who had come to Idaho to interview him, another event that had disturbed him lately. She was a bright young woman, he said once he had calmed down, and probably a good journalist, although he didn't trust her entirely. People always arrived from the outside world to try and disrupt his life, which was one of the reasons he liked Jigee and me: we didn't ask him a lot of damn fool questions about his work.

The momentary tension was dispelled by the arrival of two of Hemingway's hunting companions, Chuck Atkinson, a local businessman, and Bud Purdy, a rancher who owned some of the land where the Hemingways had gone to shoot ducks that day. Purdy, a tall young man who looked as if he might have Indian blood, owned and piloted a small aircraft which he usually used for reconnaissance, he told me, to locate the ducks on Picabo creek, a small stream that meandered through the fields of his ranch. Once he had spotted the ducks, the shooters would set out in canoes, to drift with the current through the reeds lining the creek. Ten birds were the legal limit, and because of the efficiency of their methods, the party soon had the allotted amount.

Papa enjoyed the military aspect of the operation, of which he was always in command, Purdy told me, as the war still seemed to haunt his memory. He had enjoyed certain aspects of soldiering because, I realized, he had never had to put up with the boredom and restrictions of being an enlisted man. I didn't miss the war, I told Purdy, was grateful that I had survived, and, if anything, was still haunted by the memory of the friends I had made in the Marine Corps who had not been as fortunate.

Papa overheard part of our conversation, and when Atkinson and Purdy had departed he brought up the subject of his son's capture again. He described in detail how he had sought vengeance against the "Krauts" during the fighting in the Hurtgen Forest and had even shot a German soldier at close range, only to discover that he had killed an eighteen-year-old boy, a realization that had filled him with guilt. The anecdote sounded slightly like an invention to me, mainly because I had heard an identical story from a Marine comrade on Guadalcanal. That it was vitally important to him to insinuate that he had been courageous in battle was obvious and somewhat disquieting, and there was an embarrassed silence after he concluded the anecdote. I told him that I hadn't killed anyone during the war, except maybe by proxy; I had even found that I didn't hate the Germans once I was at the front, although I had every reason to. The Nazis had killed my uncle in Poland; they had forced him to dig his own grave and then had shot him after somebody from his village had denounced his presence there.

"What was your uncle doing in Poland?" Hemingway asked.

I explained that my mother's family came from the part of the Ukraine that had belonged to the Austro-Hungarian Empire and that they had stayed on in Sambor after the Treaty of Versailles. Then in 1939 the Russians had marched into that part of Poland but had been driven out by the Germans in 1941 when Hitler attacked the Soviet Union. My grandmother had been evacuated to Moscow, but my uncle, her youngest son, had returned to Sambor to rescue the child he had had with one of the maids in my grandfather's household. His concern for her had cost him his life.

Hemingway listened with interest, but Mary declared that she had had enough of all the talk of killing and war. It was still light, and Papa suggested we take another walk before dinner; he and Black Dog were in need of some fresh air. Once we were out in the street, and alone, he brought up Lillian Ross's visit again. Apparently he had been brooding about some of the things he had said during her long interview of him. His tone was curiously self-mocking as he repeated fragments of their conversation. He had told her that he had taken on "Mr. Turgenev" and "Mr. de Maupassant" and had beaten them both, a declaration that I assumed was made to be taken humorously but that looked embarrassing in print when Ross's article appeared, quoted literally without a sufficient explanation of Hemingway's habit of making fun of himself. He went on to say that Miss Ross "was a shrewd lady" but that he didn't quite trust her.

At the risk of provoking his displeasure, I quoted Goethe's well-known statement *"Dichter, rede nicht"*—"Poet, don't talk"—and Hemingway nodded. "Yeah, but did Goethe take his own advice?" he asked.

When we stopped at the Tram for a drink, Hemingway's "black-ass mood," as he described it, vanished, and he started to reminisce about his early days. He recalled a visit he had made to the Midwest after the publication of *A Farewell to Arms* and described how he had walked across a plowed field to meet up with his Uncle Ned, who was a farmer, and how he had found him seated on his tractor at the end of a row. "I'm Ed's son, Ernie," he announced, to explain his presence. "Oh, sure, I know," Uncle Ned had replied, *"All Quiet on the Western Front!"*

Papa chuckled to himself and ordered another tequila. The anecdote, self-deprecating as it was, canceled out my momentary disillusion.

IT SNOWED THAT NIGHT, and in the morning, as we stood in our adjoining doorways surveying the transformed countryside, Papa announced his departure. It was time for him and Mary to return to Cuba; he had to get back to work. He asked me what my plans were, and I told him Jigee and I would stay on for another ten days and then would return to California, where I would have to look for a movie job, as the family finances needed replenishing.

He voiced his hesitant disapproval. Working in the "industry," as he always referred to the motion picture business, was harmful for a writer. It was all right for the "whores" like Ben Hecht, who had sold out his talent long ago, but for anyone with an ounce of integrity it was a dangerous thing to do. He had a few pals "out there on the Coast"—Mark Hellinger, who had died recently, and Coop of course, and Dietrich and Ingrid Bergman, but he had visited California only once and that had been quite enough for him. Faulkner had worked out there as a scriptwriter, as had John O'Hara and Aldous Huxley, but they had all wasted their time for small rewards, he said.

I explained that I had come out of the service with no cash and had needed to earn enough money to take care of Jigee as well as help my mother, so I had been obliged to find work as a screenwriter. It was a profession I had more or less fallen into at the age of eighteen and I felt fortunate to be able to take it up again now. Papa listened sympathetically. He urged me to cut down on my living expenses and not to go on "whoring" for too long.

That afternoon I helped stow the Hemingways' luggage and hunting gear in the Buick, and the following morning they got off to a late start. Papa was quite cheerful at the moment of departure, although somewhat apprehensive about the long automobile journey. They had had a traumatic experience on a previous trip, during which Mary had had a miscarriage in a motel in Casper, Wyoming, and had nearly died, an incident that he referred to only briefly, reaching out to touch the wooden front door of his cabin, evidence of his superstition.

Then once their car had disappeared down the road to Hailey in a mild snowstorm, Jigee and I talked about how often Hemingway, from his own accounts, had been involved in near-tragic accidents. "Miss Slim," which was how he referred to Howard Hawks's current wife, had almost shot him while hunting in Idaho the previous year. He had also been involved in several serious automobile accidents, to say nothing of all the near misses he had survived in World War II. Was he inclined to dramatize his brushes with death, we wondered, or was he accident-prone? He seemed even then to be constantly aware of the possibility of his own death, mentioned it repeatedly even though he was not yet fifty years old.

Before climbing into his heavily loaded car he had given me a bear hug and had mumbled: "Let's keep in touch, Pete," words I did not take too seriously at the time.

· · · ·

17

JIGEE AND I RETURNED to California, to the small board-and-batten house we had built in an unspoiled canyon eight miles north of Malibu with the help of a plumber, a carpenter, and the willing, unskilled weekend assistance of many friends. Jigee collected her eight-year-old daughter, Vicky, who had been living with my mother while we were in New York and Sun Valley, and I started looking for a job. We had bought the nine-acre plot on which our house stood in partnership with Kathy and Robert Parrish, a young film editor I had befriended during my very brief tour of duty in John Ford's photographic unit that for some mysterious reason was a part of the O.S.S.

The Parrishes had hoped to build a house of their own on the upper half of the land, but as Bob's profession required he live nearer the studios, they had decided that building a duplex in San Fernando Valley was a more practical solution for their needs. Bob had grown up in the movie business, had been a child actor and then an extra, which was how he had met Jigee. We often lunched together at Musso Frank's restaurant on Hollywood Boulevard along with Mike Luciano, another film editor who had put in some time with the Ford unit.

Both Luciano and Parrish were dedicated filmmakers, as they would be called today, and our lunches were usually spent discussing movies, good or bad, that had already been made or material—books and short stories—that might yet be used. The cynicism Hemingway had assumed was ever-present in the "industry" was a germ we had not been infected with, but I knew it would have been difficult to convince Papa that the same seriousness of purpose often went into screenwriting as into novel writing. Unfortunately the final product was always beyond the screenwriter's control, but that hardly justified calling all screenwriters "whores."

Life at my mother's house had changed considerably since the war, I noticed after my stay in New York and Sun Valley. Greta Garbo's early retirement from moviemaking had, strangely enough, severely affected my mother's career and lifestyle. Since acting together in the German version of *Anna Christie*—in which my mother played the role Marie Dressler had created in the American film—she and Greta had shared a friendship that spanned nearly two decades. And it was Garbo, after meeting my mother at a Beverly Hills dinner party given by Ernst Lubitsch in 1930, who had suggested my mother try her hand at writing. More than half a dozen produced screenplays were to result from this suggestion and sponsorship, most of them "Garbo pictures" and most of them successful if not entirely satisfactory in my mother's eyes. Garbo's last film, *The Two Faced Woman*, was the only failure, and it decided Greta to withdraw from the Hollywood arena which she had entered in the early 1920s at age nineteen, certainly not emotionally equipped for the fray.

My mother wrote the script for one more movie in the early sixties, but after it received a mild reception she found it more difficult to get work. The high command of the industry was prone to typecasting actors and actresses and, as it turned out, scriptwriters as well. My mother's old friends remained loyal to her in spite of this change in her fortunes, but the groups at her Sunday tea parties at Mabery Road became noticeably smaller. The European literary contingent, which included Thomas Mann and his wife, Bertolt and Helli Brecht, Bruno and Liesel Frank, and various other intellectuals exiled from Nazi Germany, continued to socialize at my mother's, as did Charlie and Oona Chaplin. Aldous Huxley, too, continued his austere visits, but the movie crowd was less in evidence.

On weekdays Garbo still came by to collect my mother for their habitual walks, but there were seldom any dinner parties. Occasionally my mother would forget her financial problems and invite half a dozen guests for a meal she prepared herself, spending most of the day in the kitchen. All these changes in my mother's lifestyle made me even more aware of our financial problems and the need to find an assignment as quickly as possible.

Then one morning in early 1948 Meta Reis, my agent, called to say that Frank Moss, a producer at Universal Studios, wanted to see me; he was associated, she said, with Mike Todd, who had formed an independent company that was financed by Universal. Moss turned out to be a friendly, heavyset man eager, so he said, to make an unusual film. What he had in mind was a gangster picture, an allegory based on the rise of Hitler and his bullyboys from jail to great power, a screenplay that he felt sure I would be able to write. He had agreed to Meta's terms, and there remained only for me to meet Mike Todd.

This was a mere formality, Moss said, and without further ado I was ushered into Todd's office. He was seated with his feet on his desk, a cigar stuck in his mouth. Without bothering to get to his feet, he accused his partner and me of being "a couple of faggots," as Moss had been exceedingly eloquent in singing my praises. I realized that Todd was trying to be funny, but I bridled at his manner. Later Moss apologized for Todd, but by the time I arrived back at Meta's office in the Berg-Allenberg agency, I was ready to halt the deal in spite of the considerable sum of money I had been offered. Meta agreed, somewhat reluctantly, with my decision. Meanwhile she had had a call from Sam Spiegel and John Huston, who had expressed interest in my working on the first film Huston was to direct for their company, Horizon Pictures. The salary would be considerably less than what Moss had agreed to pay me, but at least I would be working with one of the most brilliant directors in town, Huston having already made *The Maltese Falcon* and *The Treasure of the Sierra Madre*.

I HAD FIRST MET HUSTON when I was fifteen years old. A friend of my mother's had suggested she invite him to dinner at Mabery Road because he was a promising screenwriter and an interesting young man, although considered to be wild and amusingly mad. My mother agreed—she was always eager to meet a fellow scenarist. It was a memorable occasion. Instead of mingling with the adult guests, Huston engaged my brother and me in conversation, and upon learning that we had a boxing instructor who came to our house twice a week, he asked to be taken to the garage to look over our gloves and punching bag. He had boxed a good deal himself, he told me, and suggested we put on the gloves and spar for a few minutes. I was not too happy with the idea, but as he was a guest, I agreed.

After shedding our jackets and ties, we faced each other in the empty garage. Huston feinted and dodged, obviously intent on showing off his superior skill. His long reach and his unorthodox style kept me at bay, but eventually I closed in and he landed a jarring right. We clinched, and he apologized, holding me firmly in his arms. Both of us were bathed in sweat as we called it quits. We then realized that our shoes were covered with dog shit, for my mother's German shepherd, Prince, had a habit of using the garage as a toilet whenever he was locked in. After cleaning our footwear as well as possible, I led John to the guest bathroom where we washed up before rejoining the dinner party.

Later that evening we discovered that we had another mutual interest, horses, and Huston invited me to join him at his father's ranch in San Fernando Valley for a weekend. It was an invitation that, quite understandably, he never followed up. But that didn't bother me, for despite his paternal posturing I had felt ill at ease with him. We met again several years later outside the commissary at Warner Brothers studios. By that time he had directed *The Maltese Falcon*, and I had written my first novel and was working on a screenplay for Jerry Wald, one of the fledgling producers on the lot.

Huston was accompanied by Henry Blanke, his producer, and they both stopped to say hello. "He's the type we're looking for," John said jocularly. "Perfect for the part!" They were choosing the cast for *The Treasure of the Sierra Madre*, Blanke explained, not an easy task. It turned out later that the role Huston was referring to was the one Tim Holt played in the movie as that of Bogart's young partner, which should have been a warning of Huston's mistaken appraisal of my person. He seemed to recall our earlier meetings and invited me to his recently completed house in Tarzana for lunch the following Saturday.

It was a large, sprawling, modern house built entirely of redwood; he had designed it and was appropriately proud of it. As soon as I arrived I realized that Huston was living up to his wild, nonconformist, bohemian reputation, for Mary Astor, his former leading lady and mistress, was among the guests, to the obvious discomfort of his beautiful Anglo-Irish wife Lesley. After lunch John led us all down to the small riding ring at the bottom of the garden, where he mounted one of his jumpers. The demonstration of his skill as a horseman resulted in a crashing fall. Both of his women rushed out to console him and to see if he had been seriously injured, a complex situation that he appeared to enjoy. Somewhat reluctantly I returned the next morning to go riding with him, and although Mary Astor was no longer present, the atmosphere was far from relaxed.

After our hack around the hills John went off to take a shower, and during a long wait I could hear screams coming from his suite. I was uncertain whether he was beating his wife or making love to her. However, both of the Hustons ultimately returned to the luncheon table and appeared as unconcerned as if nothing out of the ordinary had occurred in their private quarters.

I lost touch with him after Pearl Harbor, but we met again backstage at the Grauman's Chinese theater, where the Academy Awards for 1946 were being presented. Dore Schary was in charge of the ceremony that year, and prior to the handing out of the Oscars he had arranged for ex-servicemen from all the branches of the military to make short speeches to the audience. As a former Marine I had been assigned to speak for the writers, preceding Huston, who was representing the directors who had been in uniform. He had made three outstanding documentaries while in the service—*Report from the Aleutians*, *The Battle of San Pietro*, and *Let There Be Light*, which depicted the treatment of shell-shock victims with the as yet unknown drug sodium pentothal. He greeted me like a long-lost friend, and we each did our turn in the glare of the footlights and were rewarded with solid rounds of applause.

SO IT WAS with a feeling of pleasant anticipation that I reported to Sam Spiegel's house in Beverly Hills for my next job interview. In marked contrast to Mike Todd, Huston was polite and friendly. Spiegel was more reserved, playing the part of producer to the hilt. John explained that the movie they were hoping to make was based on a segment in a book by Robert Sylvester entitled *Rough Sketch* and had as a background the revolt against the government of the Cuban dictator Gerardo Machado. It sounded like an interesting project, indisputably better than working for the flamboyant Mike Todd.

They were a strange pair, the tall, lanky Huston and the obese Spiegel, who was inclined to long pronouncements that John repeatedly cut short with an irreverent jest. Spiegel, rumor had it, had lured John into the partnership by paying him an advance of fifty thousand dollars, but there was obviously more to it than that. Despite the successful films John had made at Warner's, he was anxious to get away from the despotic rule of the executives that headed the big companies. He also hoped that by working with an independent producer he would be able to share in the profits that would be forthcoming if a movie turned out to be a hit. Above all, he enjoyed shocking the established rulers of the industry by making a deal for three pictures with a man who was considered to be a fly-by-night upstart at the very moment when he, Huston, was in great demand. Spiegel's colorful past included having been in jail in England for bouncing a few checks, a detail that amused John.

I took a copy of *Rough Sketch* home with me and read the section of the book entitled "China Valdez," which was to provide the title and serve as the basis of the screenplay I was to write with Huston. The story was based on the actual attempt of a group of Cuban terrorists to kill the dictator Machado by planting a bomb in the main Havana cemetery and exploding it while Machado and his cabinet were attending a state funeral. In Robert Sylvester's account, the plotters (which included a beautiful Cuban girl) were apprehended and shot by a firing squad, not a commercially appealing ending for our projected movie. But even in those days, long before international terrorism had reached its present alarming proportions, making a group of political assassins the heroes of a film was a daring departure from the norm of adventure stories. However, knowing that I would be collaborating with Huston, I didn't worry too much about how the story line would be resolved.

Spiegel was waiting for me in the bar of his gloomy house the next day. He told me that he had not yet decided on a writer and warned me that John was a brilliant but undisciplined man and that collaborating with him would be a difficult task, all the more so as the movie was to start principal photography in three or four months. He was already negotiating with two stars for the leading roles and would soon be forced to give them starting dates.

Then Huston arrived. He brushed aside Sam's reiterated statement on the necessity of getting a shooting script written in the next two months. Yes, he knew that they would soon have to cast the two leads, he said, but in his opinion the screenplay was more important than anything else and he certainly wouldn't start production until he was satisfied that the script was perfect. If necessary he would accept another assignment first, a statement that upset Spiegel visibly. Harsh words were exchanged between the two partners. Huston said he was not going to make a "lousy movie" just because Sam was in a hurry, and the discussion, at Sam's urgent request, returned to the problem of the script.

I felt sorry for Spiegel. He had probably borrowed the money to form his partnership with Huston, and he was justifiably afraid that if John signed to make another film prior to *China Valdez*, he might never make a movie for the independent Horizon Pictures at all. At the same time I felt it would be foolish not to voice my doubts about the way the story was resolved in the original material. Huston listened attentively to what I had to say and agreed that the ending presented a serious problem. However, he said with a benevolent smile, every story he had ever worked on had presented him with the same kind of headache. Although as literary properties *The Maltese Falcon* and *Treasure* were far superior in quality to *China Valdez*, they nevertheless had had less than satisfactory conclusions.

Spiegel, apparently eager to agree with his partner whenever possible, voiced the opinion that solving the problem of the ending of any story was merely a question of hard work. Perfectly constructed novels like *The Maltese Falcon* were difficult to find; they came along once in a lifetime. But he was nevertheless confident that *China Valdez* would make a great picture. Huston shrugged and said nothing. I then men-

23

tioned that I had met Hemingway in Sun Valley and that he was well acquainted with the intrigues of Cuban politics and might be worth talking to. My suggestion seemed to revive John's waning interest in the discussion.

Sam agreed to our eventually making a trip to Havana, and the matter of my employment having been settled, the conversation turned to the political events of the day. Former Vice President Henry Wallace was to arrive in Los Angeles to address a rally at Gilmore Stadium as the presidential candidate of the Progressive Party. John had been asked to introduce Wallace from the platform, which Spiegel had already advised against. Sam now brought the subject up again, arguing that as Huston was not a Wallace supporter it would be wrong for him to even attend the rally.

"For God's sake, Sam," Huston replied, "he was the vice president of the United States! How the hell can I refuse to introduce him?"

The argument became acrimonious. Spiegel insisted that because their independent company had not yet made a financial deal with one of the major studios, by sponsoring Wallace John was about to jeopardize the entire venture. He wasn't "sponsoring" the man, John replied. He was merely introducing him; Wallace had a right to be heard. "Are you going to vote for him?" Spiegel asked. "I don't know. I don't think so," Huston replied. "I haven't made up my mind." Spiegel glanced up at the ceiling and shook his head. Would John at least postpone his decision until that evening? Sam pleaded. He was going to Columbia to lunch with Harry Cohn and might make a deal that very day. "All right," Huston said. "I'll hold off for a few hours, but I'm not going to go back on my word."

There was an undeniable logic to Spiegel's argument. By appearing on the platform with and introducing Wallace, John would seem to be endorsing Wallace's candidacy, while in fact he had already made up his mind to vote for Harry Truman, fearing that a third-party ticket would split the liberal vote and perhaps allow Thomas Dewey to be elected. But John had already said he would introduce Wallace, and his refusal to do so would seem like cowardice. The political climate that year was oppressive. The House Un-American Activities Committee hearings were in full swing, and six months earlier Huston had traveled to Washington, D.C., as one of the organizers of the Committee for the First Amendment. The trip had ended in failure, particularly since Humphrey Bogart had changed his mind on the way back to California and had given an interview in Chicago declaring that he had been "ill advised" to join the committee. Yet Huston's friendship with the actor had survived Bogey's defection, as had John's status in the industry.

Spiegel departed for his meeting with Harry Cohn, and John and I began our first story conference. The truth contained in Spiegel's warning that collaborating with Huston would not be an easy task soon became evident to me. He seemed distracted, unwilling to talk about the problematic ending or even about the theme of the story. We went to lunch and discussed the war and horses, anything but the fate of China Valdez and her fellow plotters. Then once we were back at Spiegel's gloomy house, Huston suggested we start right in to construct the opening of the script and not worry too much about the final sequence.

By the end of the afternoon we had made little progress, and John declared that we had racked our brains enough; we should meet again at his ranch in the morning. Then Sam arrived, all smiles. His meeting at Columbia had gone well, and it now seemed that both MGM and Harry Cohn were interested in financing Horizon Pictures. "Have you decided about the rally tomorrow night?" he inquired of John. "I have," came the reply. "I'm going."

Spiegel glanced up at the ceiling, requesting divine intervention. Then he asked if we had done any work. "Well, we've started," John said. Spiegel insisted that he be present at our next story conference, and Huston reluctantly agreed to meet in Sam's bar for lunch the next day. On the way to our cars I asked John why he had become a partner of Sam's when he obviously had had a number of other offers. "Because it was the wrong thing to do, kid," he said, grinned enigmatically, got behind the wheel of his car, and drove off.

IN MY BRIEF PAST as a screenwriter I had worked on only two scripts that had been made into films: Irwin Shaw's well-conceived original screenplay for *The Hard Way* (the final version of which was far less brilliant than his first draft) and *Saboteur*, a lackluster script I had rewritten under the tutelage of Alfred Hitchcock. Hitch hadn't seemed to worry too much about in-depth motivations. He was making his first American thriller, the hero of which was a bland character played by Robert Cummings, the villain a rich fascist portrayed by Otto Kruger, and he too had counted more on casting than on characterization to tell his story.

After a lengthy discussion at lunch the next day, Spiegel and Huston decided to try to secure the services of John Garfield and Jennifer Jones for the leading roles, which they both agreed would be difficult without a screenplay to show them. However, as Huston was firmly established as one of the most prestigious directors in town, Spiegel felt that he had a good chance of signing them by submitting the original material. The only serious hurdle facing Sam would be David Selznick, who was not only Jennifer Jones's employer but her lover as well. Selznick was a close friend of Huston's, admired his talent, and might therefore be talked into loaning out the young actress for the leading role. This according to Sam, whose machinations Huston reluctantly agreed with despite his serious doubts about tying himself down to a starting date.

By the time all these matters had been thoroughly discussed it was late in the afternoon, and Huston realized that there would not be time for him to drive to Tarzana and change into his dinner jacket to appear at the Wallace rally. Spiegel attempted a last-minute persuasion for John not to honor his commitment, but to no avail. Huston called his maid and instructed her to bring his evening finery to Spiegel's house in a taxi. There was a final moment of panic when it was discovered that his dinner jacket was at the dry cleaner's. Huston was nonplussed for a brief moment and then decided he would appear in a navy blue suit. The last hour of this, our planned second story conference was spent writing a short speech with which my collaborator would introduce the Progressive Party candidate for president of the United States.

Jigee and I attended the rally. Katharine Hepburn, looking lovely in a red dress, made a long, eloquent speech; then minutes before she finished, John took his place on the platform. After the deafening applause for Hepburn had subsided, John made his way to the microphone and introduced Wallace to the enthusiastic audience. Jigee and I heaved a sigh of relief. The candidate's words seemed inconsequential after all this excitement.

IN THE DAYS that followed John and I met every morning at his house in Tarzana, where I would arrive punctually at ten o'clock. He had previously explained to me that he had never learned to type, and as his earliest ambition had been to become a painter, he was incapable of picking up a pen or a pencil without starting to sketch. These quirks of John's established our method of work. I set up my typewriter on the redwood terrace overlooking the swimming pool, and John paced while we talked.

In many respects a collaboration between a movie director and a screenwriter is like an arranged marriage. It is thought by the colluding parents that love and affection will ultimately develop between bride and groom and that an heir will be forthcoming as a result of the union. In a collaboration the writer inevitably plays the part of the bride and is expected ultimately to give birth to a screenplay that the director has contributed to sufficiently so that looking for a new wife will only on occasion be necessary. Huston was fourteen years my senior, and at the age of forty-one he was a collaborator whose leadership and guidance I expected, as he had started his illustrious career as a screenwriter.

There is also an important getting-to-know-each-other period involved in both an arranged marriage and a collaboration that inevitably consumes quite a bit of time. At least that was true of our early encounters, the midmorning sessions that were meant to result in as many pages as possible of a shooting script. John, I soon discovered, was even a better listener than a raconteur, and we found so many topics of mutual interest that the hours on the shaded terrace passed without much getting accomplished. We talked about Sam, the war, horses, our wives, and our many mutual friends without ever getting bored or feeling the need to get down to work—and soon, once more, it was late afternoon.

A certain line of dialogue in *The Maltese Falcon* is repeated quite often during the movie. "Let's talk about the black bird," Sydney Greenstreet or Bogart says on various occasions. These words became a password between John and me that we had frittered away enough time and should get back to work. However, there were so many other distractions that even this signal didn't help very much. John had bought a few brood mares, the get of which he was hoping to send to the racetrack in due time. He was also a passionate punter. Deeply in debt, he always hoped that a long shot he had wagered on would give him a little financial breathing space. If the horse lost, he reckoned that he was only a little more in debt than he had been prior to post time.

Calls to his bookies had to be made in the mornings, so our morning work sessions were interrupted. Then in the afternoon we had to be near the radio so that John could listen to the half-hourly results. We also spent quite a few hours visiting his animals—the jumpers in their stalls, the burro in the alfalfa patch, and the small monkey that was kept in a cage during the day and was occasionally released after dinner while a movie was being run in the living room. I attended as few as possible of John's dinner parties; once the monkey had been turned loose in the dark, he was apt to jump into your lap and either bite you or urinate on your trousers. Spiegel hated "the little ape" and refused to appear at the house unless John had given his word that the monkey would be locked up, a promise that was occasionally broken.

JOHN'S MARRIAGE to his second wife, Lesley Black, had ended in divorce while he was serving in the Army Signal Corps. Like Jigee, Lesley had lost a child at birth, which Huston felt was one of the principal reasons for the breakup of their marriage. Like Jigee, Lesley felt that her husband had not been equally affected by their personal tragedy. So after an unresolved love affair with Marietta Tree, who had been unwilling to leave her husband while he was still overseas, Huston had returned from the war to his rambling house at the far end of San Fernando Valley.

But his bachelorhood ended suddenly, for on a sudden whim he had married Evelyn Keyes, a young actress who had come to Hollywood like so many others to be tested for the role of Scarlett O'Hara. Evelyn was allergic to horses, cats, and dogs, so she rented an apartment in West Hollywood and visited John only on weekends. On occasion they would have dinner together in town, mostly on days when Evelyn had a late call on the set of the movie she was doing. This, my collaborator's complex lifestyle, however, was not responsible for the snaillike pace of our writing efforts.

For some strange reason John seemed unwilling to settle on the theme of *China Valdez*. In the novella the plotters were motivated by their hatred of Machado, and they justified their actions by the credo that "revolution against tyranny is obedience to God," a message that John declared was too trite as an overall theme. He felt that a better one would develop in the course of our work. So we attempted to dramatize the incidents of the story as they appeared in Sylvester's fictionalized account. I accepted this method of tackling the job because I couldn't think of a better way and because as the junior member of our partnership I expected Huston to set the pace.

But after two and a half weeks we had been able to produce no more than eleven pages, and even these were far from perfect in John's opinion. In the meantime Sam Spiegel had been fully occupied trying to make a deal with MGM or Columbia as well as to finalize his negotiations with Garfield and Jones, so he had not visited "his writers" to find out for himself how they were progressing. When he finally did venture out to Tarzana he was shocked to learn how little we had to show him, and, to make matters worse, when I handed the pages over to him for his inspection, John's pet monkey appeared as if on cue and tried to tear the pages out of Sam's grip, the little beast having escaped from its cage while it was being fed by one of the servants.

John was greatly amused by the incident, which Sam suspected was one of his partner's practical jokes, although of course it wasn't. I retrieved the two or three pages the monkey had tossed aside, and Sam glanced at them with an understandably jaundiced eye. We were well on the way to a true disaster, he declared, and suggested that perhaps it would be best if John and I went to Havana, partly for on-the-scene inspiration and partly to choose the locations where some of the film would be shot. John agreed to the trip at once, having earlier suggested that we visit Cuba to remove us from the local distractions as well as indoctrinate us with the atmosphere of the place we were attempting to write about.

All the travel arrangements were made by Gladys Hill, Sam's efficient secretary. Jigee and Evelyn would accompany us, Sam had decided, a generous gesture that he fervently hoped would ensure a certain stability during our stay. Prior to our departure John arranged a dinner party to which he invited Burgess Meredith and his wife Paulette Goddard, who it turned out had a pair of small monkeys they were hoping to board at the Huston residence while they were on a trip to New York and then Europe. It was to be a farewell party for all of us, a festive occasion.

The Merediths arrived with a long black cardboard tube in which their two monkeys had made the trip from town. John's monkey was released in the living room, and then Burgess set free his pets. But instead of a friendly meeting of primates, the Meredith monkeys took an instant dislike to the son of the household and set off in pursuit of him, emitting wild cries of hate. John's monkey chose flight instead of battle, seeking refuge on the high galleries of the living room that housed John's pre-Columbian art collection. Soon we were all racing from one corner of the large room to another, attempting to catch the falling treasures before they hit the tiled floor, a grotesquely funny scene that delighted Huston and his guests.

The going-away party set the stage for our departure. As Spiegel had not finalized his deal with Columbia, neither John nor I had been paid our weekly salary, so we were both short of cash. However, I felt certain that Sam had supplied his partner, the leader of our expedition, with sufficient funds for our trip. But once we had set out the morning after the monkey fiasco, I discovered that John was under the impression that I had been made the treasurer of our group. Art Fellows, a friend, had volunteered to drive us to the airport, and when we realized that the four of us were virtually penniless, he kindly lent us all the money he had on him, a wad that amounted to roughly a hundred and fifty dollars that Fellows had been planning to take with him to the racetrack later that day. John was furious, while Jigee, Evelyn, and I thought it was an amusing, if disquieting, way to begin our Cuban adventure.

But once we arrived in New York and moved into a luxurious two-bedroom suite at the St. Regis, John's anger abated. Nevertheless he simulated outrage when he reached Sam on the telephone. But at that distance Spiegel was not easily intimidated. After a long conversation Huston hung up, quite evidently reassured. Sam had informed him that fifteen hundred dollars was being wired to us in Havana. John had already secured a five-hundred-dollar advance from the hotel's cashier, so things seemed to be looking up. He invited Pauline Potter, one of his "social friends," as Evelyn described her, to dinner in our suite and announced we would have time the next day for "a little shopping" before catching the plane to Miami, news that pleased Evelyn, who said, she was "getting tired of travelling like a pauper."

Aware of the true state of John's finances, Jigee and I were amazed at the nonchalant way he ordered an elegant set of matched luggage from Mark Cross, and it was obvious that had we had more time, he and Evelyn would have indulged in a really serious shopping spree. He asked for the half dozen suitcases they had bought to be sent C.O.D. to the St. Regis as soon as they had been monogrammed and then invited us to lunch at 21 to celebrate our new affluence, after which we barely had time to return to the hotel, collect our belongings, and head for La Guardia. Approximately eight hours later we staggered into the humid Caribbean air and were served frozen daiquiris by a local reception committee before being driven to the Hotel Nacional, Cuba's finest, the walls of which were still pock-marked with shell holes from the most recent attempt to overthrow the government.

· · · ·

HAVANA IN THE late forties had the reputation of being a "swinger's paradise." The big gambling interests from Miami had not yet invaded Havana and built their concrete, windowless, air-conditioned bunkerlike structures, and the town still had the appearance of a Spanish colonial port. The old family residences along the Malecón, the avenue that skirts the city's seafront, had an air of past opulence that reminded me of the large, wooden-frame houses on Ocean Avenue in the Santa Monica of my childhood, melancholy in appearance and disused.

Ernesto Smith, a fat Cuban in a white suit who was the Columbia Pictures representative, came to make a courtesy call and promised to take us on a guided tour of the city the next day. Seated in a wicker armchair, a frozen daiquiri in his fat right hand, he bemoaned the inferior quality of the recent Columbia films he was being asked to sell. He mentioned several titles, adding "very bad movie" after each one. He mentioned a movie Evelyn had starred in. "My wife is in that film," John said, warning him with a false smile that he should proceed with care. "Very good movie," Smith corrected himself without a change of expression. To his discomfort, we roared with laughter.

Then John asked the question that was uppermost in all of our minds: Had any money been sent from California for our expenses? Yes, a draft had arrived that day, Smith replied and took a manila envelope out of his jacket pocket. John offered to sign a receipt for the thick wad of twenty-dollar bills, but Ernesto looked doubtful. The addressee was Señor Viertel, he explained sheepishly. "Well, sign the receipt, kid," John ordered, and I did. Although many thousands of miles removed from the theater of operations, Spiegel was still trying to control our destiny.

John invited Smith to dinner, and after the man left I suggested hesitantly that Jigee's and my presence was not really required that evening. Knowing that I had already attempted to telephone Hemingway, Huston agreed to give us the evening off. Although Hemingway's Finca Vigía was only twelve miles from the center of Havana, I was still waiting to complete the call. It came through a few minutes later, on a static-filled line. Hemingway was eager to see us, so he said, and asked us to come out to his house as soon as possible. I made no mention of our traveling companions, as John had deemed it wiser for us to make our first visit alone.

The line went dead before we had finished talking, and when Papa called back a quarter of an hour later, he suggested we take the bus from Havana to San Francisco de Paula, the village near his farm, as that day the Buick was undergoing repairs, and from there we should take a taxi, as this was cheaper than hiring a car to take us all the way from our hotel. In John's opinion that was a ridiculous way to save money; Cuba was just like Mexico, and riding a taxi would be uncomfortable enough. I didn't know Papa very well, but well enough to suspect that he would disapprove of my changing his orders. That a young writer should be able to put up with a little hardship was an opinion he had already expressed.

The bus ride was indeed uncomfortable, but it was colorful. The ancient charabanc was filled with Cuban farm workers, their chickens, and a few soldiers, and it seemed to stop at every major intersection, so that it was dark by the time we had arrived at the village of San Francisco de Paula. To our relief the Hemingways' Buick was waiting at the local bus station, as was its driver, a young black who introduced himself as Juan. He spoke very little English but was able to explain that the car had been repaired an hour earlier and that "Mister Papa" had ordered him to collect us. A few minutes later he announced with considerable pride that we were now entering the grounds of the Finca Vigía.

The main gate needed whitewashing, and the garden beyond it looked unkempt and bare. We noticed three or four roosters with shaved legs, each of them shackled to the trunk of a palm tree with a thin chain. They were Mister Papa's fighting chickens, Juan informed us. Huston had mentioned that although cockfighting had been outlawed in Cuba, the recently enacted law was not being enforced and he was anxious to witness one of these spectacles. That Hemingway was an enthusiast of this barbaric pastime was disturbing to say the least. Jigee and I just had time to exchange horrified glances before we caught sight of our host coming down the concrete steps of his villa to welcome us.

He was dressed in khaki shorts and a sport shirt, his powerful legs and arms bare. He embraced us both and led the way through a screen door into the living room. Blackie was sprawled out on the tile floor, obviously not yet acclimatized to the intense heat of his new home. Papa asked how we had withstood the bus ride, and I sensed, just as I had suspected, that this had been another small test for us to pass. Jigee, not at all intimidated, suggested that he had never made the trip himself, and Papa grinned sheepishly and admitted that he hadn't ridden a Cuban public conveyance for many years.

We were given a tour of the first floor of the house and were shown some of Hemingway's most prized possessions, Miró's painting *The Farm*, a Klee, and two canvases by Juan Gris, as well as a bullfight poster that had served as the cover of *Death in the Afternoon*. There were several African trophies on the walls, but the room itself, the furniture, and the straw carpets looked run-down and not at all what I had expected it to be, considering that its owner was the most successful serious writer in America. A large Spanish still life hanging in the dining room needed a good cleaning. The Cuban climate was hard on everything, Papa allowed, furniture and paintings and people. Yet this was where he was able to do his work without being disturbed too often by unwanted visitors.

We did not belong to that category, he assured us. "Good to see you, boy," he said, his strong right hand grasping my shoulder. "You, too, daughter," he added without looking at Jigee and commented shyly on her refreshing prettiness, her clear complexion, and her lovely hair.

I had sent him a copy of my first novel, *The Canyon*, and he said that he had read it slowly, with great pleasure, standing up in his study, a chapter every morning, to make it last. I was pleased and flattered, of course, and promised to send him my second novel as well, along with a warning that it really hadn't turned out as well as I had hoped it would. "You probably wrote it too soon," he said when I told him that it was a "war book." Once again he advised me to leave California and the movie business. "You said good-bye to the place with your lovely book," he said, which I realized was true as soon as he said it.

Mary appeared. She seemed to have blossomed now that she was in her own home. The heat suited her better than the dry cold of Ketchum and she said that she was doubtful about ever living anywhere again except the tropics. Papa mixed a glass pitcher of dry martinis, then remembered we were teetotalers. Well, his concoction would probably not go to waste, he said, as once he had removed the ice it would keep. I told him that I was working with John Huston, who was staying at the Nacional and had instructed me to invite the Hemingways to dinner the next night. Papa said he never went out to dinner but would like to take us fishing on the *Pilar*. We were there to work, I informed him, so going out on his boat might prove to be difficult. He replied that it would be a good idea for us to get used to the climate first, and then after a couple of days go to work on our screenplay.

Mary asked about the story we were planning to write, and I noticed Hemingway's expression change as I outlined the basic plot. The facts were accurate enough, he remarked in a tense voice, but he expressed concern about using the incident as the basis of a film. Nor had he approved of Robert Sylvester's fictionalized account. The president of the senate whom the plotters had killed as "bait" had been a liberal and a "good man," so the conspiracy had started out on a negative note right from the start. It was once again a matter of the means perverting the end that the revolutionaries were attempting to achieve. Terrorists were always in the vanguard of almost every revolution, but ultimately they had to be eliminated, he went on. However, he approved to some degree of political assassinations, he added with a grin after a brief pause, as they made the politicians in power realize their responsibilities more acutely and not think of politics as merely an easy way to get rich.

He suggested we devote some time to studying Cuban history and talk to some of the locals who were still involved in "the struggle," as it would be a great mistake to glorify the people who had taken part in that particular incident.

I found his comments disturbing, for I realized belatedly that John and I had accepted the basic material simply as a good yarn without thinking about the thematic content of the story we were setting out to write, and I asked Hemingway how the plotters had been discovered. Through a fluke, he explained. The night before the funeral their demolitions expert had decided to check the wire with which they were to explode the bomb once all of the mourners were grouped around the grave. A night watchman had asked the demolitions man what he was doing there and, thoroughly frightened, the man had replied that he had dropped a peso beside a grave on the previous afternoon. The night watchman, anxious to find the coin, had searched the grounds after the demolitions man left and had discovered the wire, thus foiling the plot. The terrorists were shot, their bodies dumped into the bay to feed the Morro crabs, a local delicacy.

Hemingway's account of the failure of the plot seemed like a possible ending to me; it was certainly better than any we had so far discussed. Papa went on to say that the most recent plots against the government had involved some of the football stars at the University of Havana and that the Irish-American coach of the team was at the center of much of this activity. He was a friend of Papa's and would be

34

a good man for us to talk to, as he was well informed about the political past of the island.

After dinner Hemingway volunteered to drive us back into town, leaving Mary behind at the *finca*. We stopped at the Floridita, Papa's favorite hangout, and were served frozen daiquiries. The Floridita in those days was an open bar with white, tiled walls and revolving ceiling fans. Hemingway took up his favorite position at the far end of the bar—so he could have his back to the wall, he explained, as he was often molested by drunken American tourists. One of them had challenged him only a few days ago. "You're the writer with hair on his chest," the man had said. "Let's see if that's true." Hemingway was anxious to avoid these encounters and seemed a little paranoid on the subject, although not unwilling to "cool" any of his molesters with his bare knuckles.

It was eleven-thirty in the evening by that time, and Hemingway had consumed a considerable amount of alcohol—the martinis before dinner, wine with the meal, and a vodka and tonic that René, the houseboy, had given him for the drive into the city. Yet there was no outward sign of his feeling the effects. His speech was somewhat slower than before, but that was all. Nor was he more aggressive or nastier, as he was advertised to be when drunk. A pistol shot rang out in an adjoining street, I remember, and both Papa and I ducked involuntarily. This amused him, as he took it to be evidence of my past military service. "The trouble with Cubans," he said, "is that they don't think firearms are dangerous. A knife to them calls for more respect."

He seemed to enjoy the lawless atmosphere of Havana, and he was still in an excellent mood when he dropped us off at our hotel. I was to call him early the next morning in case John Huston could be talked into spending the day out in the Gulf Stream instead of working on our script.

I WAS SLIGHTLY APPREHENSIVE about introducing Huston to Hemingway, the way one always is about introducing friends. I wanted Papa to like John, not only because *I* liked him but because it would facilitate our social life in the days ahead. Although we were spending most of our days together and I still found John to be an amusing companion, I never really felt completely at ease in his presence, probably because I was never quite sure how he would react in any given situation. I knew he could be violent if provoked. In the presence of Jigee and Evelyn he was pleasant, but slightly removed, and I had the distinct impression that he preferred the company of men.

He had told me often enough that he admired Hemingway's writing; he was also enthusiastic about many of the sports Papa had devoted a lifetime to, such as big-game hunting and marlin fishing, the latter John already having tried with limited success in Mazatlán while on his honeymoon with Evelyn. Without any hesitation he agreed to Papa's suggestion that we spend the day on the *Pilar*. "We can work on the script anytime," he said. "It isn't every day that Ernest Hemingway invites you to go fishing."

We all met the next morning at the Havana Yacht Club. Jigee and Evelyn came along. Mary, Papa explained, had chosen to remain behind at the *finca*. We had a round of drinks at the bar and then went aboard the *Pilar*, a forty-two-foot, twin-dieseled sport-fishing boat named for the heroic gypsy woman who commands the group of guerrillas in *For Whom the Bell Tolls*. The *Pilar* had a black hull, a light green superstructure, and was not very prepossessing at first glance. She could be steered from the flying bridge on top of the wheelhouse that Hemingway had added after initial construction of the boat had been completed, but the engine controls were below. The head, Papa warned us, was only partly functional. Toilet paper, if used, was to be pushed out of the head's porthole, not dropped into the bowl, as paper was apt to clog the pump.

Evelyn and John stayed in the aft cockpit, while Jigee and I joined Papa on the flying bridge. We had all been introduced to Gregorio, Papa's boatman, a rugged-looking Cuban with calloused hands that were as strong, to judge by his handshake, as Papa's. He wore a straw hat, blue work trousers, and a faded khaki shirt. He had piercing blue eyes and could see, it soon turned out, objects that we could only pick up with the help of binoculars. He was, Papa soon explained, in silent competition with his boss when it came to anything concerning the boat and fishing, and he was convinced that he knew more about the sea than his employer, Papa informed us with a sly smile.

From where we stood I could look down at the Hustons in the stern. Evelyn was a pretty blonde with a good figure and a somewhat hesitant manner now that she was out of her element. The world she was used to, Hollywood and the movie business, had not prepared her for this kind of outing, and Papa intimidated her. For Papa's part, his shyness when faced with an attractive young woman, especially a person from Evelyn's background, prevented him from being comfortable.

There was a heavy swell as soon as we were out in the Gulf Stream, and Jigee and I hung on to the painted railing of the flying bridge while Papa stood clutching the steering wheel, his big feet and powerful legs braced like the pillars of a stone monument. He wore a fishing cap with a long green plastic visor to protect him against the tropical sun. As best he could, he steered the *Pilar* through the waves that were steadily increasing in size, doing his best to minimize the roll of the small craft. Flying fish rose from the sea in front of *Pilar*'s bows, and Hemingway told us that one of his sons had become such a fine shot that he could pick them off with a .22-caliber rifle.

Soon Evelyn joined us. She looked pale and not at all happy. Catching a glimpse of the flying fish, she asked Papa what kind of birds these were that rose from the water. He explained the obvious. I could see by the expression on his face that he was amazed by her question. He glanced over at her and diagnosed at once that she was on the verge of becoming seasick. Had she brought any pills along, he asked, to soothe her *mal de mer?* No, she hadn't, Evelyn admitted; she had often gone to Catalina with friends in California and had never felt even queasy. Papa looked troubled. He suggested she go back down into the cockpit, as holding on to the railing was taking away what strength she had left.

I helped her down the rungs of the metal ladder. If she began to feel worse, I told her, it was better that we turn back, but she shook her head and assured me she would be all right after a while. I rejoined Papa on the bridge. He remarked that he had never met anyone dumb enough to mistake flying fish for birds and asked whether I thought we should head back for port. I suggested we go on for a little while longer and he shrugged and looked doubtful. The size of the swell was increasing. It would be difficult to fish under these conditions, Hemingway said, and so there was no point in continuing the exercise. "We'll go out some other day, without your friends, and maybe have better luck," he told me. Then turning the wheel, he headed the *Pilar* back in the direction of Havana. We joined the Hustons in the stern, and Gregorio took over the tiller.

Evelyn insisted bravely that she didn't want to spoil our day, but Papa shook his head. He knew what it was like to be seasick. Despite his earlier remark about the flying fish, he seemed concerned. The *Pilar* was rolling less by this time, as we were moving through a following sea. Papa suggested Evelyn drink a beer, and she agreed shakily. He took over the helm, while Gregorio made drinks for all of us and then reeled in the lines that had been attached to the two outriggers, stowed away the rods, but left the big horn teaser that moved back and forth in the center of our wake in its place. Once he had completed these chores, he took over the helm from Papa.

I mentioned how effortlessly Gregorio moved around the slippery side decks, hardly bothering to hang on to the safety rails. It was as if he had suction cups on the bottoms of his feet. Like the tentacles of an octopus, Papa agreed. They had been together for years, and Hemingway said he had never seen Gregorio off balance, no matter what the weather. He was a perfect deckhand, close-mouthed and uncomplaining, with a great respect for the ocean and its dangers. Even when the *Pilar* had patrolled as a Q-boat early in 1942 and had carried a crew of ten to twelve men, Gregorio had put up with all the hardships of crowded quarters without ever asking for a day off.

We were all relaxing in the cockpit, with the water smooth now that we were inside the bay, and I wanted to ask Papa about his attempts to sight an enemy submarine, but the conversation somehow veered off onto another subject. American gambling interests, sponsored no doubt by the Mafia, were about to invade Havana, and this prompted John to go off on a long, rambling story about the mysterious personage of Virginia Hill, Bugsy Siegel's presumed mistress. I had known John to be a good raconteur, but on this occasion, perhaps because of alcohol, the movement of the boat, and the hot tropical sun, he seemed to be rambling on pointlessly, and although we all listened to him in silence, it was apparent to me that he was not his usual self.

We picked up our mooring, berthed the *Pilar*, and the Hustons excused themselves and went ashore, as Evelyn was understandably eager to get back to the hotel, while Jigee and I stayed on with Papa. He wanted to take us to lunch at his favorite Chinese restaurant, a place called El Pacífico, located on a rooftop in downtown Havana. Mary joined us there, and Papa ordered a lavish meal. He was much more relaxed now that we were on our own. "Lucky that John has 'the industry,' " he said with a malicious chuckle, adding that as a storyteller he seemed not to be too well endowed. I explained that the roll of the boat had in all probability affected him, and Papa shrugged, unconvinced. It was time I "quit whoring" and wrote my own stuff, he said. Working with Huston was hardly that, I replied. "You're still hiring out," Papa said, "and that's enough to destroy any writer." He didn't dwell on the subject, and he and Mary suggested I invite the Hustons to dinner the following night, to make up for the fiasco of our fishing trip.

WORK ON OUR SCRIPT did not progress. I told John what I had learned from Papa about how the plot to assassinate Machado had been uncovered, and although he showed interest in the anecdote, he said that it would not help us with the ending of our story. He was aware, he said, that there was an inherently negative quality in the material that seemed to preclude both a catharsis or some kind of ironic comment that might be satisfying for an audience. The ending of *The Treasure of the Sierra Madre*, which had the wind blowing away all the gold dust the prospectors had worked so hard to acquire, expressed the central theme of a story that was basically about cupidity. That the old prospector could roar with laughter at his loss was somehow satisfying, as it demonstrated the grandeur of the human spirit. The failure of our plotters, even if we allowed them to escape a firing squad, would merely leave the audience with a bitter taste in its mouth.

This, however, did not seem to lead him to the obvious conclusion that the entire venture was a mistake, a thought that was seriously beginning to bother me. Then what the hell are we doing here? I asked him. I don't know, kid, he replied, grinning. Then he went on to recall how Sam, during their initial meeting at MGM, when they had faced Louis B. Mayer and what was then laughingly referred to as the "college of cardinals," the studio's hierarchy, had been asked by L.B. how the story they were trying to sell was to end. Desperate to conclude a deal, Spiegel had extemporized, declaring that in our version an American destroyer would come sailing into Havana harbor, dispose of the dictator, and save the lives of our heroes. It was an amazing show of pure guts, John said, highly amused in retrospect.

He decided that we should stop work for the day and go location hunting. There was no greater mental torture in his opinion than to be bogged down while working on a script. But once we had adjourned to a chauffeur-driven limousine and were being taken around Havana, the picturesque surroundings of the city appeared to revive his interest in our project. We were driven to the Hemingways' house for dinner, where we were cordially welcomed by host and hostess.

John, with his infallible instinct for doing the unexpected, made a great fuss over Mary, undoubtedly sensing that he had yet to win the approval of Papa. He was most complimentary about the house, the paintings, and the hunting trophies, and the evening seemed to be going quite well. Papa mixed his lethal martinis, and everyone was in a most congenial mood as we sat down to dinner. Then once the meal had been concluded, we all went out on the terrace for coffee. Inevitably, modern literature came under discussion, and after stating his admiration for Jean-Paul Sartre, John told Hemingway that he had directed a Sartre play, *No Exit*, which had failed on Broadway. "Have you read his novels?" Huston asked.

Papa got slowly to his feet, braced himself on his powerful legs, and took a deep breath. "I'll tell you about Sartre, John," he said. "The best thing he ever wrote was a short story called *Le Mur*. That was one of his early ones. Then once the rest of his books had been translated, Blanche Knopf, his publisher, decided to put out his complete *oeuvre*. Only she chose to publish his stuff in the reverse order in which it had been written, and all the critics pointed out how much Sartre had grown."

It was, of course, an outrageous statement, made half in jest, and was undoubtedly meant to annoy Huston. John did not rise to the bait. Instead he turned to Mary and asked what she thought of *The Age of Reason*. Mary, quite wisely, said she hadn't read the novel. I felt nervous, sensing that we were approaching troubled waters. Jigee said nothing and lit a cigarette, a sure sign of nervousness.

There being no meeting of the minds on the subject of modern literature, the conversation returned to the world of sport. Hemingway recalled a recent visit by Gene Tunney to the *finca* and described how they had sparred for a few rounds out on the tennis court. John mentioned that he had boxed professionally as a light heavyweight, and Papa began to question him pointedly as to where and when he had fought in that category. I don't remember exactly who it was that proposed putting on the gloves, but I know that the suggestion filled me with immediate alarm. It was dark by this time; the crickets were chirping in the garden, and I could imagine nothing worse than John and Papa stepping a few fast rounds on the terrace. Mary Hemingway was equally appalled about the prospect of her husband taking on one of his guests.

"Pete . . . do something to stop Papa," she whispered in my ear after Hemingway had gone into the house, ostensibly to get the boxing gloves. I followed him and found him in the guest bathroom, stripped to the waist and daubing water on his eyes.

"I'm just going to cool him quick, Pete," Papa mumbled.

"Please, Papa," I said. "John's a friend of mine, and he's had a little too much to drink. And so have you," I added.

"He said he was light heavyweight champion of California," Hemingway replied, scoffing.

"He didn't say that. He said he fought a few professional bouts, that's all." Hemingway was toweling down his torso, drying his face. "Please, Papa," I implored him. "You can box with him some other time."

Finally he relented, slipped on his white shirt, and returned with me to the terrace. The two men shook hands, and the atmosphere became somewhat more relaxed.

Half an hour later we said our good-byes. Huston stumbled on the concrete steps on his way down to our waiting limousine, fell, picked himself up, kissed Mary on the cheeks, waved to Papa, and eased himself painfully into the front seat of the car. Then the four of us, Evelyn, Jigee, John, and I, drove back in silence to the hotel through the warm, tropical night.

JIGEE AND I were sure that there would be no further social contact with the Hemingways, yet John, when he joined us at the hotel's swimming pool the next morning, seemed to remember the evening only vaguely. When I told him that Papa had mumbled that he planned only to "cool him quickly," he laughed appreciatively. For his part he had no intention of inflicting punishment on his opponent, he told me, and had agreed to box with Hemingway because it would have made for a great after-dinner story once we had returned to Hollywood. Papa, who was almost fifty, was overweight, John stated, and would have been "easy to hit." I said nothing, although I was tempted to point out that he was not really all that fit himself, even though he was seven years younger.

What troubled me most was Papa's behavior. Irwin Shaw had warned me that the bully in Hemingway was apt to surface after a few drinks; he had knocked down a journalist, Bruce Grant, as a result of Grant's baiting him in Rambouillet, where Papa and a group of fellow journalists were waiting to enter Paris with the liberating troops. Why Papa still felt the need to prove himself with his fists was puzzling and disconcerting, as he must have been aware that John was drunk.

That afternoon Mary Hemingway telephoned and, without reference to the shambles of the previous evening, informed me that the weather at sea had improved and that Papa would like to take us all fishing again. John accepted the invitation without a moment's hesitation. We weren't making much headway with our work, he said, so we might as well enjoy ourselves. Evelyn had been called back to California to start a movie, and once she heard that a second sortie on the *Pilar* was being planned, she was a good deal less sorry to be leaving. John instructed her to call Sam Spiegel as soon as she arrived and to tell him that we would soon be in need of more funds. The Hotel Nacional was not inexpensive, and there were three of us in residence.

We went to the local fronton after dinner, as the jai alai games in Havana seemed like a good locale for a scene in our movie. John had become interested in this sport many years ago while spending time in Mexico City long before the war. The betting, which involved rapidly changing odds as a game progressed, seemed complicated to me, compounded by our unfamiliarity with the language and the players. Piston was the name of the most brilliant forward, we decided, after the first doubles match had been concluded, and John backed him heavily in the quiniela that followed, which pitted one individual player against another. Before the evening ended, we had lost several hundred dollars, not really a lot when compared with John's losses at the races, but in our present financial condition, a considerable sum. He seemed unconcerned, however, assuring Jigee and me that we would soon win it all back.

The sea was calm the next day, but the marlin were reluctant to take our bait. We anchored for lunch in Papa's favorite cove, and while Gregorio was busy preparing the midday meal, we sat in the shade of the wheelhouse drinking cold beer. Mary had come along, and the atmosphere on board was genial and relaxed. Papa amused us with various Cuban anecdotes and after a while got out a .22-caliber rifle with which we practiced our marksmanship on the empty beer bottles Papa tossed overboard and allowed to drift away from the boat.

Jigee delighted Hemingway with her accurate marksmanship, shattering quite a few bottles at a range of more than a hundred yards. As a little girl she had been taught to shoot by her father, an Irish reprobate who had crossed the country in a covered wagon as a boy and who besides teaching them marksmanship had done very little for his daughters after leaving their mother in the lurch. Gregorio came out of the cabin and pointed out a huge iguana that he had sighted on the shore. I could barely make out the shape of the reptile sunbathing on a rock, and Hemingway handed me a pair of binoculars so that I could serve as spotter. His first shot was low, and I gave him the correction I thought was required. On the third shot the animal leaped high into the air and disappeared.

Lunch was ready, but Hemingway was reluctant to leave the wounded reptile without finishing it off, and John and I volunteered to swim ashore to find it. The midday sun was at its fiercest, and I was concerned that John would catch a sunburn on his untanned body, but he too had realized that Papa would not rest until he had had his way. We swam ashore nevertheless. After a long search we were both ready to abandon our efforts when we saw that Hemingway was swimming toward us, holding the small rifle above his head in one hand.

Without mentioning our failed efforts, the three of us now continued the search. After a quarter of an hour Papa located what he said was a drop of blood on the hot sand. He took a dried stick, broke it into small pieces, and patiently staked out the blood spoor he had found. It led to a big boulder thirty yards or so higher up on the beach. Kneeling in front of the overhanging stone, he heard a slight movement in the natural cave formed by the boulder. Very carefully he sighted the rifle into the cave's opening. I cautioned him that the bullet he intended to fire might ricochet, but he shrugged off my warning. He would give the animal "the gift of death," he replied. John and I stepped back, and Hemingway fired. There was the sound of a violent movement from inside the cave, and Papa declared that the iguana was dead.

Following his instructions, I found a long stick on the beach, and together we extracted the dead reptile. Delighted with our success, Papa declared that it was one of the biggest iguanas he had ever seen. Then the three of us swam back to the *Pilar*. I was entrusted with the rifle, while the victorious Hemingway managed to get back to his boat without getting his trophy wet. We were welcomed by a visibly pleased Mary, who declared that she would have a handbag made out of the iguana's hide.

It had been an impressive performance. John and I admitted that we had been ready to abandon the hunt just as Papa had arrived on the scene. Hemingway grinned happily, and as soon as we had finished our lunch he climbed back onto the flying bridge while Gregorio hoisted the anchor. Mary told us that knowing Papa as she did, she had feared that we would have remained in the cove until dark if necessary, as he would never leave behind a wounded animal that he had shot. She carried the iguana handbag for many years, I remember, as a souvenir of that day. "And how is dear John?" she would ask whenever the handbag was mentioned.

OUR HEDONISTIC LIFE continued. Long evenings at the fronton were followed by late-morning story conferences that were brief even compared with our Tarzana routine. The intense heat that arrived in the middle of the day inevitably caused us to adjourn to the side of the swimming pool, and once there we found it virtually impossible to continue working. John had purchased a copy of Emile Zola's *Nana*, and he soon seemed more eager to finish the novel than discuss *China Valdez*. There was a pretty young woman staying at the Nacional who sang in the hotel bar at night, and John often invited her to lunch, which put an end to all discussion of the problems facing us. The strangest thing about his behavior was that he did not appear to be concerned about what lay ahead, seemed certain that in the end it would all sort itself out, that either the movie would be called off or that we would somehow be able to write a script once production had started.

Papa arranged for us to meet the Irish football coach at the University of Havana to complete our research on the revolt against Gerardo Machado. It was not a particularly rewarding expedition. We were taken first to the office of the president of the university, where we waited for more than half an hour in an anteroom that was filled with *pistoleros*, the president's body guard. Finally we were granted a three-minute interview with the harassed-looking president, who assured us of full university cooperation once we returned to film our movie. Then we were escorted to the office of the football coach, an elderly, nervous man, who told us that he had scant knowledge of the Machado regime, as that was well before his time. He seemed reluctant to discuss Cuban politics, quite apparently frightened of losing his job. The interview lasted only fifteen minutes and added nothing that might help us with our story.

John seemed pleased that Hemingway's tip had resulted in failure. We would have to rely on our "powers of invention," he said, and not ask anyone for advice. Our trip had supplied him with a view of the locale of our story, and that was quite enough in his opinion. He now seemed anxious to return to California to deal with his own financial problems and to check on what Sam was doing. There was no use even discussing our story. He arranged for us to visit a cigar factory, another possible locale for a scene in the movie, but the place turned out to be not a very picturesque setting. It did afford John the opportunity to order two dozen boxes of cigars that he forwarded C.O.D. to Spiegel in California.

We spent the remainder of the second week of our stay at the side of the hotel's swimming pool, in the evenings going to the fronton, where John lost quite a bit more of our petty cash. A few days before we were scheduled to fly home, he invited the Hemingways to our suite for cocktails to repay their hospitality. He also asked Ernesto Smith and his wife to join us, as the deal with Columbia Pictures had finally been signed. The rest of the guest list included the young American singer from the hotel bar, the U.S. consul and his wife, and a couple of American tourists we had befriended at the pool.

Papa arrived punctually with Mary and told John that he had taken the liberty of asking Pauline, his second wife, to join us, as she had recently arrived in Havana. He was dressed for the occasion in a starched white *guayabera* and clean khaki slacks and looked respectable and handsome, his face cleanly shaven. Mary appeared in a summer dress that suited her and gathered more extravagant compliments from John. Pauline appeared a few minutes later. She was surprisingly small of stature, with closely cropped brown hair, not at all as I had pictured her—the femme fatale for whom Papa had left "the lovely Hadley." Quite casually she told us that a man with a knife had tried to rob her while she was sitting in her car on a Havana street and that she had rebuffed him and frustrated his attempt to rid her of her money.

Papa was amazed and disturbed by her story. He commented on how ridiculous it was to resist an armed, desperate man and seemed not at all impressed by his ex-wife's display of disdain for her personal safety. He remained civil, nevertheless, although her account of the incident had displeased him. "Christ, how important can money be?" he mumbled to me. The guests were all seated in the living room of our suite, drinks in hand, when the conversation turned to the Spanish Civil War and the documentary movie Hemingway had made with Joris Ivens. John complimented Papa on his narration and the underplayed tone of voice with which he had read his own words. "What made you decide to narrate the film yourself, Papa?" Huston asked, with apparently keen interest.

"Orson Welles was supposed to do it," Hemingway said, his mouth twitching a little, a sign, I had learned, of extreme annoyance.

"Orson, eh?" Huston said, nodding. "And why didn't he do it?" Everyone in the room was listening by this time.

"Well, John," Hemingway replied in his gravelly voice, speaking very clearly and slowly. "Every time Orson said the word 'infantry' it was like a cocksucker swallowing."

There was a hush. John, rising to the occasion, managed to chuckle politely. Then after what seemed a long while, the shocked guests resumed their small talk.

Those were different times. Films and books were not nearly as explicit as they are today. And even today the use of that particular word in any but the most bohemian circles would in all probability shock most people. But on that sunny afternoon Papa's statement was like a grenade exploding in the living room of our suite, leaving everyone a little dazed. The U.S. consul and his wife excused themselves five minutes later and departed, as did Ernesto Smith and his Cuban spouse. The rest of us recovered our composure once the "official" guests had departed, and the evening ended on a generally friendly note. Papa declined John's invitation to join us for dinner, and the three Hemingways departed for their *finca* and what would in all probability turn out to be a strange family dinner.

The next morning Papa called and asked Jigee and me to meet him at the Yacht Club for lunch. He was leaving, he explained, on a week's fishing trip with his old friend Tommy Shevlin and his new wife, Doreen. Shevlin, a wealthy playboy and sport fisherman Papa knew from his Bimini days, made frequent visits to Cuba from his home in Palm Beach. His bride turned out to be a pale, pretty young blonde who arrived at lunch in white slacks and shirt, with her face well powdered in preparation for the fishing trip. She didn't look like the hardy outdoor type to me, nor to Papa, to judge by the way he scrutinized her. Shevlin was handsome in a fading way, with a lithe body that had obviously withstood many years of heavy drinking.

Lunch was a friendly occasion. I was seated next to Mrs. Shevlin who, whenever the conversation at the other end of the table was lively enough so that she would not be overheard, asked me what the *Pilar* was like and whether we had spent a night on board. She was apprehensive about the trip, as the yachts and fishing boats she had been a guest on had all been considerably larger than Papa's boat. I told her that Jigee and I had gone out only a couple of times on the *Pilar* and that except for the head not functioning too well had found her to be seaworthy and comfortable enough, although anything but luxurious. I reminded her that Papa and a crew of eight had spent two months at sea on the forty-two-foot craft while supposedly chasing German submarines and that they had all survived. "Yes, I've heard that story," Doreen Shevlin said caustically. "From Winston Guest," she added, "but he's too much of a fan of Papa's for me to trust."

Jigee and I said our good-byes as coffee and brandy were being served. Papa rose from his place at the head of the table, kissed Jigee affectionately, and gave me a paternal hug. "Sorry you guys are going," he said. "Would have been good to have you along." It was a sentiment the Shevlins echoed, particularly Doreen, who seemed to look upon me as an ally against the perils that lay ahead. Papa accompanied us to the entrance of the restaurant. "Work well, Pete," he mumbled, giving my shoulder a final squeeze. "And give my best regards to the light heavyweight."

AT THE TIME, William Wyler was considered by most people to be the best director in Hollywood. John Ford had had his day, as had Capra and Stevens. And although the others were still highly regarded, the consistent quality of Wyler's films had won him a greater acclaim inside the business. Frame by frame his movies were considered to be technically perfect, comparable to the work of an artistically endowed Swiss watchmaker, the obvious comparison as Wyler was half Swiss by birth and half Alsatian. Huston had worked on the screenplay of one of his movies, *Jezebel*, and during that collaboration they had become close friends. Together they had shared, according to John, quite a few flamboyant and amusing escapades that had given the nickname "Wild Willy" to Wyler. They had gone skiing together at Lake Arrowhead without any previous instruction and had never bothered to make a turn, crashing through the trees as if bent on their own destruction. Both enjoyed driving fast cars, and, as if that was not enough, Willy was fond of riding a motorcycle.

Considering the requirements of his profession, Wyler was known to be anything but an articulate director on the set. He was famous for saying, "That's fine, let's do it again," a habit that invariably caused consternation among his actors, although not one of them ever refused to accept a role in a new Wyler movie. Close-mouthed and shrewd, he was a roly-poly little man with sparkling eyes and a fairly basic sense of humor. A dictum that he was fond of repeating was that there were hundreds of stories that had a great beginning, but very few with an equally good ending. Now as we continued our labors on the script of *China Valdez*, Willy's words began to take on an even more ominous significance.

But there seemed to be no turning back. Despite Huston's repeated declarations that he would never begin principal photography until he was satisfied with a completed final draft of the script, we soon faced a starting date that Spiegel had been forced to accept by the agents representing Jennifer Jones and John Garfield. Both actors were so eager to work with John that they had waived their script-approval clause, a flattering confidence in his talent. Sam had given them the first forty pages of our screenplay and that had been sufficient for them to report to work. Their decisions appeared to be justified, for as soon as we started shooting, John's lethargy changed into a dedication that was most impressive. Once he was on the set he became a completely different person, lively, brilliant, and committed to the task at hand.

The casting of the minor roles was soon accomplished. John delighted in choosing some Latin leading men of the past: Ramón Novarro and Ricardo Cortez as well as Pedro Armendariz, a Mexican screen idol, now bald and overweight, were all given character parts. I suggested Gilbert Roland for the role of one of the minor figures in the assassination plot; he was also a former screen lover and was a tennis partner and friend of mine. He was still devastatingly handsome, with an imposing black mane. But when he reported to work, Huston told him to cut his hair as short as possible, a demand Roland accepted with pained reluctance. It at first seemed that John was merely being sadistic in wanting Roland to part with his full head of dark hair, but I soon realized that John knew exactly what he was doing. Overnight Roland was transformed into an impressive-looking character actor who would steal all of the scenes he was asked to play.

The shooting of our movie progressed, the dailies looked promising, and even Spiegel seemed a little less desperate about the final outcome of our venture. Still John and I had no idea how we could effectively end our story. We tried to work each night after the day's work but made little headway. One Sunday afternoon John suggested we go to see Wyler, who he thought might be able to help us with our predicament. Willy listened attentively while John outlined our story, as there was not enough time for Wyler to read the eighty-some pages that were already in the can. Then he shrugged. "It sounds to me like you guys are making what we used to call a 'lighthouse story,' " he said. "Always, in a lighthouse story, your characters are trapped in the same locale and to get them out of it is a bitch. It's the kind of movie I've done my best to avoid making for thirty years," he added, scratching his head with a sympathetic grin.

"Thanks, Willy," John said. "That helps a lot." We drove back to John's ranch in the San Fernando Valley, an hour's drive from Wyler's rented house in Malibu. We didn't speak much, but as we approached Tarzana Huston's mood suddenly brightened. "You know, there's a yearling sale at Hollywood Park next Saturday night. We ought to go. It'll help us relax and give our minds a rest."

I was amazed. Huston was deeply in debt and the success of *China Valdez* was his only chance of salvation, quite apart from the damage a resounding failure might do to his reputation.

"What's the point of going to a yearling sale if you have no money to buy a horse?" I asked him.

"You like to look at expensive cars even though you can't afford to own one, don't you, kid?"

There was a certain logic in that, but as I felt quite sure he wouldn't remember the date of the sale, I made no attempt to argue with him. Then on Saturday morning his secretary called from the set to tell me that Mr. Huston expected me to join him at the Hollywood Brown Derby for an early dinner that evening. We dined at six-thirty, and Jigee and I drove with John to Hollywood Park. On the way to the racetrack he informed me that Mrs. Walls, his business manager, had confiscated his checkbook and that if he did decide to buy a yearling I would have to pay with a check of my own that would be reimbursed the following day. Not too happy with this plan, I warned him that there was little more than two thousand dollars in my account.

"Oh, that's fine, kid," he said. "We're just window-shopping anyway."

The sale took place in a paddock over which a tent had been erected, with wooden folding chairs set up in rows for the potential buyers. One glance at the people around us was enough to confirm my suspicion that we were trespassers in a world of wealth and equine knowledge. However, John seemed not to be the least bit intimidated. Armed with a glossy program, he busied himself with studying the breeding of the yearlings that were being led out for the inspection of the buyers. Jigee and I were content to admire the beauty of the animals.

Ultimately a chestnut filly was led out into the paddock. Her shiny coat and lovely head set off her perfect confirmation. The filly, I remember, was by My Babu, a fashionable stallion, and the bidding started at fifteen hundred dollars. In a couple of minutes it had exceeded two thousand five hundred, and not very much later the filly was sold for seven thousand five hundred dollars, by today's standards a modest sum, but in those days a good price.

"What a shame," I whispered to John, who was seated on the other side of Jigee. "That's the best-looking thing we've seen so far."

"I agree with you, kid," he replied, grinning. "I just bought her!"

"But for God's sake, John," I said, "I told you that I only have a couple thousand dollars in the bank."

"I know," he replied. "But she was too beautiful to resist."

"How are we going to pay for her?"

"Write a check, what else do you suggest? I'll cover it somehow."

The sale was concluded an hour later, and the buyers rose from their chairs. "Come on, kid," Huston said. "You've got your checkbook with you, haven't you?"

I followed him nervously to the table at the front of the tent, and we waited for our turn to pay. The two men in charge agreed to accept my check, as they had recognized my companion. At the last moment I had a brilliant idea. I suggested that Mr. Huston, the actual buyer, endorse the check I had written. John gave me a withering glance and signed the back of the worthless slip of paper.

"I didn't want to go to jail alone," I explained to him as we walked back to his car.

"Are you worried, kid?" he asked, enjoying my discomfort.

"Sure. Aren't you?"

"Not a bit," he replied, airily. "We'll get the money from Willy first thing in the morning. Then you can deposit his check on Monday."

At nine o'clock Sunday morning, John picked me up and we drove to the Wylers' house in the Malibu Colony. Willy was still asleep, the Mexican maid informed us, but that did not deter John. He tiptoed into the Wylers' bedroom, leaving me to wait in the backyard. Five minutes later he rejoined me, grinning broadly. Unwilling to interrupt his rest, Willy had signed a blank check without asking any questions.

"I told you there'd be no problem. Now we can have some fun with Willy by not telling him the amount I borrowed."

It was a typical Huston gambit. But Willy was not the least concerned when I went to see him later in the day. "What John doesn't know is that I keep only about ten thousand dollars in that account," he said, smiling mischievously. I warned John we still might be in jeopardy, but in the end the check cleared, and the My Babu filly turned out to be one of the few horse investments that paid off. She won some stakes races as a two-year-old, but John was forced to sell her and was unable to profit more than "a few thousand bucks," in his words.

I spent much of my time on the set; often there were last-minute changes to be made in the scenes as they were being shot. Although everyone wanted to know how the story was to end, the atmosphere on the soundstage was relaxed and enjoyable. Garfield even said that as the real plotters themselves hadn't known what was going to happen, Huston's keeping the actors in the dark was beneficial, an opinion Jennifer didn't quite share. The actors and crew, as well as John, who indulged himself in a variety of practical jokes, worked well and enjoyed themselves. Sam Spiegel seldom appeared, choosing to remain in his office where he received hourly bulletins of our surprisingly rapid progress. Huston and Spiegel's relationship had worsened, as from a distance Spiegel overrode John's choices of which takes should be printed and pressured John for speed rather than quality.

Then one memorable afternoon when we had finally finished an underground sequence and were shooting on a big set that represented the main marketplace in Havana, Sam arrived. He came with Johnny Hyde, one of the most powerful men in the William Morris Agency, a midgetlike creature with a Napoleonic bearing, dressed in an expensive double-breasted suit. With them was a voluptuous blonde in a flimsy summer dress that revealed her well-endowed figure. It was not an unusual sight in Hollywood, beast and beauty out on the prowl.

Although he was in the middle of directing a scene, John stepped away from the camera as soon as he recognized Hyde and greeted the trio with the usual warmth and graciousness he reserved for nearly all visitors. There was a brief conference among the three men, during which time the blonde stared vacantly into space. A few minutes later the visitors departed, and once they had gone the big street doors rolled shut again and work was resumed. It was quite obvious to nearly everyone on the stage that Hyde had introduced the blonde to Huston in the function of the girl's agent and possibly lover.

That evening, after the last shot was in the can, John called John Garfield and me aside. Spiegel had requested that Huston make a silent test of the blonde but had emphasized that he wanted to waste as little time as possible: have Russell Metty, our cameraman, photograph the young woman and that was all. John said that he thought it would be funny if I wrote a small scene which Garfield would play with the girl. Although it would cost us an hour or two of shooting time, he felt it would be worth it to teach Sam a lesson not to flaunt his power.

The next morning we shot the test scene I had written while fifty or more extras were kept waiting. Spiegel was annoyed but managed to control his anger when he arrived on the set at noon. Later I was called to his office, where he reminded me that we still did not have an acceptable ending. He was furious that John's prank had held up work on the set as well as on the script.

"It was your idea to test this girl, Sam," I reminded him.

"I was doing Johnny Hyde a favor," he replied. "He's helped us enormously in setting up our deal at Columbia." Sam told me I should have warned him of John's irresponsible plan. "I can't be your spy," I replied. "That's not a part of my job."

He shook his head and lit a fresh cigar. "Sometimes I feel that I'm involved with a maniac," he muttered. "All right. Go back to your office and get to work."

The young actress's name was Marilyn Monroe, and John, immediately aware of her inherent talent, used her in his next film, *The Asphalt Jungle*, which was the start of her prodigious career.

Quite understandably Sam was growing even more desperate about the last sequence of our movie as each day passed. He suggested that we meet with Billy Wilder, an old friend of his from their early days in Berlin and Paris and the writer-director Sam most admired after Huston. Wilder was known to have an inventive story mind, and Sam thought he might come up with a good idea for our ending. Evelyn Keyes, John's wife, had had a brief romance with Billy, which I suspected made Huston somewhat reluctant about seeking his help. Nevertheless, he agreed to Sam's setting up a story conference with Wilder.

We met on a Saturday afternoon at Sam's house, and for several hours the four of us discussed our problem. Although Billy came up with a variety of suggestions, none of them proved to be of much help. "What the hell made you choose this story?" he asked Huston as our conference drew to a close. It was a question John and I had been asking ourselves for quite some time.

Like a married couple who have sought advice from mutual friends and have found none forthcoming, John and I decided to try once again to solve our difficulties by ourselves. Again I suggested the incident Hemingway had told us about, the discovery of the wire in the cemetery and the ensuing arrest of all the plotters. The film had to end, I argued, with the execution of our heroes by a firing squad. Huston shrugged. "You can suggest it to Sam if you like," he said. "He might just be desperate enough to go for it."

"Was this your idea or John's?" Spiegel asked suspiciously after I had outlined a possibly tragic ending.

"Mine," I admitted.

"Baby, have you taken leave of your senses?" he exclaimed. Then he went on to prophesy a disaster at the box office if the movie ended on anything but a positive note. He hinted darkly that perhaps he should look for another writer, a threat that annoyed me. I said: "Why don't you? Just let me know so I can stop racking my brain and go out and look for another job."

"Baby!" he thundered. "Sometimes I think I'm losing my mind. You're beginning to behave like Huston!" Then his tone of voice changed to one of pleading, and he begged me to return to my office and write the ending John and I had decided upon without any real conviction. I did so and was released from any further obligations and rewarded with my final check, which arrived two weeks late.

Spiegel was not a man who believed in open covenants openly arrived at. Without notifying me, he hired Ben Hecht at Hecht's favorite salary of a thousand dollars a day, which was the normal procedure in Hollywood, and probably still is. John had departed for Havana to shoot exteriors, and it was only by chance that I met Hecht at a dinner party and he informed me rather shamefacedly that he had "added a comma" to mine and Huston's script. Then at the first preview a couple of months later, I saw what his comma had entailed. With a total disregard for the history books, Hecht had the revolution break out in the streets of Havana just as our plotters were being apprehended, so that neither Garfield nor the beautiful Jennifer had to face the firing squad.

Many months later the movie, released under the title *We Were Strangers*, turned out to be less than a success, but not quite a total disaster. Faint words of praise were here and there forthcoming, plus one openly hostile review in the *Hollywood Reporter*. Not content to pan the film on its artistic merits, the critic accused the movie of being pure Communist propaganda that was being foisted on the public by three well-known 'Reds,' John Garfield, Huston, and myself. It was a vicious attack, but John shrugged it off without undue concern. He felt that Billy Wilkerson, the owner of the *Reporter*, was merely getting back at him for his having been involved in the formation of the Committee for the First Amendment. "Who cares what the *Reporter* has to say?" was his only comment. Years later I learned to my alarm and amazement that he was seriously mistaken.

THROUGHOUT the hectic months of shooting I had corresponded regularly with Papa. I looked forward to his letters, typed on thin airmail paper, which described his life with Mary, his fishing exploits, and his health as well as containing much literary advice. Then a long letter arrived with a surprising offer. Although he had never collaborated with anyone, he now suggested that we write a novel together so that I would "never again have to work for the movies." The book would be based on his experiences in the early part of World War II, during which time he had sailed the Caribbean on his small fishing boat in an effort to locate German submarines for the U.S. Navy. The plan he suggested was that he would write the part of the story that took place on the *Pilar*, and I would write the interlocking sections that would describe the activities on board the enemy submarine. As the result of thorough research, made possible by my knowledge of German, my part of the novel would complete the whole picture, which was to end in a battle between the Q-boat and the sub. The finished product would be published under both of our names and, judging by past performance, I would never be forced "to whore for Hollywood again," as he and I would split the proceeds fifty-fifty.

It was a generous and flattering proposal, but I realized that I could not accept it. The two novels I had written had been based on my own experiences, and I was doubtful, to say the least, that even the most thorough research would make it possible for me to present a true picture of life on board a German U-boat. I also foresaw that collaborating with Papa would not be an easy task. Working with Irwin on our ill-fated play had not posed any serious problems, as the age difference between us was a scant seven years. Our relationship had always been one of straightforward give-and-take. Then, too, writing a play was quite different from trying to write a novel. Irwin and I had written a long outline in which we had determined the structure and invented the characters, and once we had accomplished this we had divided the work of writing the principal scenes, "the main arias,"

Irwin had called them. The interlocking material we had written together, taking turns sitting before the typewriter.

In many ways the novel Papa was proposing could be written in a similar manner, and yet I knew the end result would probably not be satisfactory. Whatever disagreements would inevitably arise would jeopardize our friendship, and eventually it would turn out to be a waste of time and effort. I spent a couple of sleepless nights trying to decide just how to reply to his offer, for I didn't want to offend him. Finally I sat down and wrote him a long letter in which I explained all of my misgivings.

Ten anxious days later his answer arrived. He was not in the least offended, he wrote, merely thought I was making a big mistake. The next time we got together, and he hoped it would be soon, we would discuss the project some more.

THE TRADITIONAL PARTY given at the end of principal photography took place a week after Ben Hecht's new version of the final scenes was shot. It was the usual catered affair. I arrived on the set a little late, and the festivities were already in full swing. Beer and wine were being served, as well as spaghetti bolognese, furnished by a neighborhood Italian restaurant. As is customary, the highly paid help gave presents to the crew and to each other. I received from Jennifer a beautiful straight-grained Dunhill pipe that I still smoke on occasion today. It increased my already abundant admiration for her, as it proved that she was not only observant, but conscious of my adoration, which I had kept in check by a normal amount of shyness. Jigee had already complained that she was growing tired of my accounts of our leading lady's beauty and talent.

Then at the height of the festivities, a cage containing a young female chimpanzee was carried onto the set, Jennifer's present for her director. The chimp's name was Trudy, and it was love at first sight. John insisted on opening the door of the cage, and the ape emerged, embraced her new owner, and settled down in his lap. It was an extraordinary scene that I watched from a safe distance, for besides her strong, wild smell, Trudy was a good deal less than affectionate with anyone who dared approach the deck chair on which she and John were seated. Obviously there was something about him that reassured the animal's female instincts, a sexual attraction that made her cling to him and snarl at anyone else that came within her long reach. Spiegel hurriedly finished his drink and fled to the safety of his office.

"What are you going to do with Trudy?" I asked John.

"Take her home, kid, of course," he replied.

And take her home he did. As his house in Tarzana was too far from the studio, he was at that time residing temporarily in an apartment on Sunset Boulevard that Mitch Leisen had leased Evelyn. It was a luxurious flat, decorated in a rather effeminate style, with white carpets and curtains. Not long after John and Trudy arrived, Evelyn moved to Paulette Goddard's apartment upstairs, threatening not to return until her husband had "gotten rid of the ape."

I dropped in the next morning to collect John and drive with him to the studio to begin the first day of editing our film. John and Trudy were in the shower, Evelyn, who had come down to collect some of her clothes, informed me with a tense expression on her face. She disappeared a few minutes later. John emerged in due time, naked and wet, and proceeded to towel down the chimp as well as himself. "Aren't you afraid Trudy will catch cold?" I asked him. "I've read somewhere that you're not supposed to bathe chimps."

"That's an old wives' tale. Trudy will be all right."

"What about Evelyn?"

"Oh, they'll make friends sooner or later. Things were a little tense last night when we got home, but that was only their first meeting." He chuckled to himself. "It was a scene I've had to write quite a few times, when the husband introduces his wife to his mistress. I wish you could have been here, kid," he added. "They just stared at each other . . . then Evelyn put out her hand, and Trudy bit her."

"What happens to the chimp while we're at the studio?" I asked.

"She's coming with us, kid. She can't bear to be separated from me. Then next summer we're all going to Europe together—Evelyn, Pablo, Trudy, and I," he said, grinning. "A nice little family."

Pablo was a Mexican orphan who had attached himself to the crew during the filming of *Treasure of the Sierra Madre* and whom John had ultimately adopted upon his return to California.

I followed in my car, as we started off down Sunset Boulevard in the direction of Gower Street. John had recently acquired a yellow Jeepster, a convertible four-seater that he usually drove with the top down as putting it up was too difficult. Trudy sat nestled close to him, one long arm draped over John's shoulders. I noticed that there were several near accidents in the oncoming traffic as drivers stared at the strange sight and forgot to look where they were going.

John moved back to his ranch the next day, a large cage having been purchased for Trudy and installed at a healthy distance from the smaller cage that housed the other primate already in residence. Thoroughly unnerved, Evelyn had decided to stay on with Paulette Goddard, as she sensed that her troubles were only beginning. She was right. Trudy separated the flimsy bars of her cage and wandered off to visit the neighbors. In the end John was obliged to give his adopted daughter to a nearby zoo, but the harm the incident had done had a lasting effect on his and Evelyn's marriage.

He probably knew their relationship was doomed. At a party in Hollywood he had met Ricki Soma, the daughter of Tony Soma, a Manhattan restaurateur, and, according to the local gossips, took her under his wing, not quite promising her a career in the movies, but stating that she was undeniably photogenic. Ricki was nineteen years old, an aspiring ballet dancer with an Italian Renaissance face and a tense manner that gave promise of a temperamental nature. John brought her, unannounced, to our house one Sunday afternoon, much to the surprise of Jigee, who guessed at once that his interest in the young woman was not purely professional. Having been informed of John's latest conquest, but fully aware of the cabalistic nature of the local "wives club," I had kept this bit of gossip to myself. Ostensibly he had dropped in to bring me a copy of Frank Harris's autobiographical *Reminiscences of a Cowboy*, a book whose screen rights John and his father, Walter, had purchased and which he suggested I read as a possible future project for us to collaborate on. But I suspected that the true purpose of his visit was to introduce us to Ricki, knowing that he could count on our discretion.

I was pleased that John was willing to involve me again in one of his projects, and we spent a relaxed hour talking about the story. Walter Huston was to play the part of a cattle baron, and Bogart a mean, nasty cowboy, thus uniting John's two favorite actors in an unusual western that John hoped to start sometime in the near future. Sam, he said with a grin, was not too enthusiastic about "cowboy movies" but was willing to pay me a small fee to write a first-draft screenplay. I promised to read the Harris book, although I was slightly apprehensive about what Sam might consider to be a "small fee." The proposition sounded like one of Spiegel's schemes to pacify his partner, but knowing that John usually had his way when he wanted to do something, I agreed that it was worth a gamble. The fact that Walter Huston had purchased the rights was an added lure.

"She's quite a gal, Ricki Soma, isn't she?" John said to me as I walked him to his car. Ricki was still standing on our front lawn saying good-bye to Jigee and Vicky, Jigee's daughter.

"She's beautiful," I agreed. "But a little young, don't you think?"

"What's wrong with that, kid?" he asked, grinning.

"Nothing . . . as long as her father doesn't decide to shoot you." Tony Soma was known to be an excitable Italian, given to standing on his head late at night on the floor of his restaurant and singing arias from his favorite operas.

"Well, he might do that, and he might not." John said, turning to face our house. "Come on, Ricki," he called out. "We've got to get back to town."

Once John and Ricki had driven off, their departure brought on the usual discussion about the double standard that men applied to marital infidelity. Jigee liked John and enjoyed his company, but she thought that he was quite impossible to be married to. "John wants a wife not to come home to," she said drily.

I knew that we were approaching dangerous ground. John had had several love affairs while he was married to Lesley, but I told Jigee he continued "to adore her" and genuinely regretted the dissolution of their marriage. He was by nature unsuited to matrimony, I argued in his defense, as well as being led into constant temptation by his profession. Hardly anyone was "made to be married," Jigee replied, men *or* women, a statement that was quite obviously a reference to our own troubled past. She had had several lovers while married to Budd Schulberg, men with whom she had remained on good terms and whom we inevitably encountered in our circle, a fact that always bothered me. Neither of us had been faithful to the other during the war, and whenever the subject of infidelity came up Jigee never failed to remind me of Lucy, my "Red Cross girl," whom I had met in the early months of the campaign in the South Pacific. She had opened a letter addressed to me that had arrived at our house one day while I was at the studio. The letter had not been at all compromising; it had been an affectionate, nostalgic note that had contained one unfortunate sentence. "I can still remember you storming into our Club in Noumea," Lucy had written, "looking like Heathcock," an error that Jigee thought was hilariously funny at first, a Freudian slip in her opinion that proved my relationship with the young woman had not been platonic. Endless questions followed. These had led inevitably to mutual confessions, and finally to bitter recriminations.

In those days the concept of an "open marriage" was unheard of in the predominantly middle-class society whose mores, contrary to the public image of Hollywood, still dominated the movie colony. People had affairs but, once discovered, usually divorced and remade their lives with a new partner. Realizing that the war had been responsible for our infidelities, neither Jigee nor I wanted such a radical solution. We were still in love with each other, but our past misdemeanors rankled just the same, and John's visit that day opened some of our old wounds.

I remember that Marian and Irwin Shaw came to dinner that night, and when Huston's behavior was brought up again Irwin withheld comment. He had already documented his point of view on the subject in his brilliant short story "The Girls in Their Summer Dresses," and so he really had no need to say any more. It was quite apparent that he thought discretion was the answer to the problem and that the most important thing was not to get caught. Matrimony, he had often declared, was not conducive to broadening a writer's experience. Nothing ever happened to a man while he was traveling with his wife, a statement I agreed with but didn't dare second in mixed company. Irwin much preferred his wife to other women, he once told me, but being faithful to her when temporarily separated was too much to ask of him or any normal man.

Lewis Milestone, with whom Irwin was working on *Arch of Triumph*, had once quoted Pushkin on this subject to both of us. "You cannot possibly have all the women in the world," Pushkin was allegedly to have declared, "but you must try." For better or for worse, Irwin and I decided, we were both Pushkin men, as were most of our acquaintances, John Huston being the prime example.

IN THOSE DAYS, long before the advent of smog and gridlocked traffic, Malibu was, it seemed to us, one of the most consistently pleasant places in the world. Irwin and Marian had rented a cottage on the beach a few miles south of Zuma Canyon, and almost every Sunday a large luncheon party *chez les Shaws* was the order of the day. Irwin and I had been close friends since the day we met at the Beverly Hills Tennis Club in the spring of 1940. I was nineteen and he was twenty-seven, and I seem to remember that he expressed surprise that as well as being able to play a fair game of tennis, I had already written a novel.

I invited him to Mabery Road, and he became the first of my "tennis friends" to meet with my mother's wholehearted approval. That he was enamored of the theater was enough to please both my parents, who enjoyed his youthful enthusiasm for life and literature as well. Irwin's wife, Marian, had been one of Busby Berkeley's dancing girls, as had Jigee, so their friendship predated Irwin's and mine. The four of us were united in a common front against the European regular guests, who, no matter what innovative American play, or even film, was mentioned, would dismiss it with the words "Oh, that was done in Berlin in the twenties" or "We've seen that done before." Jigee said: "I suppose if fascism ever comes to America, they'll say, 'Oh, we had that in Germany long ago,'" a flippant remark that provoked only polite laughter at the tea table.

The Shaws' festivities at the beach on weekends included their theatrical friends from New York, who were less dismissive of American art. It was there that I first met Harold Clurman, Boris Aronson, Louis Calhern and his former wife Nataly Shaeffer, as well as some of Irwin's movie friends, George Stevens, Chester and Sally Erskine, and many others. Also present whenever they were in California were Martha Foley and her husband, Whit Burnett; Foley's yearly anthology of the best American short stories invariably included one written by their host. As a rule, those of the Shaws' guests who lingered on after sunset would wind up at our house for a spaghetti dinner that Jigee would prepare.

On his frequent summer visits to the West Coast Irwin had become an enthusiastic horseman and had hired two horses that were quartered in the corral Bob Parrish and I had erected fifty yards or so behind our residence, primarily to house the thoroughbred mare I had bought for Jigee before we were married and a smaller mount for Vicky that we had more recently acquired. Our Sunday outings on horseback once the heat of the day had subsided became a part of our weekend entertainment. The task of feeding and grooming our horses had fallen to me, a chore that involved my getting up an hour earlier every morning before setting out on the long drive to work.

One memorable, bright Sunday afternoon I had left the beach to prepare our mounts when a gleaming Chrysler convertible pulled rapidly into our gravel driveway. A small bald man was at the wheel, and once the dust had cleared he came striding toward me, dressed in a pair of sky blue frontier pants with a cowboy shirt to match. He put out his hand and said, "Lazar" and then squinted searchingly up at me through his thick-lensed glasses.

He had arrived at the beach too late for lunch, he explained, and being uncertain of Irwin's address had driven on to our place in Zuma Canyon, where he had been told we would all be having dinner. I recalled that the Shaws had had mentioned that they might be bringing an added guest and suggested to Mr. Lazar that he go into the house and pour himself a drink and wait for the other Sunday guests to appear. In the meantime I would finish saddling up, I told him, as some of us were planning to go for a short ride along the beach before the evening meal. To my amazement Lazar declared that he was hoping to join us if by any chance a spare mount was available.

Vicky was visiting her father in town that weekend, and rather hesitantly I told Lazar that he would be welcome to ride her miniature mare. "How old is Vicky?" he asked, somewhat contemptuously.

"Eight," I told him, but warned him that she was an expert rider. "That's her little mare over there," I added.

Lazar informed me that he had ridden quite a lot himself, a statement that sounded dubious to me when, without a moment's hesitation, he crossed to where the mare was standing and attempted to mount from the wrong side. I hastened to correct his error and helped him up into the saddle. Standing beside him I told him to wait for a minute so that I could attach a lead rein to my mare's bridle as an added precaution, but as I stepped back Lazar dug in his heels, and he went shooting off toward the main gate at what is known in equestrian circles as a hand gallop.

I quickly mounted another horse and set off in pursuit of the runaway. Once outside the gate the little mare turned left, heading down the Zuma Canyon road in the general direction of the coast highway. By some miracle her rider stayed in the saddle as I galloped after them. Knowing the pace would increase if I came up from behind too quickly, we went on for a mile or so toward the tunnel under the main road that led to the beach. I was gaining slightly on the sky blue horseman when the little mare stopped abruptly, wheeled like a polo pony, and, realizing that she was in full command, headed back for the barn.

The Shaws and several of our other guests were just getting out of their cars as Lazar, holding on to the saddle for dear life, galloped up to the corral behind our house. He dismounted with all the panache of a Tom Mix and dropped the reins of his mount. "I want to meet the eight-year-old girl who rides this animal!" he declared to the alarmed group of bystanders that had scattered to make way for his arrival.

To my knowledge it was Lazar's last ride, but it was not the last time he chose to risk life and limb that summer. Although no one demanded that he demonstrate his physical prowess, he seemed determined to show us in the weeks that followed, after he had become a regular weekend guest, that he was capable of taking part in whatever sports the rest of us indulged in. Irwin had purchased a Navy life raft in which we rode the breakers in front of his rented beach house, a not undangerous pastime when the surf was up. To avoid being ground into the wet sand once a wave had broken on the raft, we would dive off it. Soon we noticed that "Swifty," as Lazar was called by his friends, hung on to the bitter end rather than abandon ship. When he finally explained that he was a poor swimmer and chose to hold on to the raft rather than risk drowning, we thought it best to discourage his joining our boat rides on stormy days.

That he was equally fearless in his business life soon became evident. His frequent, heated confrontations with the heads of studios was in a minor way the talk of the town, and before long he became Irwin's agent. *The Young Lions*, Irwin's first novel, had recently been published to glowing reviews. The book was a literary event and an immediate best-seller and had been sold to the movies by Leland Hayward prior to Hayward's leaving MCA to become an independent producer. Lazar, sensing that Irwin was not altogether satisfied with Hayward's replacement at the all-powerful agency, stepped quickly into the breach and stole Irwin away; along with Moss Hart, George S. Kaufman, and a few others, Irwin became one of Lazar's most valuable clients. In the jungles of Hollywood this diminutive lion was making himself heard with a shrill roar.

I ran into him outside an ice cream parlor on South Beverly Drive that fall and, cones in hand, we walked to his office, situated in a back alley. It consisted of a single room equipped with a desk and two armchairs. His light blue stationery was piled on one corner of his "workbench," and I noticed that his name, irving paul lazar, was engraved on it, the letters all in lowercase, an unusual departure from the norm. He talked briefly about his past: he had graduated from law school in 1929 and, in consideration of the financial disaster of that year, had decided to make bankruptcy litigation his specialty, a shrewd decision. But he drifted quickly into show business, abandoned practicing law, and devoted himself to booking musicians into the eastern nightclub circuit that was dominated at the time by minor gangsters. It was by his own account a good proving ground for dealing with the

62

czars of the motion picture business, whose bullying methods of negotiation were somewhat less dangerous.

World War II had come along, and he had been drafted. As a university graduate he qualified for Officer Candidate School and completed the course in the same class as Clark Gable. Through the help of Moss Hart he became the booking agent for *Winged Victory*, the Army Air Force show that Hart had helped author, and rose to the rank of captain, a considerable accomplishment. After VJ day he had come West, having decided that his ability as a salesman of talent would be better served in the rich killing fields of Hollywood. Early on he had decided it was better for him to specialize in the "handling" of writers because representing actors was more time-consuming. "If you ever decide to leave Bert Allenberg," he told me that day, "I'd be pleased to take you on, too. You won't regret making the move," he added, and, as things turned out, I never have.

But long before that we became close friends. He was, above all, a most amusing man. His aggressive spirit was directed mostly at the bosses of the business whom he dealt with day in and day out, championing talent against their entrenched power. In contrast to the subtle and quiet bargaining procedures of Bert Allenberg, or even Lew Wasserman, he played an angry rebel, a small package of dynamic effrontery. Irwin succinctly explained the nature of his being: "If you had been born that size, you'd be permanently angry, too."

I remember that that fall Leland Hayward, with gentlemanly disregard of Irwin's defection from MCA, was quoted in the New York press as saying that *The Young Lions* compared favorably with *War and Peace*, extravagant praise that enraged Hemingway. In one of his letters to me he referred to Irwin as a "Brooklyn Tolstoy," a snide comment that he must have repeated to some of his cronies, for it soon cropped up in one of the New York gossip columns. In a second letter, Papa tried to justify his ungenerous remarks by accusing Irwin of having libeled his brother Leicester with an ill-concealed portrait in *The Young Lions* that made Leicester out to be "a jerk." "He is a jerk," Papa wrote, "but he's still my brother."

Shaw shrugged off Hemingway's vindictive remarks. "Papa doesn't like anyone to invade what he considers his literary terrain, war," Irwin declared. Nevertheless the incident widened the rift between the two men. With typical generosity Irwin did not expect me to take sides. Nor did all the sniping from Cuba lessen his admiration for

Hemingway's early work or deny the influence Papa had had on him as a writer.

Superficially there was a similarity between them: both were physically robust and athletic; both were bons vivants in the best sense of the word, lovers of wine and pretty women, writers with hair on their chests. But the deep differences in their natures were much more striking than the surface resemblances. Irwin was exuberant, optimistic, generous in every aspect of his nature. He was more inclined to like a friend's work than to criticize it, so much so that his affection for a fellow author often impaired his critical judgment. I could not envision his commenting unfavorably on the work of a friend.

But there was also a veiled anti-Semitic overtone in the term "Brooklyn Tolstoy," or so it seemed to Irwin and me. Papa had undoubtedly been anti-Semitic in his youth, as evidenced in *The Sun Also Rises*, but he seemed to have gotten over it. His admiration and affection for the poet Edwin Rolfe, which dated back to the Spanish Civil War, was evidence of a sort that he was not a Jew hater. Nor had he expressed any bias in his more critical stories about the photographer Robert Capa, and he had, after all, gone out of his way to befriend me. Irwin was a little more skeptical about Papa's degree of tolerance, but even he felt that Papa was much too intelligent to fall prey to any kind of serious racial prejudice. Jake Barnes, the hero of his early novel, was after all a fictional character, an invention of the author's imagination. That Jake ascribes Robert Cohn's irritating personality to his being Jewish was evidence of a snobbism that probably existed in the circles Hemingway frequented in the Paris of the twenties.

I remember a prolonged discussion on the subject one Sunday afternoon at the Shaws' beach house. Boris Aronson, the set designer, was there, as was an old friend of Irwin's, an Irishman named David Driscoll. Driscoll, influenced by a few too many drinks, launched into a long dissertation on Israel and the Jews, the gist of which was that the Jews should stop wanting to be like everyone else, that they had proven themselves to be more intelligent than Gentiles, and that their desire to be farmers and work the land was a big mistake. "What the hell do farmers talk about?" he asked rhetorically. "Will it rain, or won't it rain? That's about the extent of their conversation!"

Aronson answered in his heavily accented English with his usual eloquence, accusing Driscoll of inverted anti-Semitism. When a Jew was accused of being a gangster or a thief, he should be called just that, not a Jewish thief or a Jewish gangster. Religion and race were of no importance, neither negative nor positive qualifications. "And don't forget," Boris concluded boisterously, "it takes five hundred or more years of 'will-it-rain-won't-it-rain' to produce a Tolstoy!"

SECURELY SETTLED in our small homestead, I never would have imagined wanting to leave after less than a year and a half of residence. Mine was a geographical complacency that Irwin didn't share. He and Marian had begun to long for New York and all the pleasures city life provided—the theaters and restaurants and his many East Coast friends. He quoted Ludwig Bemelmans, the Austrian-born writer and painter, as saying that "no matter how hot it gets during the day in Los Angeles, there's still nothing to do at night." Bemelmans was also reputed to have said, that "in California, if you go out to take a sunbath, when you wake up you're middle-aged." Although I didn't hold with Bemmy's jaundiced view, it was not an unfamiliar one. My father used to complain: "There's no *Kaffeehaus*, no place to sit quietly and think. The streets are made only for cars, and it's impossible to go for a walk."

For Jigee and me, living near the beach thirty miles removed from the city was perfection, a comfortable exile that most of our acquaintances looked down upon with a tolerant superiority, as if locking ourselves away in Malibu was nothing more than an escape to a sandy Shangri-La. Chester and Sally Erskine shared our isolation after the Shaws had departed for Manhattan. Chester had been a successful Broadway producer and director in the late twenties and early thirties, and his fall had been as rapid as his rise. He had come to Hollywood after the war and had coproduced *The Egg and I* at Universal, a film that provided for his immediate economic future. He had purchased a house in Trancas a few miles north of Zuma Canyon, refurbished it, and built himself a studio above the garage where he wrote plays and screenplays while his wife painted. He was generally cynical about show business, having shed his illusions long ago in New York, but he was a friendly, highly intelligent man. He had directed Spencer Tracy in his first Broadway success, and Tracy often visited the Erskines and then eventually rented a house a mile or so up the beach from them.

Spence, as he was known to his friends, was already a myth at the time we met him through Chester. He had had a bout with alcoholism, which as a result of his friendship with Katharine Hepburn he had finally won. Of Irish descent, he had many of the Irish virtues: he was a wonderful storyteller and had a pixieish sense of humor, as well as a fair complexion that made him allergic to the bright sun. He seemed also to possess the chronic Irish melancholy, but instead of staring out at a bog was given to staring out across the Pacific. A nonpracticing Catholic, he had remained married to a wife he no longer lived with and provided for her and their children, one of whom had been born a deaf-mute. He avoided the social life of Hollywood and for that reason had rented the house in Trancas as a hideaway. Except for the Erskines and one or two of their friends, he saw very few people and was content to sit on his terrace by the sea or in the dark living room of his house once the sun had broken through the morning fog.

Hepburn came to visit him frequently. Although she had known my mother at MGM, it was at Tracy's that Jigee and I first made her acquaintance. It was soon apparent that Kate, as she was known, was a woman endowed with an amazing amount of physical and mental energy as well as a sharply critical intelligence that occasionally made her sound like a schoolteacher, the kind you would inevitably have a crush on. She took care of Spence in a good-natured, sometimes comical way that complemented his lethargic lifestyle, almost as if he knew that by letting Kate manage things he was pleasing her most. He would watch with amusement while she took care of the household chores, the shopping, the driving, and even bringing in the logs for the fireplace, an unusual chore for a glamorous Hollywood leading lady. Spence basked in her admiration of his talent, as well as her affection for him, although they were both diligently discreet in showing any sign of their devotion.

I had seen little of Huston since the release of our movie, as he was busy making a film at MGM based on a novel by W. R. Burnett, *The Asphalt Jungle*, which had been adapted by Ben Maddow, a talented young screenwriter. I envied Maddow his good fortune, as the material he had been given to work with was far superior to *China Valdez;* all the more as word was out around town that John's new effort was turning out to be an exceptional motion picture that was certain to reestablish his reputation. Then one Sunday morning he appeared unexpectedly in his yellow Jeepster. He explained that he had been invited to lunch by Anatole Litvak, who lived ten miles down the beach, and he suggested that I come along, assuring me that Litvak would be delighted to receive me. I said that I didn't think that was such a good idea.

"Why, kid?" he asked.

"Because I haven't been asked."

"Well, if Litvak looks unhappy when we arrive," he replied with a grin, "you can wait in the car until lunch is over."

Reluctantly I agreed to join him. I had met Litvak in 1936 at my parents' house. His first internationally successful movie, *Mayerling*, had just been released in the United States, and he had come to Hollywood with Jeff Kessel, the Russian-born French novelist who had written the screenplay. The white-maned director and the flamboyant writer had enjoyed a remarkable social success for several weeks, after which Kessel returned to Paris, while Litvak stayed on, having signed a contract with one of the major studios.

Litvak had met Miriam Hopkins at our house and a few months later had married the talkative blond actress, malicious rumor had it because this helped him obtain U.S. citizenship. Once established he had made half a dozen successful movies, and although he was well past draft age and was suffering from asthma, he had applied for a commission in the Army Signal Corps at the beginning of the war. John Ford, Huston, George Stevens, and Willy Wyler were already in uniform, and soon Litvak was brevetted to the rank of lieutenant colonel. Although he did not made a movie while in the service, he served overseas, mostly in London and Paris. I met him briefly in the French capital a few weeks after VE Day, when along with Kessel, Josh Logan, and Irwin he was about to set out on a tour of Germany, a trip his commanding officer had agreed to, although apart from sightseeing there had been no specific mission connected to their journey.

Several years before going off to the war, in 1943, Litvak had been the victim of a malicious canard that had been circulated in Hollywood and that had actually threatened to put an end to his career as a director. Divorced from Miriam Hopkins, he had romanced several well-known actresses, one of them being Paulette Goddard, who at the time was unhappily married to Charlie Chaplin. One evening at Mocambo's, the fashionable nightclub of the period, Litvak, it was rumored, had exceeded himself in showing his affections and had perpetrated a sexual act under the table at which the young actress was seated. Unidentified eyewitnesses were said to have testified to the truth of this outrageous story, and by innuendo Litvak had even been castigated in the local press for his alleged improper behavior.

Somehow he had survived this unpleasant experience, the injustice of which had outraged Huston, and on our drive down the coast highway, John mentioned again how pernicious these false accusations had been and how difficult to combat. I agreed with John that Litvak was hardly a man to lose his self-control to that extent and that the self-declared eyewitnesses were merely liars vying for self-importance or, worse, were being malicious purely for malice's sake. The fact that Litvak was a foreigner undoubtedly had made him a target, I suggested, and Huston agreed wholeheartedly.

Once we had been welcomed by our host, I realized that Litvak was indeed everything John had said he was, a gentleman and a *grand seigneur* with impeccable manners, certainly not the lecherous silver-haired seducer he had been made out to be by his anonymous enemies. He assured me that he was delighted I had come along and, to my surprise, added that he was eager to discuss a story with me that might well turn out to be his next movie for 20th Century-Fox. His last film, *The Snake Pit*, had turned out to be a big hit, and he felt confident that Zanuck would not veto whatever story he might select.

The beach house he had built had the gracious charm of a villa in the south of France, the walls decorated with a number of Impressionist paintings, a celebrated picture by Rouault entitled *The Three Kings* among them, as well as several Dufys. The food, too, had a French flavor and was served impeccably by his staff, who still referred to their boss as Colonel, which was not unusual, as John's groom and secretary also addressed Huston as Major Huston, a habit that was discontinued only a couple of years later.

After lunch had been served, a couple of gin rummy tables were set up on the terrace overlooking the shining Pacific, and before joining the card players Tola led me into his study. The title of the book he was interested in, he informed me, was *Call It Treason*, a war novel that was about to be published in New York. The author was a man named George Howe, who had served as a civilian documents expert in the O.S.S.

I had already heard about it, as Howe and I had served in the same unit, and the novel had been inspired by an operations I was involved in during the last month of the war in France. It was the fictionalized account of an intelligence mission behind the enemy lines that had been undertaken by a young German soldier I had, in fact, recruited, a mission that had failed and had ended tragically with the death of the young German. These small tactical operations had been called "tourist missions" and had been launched by us at the request of 7th Army intelligence.

Litvak was impressed by the coincidence that I had been a participant in the story, and this seemed to increase his enthusiasm for the project. He thought that the time was ripe for a realistic movie about Nazi Germany during the war, a new, more political version of *All Quiet on the Western Front.*

I agreed with him but told him I was hesitant about working on a story that dealt with the same background of my own experiences in the O.S.S. that I had already started to write as a novel.

"You can always go back to your novel later," he replied, brushing my objections aside. Then he admitted that one reason the story intrigued him was that it offered him a chance to make a movie in Europe. He was homesick for London and Paris and Vienna and hadn't been back to Europe since the end of the war. "You wouldn't mind getting out of this place for a while, would you?" he asked.

IT WAS A TURNING POINT in my life, which I realized only many years later. At the time I knew that I was facing a major decision, but I had no idea that it would have such far-reaching consequences. Howe's novel dealt almost exclusively with his hero's adventures once he had been parachuted into the Third Reich. The story I was planning to write, and had indeed started, was concerned with an American officer who, like me, was involved in the strange business of recruiting and launching "Joes," as we called them, into enemy-held territory. The guilt felt by those of us who stayed behind was to be the main theme of my novel, a feeling the author of *Call It Treason* had apparently not shared.

Howe's novel had no literary pretensions. He had been an architect most of his life and had joined the O.S.S. in middle age. Apparently deeply impressed by the tragic nature of this one failed mission, he had decided to try his hand at writing an imagined account of the adventures his protagonist might have encountered behind the German lines. The theme of his book was concerned with the nature of treason, the doubts he assumed his hero might have felt at the belated realization that he was betraying the Fatherland.

Litvak, I realized, was probably right in his assertion that I would not be jeopardizing my own book by writing this screenplay. I also needed to make money, for my mother, Jigee, and Vicky. Then, too, the terms that were being offered me by 20th Century-Fox were far better than those attached to working with Huston on the Frank Harris western.

I consulted Irwin, whose advice I valued, and he encouraged me to accept Litvak's offer. Litvak, he argued, was a first-rate moviemaker. Aside from *Mayerling*, his Hollywood movies were *The Amazing Doctor Clitterhouse; Confessions of a Nazi Spy; Sorry, Wrong Number*; and his most recent success, *The Snake Pit.* "Of course it would be better for you to write your novel," Irwin said. But he knew about family responsibilities. He had written radio soap operas for a good many years because of them. "Still, it will be an interesting experience working with Tola," he added. "And the food will be excellent."

His predictions were accurate. I was well fed, the experience was interesting, but it was far from satisfying. I was better acquainted with the background of our story than the director I was attempting to satisfy, as he had only George Howe's pages to guide him. Howe had had little knowledge of the conditions inside Germany during the last few months of the war. He spoke no German and had never taken part in the debriefing of any of our agents. As a conducting officer it had been my job to take the Joes to the front and see that they were taken safely through the enemy lines; I had also taken part in the debriefing sessions because I had come to know nearly all our agents intimately. Nevertheless, Tola seemed to put more value on the novel's descriptions than the information I could offer him.

I also became aware that he was trying to inject into the script an experience he had had as a boy of fifteen. Born in Kiev, he had been sent at an early age to a military school near Moscow. When the October Revolution broke out in 1917, he had attempted to make his way home to Kiev through the chaos of a civil war. Dressed in his cadet's uniform, he was the target of abuse by the Reds, to whom a military school was a symbol of the old order. The opposing side, the White Russians, were a danger to him as well, as there was the chance they would press him into military service despite his youth. Finally he had taken refuge in a small bordello.

I realized that a counterpart of this scene was bound to find its way into our film, although to my knowledge the final days of the Third Reich had made the existence of this kind of institution virtually impossible. But Tola was an incurable romantic, and the golden-hearted whore was a valid symbol of a decaying regime as well as a valuable character in a story that was practically devoid of sex and women. Hildegarde Neff portrayed this character in the film, ultimately called *Decision Before Dawn*.

But long before principal photography began there were countless arguments about every sequence I was to write, quite a few of them

70

acrimonious. "I may not be talented," Tola shouted during one of our heated discussions, "but I'm very, very intelligent." It was an allegation I could not dispute. He was also a generous and fatherly boss who had the unusual ability to forget the bitterness of our disagreements, although I was constantly exasperated by his attempts to write dialogue with only a tenuous grasp of the English language.

As we continued working and arguing, the figure of the final arbiter loomed nearer and nearer. He was none other than Darryl Zanuck, the "big boss," whom Tola seemed to respect and even fear. Zanuck had started his meteoric rise in the business as a screenwriter, and he still read all the scripts that were being prepared for production. When we were summoned to a story conference in Zanuck's office, Tola lectured me on what my behavior should be in Darryl's presence. He urged me not to venture my opinion too often, to agree whenever possible with Zanuck, as his approval of our script was all-important. We would still have the opportunity to make all the changes we wanted, but now we needed the green light. Tola transmitted his nervousness to me.

The large, air-conditioned office we were admitted to for our first story conference was intimidating. Zanuck, dressed in sky blue coveralls fashioned, no doubt, by one of the town's expensive shirtmakers, came out from behind his antique desk to greet us and launched immediately into a lengthy critique of our screenplay. Although he referred intermittently to a sheet of typed notes, he was in obvious error on a point of continuity, and I cleared my throat to correct him. "Mr. Zanuck," I began, and he stopped me in mid-phrase. "Call me Darryl," he said. "Now what were you going to say?"

Tola sat in abject silence while I timidly made my point. Zanuck stopped his pacing, returned to his desk, and checked his notes. "You're right," he said gruffly and then informed us that the studio had recently made a survey to investigate audience attendance behaviorism, the findings of which showed that sixty percent of the moviegoing public usually arrived in the theaters in the middle of the feature, proof that the trouble writers and directors took with logical continuity were largely for their own benefit and that of their peers in the industry, a point Hitchcock had made to me more than ten years earlier on the set of *Saboteur*.

Tola and I laughed politely, the conference secretary nodded and beamed as if her boss had just served an ace, and Darryl went back to the critique of our script.

Suddenly, in mid-flight, a scene occurred to him. While on the road back to the front line, our hero, he suggested, could come across an old woman, who asks for his help. Darryl played the scene for his small audience of three. He limped over to where I was seated, transformed into the character he had invented, touched my knee with a trembling hand as he asked for alms in a cracked voice. In the background I could see Tola nodding silent approval, a signal for me to abstain from comment. I noticed that the conference secretary was nodding too.

Meeting an old woman on a bombed-out road had very little to do with the plight of our protagonist at that juncture in the movie. SS checkpoints lay ahead, as did the actual combat zone that was the greatest obstacle any returning agent had to face. However, I did not oppose the big boss again, and the conference ended on a positive note. Zanuck declared that once we had made the agreed-upon changes, he would give the go-ahead to the production office; then he warned Litvak that shooting a feature in war-torn Germany was a dangerous venture. As we were ushered out of the spacious office, Zanuck shook my sweaty hand, said he was pleased to have met me, and hoped that I would work again for his studio in the near future.

We made the alterations in the script, and a new version, marked "Final Screenplay," was mimeographed and distributed to all of the studio departments. Frank McCarthy, a graduate of Virginia Military Institute and a retired colonel in the U.S. Army who had been General Marshall's aide and secretary, was appointed by Zanuck to be associate producer on the film. He was to accompany Litvak on a first reconnaissance to Germany and to attempt to get the U.S. Army of Occupation to give us technical assistance once we began shooting.

One day while I was lunching alone in the studio commissary McCarthy joined me and over our chef salads explained that he had left the Army and gone to work at Fox hoping to become a producer, and this was to be his first actual project. Litvak, he said, rather intimidated him, and I assured him that Tola's bark was worse than his bite. A soft-spoken man with a trace of a Virginia drawl and the manners of a gentleman, McCarthy seemed somewhat out of place in the 20th Century-Fox commissary; self-contained and modest, he was most unlike the vast majority of the characters in our immediate vicinity.

I wondered what had decided him to go into the entertainment business, but I felt reassured that he was going to be a member of our team.

. . . .

LIKE HITCHCOCK AND HUSTON, Litvak insisted on a close relationship during our collaboration, a requirement that was awkward because of the eighteen-year difference in our ages. Of the three, Hitch had been the easiest to get along with, less demanding than Tola and less dominating than John. During our countless dinners and luncheons he hardly ever discussed work, as meals were a time for relaxation and enjoyment.

Hitch had already made more than twenty movies by the time I worked with him, and he knew that suspense was his forte; what he required was a good plot so that he could work his magic. He was also confident that he would make many more films and that an occasional failure would do little harm to his reputation. Nor was working at close quarters with a writer a way for him to establish his *auteurism*, a word that was not in use by the French movie buffs yet, nor the critics who have worked it to death since. With the possible exception of *Rebecca*, he seemed to know that his films would inevitably be labeled "Hitchcock movies," so his vanity was never involved in our exchange of ideas.

Working with Huston had involved a constant overtone of competition. He had turned to directing after being a screenwriter for quite a few years because he was fed up with his scripts being edited or even rewritten by directors or, worse yet, misinterpreted. And beyond wanting to satisfy his critical judgment, I always sensed that he wanted to prove that he could master words even while the pencil or pen or, to be more exact, the Royal portable was in another's hands. But he was good at constructing scenes and writing dialogue, despite his many blocks, provided there was ample time.

Because Tola was lacking in these talents, he had to possess his writer to squeeze the right words out of him. He was also convinced that there was always room for improvement. Fortunately, once a script had been mimeographed and distributed, it was a studio rule that changes had to be added on paper of a different color and passed on to Zanuck, so once I had been taken off the payroll the authorship of such changes could be queried by the big boss, which made Litvak hesitate to make alterations on his own.

Throughout the summer and early fall of 1949 I continued to correspond with Hemingway. In most of his letters he complained about the many visitors who were arriving constantly at the Finca Vigia and interrupting his work. Then in late October a letter arrived that

73

sounded more cheerful. He was near to finishing his "Venice novel" and was confident that it would turn out to be his best book. By the first of November he would have completed the final chapters, and to celebrate he and Mary had decided to return to Europe for a long holiday. Why didn't Jigee and I join them? he wrote. I would need to "cool out" after my long stint at screenwriting, and a change of scenery would be good for me, too.

He proposed that the four of us spend a few weeks in Paris and then motor down to the south of France. From there we would drive to Venice for some duck shooting and then go on to Cortina d'Ampezzo in the Dolomites, a ski resort that was frequented by many of his Italian friends and that, although his skiing days were over, he much preferred to Sun Valley. He was homesick for Europe. He wanted to walk down narrow streets that were stained with "horse-piss" in the frozen snow. There were no Austrian ski teachers there to annoy him, and the place was full of beautiful Italian girls and their handsome escorts.

It was a tempting proposition—Paris with Hemingway as a guide, as well as a first visit to Venice. I mentioned it to Litvak and he made a face. He had never met Hemingway, but from what he had heard he was not favorably inclined to him. Then on second thought he agreed that my going to Europe might be a good idea, but Zanuck would probably balk at the studio's paying my way. However, if I was already there, Tola felt that he could persuade Zanuck to hire me for a few weeks of final dialogue changes. This decided me, and I drove to the office of the French Line in Los Angeles and booked a double cabin on the *Ile de France* on the date mentioned in Papa's letter. In the interest of family economy, Jigee and I decided we would travel second class, and I sent off a hasty note to Cuba with the details of our travel plans. There were still quite a few problems to be solved prior to our departure, such as who would look after Vicky while we were away and what to do about our house in Zuma Canyon, complete with horses and Bodie, our German shepherd, who was an important member of the family. We both realized what a major decision this was, but now that our passage had been booked there was no turning back.

In retrospect I am amazed by how quickly and decisively we changed the course of our lives. Leaving California, even for a limited period, meant distancing myself from the source of our income, as well as our home. During the war we had both dreamed of having our own house and a few acres of land to graze our horses. Once I had been discharged from the service, I had borrowed money from the bank to buy the land in Zuma Canyon and build our modest home. Much of the work of building fences and nailing down slates on the roof we had done ourselves with the help of weekend visitors, principally Bob and Kathy Parrish. A rugged carpenter who had been a platoon sergeant in the 82nd Airborne Division, Bob had been one of the key figures in realizing our dream. Under his guidance, we had erected the small frame structure, a slow, laborious process, as materials had been difficult to come by. Yet despite all the work and the scrounging of money, we decided to sell the place without too much heart-rending doubt. We substituted a new dream for the old one, and that was to live in Paris, where I could write novels without the seductive lure of movie money.

My mother agreed to take care of Vicky until we had settled down in Europe, and so we put our small ranch on the market and were a little dismayed when the first prospective buyer met our price. My mother had also agreed to keep Bodie, so all that remained was to find a home for Silver Blade, our thoroughbred mare. Through Huston we had met Ed Janss, a wealthy real estate operator and horse breeder, and we went to his ranch to ask if he would accept Silver Blade as a present and give her a good home to the end of her days. Her breeding was less than first rate, but Janss agreed magnanimously to accept the animal, provided he would keep her progeny or offer whatever foal she produced for sale.

All this was accomplished in a matter of weeks, including the sale of my car, a red Chrysler convertible, another prized possession. Freed of all our encumbrances, we were ready to set out on our journey. "All adventure," William Bolitho had written in his book *Twelve Against the Gods*, one of my early favorites, "begins by running away from home," and that was exactly what we were doing.

The realization that I was leaving my brief past behind only dawned on me in mid-October, when on a Sunday afternoon I decided to drop in on my mother's house to assure her that Jigee and I were not departing for good and that we would soon return to pay her a visit or have her join us with Vicky in Europe. She had passed what was then considered an important milestone in a woman's life, was well over fifty, and was given to frequently warning us that Jigee and I might never see her again.

As I let myself in through the garden gate and was greeted by Bodie, I was conscious of the dilapidated condition of the house I had grown up in. Although it was too big a place for her to keep up, she had steadfastly refused to sell it, as it represented a past of twenty troubled but happy years. She had recently rented the two rooms over the garage to Carlton Moss, a black writer, and his white wife, Lynn, which had caused a furor in the neighborhood, and now lived alone with my grandmother, an old lady enfeebled by age and Parkinson's disease, a constant reminder of what old age probably held in store for her as well.

As I entered the living room, I saw that a tea party was taking place. Thomas Mann was there, with his wife, Katja, the elderly Nobel Prize winner seated stiffly in an armchair, while his better half shared the couch in front of the fireplace with Bruno and Liesel Frank. Frank was a less well known German writer, but an equally serious intellectual, who had fled Hitler's Germany in the mid-thirties. Liesel was the daughter of Fritzi Massary, a successful musical comedy star from the old days in Berlin. Both she and her husband were less austere than the Manns, yet the presence of their most eminent colleague seemed to influence their party manners, and I was conscious of a prolonged silence while I greeted the guests and took my place at my mother's side, prepared to listen to the conversation and not take part in it, almost as if I were a child again.

The telephone rang in the breakfast room, and Lena, our German cook, appeared to announce that there was a long-distance call from Cuba. In her heavily accented English she muttered that the caller had given his name as "Papa."

"Hemingway," my mother explained for the benefit of her guests, adding with an amused smile that he was "one of Peter's new friends."

Katja Mann, more outspoken than her celebrated husband, bridled visibly. "Hemingway!" she snorted. "Huh! Anyone who likes bull-fighting is a fascist," she then announced didactically. "Don't you agree, Tommy?"

It was startling to hear the author of *The Magic Mountain* and *Death in Venice* addressed by the nickname he shared with my younger brother. "Tommy" shrugged and replied that he thought Hemingway was "a very interesting writer," obviously not eager either to correct or to agree with his wife. I excused myself and hurried off to take the call.

Static crackled on the line from the Finca Vigía, as Papa asked how I was and then urged me to change my reservation on the *Ile de France* to first class, the purpose of his call. The difference in price was only a couple of hundred dollars, and that way we could all have our meals together, as well as use the first-class gymnasium. Once we had arrived in Paris, he added, he would see to it that we wouldn't spend too much money. We were cut off before we had finished our conversation, although I had already assured Papa I would change our booking.

By the time I returned to the living room the Manns were agreeing with Bruno Frank that Hemingway deserved great credit for his personal involvement in the Spanish Civil War. Both Malraux and Hemingway were writer-adventurers, Bruno declared, and it was no accident that they always chose to support the right side, in China and in Spain. It was faint praise, and I made no attempt to voice my opinion, even when Liesel Frank added that she thought Hemingway would endure as an influence on modern literature rather than as an author whose novels would be read after his death, the final judgment on any man's work in her opinion. They were Europeans—a status I had been eager to abandon at the age of twelve—and although Bruno Frank spoke fluent English, neither he nor Thomas Mann had entered the discussion with more than an occasional nod or a brief sentence to state their agreement.

TWO WEEKS before Jigee and I were to leave for New York, my agent, Meta Reis, informed me that Sol Siegel, one of the most respected producers at 20th Century-Fox, wanted to see me. The property he was "flirting with," Meta informed me, was a *New Yorker* article entitled "Man on a Ledge," which was based on a foiled suicide attempt that had taken place in Manhattan. Despite the plans we had made and the brief time that remained before our departure, I met with him. Siegel turned out to be a friendly, businesslike man in his fifties who was genuinely eager, so he said, to make "good movies." He asked me if I had read the *New Yorker* piece and, when I told him I had, asked me if I thought I could write a screenplay based on the incident.

I told him that I was planning to leave for Europe in less than a fortnight, which show of independence seemed to intrigue him all the more, and he suggested I postpone my trip and write a treatment based on the story that Fox had optioned for him. That way he would be able to make up his mind whether to proceed with the project. The job would take less than three weeks, he reckoned, and he offered to pay me ten thousand dollars, a considerable sum of money in those days. It would make it possible for us to stay on in Europe for at least half a year, Jigee and I calculated, and still be able to sail to France on the *Ile de France* on its next eastbound crossing. As it seemed foolhardy to turn Siegel down, I accepted the brief assignment.

I called Papa and told him what had happened. We would be able to join him in Paris a little later, I explained, somewhat better equipped with money for a longer stay. He agreed hesitantly and then suggested that Jigee stick to our original plan and sail with him and Mary on the earlier crossing. "We'll take good care of her," he assured me.

We had already sent most of our belongings to Bekins Storage and were living with my mother, so once I had discussed Papa's offer with Jigee, we decided that it was not a bad idea for her to precede me. Vicky was going to stay with her father, Budd Schulberg, in Bucks County over Thanksgiving and could thus travel east with her mother on the train, a long trip it was preferable the small girl not make on her own. It seemed like a sensible solution, all the more so as Hemingway would be less disappointed if one member of our family stuck to the original plan.

As I had already sold my car, Tola magnanimously offered to loan me his Cadillac convertible for a month. He was leaving for Munich with Frank McCarthy, and he preferred I use his car rather than put it into storage. For the first time since before the war I was on my own in California, liberated from all family obligations as well as the long drive into town from Zuma Canyon. Writing a treatment for Sol Siegel turned out to be a fairly easy job. I was assigned an office and a secretary, a luxury I had not enjoyed while working for Litvak. In a little more than two weeks I was able to complete the task, and although Siegel said he regretted that I was not willing to continue with the screenplay, he wished me luck and said that he hoped we would be able to work together in the future.

I had crossed my own tiny Rubicon; come what may, I would not turn out to be a "Hollywood writer," for better or for worse.

IN NEW YORK I stayed at the Hotel Gotham. The weather was cold and clear, and I felt reassured that I had made the right decision in leaving California. I was delighted to see Marian and Irwin Shaw again, all the more so as Irwin was in an excellent mood. The city inspired him just as it had in the past. I went with him to his favorite bars, and he introduced me to many of his friends, among them John Cheever, A. J. Liebling, and Jack Kahn. Bob Capa was in town, too, as was Bill Walton and Charles Wertembaker, all three of them still employed by *Time* and *Life*, the two powerful institutions for which they had risked their lives while covering the war in Europe.

My departure for Europe only a few days away was to me an equally hazardous adventure. Paris and London were not as readily available as they are now, although daily flights to the Continent were already well established. Nevertheless I was quite happy to be traveling by ship, a more venerable form of transport. On the day of my sailing I lunched with Irwin and Capa at the 21 Club. Marian joined us for coffee, as did Walton and Wertembaker. It was a festive occasion, and all expressed regret at having to remain behind. Wert and Bill sent their greetings to Papa, while Capa and Irwin maintained an amused silence. Both had had strained relations with Hemingway in the previous few years, a condition they refrained from commenting on.

Capa insisted on accompanying me to the pier, saying he enjoyed watching a big ocean liner leave port; it was always a meaningful moment to him, lifelong traveler that he had been forced to become at an early age.

It was not my first trip on an ocean liner. As a boy of six I had traveled to New York from Hamburg on the HAPAG liner *Albert Ballin* with a German nanny and my two brothers. Years later, in 1942, I had been shipped to the South Pacific as a Marine on the *Lurline*, a more recent and memorable crossing. This time there would be no enemy submarines lurking under the surface of the ocean, a reassuring thought.

I changed for dinner in my inside cabin and made my way to the first-class bar. There were only three passengers present, a young American called Henry Lenning and a mustachioed Frenchman with pomaded black hair slicked down on his head, who was intent on the third passenger, an American girl called Eve. The girl soon turned to me and whispered that she wanted to shake off her suitor and dine with me if I was traveling alone. She was blond and pretty, with an impish, freckled face, a few years younger than I, and I happily agreed to come to her rescue. As soon as the Frenchman had excused himself to go to the men's room, Eve and I left the bar together and remained that way for the rest of the crossing.

Shipboard romances were almost a tradition in those days and Eve was a charming companion. She had just inherited a hundred thousand dollars from her grandmother and, like me, was going off to Europe to start a new life. Neither of us had any idea of our relationship becoming a lasting one, and it seemed a fairly innocent way to make the crossing pleasant. I boxed with the French masseur whose services Papa had recommended to me, won the Ping-Pong tournament in first class, cheered on by Eve, ate too much, and was genuinely sad to leave the ship when we docked in France on a gray, wintry day. I was also eager to see Jigee. I took the boat-train to Paris in the company of Henry Lenning and a young man who had introduced himself as the Vicomte de Vallembreuse, and had twice parachuted into Normandy during the war. Lenning shared a taxi with me as far as the Ritz, where I had been instructed by cable to meet the Hemingways and Jigee.

The place Vendôme and the *porte cochère* of the luxurious hotel were intimidating enough to make me feel nervous. During our previous visit to Paris, on our return from Switzerland in December 1946, Jigee and I had only passed the famous hotel as sightseers. In those days we had observed the custom of most young tourists of stopping outside the bistros of our choice to study the prices on the posted menus and thus avoid blundering into a restaurant or hotel that was too expensive. We hadn't even ventured inside the famous Ritz bar to have a vermouth cassis, the mild aperitif we had learned to order.

To my surprise I discovered that Jigee was actually staying at the Ritz, and that the receptionist was ordering the *bagagiste* to take my luggage up to her room. On my way to the elevator on the rue Cambon side of the hotel, a bellboy caught up with me and handed me a note telling me to come to the suite of "Monsieur Hemingway" as soon as I arrived. I washed my face and hands, straightened my tie, and, after reading the price card on the bathroom door and determining that we would move immediately to a less expensive hotel, went off to find Jigee and her traveling companions.

When I entered the Hemingways' suite I thought I had arrived at a cocktail party. A young man with freckles and dark reddish hair opened the door in answer to my timid knock and introduced himself as Aaron Hotchner, "Hotch" to his friends. I judged him to be about my own age and was impressed by his pixielike friendliness. I followed him into the sitting room and was given a hug by Papa, who said, "It's good to see you, Pete." Mary too smiled and accepted a kiss on both cheeks. There was also a heavyset, dark-haired man in a black suit whom Papa introduced as Don Andrés, his private priest. "He speaks Basque and Spanish, and that's all," Hemingway warned me with a wide grin.

Jigee was seated at the far end of the room, and I arrived last at her chair. "It's about time," she said mischievously as I kissed her on the forehead. I wasn't sure if she meant it was about time I got around to her or if she was referring to my late arrival. She looked paler and thinner than when I had seen her a month earlier.

"We've looked after your girl," Papa assured me.

"As you see," Jigee said, indicating her surroundings. "I'll explain later," she added for my benefit in a lower voice.

I felt like a husband who joins his wife at a vacation resort long after the season has gotten under way. The others in the group had their private jokes, knew each other well, and had had their little adventures during *their* crossing. I experienced a sudden pang of jealousy. I knew that Jigee believed in a single standard of conduct. We had gone through that often enough, and because I felt guilty about my own behavior I was suspicious of hers. At first glance Hotchner seemed like the most obvious candidate for her to have chosen. He was young and, although not traditionally handsome, was attractive enough, bright and lively and overly friendly toward me. Looking back, I realize just how outrageous my attitude was, but there is nothing logical about jealousy.

Papa asked if I would like a glass of champagne. A bottle of Perrier-Jouët was resting in an ice bucket next to Jigee's chair. "I'll have what Jigee's having," I said.

"She's having a whiskey sour," Papa said. He went on to explain that he had found her too thin and had persuaded her to have a whiskey sour before dinner so as to relieve her nervous stomach.

I made a face and said that I'd prefer a ginger ale. But that was about the only drink that was not available in his small private bar, Hemingway said, suggesting I settle for a glass of Perrier-Jouët, a better drink to celebrate my arrival and my "joining the club." While he poured, he assured me that "nothing wrong" had taken place, that they'd all had a good time, and repeated that he had "looked after your girl." As I had already learned, and would learn again and again in the years ahead, Papa had an unfailing instinct about what was going through the minds of people around him and had the ability to say just the right thing most of the time.

He and Mary would not be able to join us for dinner that night, he went on to say. They would dine in their room as he was putting the finishing touches to his novel so that Hotchner, who was a junior editor at *Cosmopolitan,* could take the completed manuscript back to New York. The novel was to be serialized in the magazine prior to publication, which was the reason Hotch, at Papa's suggestion, had come along on the trip. "He's a good boy," Papa added. "You'll like him." Hotchner was not staying at the Ritz, but he would meet Jigee and me in the little bar, it was decided, and from there the three of us would go out for our evening meal.

As soon as Jigee and I were alone together I asked her why she had decided to stay at the Ritz. She explained that she had been persuaded by Papa to stay there for a few days to get used to the city. That same afternoon a messenger from Papa's French publishing house had arrived with a package that contained all the royalties that Hemingway had accrued during the war. Papa had been delighted by this windfall and had insisted that they divide the money three ways. Sitting on the floor of their sitting room he had counted out three stacks of the flimsy bills, one for Mary, one for himself, and one for Jigee. That way she wouldn't have to worry about the high room rates; besides, Papa had been offered a special rate for his party by Charles Ritz, an old friend from his early days.

I asked her how she could possibly have accepted such a big present. Her share amounted to almost two thousand dollars. Jigee explained that Hemingway had insisted she take a third of the money, and Mary had agreed because if Jigee refused, Mary would be deprived of her "pocket money" as well.

"What about Hotchner?" I asked, studying her face closely.

"He's on an expense account from *Cosmopolitan*," she replied, "and doesn't need extra funds."

I told her that I would pay Hemingway back, but she begged me not to mention the incident, as Papa would be offended. After all, it had been at his insistence that she had agreed to stay at the Ritz.

We changed for dinner and went down to the small room that faced the main bar of the hotel, called *le petit bar*, fittingly enough. The bartender was a short, partially bald Frenchman with glasses whose name was Bertin, and it was immediately apparent that he knew Jigee well. I was surprised to see that he served her a second whiskey sour, and she explained that as this was a special occasion, a second drink was in order. I was slightly disturbed by this but said nothing. Hotchner joined us a few minutes later. His manner toward me was even friendlier than it had been at our first meeting, and he declared that he was delighted I had joined the party, that he and Jigee had been waiting for me with impatience. I suspected that there was a hidden meaning behind his remarks and that it had to do with Papa and was in no way related to himself and Jigee. I dismissed my earlier suspicions and wound up feeling even guiltier about my own behavior.

My back was to the entrance of *le petit bar*, and I noticed that Bertin's face suddenly lit up. Turning, I saw that Papa had arrived, followed by Georges, the head bartender. A thin, fairly tall man with a ferret-like face and a receding hairline, Georges was the famous doyen of the establishment, had been there in the twenties, and had served Scott Fitzgerald and Zelda as well as many of the other illustrious habitués of the hotel. Not only had he mixed their drinks, but he had seen to it that their messages were delivered, had even loaned some of them money, and, most important of all, had advised Papa and a few of the others on what horses to bet on at the various racetracks around Paris.

While the two bartenders stood politely beside our table, the talk was all about the next day's meeting at Auteuil. Georges' interest was mainly in flat racing, but he seemed to enjoy the discussion, obviously flattered by Hemingway's presence. He had accepted the fact that his famous customers preferred Bertin's little bar now that the main room had become too popular with socialites and businessmen.

Papa looked older than he had during our stay in Havana a year and a half earlier. His jaw was covered with a gray stubble, and his stomach appeared to be pushing against his tweed jacket. He suddenly looked like an elderly American tourist, an image that was emphasized by his halting, heavily accented French. He looked a little seedy in the elegant surroundings of the bar, where all the other occupants were in dark gray or blue suits, the customary dress for an evening out in the city.

Only his language was unchanged, his slow, telegraphic style of speech, rendered in a deep voice with a midwestern twang. "Good to have you on board, lieutenant," he said with a smile and raised the double dry martini Bertin had served him with a flourish.

"Good to be here, Papa," I replied hesitantly.

He chuckled and said, "How do you like it now, gentlemen?" which I remembered was one of his favorite sayings, a famous, oft-repeated gibe attributed to a British colonel on some distant battlefield of the empire.

Then I noticed that he turned his attention to Jigee. He told her that he was sorry he was not joining us for dinner and suggested we go to one of his favorite bistros on the Left Bank, a place that was reasonable but good. He spoke to her in a low voice, shyly but with affection.

I couldn't quite catch the drift of what he was saying to her, as Hotchner had engaged me in small talk, commenting on the difficulties of being a freelance writer with a young wife and daughter to support. After a while Papa excused himself, told Bertin to put the drinks on his tab, and said that he was going back upstairs to have dinner with Mary. We all watched him as he made his way slowly through the frosted glass doors, and suddenly I realized that it was not Hotchner who was my rival, but Papa himself who had become smitten with my wife.

"SMITTEN" was Jigee's word. I recalled she had often used it in her long-ago, girlish conversations with Sonia Schulberg, her former sister-in-law and her closest woman-friend. They had their own private language, preferring the archaic "smitten" to more colloquial expressions, such as "So and so has a crush on you." "Captivated" is the meaning given by the dictionary, and that Papa was captivated by her was fairly apparent.

Once we were alone I asked her just how serious their flirtation was, and she laughed nervously, realizing that I was upset. "Don't be ridiculous," she said and went on to assure me that it was nothing more than a platonic friendship, that Papa was as protective of her as if she were his daughter, although I had noticed he didn't call her that, as he did most young women. There was a girl in Venice, Jigee told me, with whom he had fallen in love and who was the main reason for his returning to Italy. Her name was Adriana Ivancich, and Hemingway had told Jigee repeatedly that his Venetian girl was "a beauty" as well as intelligent and talented.

Despite all of his raving about Adriana, Jigee suspected that their relationship was merely an aging man's rather pathetic fixation. Adriana was an aristocrat, which appealed to Hemingway's secret snobbism. He had shown Jigee a photograph he carried in his wallet; Adriana had too prominent a nose to qualify for the term "beauty" in Jigee's judgment, but she had lovely dark hair and eyes. She had been the inspiration for the heroine of his new novel, which he had recently decided to call *Across the River and into the Trees*, a paraphrase of General Stonewall Jackson's dying words.

I asked her if Papa had let her read the manuscript, and she said that he had, proof to me of his newly established confidence in her judgment. Hotchner had read it, too, she added quickly and went on to say that they had both "tackled" Papa about a slightly anti-Semitic reference alluding to the scandal that had been caused in Washington, D.C., by one Bernard Goldfine and that had involved a vicuña coat. "How many more Goldfines were there?" Colonel Cantwell had wondered in the original manuscript, a brief passage that Hemingway had agreed to delete.

I asked Jigee what she thought of the book, and she replied that although it was "touching and sad," much of it read like a satire of his earlier work. It would probably sell well as it was his first novel in quite a few years, but she doubted that the critical response would be favorable. "What did you tell him after you read it?" I asked her.

"What could I say? He sat in the same room with me while I read most of it. So I just said that it made me feel like crying, which was true, and that he accepted as a compliment." There was a tragic undercurrent to Cantwell that gave the novel a special meaning, a confession of failure that quite obviously was Papa's way of airing his dissatisfaction with his own life. "I'm sure he'll give it to you to read if you ask him," she told me.

I said: "I think I'll wait until I'm on neutral ground."

Jigee told me that Hemingway was still working on the manuscript, curiously enough in the bathroom of his suite because nobody bothered him there until midday. Two bottles of Perrier-Jouët were stored in an ice bucket every evening, and he drank them while he made his corrections and additions the following morning. He never seemed to show the effects of the champagne, which was astonishing, Jigee added.

I asked her if she found him attractive, and she ridiculed my question. His protruding stomach and the faintly unkempt odor—that and the rash on his face would have been enough to put her off, she said, even if she were not in love with me. He was generous and paternally protective, but impossible to take seriously as a suitor.

What about Hotchner? I asked, and Jigee replied that he was a pleasant enough young man with a good sense of humor. He was struggling to make ends meet as an editor and a writer, and this assignment was obviously his big chance to get ahead. Anyway, he had only recently married a pretty young redhead and appeared to be very much in love with her. "Thank God he joined the party," Jigee added. He had defused the tensions that had surfaced during their crossing. There had been a journalist named Sam Boal on the boat, and his presence had irritated Papa and had made him ill-tempered and mean at times, which had disturbed Mary, as Boal was an old friend from her London newspaper days.

At noon the next day Don Andrés, the incomprehensible Basque priest, joined the group in Bertin's *petit bar* before we set out for Auteuil. The weather was cold and cloudy, so Mary and Jigee decided to spend the afternoon window-shopping. Papa, Hotchner, the "black priest," and I got into the Packard limousine that had been hired by the concierge for Hemingway's use. The punters, Hotchner and Papa, were equipped with a pair of binoculars and several copies of *Le Turf*, the Paris version of *The Racing Form*. Papa and Hotch had formed a syndicate after pooling some of their resources, and together they were eager to try their luck.

It was a pleasant way to spend the day, especially for Papa and Hotch, as they took their betting seriously. I enjoyed walking down to the saddling paddock and staring at the glistening horses and their owners, trying to decide on my choice based on the looks of the entries, one reason that I was less successful than my companions. Hemingway spent his time in the bar, moving out to the grandstand to watch each race after Hotchner had been dispatched to place their bets. Don Andrés participated with them in the feature race of the day and, when he won, declared that he had made more money in that one afternoon than he would have made officiating at six weddings and four baptisms.

As one of the few priests who had chosen to side with the Loyalists during the Spanish Civil War, he had been forced to take refuge in Cuba, where he lived an impoverished existence. It was quite obvious that Papa had helped him financially in the past, although Hemingway made no mention of it. On the way back to the Ritz, Don Andrés, exuberant after his winning wager, burst into a fierce Basque song which none of us could understand. Papa was pleased to have a man of the cloth in his entourage, although when I asked him about his own religious beliefs, he replied that he was *"pratiquant, mais pas croyant,"* a practicing Catholic, but not a believer, a humorous reversal of the usual response. But neither was really true.

The daily excursion to Auteuil became our way of life during that first week. It usually started in *le petit bar* with bloody Marys, and when Mary and Jigee came along, we lunched in splendor at the racetrack in the upstairs restaurant that looked down on the track and the distant Paris skyline. The food was far superior to the ham sandwiches

Berlin, 1926. My brother Hans (right) and I in our last days of German citizenship. Shortly after this photo was taken, we joined my parents in Hollywood, where my father was working on a film for the Fox studio with his countryman, the legendary expressionist filmmaker F. W. Murnau.

My mother in 1939, photographed near the Austrian mountain resort Semmering, where she was visiting her sister.

My father at his writing table in New York, where he lived and worked during World War II.

This photograph of Greta Garbo, taken in the early 1930s, evokes the woman I remember—the cheerful friend of my mother, not the notorious recluse she would later become.

Our house on Mabery Road in Santa Monica Canyon. Here my mother held her tea parties and dinners for the German and Austrian intelligentsia who had fled Hitler in the 1930s. Frequent guests included Bertolt Brecht, Thomas Mann, and others.

Christopher Isherwood in Santa Monica, 1938. His novel *Prater Violet* was inspired by his experiences working on a film my father directed.

On my way to the Officer Candidate School in Quantico, Virginia, spring 1944.

In front of the house Jigee, my first wife, and I rented in Ketchum, Idaho, in the winter of 1948–1949. The man shovelling snow off the roof is our houseguest Robert Parrish, a Hollywood film editor. A few hours after this picture was taken, Bob broke his leg skiing.

When I was growing up, Ernest Hemingway was my literary idol;
when I was older I was fortunate to have him as a friend, a mentor,
and an admirer (and thoughtful critic) of my work. Here is "Papa,"
as he liked to be called, and his wife, Mary, in Ketchum in the 1950s.
(John Bryson)

Dinnertime at our rented house in Ketchum during the winter of 1948–1949. From left to right: myself; Vicky, Jigee's daughter from her marriage to Budd Schulberg; Kathy Parrish, Bob Parrish's wife; Jigee; Bob.

Left to right: Jigee's and my daughter, Christine; Jigee; Vicky. We're celebrating Christine's second birthday in Klosters, Switzerland, 1956.

and beer we had eaten in the downstairs bar, and, as it was fairly expensive, Papa always insisted on picking up the check.

One evening before dinner, when we were once again seated in Bertin's bar and Mary and Jigee had not yet joined us, I looked up and saw Eve, the young woman from the *Ile de France*, come through the glass doors and then retreat quickly into the hallway. I excused myself and hurried after her. For a brief moment we stood together in the vestibule near the rue Cambon entrance of the hotel. By chance she was meeting someone there, but once she had seen me she had decided to leave as quickly as possible. We spoke for only a minute or two. She asked me if I was all right, and I told her that, yes, I was fine and hoped she was all right, too. She gripped my hand and told me to go back and rejoin my friends, which I did.

Papa had observed the brief incident, and when I was back at our table he asked me who the girl was. Somebody I met on the boat, I replied in an offhand manner. "I wish I'd known," he said, which seemed like a strange thing to say. But as no further comment was forthcoming, I decided to ignore the remark. I realized that he had been shrewd enough to guess that Eve had been more than a brief acquaintance, probably because I hadn't invited her in for a drink or because I had flushed slightly when I saw her. Later I gained a better understanding of his meaning, but for the moment I merely felt relieved that Jigee had not been present. We had reestablished our marriage during those first days in Paris and were quite happy, although we were feeling somewhat the strain of being members of "Dr. Hemingstein's command."

There was always a slight tension in the air when we were all together, probably because in Papa's presence I was conscious of having to choose my words carefully, as very little anyone ever said was taken lightly. We all wanted to please our leader, and only Jigee was herself. She was clearly Papa's favorite, which I couldn't help noticing bothered Mary at times. He was fond of his wife, called her "Kitten," while she referred to him as "Lamb," especially when she interrupted one of his anecdotes, which never failed to annoy him. But there were always abject apologies when he spoke roughly to her, which he was apt to do, especially when she professed a greater knowledge of the city. *"Montrez-moi Paris,"* he would say with biting sarcasm, and, thus rebuked, Mary would fall silent.

One day when there was no racing at Auteuil, Papa suggested we go for a long walk. I don't remember why Hotch didn't come along. It was a cold, wintry afternoon that convinced Mary and Jigee to remain indoors, and so we went off together. We visited Brentano's on the avenue de l'Opéra, where Papa bought a few books for his intended trip to Venice. He found a copy of *Death in the Afternoon*, which he purchased for me and signed with an apology for the poor reproductions of the photographs. "You might need to sell this someday, Pete," he said, "although I doubt it." Then he went on to say that he looked on me as one of his sons, "the one that's good at making money," which was meant to be flattering, although it fell a little short of being a compliment.

From Brentano's we took a taxi to the rue Notre Dame des Champs, where Hemingway had lived with his first wife, Hadley, and their son, Jack, in a small apartment above a sawmill. As we climbed the narrow stairs past peeling plaster walls, Papa recounted that it was here, in this cold-water flat, that he had written many of his early short stories and had worked out his style, which was intended for "people who move their lips when they read." As we made our way back down the squalid stairs, he spoke of Scott Fitzgerald, who had come to visit him there with "poor, crazy Zelda." The Fitzgeralds had been rich and like most rich people had been careless with the property of the poor. They had allowed their daughter, Scotty, to urinate on the stairs instead of taking her to the comfort station on the corner, and this had provoked a row with the Hemingways' landlady. He had loved Scott, he said, had felt sorry for him being married to "a crazy." This led him to go on and tell the by now well known anecdote about Fitzgerald's sexual inferiority complex, as Zelda had insisted that his penis was too small to ever satisfy her. To comfort his friend, Papa had ordered him to "show me his cock" and after Scott had done so had told him that "it was no beauty, but of normal size." As Fitzgerald insisted that the opposite was true and that Zelda was probably right, Hemingway suggested they go to the Louvre so that they could "compare Scott's cock with the classics."

The story was genuinely funny, although later, when it appeared in print, it seemed more like a malicious anecdote to many of the critics. It didn't sound malicious at the time. Then, too, it was not Hemingway who was entirely responsible for his book of reminiscences as it appeared after his death. Listening to his anecdotes of those early days, I felt flattered to be given such an intimate view of his formative years.

A dozen years later, after Papa's death and after Hotchner's book appeared, I realized that he had taken Hotch on the same tour a week or so earlier. It was apparent that during this, his first peacetime visit to Paris, he had become overwhelmed by nostalgia, was conscious of the myth that had sprung up around that period of his life. Or perhaps he was merely rehearsing his anecdotes so that he would be able to write them more easily later, although he had warned me on several occasions that "the stories you tell you never write."

Later that afternoon we walked in the Luxembourg Gardens, where once again he told of his pigeon hunting adventures, the same stories he had told Hotchner. That he had been so poor he had had to snare pigeons for the family supper didn't sound quite believable to me. He and Hadley might well have been strapped for money—when they lived over the sawmill Papa had been a relatively unknown author—but by his own account they had often gone to the Vel d'Hiv for the bike races, and he had had enough money to box and work out in one of the local gyms, where he got paid for being a sparring partner.

He told me that for many years he had only been able to sell his stories to *Querschnitt*, a German avant-garde magazine, in which they had appeared in translation. Because of my parents I was well acquainted with *Querschnitt* and knew that it paid very little, yet I couldn't quite believe the Hemingways had actually gone hungry. I thought that perhaps he was trying to impress on me that being poor was not the worst thing that could happen to a young writer, another argument in favor of my not giving in to the temptation of "whoring" in Hollywood.

From Les Jardin du Luxembourg we went on to Sylvia Beach's bookshop, Shakespeare and Co., where Papa was well received by the old lady who had first published Joyce. I remember her as a pale, thin woman in a worn sweater and fingerless wool gloves. She was delighted that "Ernest had come back" to see her and to browse, although we stayed there for only half an hour. Then we went on to Harry's Bar on the rue Danou. In the taxi, Papa spoke lovingly of Joyce as "poor blind Jimmy," although he made no mention of having read Joyce's work. Instead he spoke disparagingly of Gertrude Stein and Alice Toklas, with whom he had fallen out many years ago. I didn't press him to elaborate on either subject. I was too much in awe of him to ask for more than he was willing to tell.

He said he would have liked to take me to La Closerie des Lilas, another of his old hangouts, but he had gone there only a week ago and had found the place to have changed so much that it made him feel sad. He said he felt the same way about Harry's Bar, but we stopped there nevertheless. Papa had a Calvados, and I drank a beer and ate a hard-boiled egg. As in the bar we had gone to in Ketchum, there was an American Legion flag on the wall, a fact that once more didn't please Hemingway. The barman was a young replacement with no knowledge of Hemingway or the past, and he served us in a perfunctory manner, much to Papa's disgust.

For me it was a fascinating afternoon, and I told Jigee about it in detail once we had returned to the warm comfort of the Ritz. The next day, with Mary as a guide, we went to a furrier on the rue Cambon behind the hotel, where I purchased a sheared beaver coat for Jigee, a minor extravagance, while Mary bought a black Persian lamb redingote she fancied. Both of these purchases more than took care of their share of the royalties Papa had divided. Despite the fact that our wives were now better equipped to face the damp cold of the Parisian winter, there were no more guided tours into Papa's past.

MUCH HAS BEEN WRITTEN about Hemingway's inner motivations, his paranoia, his fascination with death, his suicidal inclinations, his chronic alcoholism, whatever made him tick. At the time I was conscious only of his acceptance of approaching old age, manifested by his nostalgia, a premature dwelling on his own past. Physically he had been severely marked by the wars he had participated in, although the only wound he had received in combat was at Fossalta in 1918, and that had healed long ago. In World War II he had suffered a head injury in an aircraft of the Royal Air Force as well as various bumps and bruises in automobile accidents, civilian and military. Yet he gave the impression, as Hotchner remarked to us that night at dinner, that he was "being held together by wire and glue."

He suffered from high blood pressure brought on by a nervous condition that he attempted to minimize by drinking. Alcohol was obviously responsible for the deterioration of his health. I remember that in Paris that autumn he often urinated into a glass early in the morning and then held it up to the light for a cursory inspection once the early darkness of the November mornings had cleared away. It was quite natural for a man who drank as much as he did to be concerned with the functioning of his liver and kidneys. In appearance he was still a huge man, and during our frustrated fishing expeditions in Cuba he had shown that he had bullish strength. He had stood for hours on the flying bridge of the *Pilar*, had swum ashore holding his rifle over his head for a distance of well over two hundred yards.

But then he was more used to living in the country than in a town, and the warm climate of his home base was undoubtedly better for him than the cold damp of Paris. He still worked standing up in the bathroom of his hotel suite several hours a day, but after that he remained mostly seated, in bars or restaurants or the armchair of his sitting room where he was in the habit of reading for most of the afternoon. He didn't smoke, and I remember that he warned me that if I continued to do so it would ultimately impair my sense of smell, a prediction that didn't turn out to be true. He also predicted that my legs would "go first," as they were skinnier than normal, another forecast that so far has failed. He did not sleep well, but that I have learned is an avoidable part of getting old. The rash that covered his face had probably been caused by overexposure to the harsh tropical sun while at sea, a danger we were all less conscious of in those days.

He had undoubtedly lived a harder life than any of my friends, with the possible exception of John Huston, who had served in the Aleutians and in northern Italy during the heaviest fighting. Also, Huston had started life as a frail child who in his own words had "never thought he would last very long"; had fallen off horses fairly regularly; had taken in his share of alcoholic beverages; had smoked cigarettes and cigars; and had lived under the stress of financial problems for nearly all his life. But Huston was better equipped to roll with the punches than Hemingway, possessed a survivor's psyche, undoubtedly acquired during his sickly childhood. Despite the airplane accidents that came later, it was Hemingway's essential nature that propelled him toward an early end. "There are people in this world," my father once said to me, "that spend their lives seeking death, while the others desperately seek life." It was an observation that seems truer than ever to me today.

One morning during our stay in Paris, I accompanied Papa to his bank, the Guaranty Trust Company on the place de la Concorde. He had kept an account there since his early days in Paris and was greeted with respect, although, as he said, the balance of his account was negligible. He gave the teller a letter of credit and asked for several thousand dollars worth of traveler's checks. While we waited he reminisced about some of the other people he had known in the Paris of the twenties, John Dos Passos and Donald Ogden Stewart. His friendship with Dos Passos had ended during the Spanish Civil War. José

Robles, Dos Passos's translator, had been shot without a trial by the Loyalists, which had soured Dos on the Loyalists' cause. "It's a serious matter when they shoot your translator, but during a civil war these things are apt to happen," Papa remarked.

Don Stewart had been a cheerful companion, he continued, and he still liked "old Don, although he hung around the rich too much." I told him that Stewart was a friend of my mother's, as well as our neighbor, and that he had intervened with James Forrestal during the war when I had been wrongly accused of being either a Red or a Fascist and that the letter he had written Forrestal had made it possible for me to become an officer in the Marine Corps instead of remaining a private for the duration. "He probably saved my life," I added.

I noticed that Papa changed the subject at once. As had been the case with Irwin Shaw and Bob Capa, he did not persist in his criticism of Stewart once he knew that I considered him a friend. He merely stated that it was a shame Don had gone to Hollywood. But I already suspected that his loyalties were apt to change once people exited his life. The only person he never reviled or belittled was Hadley. Whenever he spoke of her he blamed himself for the failure of their marriage. It still seemed to weigh upon his conscience twenty-five years later.

While we waited there in the bank he continued to speak of his former Paris friends and express his compassion for Scott Fitzgerald, John Dos Passos, Archibald MacLeish, Don Stewart, and "poor, crazy Ezra [Pound]," who was languishing in a mental hospital, accused of being a traitor. The only person besides Hadley, of whom he spoke with enduring affection was Max Perkins, who had died in 1947, "a bad year." Perkins had always been a loyal friend and staunch supporter, and his premature death had robbed Hemingway of the one person whose help he would never be able to repay.

He signed the traveler's checks and we returned to the Ritz bar and the daily routine of going to the races. That day Jigee and I had planned to go off on our own, as we had been invited to lunch by Marcel Achard, the French playwright, and his wife, Juliette. The Achards had been frequent guests at my parents' house during the thirties, and I had seen them briefly in Paris during the last winter of the war. Hemingway accepted our temporary defection with good grace, although I knew that he didn't like changes in the daily routine.

"We'll miss you guys," he said, glancing over at Jigee. We were all standing on the sidewalk of the rue Cambon after our midday session in Bertin's bar. The driver of Papa's hired limousine, another equally loyal Georges, had gone to fetch the Packard from where he always parked it on the place Vendôme, and Mary and Jigee were huddled in the back doorway of the hotel, keeping out of the cold. A seedy-looking man in a worn overcoat came ambling along the *trottoir*. He stepped up to Papa and mumbled something to him. Hemingway grinned and said: *"Je regrette, mon vieux, mais je suis dans le métier moi-même."*

The man looked puzzled, shrugged, and continued on his way. Papa explained that the fellow had tried to sell him some pornographic postcards, adding that he had discovered long ago that the best way to get rid of these types was to tell them that he was in the same business. Obviously quite pleased with himself, he climbed into the back of the big Packard limousine where he was joined by Mary and Hotchner and the three were driven off to Auteuil.

As there were no taxis available, Jigee and I made our way to the Métro station and were transported with surprising speed to the Left Bank and the rue de Courty, where we found our way to the Achards' apartment. I rang the doorbell, and we were admitted by Madeleine, their maid, a handsome woman from Brittany who had looked after the strange couple for years.

Achard was a small man with enormous glasses and a friendly, mis-chievous smile that was seldom absent from his round face. He was slightly hunchbacked, a handicap his talent and optimistic nature had helped him overcome. He invariably doused himself liberally with cologne, which I inhaled as he hugged me affectionately after kissing Jigee's hand. Juliette Achard had been a pretty young woman with a good figure when she had first appeared at my mother's house in California, but she was plumper now and more nervous than I remem-bered her. Living through the war in Paris had robbed her of her youth, as had, it soon turned out, Marcel's propensity for falling in love with the leading ladies in his plays. Melina Mercouri was his favorite of the moment, a fact that Juliette soon revealed to us with no small trace of bitterness. A French marriage was difficult even for the French, Jigee and I were discovering.

Achard asked me what had brought us to Paris, and I told him that we had come on a pleasure trip with the Hemingways. Marcel was duly impressed. Not so Juliette. *"Hemingway c'est un ivrogne,"* she stated flatly, *"comme tous les écrivains américains."*

Achard said: *"Juliette, quand même!"* reproaching her only slightly, but not quite prepared to correct her statement that "all American writers are drunkards." The meal that followed was a most pleasant one just the same, and we were conscious once again of how relaxing it was to be on our own, away from our eminent traveling companions. But it was not only the sensation of being absent without leave that made the day memorable, it was the atmosphere of our host's love of life. Despite Marcel's deformity he seemed assured that the gods had treated him well. He had survived the war, as had Paris, the boulevards he loved, the theaters and cinemas, the bistros and cafés. Unlike Hemingway, he wanted to forget the past, his enemies, his failures, the German occupation, the fact that he'd been born a myopic hunchback, the son of an innkeeper from Lyon. He had even survived the censure of many of his acquaintances who felt he should have left Paris once France had fallen.

He took us into his study, a small corner room crammed with books and manuscripts, with long windows that looked out onto a narrow little garden. It was here that he had written a number of his most successful comedies, and it was here that he had recently finished a new play and hoped to write many more. He said that he loved to make people laugh, it was his greatest pleasure, and he quoted "your friend Hemingway" that "if you want to send a message, you should call Western Union." "Why don't you write for the theater, Peter?" he asked. "It's so much more satisfying."

I told him that I had, that the play I had written with Irwin Shaw had failed in New York, and that the experience had been less than satisfying.

He knew Irwin, had met him during the liberation of Paris, and had found him to be a charming, energetic, "and undoubtedly a most talented young man." But there was only one serious problem with Irwin, he went on to say. He hated actors, had told Achard so during one of their long, festive dinners. "And that is impossible!" Marcel crowed. "If you want to write for the theater you must *love* actors, love them with all of their faults, all of their damned foolishness!"

Juliette had entered the small study to ask if her husband was coming home for dinner. Her English was very limited, but it was good enough to understand Marcel's outburst. There are authors who love actors too much, she allowed caustically, and bade us all *au revoir*.

Marcel raised his well-manicured hands and shrugged a wry, Gallic shrug. "Really," he said, "sometimes life can be very difficult. But you have to try to be happy just the same!"

LATER THAT WEEK we went to the Louvre and Le Jeu de Paume. Moving slowly over the creaking parquet floors, we stopped in front of all of Papa's favorite pictures. He had learned a lot from painting, he said, had written many of his early short sketches with the same inspiration as a painter, had wanted to reproduce with words the things he had seen and could not forget, all of it a part of his training himself to write "truly and honestly."

I remembered that when we had first met Jigee had not been a great admirer of Papa's work. She had often ridiculed his attitude toward women, had found his machoism offensive, and had made fun of the lovemaking scenes in *For Whom the Bell Tolls*. But now that he had become an admirer, she appeared to have forgotten her early disapproval of his work. I noticed the change in her, realized that his apparent infatuation had made her set aside her literary judgments, and was disturbed by their relationship, not so much out of jealousy but because it complicated *my* relationship with him. I couldn't help feeling that he preferred her company.

Nevertheless our last few days in Paris were enjoyable. We went several times to the Brasserie Lipp for lunch, where M. Cazes, the proprietor, received Papa like a long-lost friend. It was one of the places, Papa said, that he used to "save up for" when he was a young man. His favorite first dish was the saveloy sausage in a mustard sauce that was sharp enough to make our eyes water. I was aware that Papa's presence in the old-fashioned, mirrored room created quite a stir, although out of respect no one bothered him for an autograph.

As Christmas approached, Hemingway decided that we had spent enough time in Paris. He said that he had never left any place he loved willingly but that it was time we set out on our trip south. As the day of our departure fell on Christmas Eve, we exchanged presents on the twenty-third of December in the Hemingways' suite. Jigee and I had bought Papa a hunting knife with a horn handle, and we were all amused to discover that several other of his presents turned out to be cutlery of one kind or another. The celebration was a cheerful event. Charley Ritz turned up, and we had *pâté de fois gras* and caviar for our premature Christmas dinner. Papa was extremely fond of Ritz, a long-standing affection that was obviously mutual.

The following day I helped Georges load the Packard with the mountain of luggage the *bagagistes* in their blue work clothes had piled on the sidewalk of the place Vendôme. The car had been equipped with a roof rack for the journey, a fortunate addition as the rear trunk was soon full. *"Ça sera plus facile de changer les noms des rues,"* Georges muttered good-naturedly, as if he'd forgotten that we were on our way to Venice and that changing the names of the streets would hardly be sufficient. Jigee and Mary took their places in the back of the limousine, Hotch and I occupied the jump seats behind the glass partition, and Papa settled himself down beside Georges, the driver, while the other Georges, the barman, waved good-bye.

Our progress south was leisurely to say the least. We stopped at a *charcuterie* about thirty kilometers outside Paris and bought a supply of sliced garlic sausages and crackers that we munched on to stave off our hunger before lunch. Papa had filled his silver pocket flask with Calvados, which he passed around to wash down our hors d'ouevres. It was soon known as "throat-ease," his pet name for the strong apple brandy.

We stopped in Auxerre, a hundred kilometers farther south, for lunch and spent the first night in Saulieu, about sixty-five kilometers down the road, because neither Papa nor Georges wanted to go on once it was dark. The snail's pace of our expedition was a little enervating, although in those days before the construction of the *autoroute du soleil*, traveling by car was more entertaining than it is now. Drinking and eating a great deal without taking any physical exercise had never been one of my favorite diversions, and I soon found myself getting restless. It didn't seem to bother Jigee as much, possibly because she occupied a more comfortable place in the back of the car. Traveling through France was also a new experience for her, while I had already spent a considerable amount of time on French roads during the war.

Nor did our lack of progress seem to bother Hotchner. Both he and Jigee were delighted with "Dr. Hemingstein's guided tour," basking in his favors and flattered to be in his entourage. I was becoming more and more conscious of Papa's special attentions to Jigee, which Mary seemed quite willing to overlook. Jigee assured me whenever we found ourselves alone that I had no reason to be jealous, as Papa's devotion to her was purely platonic and he needed to be "a tiny bit in love with someone in order to feel more alive." She admitted that she enjoyed his adoration of her, but said it was absurd for me to be jealous. He was equally fond of me, she said, never failed to assert his affection for both of us. And it was only a matter of days before we would be returning to Paris by train. We had already decided to disengage from this expedition once we had arrived in Nice.

It was either in Nîmes or in Avignon that Papa's mood deteriorated at dinner when he was served a special helping of rice that Mary had ordered for him. His eyes narrowed and, grinding his teeth, he declared that he didn't "want any of that goddamn pressure food," suspecting that the rice had been an oblique suggestion of Mary's that he pay attention to his high blood pressure, a condition that she worried about constantly. Once the meal was over we took a walk through the town, where a county fair was in progress, and ended up in front of one of the shooting booths.

We all took turns aiming at cardboard targets with rather ancient .22-caliber rifles, a pastime that delighted Papa. Jigee once again proved herself to be an astonishingly good marksman, so we lingered on at the shooting stand. It was a cold, damp evening, and I was already quite fed up with all of the flirtation and flattery, and as we moved on to yet another booth I said that my feet were cold and that I thought I'd go back to the hotel.

Papa scowled, obviously annoyed. Mary intervened, saying that she too was tired, but her condition made no impression on her husband. I had apparently "blotted my copybook," as the British refer to small schoolboy misdemeanors, although I had the feeling that my rebellion was being looked upon as a more serious crime. "Shitmaru, Pete's feet are cold," Papa mumbled and stepped up to the counter of a second booth to pick up a rifle.

Sensing that I was fed up, Jigee decided that she would return to the hotel with me. She asked me what was the matter, and I told her that my feet were actually bothering me but that I also had had enough of group travel and of having to cater to all of Papa's whims. She agreed he had been difficult at dinner but felt I should make allowances for his age and his poor health. I said I would and we dismissed the incident from our minds.

The next morning Papa was his old agreeable self, making no mention of the previous evening, and we drove directly south to Aigues-Mortes, a medieval walled city that Papa wanted to revisit even though it involved a detour of about sixty kilometers. It turned out to be a worthwhile stop, as the ancient fortifications we visited on that bright wintry day were both interesting and picturesque. As our self-appointed guide Papa explained all the ancient methods of warfare employed by the defenders of the old town. They had poured hot oil on their aggressors from the battlements, he informed us, and as a last resort they kept a large granite ball in the chamber of the fort's tower and could roll it down the stone circular stairs in case the enemy managed to enter the fortification. The military stratagems of the Middle Ages seemed to fascinate and amuse him, not so much because they were another proof of man's enduring inhumanity to man, but because he appeared to relish past battles.

We spent the night in Aix-en-Provence and traveled on to Nice the next day. Before leaving Aigues-Mortes I told Papa that we wouldn't be going on to Venice as I had to get back to work, news he accepted calmly. But when it came time to say good-bye in the bar of the old Hotel Negresco in Nice, he seemed genuinely sad and upset. "I knew you guys weren't coming along to Venice," he said, "when I noticed that you didn't load your guns into the back of the car in Paris," a faulty deduction as he must have known that we didn't possess any hunting equipment and had never planned to go duck shooting in Venice.

Hotchner accompanied us on the trip to Paris that night, taking the final three chapters of *Across the River and into the Trees* with him to deliver to the editors of *Cosmopolitan* in New York. I remember that our mood relaxed once the three of us were by ourselves and that Hotchner informed us that he had taken notes on our stay in Paris, as well as on the car journey to Nice. I also remember the horrendous moment in our Paris hotel when we discovered that Hotch had left his briefcase, which contained the corrected three chapters, in his compartment on the train. He spoke very little French, and so together we called the railroad station, and I was told that the *wagon-lit* we had occupied was being serviced somewhere in the shunting yards.

Hotch set off in a panic to retrieve his briefcase. We were all at fault for Hotch's carelessness, as we all knew the importance of the manuscript. Papa had told us that many years earlier Hadley had left the only copies of several of his short stories, as well as the section of an unfinished novel, on a train and the manuscripts had never been recovered.

My last view of Papa, standing in the dark old-fashioned bar of the Negresco, was a rather pathetic one of an old man saddened by the loss of his young admirers, accustomed as he was to traveling with a group that he considered to be a command made up of volunteers. That he felt slightly betrayed by our departure I can now understand.

When you reach a certain age you are often inclined to think that some of your younger friends will have a better time without you.

GREATLY RELIEVED to have recovered the missing manuscript, Hotchner departed for New York. He would have liked to stay on in Paris, he said, but he had to get back to his family and his job at *Cosmopolitan*—his stay in Europe had been more like a vacation than anything else. In some ways I envied him. A job, I had learned long ago, was more invigorating than trying to write a novel, all the more so as the one I had embarked on presented problems I was not yet able to solve. With hindsight I realize now that I had not decided on a theme, nor had I worked out the ending. I was under the illusion that once I had gotten started, the novel would write itself, an illusion that had been encouraged by Papa's account of how he had written the first draft of *The Sun Also Rises* in six weeks, a slight exaggeration, I soon learned.

I also lacked self-confidence, that product of the ego that is almost as important as talent. We had enough money in the bank to last six months if we lived frugally. But once that was gone I knew we would be obliged to return to California and live with my mother until I had found an assignment. And even if I had finished enough of my novel to get an advance from my publishers, it would provide us with only a brief financial respite. I had received five hundred dollars as an advance on my first novel, *The Canyon*, and seven hundred fifty dollars for my second, ill-fated novel, *Line of Departure*. Based on past performances, an advance was not a very hopeful prospect.

I was well aware that Papa's account of his early financial plight was supposed to serve as an example, but even Hemingway had solved most of his money problems by marrying a wealthy woman. In any event I was not foolish enough to think of myself in the same league. Nor was living in Paris as inexpensive as it had been in the twenties, and Jigee and I were disinclined to radically change our ways and live in a cold-water flat on the Left Bank.

We did the next best thing. At the suggestion of Bob Capa we moved into a small apartment hotel called the May Fair on the rue Copernic a few blocks off avenue Kléber. A tiny, creaking elevator in this ancient building gave access to the modest two-room suites on each of its eight floors. M. Charles, an expatriate Swiss, was the manager of the place, and when the two maids who did the housework were busy, he often filled in as *bagagiste* or *chasseur*. The price of our accommodations was twelve dollars a day. Room service was available, but to save money we bought a small electric hot plate so that we could cook our own breakfast.

Capa occupied one of the choice suites at the top of the building, and he soon took Jigee and me in hand. Paris was his bailiwick, as he had lived there for several years before the war, having arrived as a penniless political refugee in 1934. Behind him lay a long trail of escapes made in the nick of time, first from Budapest where he had been beaten up as a suspected Communist by Admiral Horthy's secret police and then from Berlin which he left hurriedly after the Reichstag fire in 1933, Hitler's final step to becoming the supreme ruler of Germany. Vienna had been his next desperate port of call, but he left that city once Dollfuss came to power, and after a brief return to his native Budapest he had moved on to the City of Light.

Capa made Paris his headquarters during the early years of the Spanish Civil War, and after once again taking flight in September 1939 he was satisfied to reclaim the city as his principal residence after taking part in the liberation of the French capital in August 1944. He knew everybody—from Averell Harriman to Picasso to the Lazareffs, who owned and ran *France Soir*, the evening paper. Like Papa, he was fond of the races, although he preferred the flat to steeplechasing. He knew all the good bistros, the stylish ones that were expensive and the small, cheap places where you could get as good a meal for a reasonable price. His favorite was Chez Anna, a small bistro in Passy where the owner's pets—dogs, cats, and even chickens—were not confined to the sawdust-strewn floor. Anna adored Capa, and she always made room for him and his party. She even shared with him the inside information her well-heeled, racehorse-owner clients like Georges Courtois were in the habit of passing on to her.

Tiny in stature and nearly bald, she would scream at Capa if he chose the wrong item on her menu. "Idiot!" she would shout, "take the lamb tonight, it's better than the roast beef." Or "Listen to me, *cheri, le boudin, c'est extraordinaire!*"

Capa had a special kind of elegance. He favored gray flannel suits in the winter and always wore a shirt and tie, usually purchased at Sulka's. In the street he kept his topcoat draped over his shoulders, European style. He had longish black hair and furry eyebrows that were almost joined over the bridge of his nose. He was short but well built. He spoke French with a marked Hungarian accent, and his English was what he called "Capanese," a picturesque language unhindered by the rules of grammar. He had a special chuckle, low and amused, and invariably he had a French cigarette stuck in a corner of his mouth that was formed by thick, almost girlish lips.

His closest friend, who was nearly always in attendance, was a young man named Noel Howard, the son of a Breton sculptor and a former night-fighter pilot in the RAF. Tall, angular, with a prominent nose, Noel was one of those sweet and kind human beings who are not equipped to handle the two most important problems in life: money and women. As Capa was a self-confessed disaster behind the steering wheel, Noel always drove his dark green Ford convertible, which looked even more beat-up than Howard, who appeared to be chronically hung over. He had a pale, mottled skin, and although he was sinewy and strong, cigarettes and alcohol had already taken their toll. He accepted Jigee and me as friends because Capa approved of us, and he was always willing to help out with the various chores that were a time-consuming part of settling down in a city where nothing was easy to accomplish.

Noel had a talent for painting—his miniature oils were remarkable —but he wanted to be a movie director, an ambition that for a Frenchman was even more difficult to realize in 1949 than it is today. But it was his dream, and he clung to it. Jigee and I grew to like him, although he was fairly unreliable and always late for appointments. Jigee said that he was a "born loser," in her opinion the only one in our group, which soon included Arthur Laurents, Arthur and Joan Stanton, and Farley Granger, who had all taken up residence at the Hotel May Fair. Paris was bitterly cold that winter, and Jigee and I found ourselves longing for southern California, all the more so as my work wasn't going very well. Once the Christmas holidays were over Capa suggested we all go skiing, and I agreed at once, thinking that a change of scenery might help rid me of my writer's block.

We had bought a car out of the Citroen showroom on the place Vendôme, a black *onze chevaux* with yellow wheels, which made us feel less *dépaysé*, as we had both been used to owning an automobile since we were young. The Citroen cost eleven hundred dollars. We loaded it to the gunwales with all of our possessions and, with M. Charles reassuring us that there would always be an apartment available for us at his hotel, set out for the Alps in the wake of Capa's Ford, with Noel at the wheel and Bob next to him.

We arrived in Zürs am Arlberg during a snowstorm and moved into the Zürserhof, the best hotel in the small Austrian village, which, as the season was just beginning, was half empty. The snowstorm turned into a blizzard, and skiing, even on the beginner slopes, was out of the question, as all the lifts were closed. For six long days the swirling white flakes continued to fall. Only Sepp, the hotel porter, ventured out of doors to clear a path in front of the hotel's entrance. After the third day our Citroen was buried so deep in snow that only its black top was visible, and a day later it had disappeared from view. The village road was closed. Escape was impossible.

I had left my typewriter in the Citroen, so there was nothing left to do but eat, read, and talk. Capa wanted to hear all about our trip with the Hemingways. His questions were laconic, and he listened to our description of our journey with a knowing grin. He said that he was still fond of Papa, regretted their estrangement, but thought Hemingway was a difficult man to be friends with for any long period of time. He knew that his advising Papa not to rush into marriage with Mary had caused the rift between them, and he said he felt certain that things would never be "patched up" as a result of his tactless remark.

Once we were alone I again questioned Jigee about her relationship with Papa and pressed her to tell me the truth. She admitted that Papa had suggested she marry him, and if they should have a daughter they would call her Petra as a reminder of their fondness for me. It was not a serious proposal, but merely the result of a long, intimate conversation during which she had told him of our difficult period of readjustment after the war. She also told me that Papa had been shocked to learn that I had urged her to have an abortion a few months after our first child had been stillborn, not because it violated his religious principles but because he was opposed to interfering with nature. I was disturbed that she had revealed the most intimate details of our married life to him and reminded her that her own doctor had thought it wiser to interrupt her pregnancy because of her run-down physical condition and that I had agreed with him mainly because I couldn't face the possibility of another tragedy immediately after the one we had just been through.

All of our old wounds were reopened by the discussions that followed in the snowbound village. I felt that I had been betrayed by both Hemingway and my wife, and the fact that she had never countenanced him as a lover or husband seemed unimportant to me. As soon as it stopped snowing and the road had been cleared, we left Zürs, having ventured out on the slopes only once. It had been a disastrous week all around.

We drove to Davos and checked into the Parsenn Hotel opposite the Talstation of the Parsennbahn. Capa and Noel had stopped in Klosters, where Capa said he knew of a charming hotel that was preferable to the rather austere surroundings of the town that had inspired Thomas Mann to write *The Magic Mountain.* By that time we were a little skeptical about our leader's knowledge of winter resorts, but a week later, having skied down to Klosters, we joined him and Noel at the Chesa Grischuna, which turned out to be as pleasant a place as he had promised. The Gotshnabahn, the funicular that linked Klosters to the Parsenngebiet, had just been completed, so the skiing was just as good as in Davos. The price was right, too, at five dollars a head for room and board.

The village, under a thick blanket of snow, was both picturesque and friendly. The Chesa Grischuna, with its carved ceilings and clean smell of wood and furniture wax, was the center of our social life and more suited to us than the more formal atmosphere of the Zürserhof, where people wore a jacket and a tie in the main dining room and underground bar. Colette Harrison, Rex Harrison's first wife, was one of the permanent residents. A thin, pretty blonde, she appeared to be as lightly involved with Capa as many of his Paris girlfriends had been, and she accompanied us on our daily runs down the packed powder slopes of the Gotshnagrat, the local mountain.

Capa was everyone's favorite. The owners of the Chesa, Hans and Doris Guler, adored him, as did many of the shopkeepers, the garage owners, and everyone else in the village. In direct contrast to Papa, Capa hardly ever mentioned his "foxhole time" and was content to muse on his future rather than dwell on his heroic past. He was tired of going to the wars; Hollywood, where he had spent a few months in 1947, was obviously not for him. Like my father, he missed the street scene of a real city, which was not to be found in Los Angeles. The photographic agency he had founded, Magnum Photos, which also represented Henri Cartier-Bresson and Chim Seymour, among others, might provide a little necessary cash, but it was not a guarantee of a rosy future. "The important thing is to break even" was the slogan he had adopted for his work and gambling, hardly a formula for lasting security. He appeared to be full of doubts for the years that lay ahead, and so skiing and the mountains provided him with a rest from reality, albeit a temporary one. One day the snow would melt, I realized, and then we would all have to face real life again.

·   ·   ·   ·

BUT LONG BEFORE that happened Tola Litvak telephoned from Paris. He was staying at the Hotel Lancaster and was about to set out on a final reconnaissance of locations for *Call It Treason,* and he felt that it was vital for me to accompany him, as many of the scenes we had written would have to be altered to fit the actual locales. He had already called Noel, he informed me, and had hired him to act as his personal assistant, so Noel would be returning to Paris immediately, leaving Capa to fend for himself. Jigee and I were to wait in Klosters, where Tola planned to collect us.

I was not eager to leave our Alpine retreat. I had managed to make some progress on my novel and I knew the interruption would be damaging. Yet I was to be paid an additional twelve thousand dollars for my work for Litvak. Jobs for a screenwriter resident in Europe were not that plentiful, and with any luck I would be able to return to my own work in the spring. I called Litvak back that evening and agreed to his terms. But several days before he arrived in our village, a more serious problem presented itself.

It came in a brown envelope, duly forwarded by M. Charles, and the return address showed that it had been sent by the Department of the U.S. Navy. It was ominously addressed to Second Lieutenant Viertel. The text of the letter was brief. Reserve officers on inactive duty were hereby requested to inform their naval reserve districts of their permanent addresses in case the Marine Corps would find it necessary to transfer them back to active duty. The two short paragraphs struck terror in my by now thoroughly civilian heart.

A little more than four years had passed since I had been released from active duty by order of the commandant in Washington, D.C., and I had come to look back on my period of military service with what amounted to an inexplicable nostalgia. All of the places I had been, as well as the Marine Corps itself, were wrapped in an almost affectionate glow: the base in San Diego at dawn, with the platoons of boots marching to the distant chants of their drill instructors; Camp Elliot in the dry California hills where I had put in my time on the rifle range and from where I had shipped out with the 8th Replacement Battalion; Nouméa, New Caledonia, where my romance with Lucy had taken place; Tassaforanga; our campsite on the northern tip of Guadalcanal, a coconut plantation near the beach where more than a dozen Japanese ships lay half buried in the sand, their steel hulls marking the failure of the enemy's last attempt to land reinforcements; Efate, a small island in the New Hebrides where I had helped film a documentary about the evacuation of Navy and Marine Corps wounded; even the dawn landing I had witnessed from the flying bridge of a destroyer lying in the tranquil waters of Empress Augusta Bay on Bougainville, which was where I had caught my first and last glimpse of the face of the enemy in the person of a Japanese pilot swooping past at an altitude of thirty feet, who seconds later dropped a personnel bomb near enough the fantail of our ship, the U.S.S. *Wadsworth*, to kill and wound more than a dozen members of our crew —brief memories of a period of my life that had seemed endless then. "Golden Gate in '48" had been our slogan.

The prospect of putting on my green uniform again and rejoining the Corps filled me with true dismay. Ever since my return to civilian life I had been plagued by a recurring nightmare. In my dream I was on a troopship waiting to sail to the South Pacific. Orders had come through transferring me to shore duty—I had five minutes to pack my sea bag, but I found myself unable to collect my gear, and the ship was beginning to weigh anchor. That was always the moment I would wake up, bathed in sweat. Now, suddenly, the nightmare was threatening to come true.

While in the Pacific in 1943 I had applied for Officer Candidate School, mainly to get sent home, and at the expense of the U.S. government I had been trained to be an infantry unit commander. But I had never performed that function, having been transferred at my own request to the O.S.S. and sent to Europe to serve in tactical intelligence operations during the last six months of the war. Leading an infantry platoon in Korea was the last thing I wanted to do now that the war against Hitler had been won.

Jigee was even more upset by the prospect of my going back into the service. She urged me to disregard the letter from the Navy, pretend that it had never arrived. But I knew that I had no choice but to reply. So I wrote back that I had moved to Europe and gave the Hotel May Fair in Paris as my current address.

I showed the letter from the Navy Department to Capa. He frowned and squinted at me through the wisp of smoke curling up from the cigarette in the corner of his mouth. "Vy the hell did you join the fockin' Marines in the first place?" he demanded rhetorically. It was a question that I had been asking myself, on average, at least twenty times a day.

A few days later Litvak arrived in town at the wheel of his black Cadillac convertible that had been shipped from California. Sitting in the open car beside him, dressed in a fur coat and shivering under several blankets, was a strikingly pretty blonde half his age, a fact that was made glaringly apparent by Tola's prematurely white mane. Her name was Monique Davalou and she was a native of Brittany, as was Noel Howard, which accounted for a noticeable sympathy between them that did not seem to bother Tola. That his young assistant was a little bit in love with his mistress obviously flattered his ego.

We set out on our reconnaissance the following morning, Litvak leading the way in his Cadillac with Noel and Monique his frightened passengers. Jigee and I followed in our small French car and were thus able to witness Litvak's frequent madcap violations of the traffic laws. On our first stop I confided in Noel that our boss left behind him a multitude of angry motorists and pedestrians shaking their fists or pointing to their heads to protest our leader's insane driving. After a hectic three-hour drive, we checked into the Grand Hotel in Kitzbühel, the very same place where Göring had taken refuge at the end of the war and where he was arrested by the provost marshal of the 36th Infantry Division. I was there that day, heard the groans of the GIs when General Dahlquist, the commanding general of the division, shook the fat air marshal's hand before seeing him off in a small airplane. Poor Dahlquist had thoughtlessly accepted Göring's outstretched hand, for which error he was relieved of his command of the division. It was a sad incident—Dahlquist had been an excellent leader of one of the best units in the 7th Army. Later that same week Carl Muecke, a Marine lieutenant with whom I shared the command of our irregular section made up mostly of German defectors, arrested Leni Riefenstahl as well as Field Marshal Schörner, a Nazi general, who was known as the "beast of Silesia" for the war crimes he and his men had committed against Polish civilians and his own soldiers.

Riefenstahl had shed bitter tears when Muecke had taken her into custody, had declared that she had never been a Nazi. The fact that her name was on our list of people wanted by the U.S. authorities was a terrible mistake, she protested. Schörner, who had been denounced by his own batman, had attempted to hide his identity by changing into civilian clothes, but when Muecke searched him he found his Wehrmacht paybook inside his Austrian jacket.

The following day Colonel Quinn, of 7th Army intelligence, arrived in a light aircraft, the same airplane in which Göring had been flown to Augsburg and 7th Army headquarters. Schörner, in turn, was loaded into the Piper Cub and was ultimately delivered to the Russians as was required by the Yalta agreement, because he had commanded an army corps on the eastern front where his war crimes had been committed. That procedure had turned out to be a grave mistake, as instead of hanging the field marshal the Russians incorporated him into the Von Paulus Military Academy in Moscow, which ultimately led to Schörner's supervision of the North Korean armored attack across the Thirty-Eighth Parallel.

The village of Kitzbühel had been designated a rehabilitation center by the Wehrmacht, and I had memories of German soldiers with amputated arms and legs sitting on the sunlit terraces of the various small hotels staring at us, their conquerors, with pale faces hollowed by lack of food. At the eastern end of the town a large sign had been painted on the wall of a wooden barn. *"Kitzbühel Wünscht Keine Juden,"* the sign had read in black letters that were hastily painted over by the newly arrived men of our military government units. "Kitzbühel Wants No Jews" was the final message that the local Nazi Gauleiter had left behind him, and I couldn't help wondering whether the local populace still sympathized with those words.

Tola shrugged when I told him the story—he was determined not to let the past spoil his enjoyment of Austria's charms. He liked the rich food and the general atmosphere of gaiety that was characteristic of the resort, as if all the pretty girls from Munich and Vienna with their suntanned escorts were bent on blotting out Anschluss and all the troubled years they had lived through. "Sure, they were probably all Nazis," Litvak said, adding that most people usually went along with whatever government was in power. To collaborate was easier than to resist the regime of an occupied country, whether it happened to be Austria or France.

As is the case with most men Tola's age, I realize now, enjoying life was almost more important than anything else. Inviting Monique to join us on our reconnaissance was ample proof of his intention to mix pleasure with business whenever possible. Fortunately, she was a welcome addition to our group, amusing as she was pretty, without being flirtatious. She charmed even Jigee. Every night during our brief stay she sang with the small band in the hotel dining room after dinner, humming the tunes whenever she forgot the lyrics. Many of the patrons of the restaurant assumed her performance was a professional act, so whenever she hesitated before moving to the bandstand from our table, the people around us would applaud and demand she sing until finally she had to accede.

She sang "Parlez-moi d'amour" and "Est-ce-que c'est ma faute à moi?," and even "Lili Marlene," all in French (which delighted the many veterans of the Wehrmacht in the audience) as well as a score of other songs, until her voice gave out and she was forced to retire to tumultuous applause and Tola's and Noel's fond kisses on her glowing cheeks. Her spontaneous performance was all the more endearing because it was slightly amateurish. It didn't matter when she forgot the words because she was so completely adorable.

Then suddenly Monique returned to Paris. Noel, who it turned out had known her before she met Tola, explained that for many years she had lived with a wealthy French playboy who had been reluctant to marry her and that to break the deadlock of their relationship she had gone off with Tola. The stratagem had obviously worked—at least it seemed that way for the moment—as her former lover was now less hesitant about changing her status from mistress to wife. The young woman left behind her a terrible void, and Litvak changed overnight to irritable and demanding. It was time we got to work, he declared, and a couple of days later we left Kitzbühel for Munich.

The Bavarian capital was being rebuilt, but the damage left behind by the war was still visible everywhere. We inspected the studio facilities at Geiselgasteig. The soundstages and offices had been spared by our bombers, and the German staff, those who had survived, were eager to serve their conquerors. To a man they assured us they had never been Nazis, assertions Litvak received with skepticism. He was there to make a movie and was not interested in the political past of the people he would be working with.

The U.S. dollar was a strong currency, and so we spent a considerable amount of time window-shopping, looking mainly for shoes for Tola and ski boots for Jigee and me. One afternoon we found ourselves in the same department store where five years earlier I had requisitioned winter clothing for the Joes assigned to my command. Tola and Noel were amused when I led them unfailingly to the section of the shop where I had committed my "soldier theft" a week before VE Day.

Then suddenly I found myself haunted by a troubling memory I had half forgotten. One of the men I had equipped with winter gear that day in early May 1945 was a forty-year-old Austrian lieutenant I had recruited to assist us in our search for war criminals in the Austrian Alps, which were to serve as Hitler's redoubt, the last of the Führer's plans that had misfired. Unlike the other men I had recruited, I had known little about his background. He was the only commissioned officer who had volunteered to serve with us, and I was appalled when on the morning after VE Day, in a small hotel in Salzburg that we had requisitioned, he put a bullet through his head with the pistol we had assigned to him. He had obviously been the victim of an overwhelming depression, caused perhaps by his realization that his betrayal of his country had served no purpose now that the war was over.

I described the horror I felt when we carried the man's body in a blood-stained mattress cover down the stairs and out into the sunlit street full of wildly celebrating GIs. But Tola was only vaguely interested. I was trying to impress upon him the tortured doubts suffered by many of the German and Austrian agents who had chosen to serve us. Litvak maintained that the hero in our film was too politically indoctrinated to waver in his loyalties, although it was, he admitted, a part of the theme of our story. As we left the Munich sporting goods store with our purchases, he added that it would be a mistake to complicate our protagonist's motivations, as there was the danger that an American movie audience would lose patience with him. "But I'm glad you think of our story once in a while just the same," he added sarcastically.

That evening we were to meet in the elegant bar of the Bayerischer Hof, where we were staying, and as Jigee and I sat waiting for Tola and Noel to arrive I noticed that Leni Riefenstahl was occupying an adjoining table with a group of friends. She had obviously been cleared by the denazification board of the U.S. military government in 1946 and was a free citizen once again, which did not altogether surprise me, as she had been a Nazi sympathizer and not an active war criminal.

Litvak and Noel joined us after a quarter of an hour. The "boss," as we called him, seemed rather dejected, and Noel was strangely silent. I drew their attention to the woman at the next table, and Tola shook his head. "I have some bad news," he said. "You and I, and Jigee of course, are under investigation by the FBI for presumed un-American activities." He shook his head. Frank McCarthy, who had just arrived in Munich, had informed him of a letter that had been forwarded to the intelligence officer of the U.S. military government command, informing him of our doubtful status. "It's unbelievable, isn't it?" Tola muttered. "That woman is sitting there, and you and I are about to be investigated." He was worried that now he might not be able to obtain U.S. Army cooperation for our movie.

ONCE THE ARRANGEMENTS had been made for the leasing of stage space at Geizelgasteig, we motored on to Frankfurt. The I. G. Farben skyscraper in the middle of the city had been left undamaged by the U.S. Air Force and the RAF, and it now served as the head-quarters of General Lucius B. Clay. Tola, elegantly turned out in navy blue trousers, black leather jacket, and white silk scarf, set out with McCarthy to win over the authorities. McCarthy was dressed in a gray flannel suit with the Legion of Merit discreetly visible in his lapel. They must have made a favorable impression on the high-ranking officers, for in less than an hour they reappeared smiling and in high spirits. Full cooperation had been granted our production, and there had been no mention of the damning FBI accusations against us.

His mission accomplished, McCarthy elected to fly back to Califor-nia, thus avoiding any further travel in Litvak's Cadillac. Jigee and I were free to return to Klosters for a few days of spring skiing before I started the rewrite that had been decided upon. Noel, looking envious and somewhat nervous, was to accompany the boss back to France by road. Even the threat of my being called back to active duty with the Fleet Marine Force failed to dampen my spirits, as the end of my work on *Call It Treason* was now in sight.

Paris, when we arrived two weeks later to meet Litvak, was more beautiful than ever. The chestnut trees were in bloom, and Bob Capa as well as the rest of our expatriate group at the Hotel May Fair were there to greet us. Tola had reverted to his role of *grand seigneur*, and he delighted in showing us his favorite haunts, the Russian restaurants and nightclubs where he was received like an old friend. A nostalgia for Russia and all things Russian was part of his exuberant personality, which was perhaps the cause of his problems with the FBI. With Jeff Kessel and Maurice Drouont, Kessel's nephew, we went often to Novy's and Monseigneur, two Russian nightclubs.

Litvak, I soon discovered, was a passionate gambler, and on most weekends he would go off to Deauville or Enghien. He insisted that Jigee and I and Noel join him on one of these excursions, and we set off one Friday night in two cars for Normandy. I had sold the Citroen after M. Charles had destroyed its gear box and had replaced it with a much less practical MG two-seater, Jigee having sent for her Chevro-let convertible that was still in storage in Los Angeles. The Chevrolet was to serve as our family car once Vicky had joined us, and the MG was to be my own toy, a rather frivolous extravagance.

When we set out that afternoon, Jigee and I in the new roadster and Tola leading the way with Noel as his copilot in the Cadillac, the weather was clear and fine. But on Sunday evening when we started back, Tola having lost heavily at the Deauville casino, ominous clouds appeared. As the MG was equipped with side curtains and no heater, we decided that Jigee should ride in the more comfortable car. Tola passed Noel and me less than half an hour after we started back, so we followed doggedly on our own through the dense rain. We arrived at the May Fair at nine o'clock that night and were surprised to discover that Jigee was not in our suite. Somewhat worried, Noel and I repaired to the corner bistro for a drink and a ham sandwich. Still there was no sign of the rest of our party.

More and more worried, we decided to wait in the hall of the hotel and strolled outside at intermittent intervals to look for a sign of the late arrivals. At eleven-thirty a dilapidated taxi clanked up the rue de la Boétie and stopped in front of the May Fair. Tola was the first to disembark, and we greeted him with laughter that soon changed into serious concern when Jigee was helped out of the taxi by its driver. Her head was bandaged, and although she assured us that she was all right, I could see that she had had a severe shock. Tola explained that he had lost control of his car on the wet cobblestone road near Evreux and had gone into a ditch after hitting a small tree. Seeing that Jigee had been hurt, he had taken her to a hospital in the small French town, where the doctor on duty had diagnosed her injury as being a slight concussion and had bandaged the severe cut on her head.

Noel suggested that we take her at once to the American hospital in Neuilly, but Jigee would not hear of it. She seemed more concerned by the fact that the doctor in Evreux had had to cut off some of her hair to dress the wound than anything else, even the dizziness that she had not recovered from in the three hours that had elapsed since the accident. She said that she only wanted to go upstairs to bed and rest, arguing that there was nothing anyone could do about the concussion and that the effects of the injury would soon wear off. Noel and I did our best to convince her that a second, more competent examination was necessary, but in the end she had her way. I helped undress her and put her to bed, cursing myself for having allowed her to drive with a man whose prudence and skill I knew to be sadly lacking.

She seemed to recover in a few days, went off to a hairdresser and returned home with bangs, a brown fringe that hid the damage done by the doctor, and was soon herself again. As she had always had trouble sleeping, she continued taking the strong pills her doctor in California had prescribed and with which she was well supplied. Tola was suitably contrite, although Jigee assured him it had not been all his fault, as the Cadillac had never been meant for use on the narrow and slippery European roads. Soon the incident was forgotten, the Cadillac repaired, and we returned rather hesitantly to the task at hand, the final, *final* draft of our script.

Less than six months later, while getting ready for bed one night, Jigee suddenly collapsed on the floor of the bathroom of our small suite. I heard the dull thud of her fall, and fearing that she had slipped on the steps of the sunken bathtub, I leapt out of bed and ran to her side. I discovered that she had collapsed in front of the washbasin while brushing her teeth in what we were later to learn was her first epileptic attack. The doctor I took her to the next day said that she had fainted and suggested a further examination that Jigee vehemently declined. We were soon to depart for Klosters, and she did not want anything to interfere with our winter's skiing.

BUT THAT SPRING in Paris our stay was soon disrupted by a further medical incident. Tola was not an early riser, and our workday usually began at eleven-thirty. Lunch followed at one o'clock, so our progress on the revisions of the script was painfully slow. It was apparent that Litvak wanted to nail down every detail of every scene he was going to direct, and I had the suspicion that he was unsure of himself. The events he would have to create for the benefit of the camera were outside his ken, although that had never disturbed him in the past. Unlike Huston, he had no confidence in last-minute inspiration once he was standing next to the camera. The difference in our ages, I began to suspect, made him distrust my opinions, although I had lived through many of the events included in our story. He even insisted on changing the GIs' dialogue, of which he had no experience at all.

We worked on Sundays as well as weekdays, and early one Sunday afternoon, after a big meal, while he was being attended to by a masseur, the script on the coffee table in front of me began to look hazy, and I started to sweat profusely. I also felt a violent pain in my lower abdomen. Tola dismissed my complaints, attributing them to indigestion and a desire to stop work. I sat for a while listening to the sound of slapping and grunting that came from the massage table, then tried to rise, and discovered I couldn't. Convinced at last that something was seriously wrong, Litvak dismissed the masseur and began calling in search of a doctor.

Finding a physician on a Sunday afternoon in Paris was not an easy matter, but after many calls Dr. Diamant-Berger, a surgeon, appeared in Tola's top-floor apartment at the Hotel Lancaster. He stretched me out on a couch and diagnosed acute appendicitis that required immediate surgery. Litvak called Jigee, and together we drove to a private clinic in Neuilly, where I was operated on late that same afternoon, just as my appendix started to rupture.

Pampered and well looked after by the hospital staff, I recovered rapidly. Capa came to visit me with Noel Howard, as did Jeff Kessel, Tola, and Juliette Achard. Marcel, who hated hospitals, couldn't bring himself to come, but he sent books instead. Gene Kelly, who had recently arrived in Paris, came by with his wife Betsy, and as he was already a favorite in France, his appearance raised my status with the staff. Curiously enough, Gene was operated on for the same disorder only a few months later, which led us all to assume that the rich Parisian food was disrupting our American intestines.

As soon as the drain from the incision had been removed, I left the hospital to resume my sessions with Tola. By this time, however, he had decided that Paris was not a good place to work and, as part of my convalescence, suggested Jigee and I go to Biarritz. Unfortunately a June heat wave had engulfed the Pyrenees, and after a sweltering weekend in St. Jean de Luz, Tola suggested we go to St. Gilgen in Austria as a suitably cool and quiet place. Vicky was spending the summer with her father in Bucks County, and so the four of us set off in caravan: Tola and his loyal secretary Annie Selepeno in the lead, with Jigee and me following in her Chevrolet.

There was a certain logic in Litvak's choice of St. Gilgen, as it was only a two-hour drive from the Austrian mountain resort to the Geiselgasteig studios in Munich, which would make it possible for him to supervise the building of the sets, which had already started. For the first time I began to feel fairly certain that all of our labor would ultimately bear fruit.

A tedious six weeks of work followed in the pretty resort. After St. Gilgen we moved on to Munich for three weeks, where I was at last released by my affectionate, though demanding, taskmaster. As a reward for all the hard work, he invited Jigee and me to join him on a trip to Vienna, where my father was working as a director in the

Burgtheater. Helping him with the casting was the excuse he could give 20th Century-Fox to entice the studio to pay my expenses. After he had flown ahead by plane, Jigee and I boarded the train to the Austrian capital.

Friedrich Ledebur, a tall Austrian count, a family friend since our Santa Monica days who had turned up in Munich, joined us on our journey, ostensibly to show us around Vienna. Late in an adventurous life dedicated wholly to pleasure, Ledebur had decided to try his hand at becoming a movie actor, and he was vaguely hopeful that I could convince Tola to give him a part. I warned him that his rather special appearance would hardly suit our story, but he muttered in his deep voice that there must be a "tiny role" for him in the movie.

At the Enns bridge where the train entered the Soviet-held sector, Russian soldiers boarded our Pullman and began examining the papers of all the passengers. Both Friedrich's and my green passports caused the two rather grimy soldiers to pause ominously. The reason for their doubts became immediately apparent. I was born in Dresden and Ledebur was born in Czechoslovakia. *"Niet Amerikansi,"* one of them muttered, but once Jigee had presented the pair with two packs of Lucky Strikes, they shrugged and went on their way. Litvak had been wise to travel by plane, I thought to myself, as he had been born in Kiev, which might well have caused him even more serious complications.

MY FATHER HAD AGED since I had seen him a scant three and a half years earlier in New York. He seemed shorter than I remembered him, and his hair, which he wore longer now that he was back in Europe, was completely white. His deeply lined face had an unhealthy color, and he moved slowly, like a very old man. The Hitler years had exacted a terrible toll on his nervous system, as had his diabetes. Yet his professional career had improved immensely, along with his personal life. He lived in a small but comfortable apartment with Liesel Neumann, a stout, lively Austrian actress who had been his companion for a decade and whom he married in 1948, after obtaining a friendly divorce from my mother. His work at the Burgtheater was a great success. He had translated and directed Tennesee Williams's *Glass Menagerie* as well as *A Streetcar Named Desire* and was at that moment rehearsing a play by Strindberg in which he had cast Werner Krauss in one of the leading roles.

Krauss, along with Emil Jannings, had been an ardent Nazi sympathizer and had played the title role in *Jew Süss*, a violently anti-Semitic film. My mother, as well as some of our other refugee friends, thought it outrageous that my father should have consented to work with him and had recently expressed her doubts in a letter from California. My father brought up the subject during our first meal in one of his favorite restaurants. "I decided that it was bad enough that Hitler ruined my life and that I was not going to let him ruin this production as well," he said.

"What does Uncle Joseph think?" I asked. Joseph Gielen had returned from exile in Buenos Aires to take over as general manager of the Burgtheater. He was a Catholic, a staunch anti-Nazi who had married my mother's sister Rosa and for both those reasons had chosen to leave Austria after the German takeover.

"Gielen has left the decision up to me," my father said.

Realizing that my father was still troubled by the choice he had made, I refrained from comment, all the more hesitant to voice my opinion as I knew that Litvak had decided to cast Hilde Krahl as the female lead in our movie over similar objections. Ultimately Darryl Zanuck vetoed Tola's choice, not because she had been a Nazi, but because he didn't think she was pretty enough to play the role.

My father went on to describe his mixed emotions about his return to Vienna, the city of his birth and early youth. He enjoyed the food and the old streets he had wandered through as a boy, and yet he felt estranged. People would stop in the street, he told us, and point to him and say, "Look! A Jew," not with any apparent dislike, but seemingly amazed to find someone who belonged to that ostracized race walking around their city once again.

As our meal drew to a close, one of the familiar scenes of my childhood was replayed. My father recommended the *Apfelstrudel*, one of the restaurant's specialties, and after Jigee and I had ordered two portions my father told the waiter to bring a small piece for him as well, which provoked a vote of censure from Liesel, my stepmother. "Berthold," she warned, "you know you shouldn't! For you it's poison."

"Just this once," my father replied, "to celebrate my reunion with my son." And despite Liesel's disapproving glances, he chose "to sin again." "*So eine kleine Sünde*," he said, such a small sin.

The war that had ended five years earlier was still in evidence in the Austrian capital. The city was divided into four sectors—Russian, British, French, and American—and the four-man jeep patrols, manned by one soldier of each of the occupying powers, rolled con-

115

stantly through the old streets. Unlike the situation in Berlin, it was easy for civilians to travel from one zone to another. Still, taxi drivers usually warned their patrons when asked to be taken into the Soviet-held zone. *Der erste Bezirk*, the first borough, had been declared "international." It included the Hofburg, the Opera, the Kärntnerstrasse, and the Graben, the most picturesque part of the old city. The apartment on the Zedlitzgasse that had been allotted to my father and his wife because he was employed by the Burgtheater was in this international quarter. But the house where my grandparents had lived was on a street in the Russian sector, as were the two apartment houses that the family had owned and that had been confiscated by the Nazis. They were about to be returned to their legal owners, but my father had no interest in the recoupment of the family real estate. He was not and had never been a man of property, although even then the buildings were estimated to be of great value as soon as the Soviet occupying forces had withdrawn.

My father was concerned only with his daily work in the theater, perhaps knowing that he would never live to see the day when Austria would be free. I noticed the sharp, dartlike glances he shot in Liesel's direction across the round wooden table of the low-ceilinged, folklorique restaurant when she mentioned the small inheritance that would be coming my brothers' and my way once the political situation had been stabilized and the apartment houses in the Russian zone were marketable. Liesel warned me that I would probably be asked to turn over my share of the profits from the eventual sale to my cousins, who were "not well off at all." "You probably know the old Jewish saying, *lieber* Peter," she said with a smile, "that the worst thing to be is the richest member of the family." She laughed cheerfully. She had a calm, winning nature that complemented my father's fiery character far better than my mother's equally stormy disposition. "Your father looks tired," she said. "I think we should go home now."

We walked down the deserted streets to the Zedlitzgasse, Jigee and my father in the lead, Liesel and I following behind them. In his dark overcoat, with his white hair sticking out from below the brim of his gray hat, he maintained a slow pace, stopping whenever he was short of breath. He was still a heavy smoker, a self-destructive habit he shared with Jigee, although it was not their only bond, and I saw them both stop to light cigarettes, each his own because a breeze had sprung up. Quite selfishly I found myself thinking that, come what may, I would never wind up like that, would never let myself deteriorate physically because of a lack of personal discipline. I suppose we all draw our own conclusions from the examples of our parents, although what we inherit from them usually comes to the fore in the end.

The old Vienna that he had known as a boy and that had still been ruled by the Hapsburgs was of no interest to him. He was not the least nostalgic for an era he had despised as a young man for its corrupt decadence, an opinion that had made him a disciple of Karl Kraus, the brilliant and prophetic editor of *Die Fackel* (The Torch), the magazine in which my father had first been published before being called for service in World War I. Students at the University of Vienna in those days were required to join the military and received a kind of basic training to make them members of the officer corps should war break out. Thus in the summer of 1914 my father was assigned to a cavalry training center on the outskirts of Vienna.

"My father was a cavalry officer . . ." As a boy, my head filled with romantic daydreams, I used to fantasize that he had been a hard-riding martinet, covered with dust and glory, when quite the opposite was true, for he had been an intellectual even then, with no taste for sports or physical exercise. Nor did he have any desire to serve the reactionary rulers of the Austro-Hungarian Empire and their Prussian allies, believing the war to be the utmost folly. Despite the fact that he wore the high-collared uniform of the old Emperor, he was a poet, a pacifist, and a Jew, attributes that have never proven to be much value in any military organization.

He was also an ardent nonconformist, incapable of keeping his strong opinions to himself, and it was probably due to this that I was fortunate to be born at all, for if he had learned to keep his mouth shut, he might not have survived the senseless slaughter that was soon to begin. He was fond of telling the story himself, and it returned to my mind that evening as we strolled past the historic buildings that were the remnants of Austria's past.

It so happened that a few weeks after the first Austrian retreat in Serbia in 1914 my father and a group of his fellow junior officers were summoned to appear in front of a colonel of the high command who was known to be a strict disciplinarian. The colonel told the assembled officers that he had only one question to put to them; he wanted to know how the horses and pack animals had been treated during the recent debacle. One by one the quaking junior officers replied with what they considered the politic answer: that throughout the campaign the animals had always been treated humanely, almost better than the men. Finally it was my father's turn to speak. Bristling with indignation, he blurted out the truth, that the wounded horses and mules had often been left to die in agony on the battlefield and had seldom been given the obligatory coup de grace that a decent code of behavior required.

The colonel nodded and then summarily dismissed the formation, except my father, whom he decided immediately to appoint as his aide. The remaining officers were transferred to the western front, there to play their unwilling roles in the carnage of the war of attrition that is undoubtedly one of the saddest chapters in the history of our century. My father accompanied the colonel, who loved horses more than men, to Galicia, which had been liberated by Hindenburg's offensive in the spring of 1915, or in any event retaken from the Russian forces that had invaded that part of the Austro-Hungarian Empire in 1914, just as they would do in the summer of 1939. It was a relatively quiet sector of the eastern front, and by a strange coincidence my father was stationed briefly in the town where Augustus Steuermann, my mother's father, lived—a prosperous lawyer and landowner, the first and probably the last Jewish mayor of Sambor.

Until my mother's memoirs were published in 1969, I was certain my parents had met in a field hospital in Sambor in 1915 where my mother was working as a nurse's aide, a romantic notion probably inspired by my reading of *A Farewell to Arms*. In fact, they met in Vienna, where after being relieved of her wartime duties my mother, much against the wishes of her parents, had resumed her brief theatrical career. In those days a wealthy young girl's ambition to become an actress was only slightly more desirable, in my grandfather's opinion, than her wanting to dedicate herself to a life of prostitution, but as my mother had always possessed a will of iron, she ultimately had her way and went off to Vienna.

She was appearing in *The Lower Depths* in the role of Vassilia, when friends arranged an introduction at my father's request. He was on leave, was married but separated from his wife and on friendly terms, a fairly unusual situation in those days. They went to a restaurant after the performance in a large group. Not only was my father impressed with my mother's talent, but he was also familiar with the countryside where she had grown up, two immediate bonds. After supper he accompanied her to the boardinghouse where she lived and, before saying good night, assured her that someday they would be married. She told him that she was in love with somebody else and pointed out that he already had a wife, two objections that he brushed aside. Amazingly enough, three months before the armistice in November 1918, they married.

Needless to say, my father did not have a distinguished military career. He was released from active duty after having spent eighteen months on the eastern front and returned to civilian life and the theater. It seems incredible today that an officer could be released from his duties before the end of hostilities, but those were different times. Three years of active service entitled an officer to return to the inactive reserve if he wished to do so; thus my father was able to sign a contract with the Royal Saxonian Theater in Dresden, where both my older brother and I were ultimately born. By that time Germany and Austria had been defeated and even harder times had come to Central Europe, namely famine and inflation.

That evening in Vienna we sat for another half hour or so in the cluttered study of my father's small apartment. He asked about my work with Litvak and about my friendship with Hemingway, whose writing he admired more than his lifestyle. He did say, however, that he agreed with Papa that I should work as little as possible for the movies. He, too, had neglected his own work to make money in Hollywood and London and had always been torn between theater and film work and literature. He regretted that he had never been very astute about his finances, had lost nearly all of the money he had made in California during the crash of 1929 by investing in Paramount stock.

Liesel interrupted him to say that it was no use looking back, that at least he had written his poems, which was just as important as making money. I realized that she was the perfect wife for him, practical and self-sacrificing, who knew that it was pointless to live in the past and regret mistakes. The present was what counted, she said, and he should feel satisfied with the work he was doing, the contribution he was making to the postwar theater in Vienna. He paid little attention to her, although he obviously knew she was right. "I'm going to have to give up my American citizenship," he told me sadly as we were preparing to leave. He had run afoul of the existing law that forbade a naturalized citizen to return to his country of origin for more than two years. He would end his life as an Austrian, he said, shrugging.

Not that it really mattered. For the short time he had left the color of his passport was unimportant. "At least I have three American sons," he added with a bitter smile.

We kissed and said good night. "Give my regards to Litvak," my father said while we stood at the door. "And tell him that I'm grateful he made it possible for me to see my son again before I die."

Jigee made a face and said: "Oh, come now, Berthold, none of that." My father shot her an angry glance, obviously annoyed at her disapproval of his brief show of emotion. I realize now that he was well aware of how little time he had left.

WE RETURNED BY TAXI to the Hotel Imperial and stepped back into another world. As members of Litvak's entourage we lived in a luxurious room that was in sharp contrast to the modest residence of my father. We ate in the best restaurants, accompanied the director to the most expensive shirtmakers and tailors. The dollar was the currency of the victors, and Vienna was astonishingly cheap in those days. I bought a Hungarian sheepskin coat for Jigee and, following Tola's lead, ordered a half dozen shirts from a shop on the Kärntnerstrasse. As is always the case in an inexpensive city, we spent too much money and wasted our time with fittings and alterations, until our closet was crammed with new acquisitions and we were obliged to buy an additional suitcase.

Litvak had decided on Oscar Werner to play the lead in our movie and wanted me to meet him to endorse his choice. Werner was already considered to be the most talented young actor in Vienna. He was a strange young man with a pixieish sense of humor, as I discovered when he joined us the following day at Die Drei Husaren, one of the best restaurants in Vienna. He didn't look like Jacques, the code name of the young German soldier who had inspired George Howe's novel and who had drowned trying to cross the freezing Rhine on his way back to our lines. Werner shared Jacques's anti-Nazi convictions but had been clever enough to avoid service in the Wehrmacht. He seemed a little too soft-looking to play the part, but Tola assured me that he was a brilliant actor and would do well in the role.

The restaurant where we met was also one of my father's favorites, and that same morning I had suggested I take Liesel and him to dinner. But Liesel had informed me that on their last visit to Die Drei Husaren, the manager had asked my father to sign the golden book, as my father had become a celebrity in Vienna's new theatrical circles. Unfortunately he had come upon Göring's name in the back pages of the thick volume and had angrily declined to sign a book that contained this infamous signature. Tola was amused when I related the incident but later signed his name just the same.

"You have to forget the past if you want to work in this country," he said, a statement with which Oscar Werner disagreed. That was the reason he had decided to live in Liechtenstein, he declared, and only worked in Vienna. "They were all Nazis here," he added in his marked Viennese accent. "Much worse than the Germans."

"They're paying for it," Litvak said.

It was the kind of conversation I heard repeated quite often in the next few days. Friedrich Ledebur's sister-in-law, a pretty blond actress who had been in great demand during the early years of the war, confessed to me that she had joined the Nazi party as a girl in her late teens. "It was easy to get in," she said with a sad smile. "It was very difficult to get out."

Years later I heard a third-rate New York actor give this same excuse to the Un-American Activities Committee during one of its California hearings, applying this even more doubtful apology for his stay in the Communist Party, a less menacing organization, not to mention the very minor role it had played in the political scene on the West Coast. But in Vienna that year, the plea of innocence sounded like little more than a weak excuse. It was probably true that a majority of Austrians had joined the National Socialist Party out of fear or weakness or, even worse, a certain opportunism. But a few of the basic planks of the party's program were fairly evident right from the beginning: the anti-Semitism that was Hitler's rallying cry as well as his bellicose appeal for revenge of the earlier defeat of the kaiser's army.

Yet the charm of the city was irresistible. In contrast to Munich, where I had felt myself to be on the enemy's soil, there was an undeniable atavistic atmosphere floating in the autumn air that I found seductive. Maybe it was the Viennese accent mixed with the beauty of the old buildings, the food that reminded me of my mother's cooking, and the elegance of the street scene, even the liltingly sweet nostalgic music. I might have lived here quite happily if Hitler had not come along, I found myself thinking. But thanks to my mother's insistence that the family remain in the United States, a viewpoint that had nothing to do with politics, I had become an American, and finally a more dedicated patriot than had I been born in the U.S.A.

At the end of the week Jigee and I said good-bye to my father and Liesel and joined Tola and Annie Selepeno on an Austrian Airlines flight to Munich. Darryl Zanuck was soon to arrive in the Bavarian capital from the south of France for a final inspection of our production company, so Litvak had no choice but to cut short our stay. We arrived at the Hotel Vierjahreszeiten on the same day as the big boss, and Litvak was soon involved in conferences with Frank McCarthy and Darryl, who immediately vetoed Hilde Krahl and chose Hildegard Knef as the female lead.

Satisfied that he had made an important contribution to our venture, Zanuck returned to California, leaving Tola in charge. "What's he like, Zanuck?" Oscar Werner overheard one of the Bavarian studio employees ask a fellow worker. "Just another Hollywood Jew," came the quick answer, a statement that was as inaccurate as it was offensive, for he was just about as Waspish as it was possible for anyone to be.

There comes a time when almost every movie director is quite happy to see the last of his scriptwriter, and Tola was no exception. A writer comes under the heading of "unnecessary luggage" once the shooting of the film is about to begin. I had been involved with Litvak and the script for a little over a year, and I was anxious to be my own master again. Jigee and I said our farewells and departed for Klosters. The first snow had already fallen in the valleys of the Prättigau, and we moved into a small apartment we found in the as yet half-deserted village. I decided to start all over again on my novel about the O.S.S., to tell the real story instead of the one I had hired out to write.

ONCE WE SETTLED DOWN in our new winter quarters I noticed that Jigee had undergone a marked change. She had always suffered from the cold that skiing inevitably involves, and because of a freak accident on a T-bar lift in Davos the previous season she had lost some of her enthusiasm for the sport. The steel cable attached to the wooden hanger that was taking her up the slope had snapped, and when she fell, one of the skiers behind her had run over her with his skis. Although not seriously injured, she had been bruised and frightened and now seemed reluctant to go skiing on anything but a perfect day. She was not yet bothered by the fainting spells that her accident with Tola would bring on later, but as Vicky had joined us, she now preferred to stay home so she could have lunch with her daughter when she came home from school. Jigee was still following the cure for her nervous stomach that Hemingway had prescribed—a whiskey sour before dinner—then went on to a glass of Kirsch with her coffee, a local custom.

I had established a routine of remaining at my typewriter every morning but was discovering that when my work didn't go well, it was a relief to flee to the beckoning slopes. Incredibly, as I look back now, improving as a skier seemed to offer some sort of consolation for failing to make headway with my novel. Another excuse I made for myself was the threat of being recalled to active duty, which was still a distinct possibility. The "have fun while you can" mentality from the war was easy to fall back on.

A paradise, even one with subzero temperatures, is a dangerous place in which to reside. And even if it was not quite an Eden, Klosters was certainly a Shangri-La, a small world that often lay above the clouds in brilliant sunshine. As Jigee repeatedly declined to join the group on the mountain, Colette Harrison took her place as my skiing companion. A few years older than I, Colette was still a slim, attractive woman with a round, catlike face. She had a good sense of humor and tireless legs, and we skied together every day until late in the afternoon.

Like one of the women in Hemingway's novel *The Garden of Eden*, published posthumously, Colette was equally fond of Jigee and was delighted to act as both her drinking companion after dark and my skiing companion during the daylight hours. Her son, Noel, often joined us on his school holidays, which defused the obviously dangerous situation to some extent, but ultimately my relationship with her went beyond the limits of a platonic friendship, and we became lovers.

Jigee knew at once what was going on. In fact, she suspected what would happen long before it did but showed only a reluctant jealousy. One evening, I remember, Colette, on her way to her room, asked Jigee to loan her a copy of the current *New Yorker*, and Jigee replied testily: "You've borrowed my husband, so you might as well help yourself to my magazine." After that we curtailed the passionate side of our relationship, and the two women declared what appeared to be an armed truce.

I knew that I had spoiled our stay in the idyllic village, so I was greatly relieved when John Huston called from London and asked me to join him on a trip to Africa that would also entail rewriting the script of *The African Queen*, his second movie for Horizon Pictures, the company that he still owned in partnership with Sam Spiegel. He insinuated that I would not be making a lot of money, but I knew that going off to work with him, first in England and then in Africa, would provide me with an escape from the mountains that had begun to close in on me. Jigee, John suggested, could join us once we had set off for the "dark continent." In the meantime he wanted me to meet him in London for a few days of preliminary talks after I had read the script.

"When do you want me to come?" I asked.

"What about tomorrow, kid?" came the jocular reply. "Don't tell me you have to think about it. How often do you think you'll get a chance to go big-game hunting in Africa?"

We settled on a date. No matter what the job would entail, I knew it would be a more satisfactory experience than working with Tola. Huston was a collaborator who pulled his own weight once he decided to go to work, and to accompany him to Africa would undoubtedly prove to be anything but boring.

Curiously enough, it had been Jigee who had urged Sam Goldwyn to purchase the Forester novel a few years earlier during her brief stint as Goldwyn's story editor during the war. Later, after she had moved on in the same capacity for Milton Sperling's newly formed unit at Warner Brothers, she had urged her new boss to take on the same project, as Warner's already owned the rights. John Collier had worked for more than a year writing a first-draft script for Henry Blanke, the producer who had made *The Treasure of the Sierra Madre* with Huston. The fact that Spiegel now owned the rights was another odd coincidence, and Jigee was delighted that I was going to work on it, as she felt certain it would make a good movie.

UPON MY ARRIVAL in London I found Huston more ebullient and eccentric than ever. He had started his dangerous career of fox hunting and, partly as a result of his enthusiasm for this strange sport, had bought all of his fancy new wardrobe at Tautz's, a sporting tailor frequented by the English gentry in the West End. He looked slightly ridiculous in his drain-pipe cavalry-twill trousers and flaring tweed hacking jackets and seemed to have embraced a new identity. He had rented a fairly hideous house in Belgravia that he enjoyed for its ugliness, and I was taken there upon arrival by his new secretary, Jeannie Sims. Claude Cockburn, an eccentric Irish novelist, was already installed as John's houseguest. A former left-wing radical, Cockburn was the author of *Beat the Devil*, a witty novel he had written recently under his pen name, James Helvick.

Sam Spiegel was living in splendor at Claridges. He had made a coproduction deal with two English producers, the Woolf brothers, who owned a company called Romulus Films. *The African Queen* was to be made under the Eady Plan, a British government scheme designed to stimulate the rebirth of the local movie industry by making available a percentage of any British-made film's box office returns for future investment in new projects. The Woolfs, Jimmy and John, were polite and gentlemanly, unlike the American film producers any of us had dealt with in the past, and they were understandably apprehensive about joining forces with their unusual American partners.

Huston insisted I attend all of the preproduction meetings, the first of which took place in Sam's suite at Claridges. Lunch was served to the dozen or so key men involved in the project at that stage, and I remember that asparagus was the first course. While it was being served, John got to his feet to address the group. In his opening sentences he made it quite clear that he thought the film should be shot in Africa, and he ended his opening statement by announcing that if it was decided by the producers to shoot the story in England, they would have to look for a new director, a declaration that was followed by an astonished silence.

The next subject on the agenda was whether the film should be shot in color, which in those days would involve an increased budget. Again John got to his feet to inform his British partners of his views. But noticing that Sam had already started on the first course of the meal, Huston stopped in mid-sentence and said: "I'll wait until my partner has finished going down on the asparagus and then proceed," a remark that provoked a ripple of uncomfortable laughter and caused Sam to glare across the table at John with an air of injured and outraged disapproval. I knew then that their partnership was in for some rough sledding and would probably not survive.

Ultimately, after several more production conferences and late-night dinners given by the Woolf brothers, who for some reason felt they should entertain us every single night, Huston and I spent a few hours discussing the story. James Agee, a respected film critic and later the author of two brilliant novels, had written a first-draft screenplay with John's help in Santa Barbara. They had played tennis and indulged in some fairly heavy drinking, and Agee had subsequently suffered a heart attack, which was the reason he had had to abandon the project. His incomplete effort was heavily laden with brilliant descriptions, but there were practically no dialogue scenes, which Huston explained was the reason I had been hired. There was no copy of the John Collier script available, Spiegel assured me, and in any event what he needed was a new version to show Humphrey Bogart and

Katharine Hepburn, who had tentatively agreed to appear in the film. Neither of them had signed a contract, reason enough to make Spiegel nervous.

Because of Huston's close friendship with Bogey he felt confident the actor would not back out, regardless of whether he was given something to read. Hepburn, however, might well refuse to leave Hollywood for England without seeing a script. Despite the pressure of this situation, John was surprisingly casual about going to work. We made the rounds of gun makers and sporting tailors, and my collaborator assured me we would begin our rewrite as soon as we arrived in Africa and that a new script would require no more than four weeks of concentrated effort. However, after a few hurried conversations I became aware that Huston was less than fascinated with the basic story. He confessed to me that *Treasure* and *The Maltese Falcon* were more the kind of movie he wanted to make, more in tune with his view of life as an adventure. The Forester novel was basically a love story, a culture clash between Charlie, a British reprobate, and Rosie, a staid parson's daughter obsessed by her desire to strike a blow for England.

Sam Spiegel was alarmed by his partner's reluctance to start working on the final screenplay, but he had agreed to Huston's purchasing guns and ammunition for an African safari, for he knew this was the main reason John had agreed to make the movie. He appealed to me to make Huston settle down to work once we left London and its various distractions. I assured him that ultimately John would begin to function as a moviemaker, and Sam warned me that if we didn't get something down on paper soon, the whole project might well be suspended. He was obviously desperate about the way things were going, but that I could help him out of his predicament seemed a foolish hope, and I told him so in no uncertain terms. I was no more of a match for Huston's strong personality than he was, and if he had hired me for that purpose he had made a serious mistake.

"But baby!" he replied. "I know you can't *control* John, but at least he seems fond of you, while he seems to hate me for some unknown reason."

I could have explained to him just what it was that irritated John about his partner's lifestyle, but I decided not to do so. The Machiavellian aspects of Spiegel's operating procedures amused Huston as long as they were applied to other people; when the lies and the evasions were directed at him, he became annoyed. A con man's antics are a lot less entertaining when you discover that you're the sucker,

John informed me. I was fully aware of what he meant. The small expense allowance I had been promised was rarely forthcoming, not to mention the minute salary for my efforts that Sam and I had orally agreed upon. In the end the Woolf brothers came through with the pounds I required for London, while the dollars I was to receive continued to be a vague promise.

I couldn't help liking Sam. He had the ability to appear as a father figure, was a good listener, and, like everyone else in the world, loved to give advice. He was shrewd, not only in business, but in his dealings with his friends as well. His greatest weakness was obvious: he was attracted to women chiefly for their looks, a not uncommon failing among homely men in the business we were in, and that was why he had married the tall Texan beauty who was his wife at that time and who was certainly not in love with him. As a "story mind" he was, in my opinion, inadequate. His greatest forte lay in choosing talented co-workers, and subsequently he never produced a movie of any merit without a first-rate director. His ability to convince men of proven talent to work with him was his trump card. After John came Elia Kazan, David Lean, Joe Mankiewicz, and David Lean again. The films he made with less-qualified directors were all disasters.

He probably resented this dependence on the talents of his partners, for his friendship with Huston, Kazan, Mankiewicz, and Lean all failed to survive working together. Undoubtedly Spiegel's venality destroyed these important relationships one after the other. Billy Wilder, who never directed a movie produced by Sam, once remarked that "Spiegel is a modern-day Robin Hood . . . he steals from the rich and he steals from the poor."

During one of their violent quarrels in Sam's suite at Claridges, John asked him why he was such an incorrigible liar, and Sam replied: "If I hadn't lied during all these years, I would now be a cake of soap," a guileless admission that delighted Huston and brought about a temporary cease-fire in their relationship. To put a seal on this benevolent moment, Spiegel suggested that Huston set out for Africa on a reconnaissance, to which John agreed immediately. When Sam discovered that his director had flown off to Nairobi without a copy of the old script, however, he was once again plunged into a mood of deep despair.

I did my best to calm him. "He wouldn't have time to work on the script anyway, Sam," I said. But he was not to be placated that easily. "I'm hooked up with a madman," he muttered, as we took our places in the back of his Rolls-Royce and drove back to Claridges from the airport.

TO EVERYONE'S AMAZEMENT, Huston returned to England little more than a week later. He had discovered, he said, that Kenya was not the right locale for our movie. He had looked for a river through the jungle and had not found one in British East Africa. He wanted to shoot the film in the Belgian Congo, but this was not a sterling area, which would greatly complicate the financing of our venture. He also brought with him the usual complaints about not being paid for his services, as he had received a series of cables from his wife, Ricki, and his business manager, each one of which began with the words "Situation desperate." After a few more tense meetings, arrangements were made by Spiegel and the Woolf brothers to shoot most of the movie in the Congo; Ricki Huston was sent enough money to live on for the next few months, and it finally looked as if we would soon be on our way.

Bogart and Hepburn had arrived in London, and the usual parties and press conferences took place. Bogart and his wife, Lauren Bacall, were the delight of the British newspaper crowd, and even Kate Hepburn was charming and amusing. On the way out of the conference a reporter cornered Huston to ask the usual irritating questions that had little to do with making a film.

Did Huston anticipate trouble with the strong-minded Miss Hepburn? the reporter asked. John frowned. "Not really," he replied. "As long as I don't get the clap from one of my leading ladies I'm satisfied." The reporter was taken aback, then realized it was a joke, and retired somewhat shaken. It was not the kind of response that reassured Spiegel as to the sanity of his director when it was repeated to him by one of his spies.

But that Huston was well aware of the realities of production soon became apparent. He helped choose Hepburn's and Bogart's wardrobes; met with Jack Cardiff, the cameraman, and went on to dispose of all the irksome preproduction tasks that are heaped upon a movie director. I went along supposedly to discuss the script, but running from place to place was hardly conducive to the holding of a story conference. I realized that what Huston really wanted to impress upon me was his greater than ever passion for big-game hunting. Now that he had tread the actual ground of the wild beasts, he was determined to go out on safari.

We revisited the various gun makers to correct some of John's earlier ideas of what was needed by way of armament and doubled our orders of ammunition for the five or six rifles John had originally purchased, a wise move as it later turned out.

I could understand skiing on less than safe terrain, driving too fast in an automobile, and, later on in life, surfing in waters that were beyond my strength and skill. But the danger of facing a lion or a buffalo or an elephant on an African plain was not one that tempted me in the slightest. Nor was I looking forward to decorating the walls of any future residence with the heads of dead beasts and I hoped that once the film was under way Huston would forget about stalking dangerous animals. The whole matter of bravery had undergone a distinct change for me since the war. I knew my basic wish to live to a ripe old age transcended any desire to prove to myself and my friends that I was physically brave. In addition, my natural repugnance at taking the life of any animal, with the possible exception of pheasant, quail, or duck, made me skeptical about standing at John's side with a rifle or a shotgun in my hands.

In all probability he would not have believed me had I stated my reservations at that point. He was under the illusion that I was a kindred spirit, adventurous and devil-may-care, eager to live life to the fullest, which per se included hunting, fishing, womanizing, traveling to exotic places, as well as the as yet unmentioned adventures of the mind. I admired Huston for his intelligence, his enormous talent, his sense of humor, and his independence of spirit more than for his strange desire to mount difficult horses or face dangerous beasts in some remote region of the globe.

But when we took off from London for Entebbe, the capital of Uganda, I now realize I was traveling under false colors, a premature conservationist instead of a backup gun, a screenwriter hoping to have a hand in the making of a good movie that his favorite director was planning to use as a pretext for a personal adventure. Huston was undoubtedly more honest in stating his purpose than I was, but then he was the boss.

AS WE FLEW SOUTH, John was funny, charming, light-hearted. He was obviously delighted to leave the problems that had besieged him in England: his desperate partner, the apprehensive coproducers, the secretary who was in love with him, as well as all the other women striving for his attentions and his affection. Once again I was caught up in the magic of our old friendship, the infectious irresponsibility he maintained as a defense against all mundane problems—money, career, family.

The Harley Street physician who had administered the half a dozen shots that were required for a visit to the Belgian Congo had warned us not to drink any alcoholic beverages, advice that John chose blatantly to ignore. By the time we landed in Rome he had had several Scotch and waters and was completely engrossed in a book on big-game hunting that for the time being seemed to have become his bible. He even read various passages from the book aloud to me, and I began to be aware that the only game that interested him were the animals that were dangerous.

At the shabby airport in Cairo we sat in the lee of a Quonset hut and drank Coca-Colas, his laced with whiskey. "Feel the mystery, kid?" he asked, mocking this, our first African night. I felt reassured. The trip was fun.

Six or seven hours later we arrived in Entebbe, and our adventure began in earnest. What followed were weeks of work on the script, with strange people moving in and out of our lives, while we were quartered in the Sabena Hotel wrestling with the story of Rosie and Charlie Allnutt. In the midst of all this, Jigee arrived. Then Hepburn and Bogart landed in Stanleyville, the assembly point for the unit. Spiegel, too, made his appearance in that hot, humid town, taking over the command of the disorganized company in a manner that was truly impressive.

By that time my disenchantment with John was complete. I had seen him work his charm on strangers once too often, was finally outraged by his irresponsibility to the work we had been sent to Africa to do, and was truly upset by his uncharacteristic blood lust. We had spent only ten days out hunting, but that was enough for me. I wanted to get the hell out of there, leave Africa forever, put the heat and the racism and the jungle behind me. I knew that I could make no further contribution to the script and told Spiegel so during our final conversation in his suite at the Sans-Souci hotel in Stanleyville. Shrewder than I was, which wasn't difficult at that point, he asked me about the ultimate screen credit on our script, and I told him that I didn't give a damn whether my name was included or not. Irwin Shaw had always referred to that aspect of working in the movies as "screen blame," and I quoted his remark to Sam. "Would you be satisfied with academy credit?" he asked, which meant that my name would be included in the film yearbooks the Academy of Motion Pictures sponsored.

"Anything you say," I replied, voicing a costly decision. My contribution had mainly been sitting for hours with John while we laboriously invented the sparse lines of dialogue he required.

"All right, baby," Spiegel said, mopping his sweaty brow. "We'll leave it at that." And he handed me the two return tickets to Paris.

I had no idea, of course, that John, as was his custom, would pull himself together and finally make a memorable film, but even if I had vaguely suspected that this might happen, I don't think I would have acted differently. Sam also said that he thought it would be nice to award credit to James Agee, who had not yet recovered his health after the heart attack Spiegel said his collaboration with John had caused. Magnanimously, halfway out the door, I agreed with Spiegel and fled.

Betty Bacall called me a traitor for leaving them all to fend for themselves in the jungle. Kate Hepburn seemed to regret my departure on a personal basis, as we had struck up the beginnings of a lasting friendship. Bogart was only anxious to find John, hoping that the presence of a large unit would make his friend give up his elephant hunting and begin to act the part of movie director.

WHEREVER I GO,
I go too,
And spoil everything.
These sad lines, entitled *Proem* by Samuel Hoffenstein, have often come back to haunt me when looking back over the decades that have passed since the spring of that fateful year. Jigee and I returned to the Hotel May Fair on the rue Copernic instead of looking for another apartment, as summer was only a few months away. Vicky was again spending the summer with her father, and Jigee and I were hoping to escape to the seaside once the heat set in. Arthur Laurents still occupied a small suite a few floors above us, as did the actor George Tyne and his wife, who had decided to escape the Hollywood witch-hunt by living temporarily in Europe. We all dined out every night in the less expensive bistros the city had to offer, with a changing cast of friends, and after dinner the "group" were inevitably drawn to the bar of Maurice Carrère's elegant nightclub on the rue François Premier. André, the redheaded barman who later moved on to Maxim's, seemed to enjoy the custom of this mixed lot of American expatriates, and Carrère, a jovial, friendly man, sometimes invited us to sit at the tables

131

bordering the dance floor so as to "dress up" the place prior to the arrival of his more affluent customers, who could afford the cover charge as well as the more expensive drinks served in the main room.

Thus it was in the bar of Chez Carrère that I first met the cherubic Art Buchwald. Art was starting his career as a stringer for *Variety*, a modest post in which he did not yet display his humoristic talents. He had served in the Marine Corps during the war and had been stationed in Hawaii. A quiet, amiable young man with a permanent grin on his round face, he appeared content to observe the goings-on and digest his observations for his future use as a columnist of the Paris *Herald Tribune*. He quite obviously shared my admiration for Irwin Shaw as both a writer and a human being, and it was largely due to Irwin that he established himself as a member of our group.

Maurice Carrère was also the owner of a small hotel and restaurant at Monfort l'Amaury, fifty miles outside Paris, where we often went for Sunday lunch. The prices on the menu were not prohibitive but were high enough to discourage regular visits for Jigee and me except when we were invited by Tola Litvak, who was already established as a member of *le tout Paris* who frequented Carrère's *moulin*. Capa, with his habitual disregard for the value of money, was a weekly Sunday visitor, accompanied by Noel Howard and Chim Seymour, one of the star photographers of Capa's Magnum Photos agency. It was good business, Capa explained, to mingle with the Lazareffs, Pierre and Hélène, the editor of *France Soir* and *Elle*, a newly established woman's magazine.

Then as now, Paris was an expensive city, despite the relative strength of the dollar, and I soon realized that I would have to find a movie job rather than devote myself once again to the writing of my O.S.S. novel. Papa's warning that whoring in the movie business was not something you could recover from overnight often came to mind as I faced my typewriter in the small sitting room of our apartment.

Getting started in the routine of writing was turning out not to be easy; even my hunt-and-peck skill had become rusty and I found myself hitting the wrong keys with annoying frequency. All indications were that it would be better to make some additional money before the winter of that year when we were planning to return to Klosters and a simpler, less expensive lifestyle.

None of my friends appeared to be as plagued by financial or artistic pressures: Irwin had rented a hotel room on the avenue d'Iéna and was writing a new novel, spurred on by the success of *The Young Lions*, which he had already adapted for the screen; Arthur Laurents was writing a play that he had almost finished; Marcel Achard had completed several acts of a new comedy that his producers were anxiously awaiting; Bob Capa was mainly involved with Magnum Photos as well a piece for Ted Patrick, editor of *Holiday* magazine. Everyone I knew seemed to be working away on some project and was happy and relaxed whenever we met for dinner.

In addition, my marriage was not going well. The trip to Africa had healed some of the wounds I had inflicted on Jigee during the past winter, but there were still some traces of bitterness. My lack of confidence in my work and the financial pressure of perhaps winding up broke in a foreign city made me decide that I should once more escape to the movie business, return to Hollywood where I felt more at home and where I knew I would be able to earn some money.

Part of my deal with Sam Spiegel had been that when my job on *The African Queen* was finished he would provide me with transportation back to California, so I packed my bags and bought a ticket to London, where the unit had returned and Huston was shooting some additional scenes to complete the movie. I also knew that Colette Harrison was there, which Jigee suspected was one of the reasons I wanted to go to England. But she seemed quite happy to stay on in Paris while I went off to seek funds for our future together in Europe.

Spiegel was once again installed at Claridges, my first stop, and he was more relaxed than he had been in the Belgian Congo. The film was almost completed; John had pulled himself together, he informed me, and had made what already looked like an unusual movie. He agreed at once to buy me a ticket to California, an expense he could write off as part of the budget of *The African Queen*. He was exceedingly friendly and even praised me for the minor contribution I had made to the script. As far as he was concerned, the worst was over. I spent the night in one of the maids' rooms at Claridges at Spiegel's expense and was driven out to Shepperton Studios, where Huston was shooting, in Sam's hired Rolls-Royce the next morning.

The morale of the unit was high, I discovered, in striking contrast to what it had been at Stanleyville prior to the start of the principal photography. Huston, who had always been popular with his crews, had won over his truculent staff once he had settled down to work. Even Kate Hepburn, his severest critic, had been seduced by his charm and no longer complained to me about John's past "foolishness." Bogart was unchanged, slightly doubtful about what would ultimately appear on the screen, mainly anxious to return home to his yacht, the *Santana*, to recover from the ordeal of living in the jungle. Hepburn told me in private that both Bogart and Huston had been the only ones to avoid the dysentery that had plagued all the other members of the unit, probably due to their daily intake of whiskey, another of life's injustices in her opinion.

Finally John arrived on the set, a huge tank that had been set up on a soundstage for the final sequence of the movie, which finds Rosie and Charlie Allnutt in the water after the *African Queen* has been sunk. "Well, Pete!" he said, cocking his head to one side, "how the hell are you?"—this familiar greeting accompanied by a jocular smile and a warm handshake. But I sensed that his bonhomie was forced. He seemed only vaguely interested in my plans, which was not like him. I was an outsider, I realized, a friend still, but one that had not lived up to his rules of friendship, for I had turned against him in Africa. He grinned and expressed approval of Sam's decision to pay for my return to Los Angeles. His own plan was to stay in England where he was soon to make a movie based on the life of Toulouse-Lautrec, "without Sam this time," he added pointedly.

I was driven back to London in a company car and spent the weekend in the country with Colette Harrison and her son, Noel. We both knew that our love affair was over. It was just a matter of saying a fond farewell. She sent her best regards to Jigee, as if her betrayal of their friendship had been a mere accident, a winter romance of no lasting consequence, which was actually a pretty good assessment of our relationship. Feeling less guilty than I should have, I boarded a BOAC airliner, delighted to be traveling first class like a screenwriter on assignment.

MY AGENT, Meta Reis, had left the Allenberg agency to marry George Rosenberg and was planning to go into business with her husband. Recalling my conversation with Irving Lazar a couple of years earlier, I asked him if he would like to be my agent. He had a list of distinguished writers, and I felt I would do better with him than with Bert Allenberg, the likable dean of agents who was usually on the telephone with Spencer Tracy whenever I wanted to see him. "We'll get plenty of action," Lazar promised, and it was not long before he was able to keep his word.

I had recently read a novella by Simenon entitled *The Brothers Rico*, which gave an accurate and penetrating picture of the workings of the

Mafia. It was the story of a clerkish brother who is forced to betray his younger sibling, who was a hired killer. Realistic and sparingly written, it was a devastating story.

Knowing that Lazar would never have time to read the novella, I outlined the plot for him, and he immediately went to work. He sent the book to William Goetz, one of his close friends, and a few days later reported that Goetz was interested in making the story into a movie. Goetz, one of the founders of 20th Century-Fox, had quarreled with Zanuck and his partners and had moved to Columbia, where he had founded a unit of his own. I had given the Simenon story to Bob Parrish to read, and he had expressed enthusiasm for the material. Parrish, who had won an Oscar as a cutter, had recently completed his first feature as a director—a gangster picture that had been well received—and I told Lazar that we would like to make the Simenon story together.

In short order Lazar saw to it that Parrish and I were asked to a Hollywood party at a mutual friend's house, a soiree to which neither Bob nor I would normally have been invited. Bill Goetz was there with his wife, Edie, as was Frank Sinatra, who at the time was still struggling to make a career as an actor. Goetz was an amusing man of great personal charm, and he seemed taken with the notion of making an inexpensive film with a young writer and director. The business of casting and launching projects was in those days quite often conducted during social engagements of this kind, and Goetz told Bob and me that he was prepared to go ahead with *The Brothers Rico* as soon as he could secure the rights.

Sinatra overheard the conversation and expressed his interest in playing the role of the Mafia bookkeeper. Goetz seemed to like the idea but counseled caution. Sinatra was a close friend of his, and he didn't want to antagonize him in case we ultimately wanted to cast someone else. Parrish and I felt Sinatra would be ideal for the part and would have promised the role to him right then and there, but Bill restrained us, mumbling that Cary Grant might just be willing to play the role, an idea that seemed ridiculous to Parrish and me. However, it was neither the time nor the place, Swifty maintained, for us to voice our objections.

"Let's get Billy to buy the book and hire you two guys before we start an argument about the casting," Lazar counseled us in a far corner of the room before we were called in to dinner. Half-convinced by Lazar's tactics of striking while the iron is hot, Bob and I agreed to swallow our misgivings. Had Lazar read the Simenon novella he might have agreed with us that offering the role to Grant was an absurd idea, even if Grant was the most desirable freelance actor in the business at that moment. Sinatra was the perfect man for the role.

For the first time I was collaborating with a director my own age who was ambitious and talented without being a selfish megalomaniac; we were involved with a work of fiction that had great merit and had been written by a brilliant author. Our producer was a most sympathetic man who was already very rich and successful, in contrast to his two charges, and had no need to make a name for himself. We worked most days in his luxurious mansion in an elegant study with a van Gogh painting of sunflowers in a vase looking down at us.

We lunched in unaccustomed splendor; Bill Goetz was a gracious host with a wry sense of humor and a pleasant manner. In Cuba Papa had once stated that of all the "Hollywood characters" he had met, Edie and Bill were the two he preferred above all the others. But Goetz was doubtful right from the start about the tragic ending of the Simenon novel and was dogmatic in his belief that an audience never liked to leave the theater in an unhappy state of mind, a conviction Parrish and I hoped to be able to change. He agreed to my writing the first draft of the screenplay in Europe, provided I was willing to return to make the changes that would surely prove necessary. Bob was doubtful about the wisdom of my going that far away from "command headquarters," and I too was concerned that it might not be the right thing to do, as I was reluctant to leave Jigee and Vicky to fend for themselves in Paris.

But before leaving I found myself being asked to parties that were amusing and supposedly good for developing business contacts. Edie and Bill Goetz's house was one of the prime social arenas to which access was sought by a good many Hollywood strivers, and as I was now frequently invited I began to enjoy my temporary bachelorhood. On one occasion I ran into Bert Allenberg, and without trying to hide his surprise he asked: "What the hell are you doing here?" Screenwriters, except for the most successful of them, were not asked to the kind of glittering assembly that Edie sponsored. "My new agent is looking after me," I replied. Allenberg said: "So I see."

Prior to my departure the Bogarts returned from England and were welcomed by their intimates as if they had found Livingstone instead of merely having retrieved Huston from the jungle. Betty Bacall asked pointedly if I planned to see John once I was back in Europe, and I allowed that our paths would undoubtedly cross somewhere. Her attitude suggested that Huston would not be all that pleased to see me, so I asked if he had made some kind of negative comment about me. "No," she said guardedly. "He just seemed less enthusiastic about your friendship. I don't know what happened between you guys," she added, "but he'll probably get over it."

I had other worries to occupy my thoughts, and they presented themselves soon after I arrived in Paris. Separations, I knew, were always dangerous, and Jigee had enjoyed being on her own in Paris as much as I had enjoyed my stay in Hollywood. Harry Kurnitz, a screenwriter I had met only a few times, had taken Jigee to dinner frequently, and I began to suspect that she had become involved with him. Harry was a gentle, witty man who during the late thirties had sporadically attended some of the Communist discussion groups that had been in vogue, although he had never been a member of the party. He had always admired Jigee, even before her marriage to Budd Schulberg, but he had never been a suitor. Not wanting to testify in front of the Un-American Activities Committee and name those of his friends who had attended these innocuous meetings, he had decided to go to Europe and seek work as a screenwriter. Under a pen name, he had written several mystery novels, and if worse came to worst, he planned to resume his work in that field. Earlier in his career he had been much in demand, having written several of the *Thin Man* series that had starred William Powell and Myrna Loy. As an intimate friend of Jigee's he knew that our marriage was in trouble, and he counseled patience and tolerance.

As is often the case with the close friend of an unhappy couple, his words fell on deaf ears. Jigee questioned me insistently on my comportment in Hollywood and then admitted that she had been briefly unfaithful with Noel Howard. I had not been completely faithful either, quite apart from the weekend I had spent with Colette Harrison in England, so I really had no right to complain. And once the mutual recriminations subsided we both agreed that the repeated pattern of infidelity was threatening to destroy whatever feelings of affection we had for each other. We were quite obviously too young and possessive to carry on an open marriage and were even inclined to doubt that such an arrangement was ever possible for two people who really cared for each other. Even Marcel and Juliette Achard, who at least were holders of the right kind of passport for that lifestyle, seemed constantly to be bickering. Marcel was still involved with Melina

Mercouri, while Juliette was having an affair with André Bernheim, Marcel's agent.

We finally decided on a trial separation, a concept we had both scoffed at in the past. During the war while Jigee had been working for Samuel Goldwyn as a glorified reader, Frances Goldwyn, who was an éminence grise in her husband's company, had told Jigee that she would be welcomed back at any time. So Jigee wrote her a letter saying she was ready to resume her independent career. A positive reply was forthcoming, and within a month of my return to Paris, Jigee and Vicky left for California. Neither of us was sure that she was doing the right thing, but the die seemed cast, as we both felt that work was probably an answer to our problems. Jigee planned to live for a while with my mother, who was having trouble maintaining the house on Mabery Road, and with her salary from Goldwyn Studios she hoped to help solve the problem of the family's finances.

TO LIVE THE LIFE of an unattached bachelor in Paris, I venture to say, has been the dream of many a foreign visitor, especially those who have arrived in the company of their wives. I was no exception, and I discovered in short order that nothing is ever quite what one imagines it will be. I saw a lot of Irwin and Marian Shaw, Arthur and Joan Stanton, and Capa, as well as some of the other refugees from Hollywood, and of course the Achards. But I was always the extra man, a status to which I had never really aspired and in which I now joined Harry Kurnitz.

To escape my immediate past I moved to the Hôtel de la Trémoille, a few blocks removed from the Plaza-Athénée on the avenue Montaigne. Before it was renovated, the Trémoille was a somewhat tacky establishment frequented by *poules de luxe*, or women who looked as if they belonged to that profession, and their well-brillian-tined South American escorts, so that the rather gloomy lobby always smelled faintly of perfume. I breakfasted at the corner café every morning, and by generously tipping the Portuguese maids I ensured that my ill-lit room was ready for me to begin my work in the early morning.

The masterful construction of the Simenon novella facilitated my job of adaptation, although I discovered that even that accomplished novelist had a tendency to write the same scene over and over again. Nevertheless I made good progress on the screenplay. Irwin and Marian were soon off to the French Riviera, where they had rented a villa, and Kurnitz followed them south. The Stantons left for the States, and I became almost solely dependent on the Achards for company. As proof of friendship they introduced me to a pretty, vivacious French-woman about my own age, and she temporarily cured my loneliness. But a fortnight later she went off to Rome to open a nightclub and I was once more alone with my screenplay.

Peter Van Eyck, a strikingly handsome German actor who had come to California to get away from Hitler's Germany, was living in the country with his new wife, Inge, an equally aristocratic Prussian who had shared his anti-Nazi convictions, and I visited them regularly on weekends. Henry Hyde, my former boss in the O.S.S., appeared in Paris for a brief visit, and he assured me that he would use his influence to get me assigned to the intelligence service should the Marine Corps call me back to active duty, still a remote possibility. Capa had gone off to Nice to photograph the aging Matisse, so after finishing my screenplay I decided to accept Marcel and Juliette Achard's invitation to join them in their house near Blois, where Marcel said it was "frighteningly quiet" and I would be doing him a favor by coming.

Juliette's most prized possession was a brand-new Peugeot sedan, which she would at times shift doggedly into reverse instead of first gear, a dangerous error in the Paris traffic. During the drive she entertained me with the current Paris gossip, anecdotes that Marcel appeared to be only vaguely interested in. Their house, I discovered, was comfortable, and the climate was indeed cooler than that of the city. I went along to the imposing mansion of Prouvost, one of the press princes of France who lived in the Sologne, for a rich but dreary luncheon that made me long for friends my own age and a simpler social life.

Then, as the first week of my stay drew to a close, Juliette insisted that Marcel and I go with her for a day to the small château of a couple who lived nearby, a visit she assured me would be amusing. The woman who owned the miniature castle had been a great beauty before the war and had married a handsome playboy who had been flagrantly unfaithful to her. Rather than compete with the women he betrayed her with, she had decided to withdraw to the country and wait until his libido had subsided so that they could share a peaceful old age. Her strategy had worked; they both lived now in serenity, devoted entirely to each other. It was an example with which Juliette hoped to impress Marcel.

The small château, set in the middle of a lovely park, was strikingly peaceful; our host and hostess were gracious and charming, and as we all sat together on a stone terrace after lunch, the lady of the house produced a recently baked *galette*, and her husband opened a hundred-year-old bottle of amber wine in honor of the special occasion of our visit. The wine was slightly sweet and corked despite the slow pouring of it, but the afternoon was memorable and somehow touching.

Then as we drove off through the park toward the front gate, Juliette asked me if I had noticed the special smell that permeated the ground floor of the house. I told her that I had assumed the odor was due to the extreme age of the castle, and she chuckled happily. That wasn't the cause, she informed me. It was the smell of opium that lingered in all of the rooms, for now her two friends spent their evenings in an opium haze to stave off the interminable boredom of their lives.

Marcel roared with appreciative laughter. It was added proof of his most basic conviction, that living in the country was a snare and a delusion and invariably caused him to be visited by hopeless depressions that were unknown to him in his beloved Paris, where there were always the well-lighted boulevards, the bars and restaurants to help you forget that death was the inevitable end for all men on this earth. Paris represented life, and he was anxious to return there despite the heat.

The next day we visited the small cemetery on the banks of the Loire where Juliette and Marcel had reserved plots for their final resting places. Once that chore had been disposed of, Marcel announced that he was driving back to the city with me in the car I had rented for the trip. Less than ten minutes after we left Blois, Marcel's optimistic joie de vivre was in evidence again. He invited me to dine with him that evening at Chez Alexandre on avenue George V. As if by divine providence, Marcel Pagnol came strolling past the terrace after we had finished our meal, and Achard called out to him to join us. I had for many years admired *The Baker's Wife* and his many other plays and movies and novels, and I sat in mute admiration while the two famous writers gossiped about the theater and the political events of the day. Long after midnight, when I at last drove Marcel back to his apartment, he confessed that he couldn't exist anywhere else in the world. "I die a slow death as soon as I depart from here," he said. "Even the Germans couldn't spoil Paris for me."

.   .   .   .

A WEEK LATER I mailed off my freshly typed screenplay and caught the *train bleu* for the south of France, where Irwin and Marian had invited me to spend a week with them. They met me at the Antibes railroad station and we drove off through the splendid sunshine of a perfect day to the Domaine de la Garoupe, a millionaire's residence with an imposing park, the guest house of which Irwin and Marian had rented. Slimmed down by their daily rounds of swimming and tennis, they both appeared to have found a connubial bliss that made me even more conscious of the failure of my own marriage. The villa that looked down upon the glistening Mediterranean had the aura of a stage set for a romantic comedy about a healthy and handsome couple of American expatriates who had made a success of life abroad. Once again I was impressed by Irwin's exuberance, his enjoyment of an existence that included work and exercise and friendship. Marian, freckled and dazzlingly pretty in a bathing suit or a tennis dress or a summer frock, was quite obviously a perfect partner for this robust, gifted man whose short stories and plays reflected a more troubled view of the world than was apparent in his present lifestyle.

As night fell that first day, the first small imperfections of my friends' idyll began to surface. The mosquitoes that plagued the park on the property had a propensity to choose Marian and me as their victims, while somehow Irwin remained unscathed. He laughed uproariously when we accused him of being a less sensitive human being, covered with a thick enough hide to withstand the insects' vicious bites. Even the nets under which we slept were no protection. We lunched the next day at Eden Roc, Irwin seemingly oblivious of the high prices on the menu. That evening Irwin decided we would dine at a small bistro called Félix au Port, famous for its bouillabaisse. Five sets of doubles in the late afternoon had restored our appetites and our thirst, and while we waited for the fish soup to be prepared we drank several bottles of Tavel, the rose-colored wine of the region.

The mild evening air, the sweetly sour smell of the waterfront, the other sunburned diners who filled the terrace, most of them British or French, provided a magic to the moment that probably stands out more vividly in my memory than the many evenings like it that followed through the years in Paris or in St. Jean de Luz. Perhaps it was the sudden change of mood that occurred. I cannot recall exactly how it started, but somehow the conversation got around to family finances and the large amounts of money we all tended to spend on motorcars. The Hillman Minx Irwin had purchased a few years earlier was the

Shaws' only mode of transportation, and Irwin maintained that it served its purpose adequately. With the top down he didn't want to go any faster than the sixty miles an hour that was its top speed.

Marian disagreed, said it was really an awful little car, and regretted that they had not brought their Ford convertible over from New York, where it was standing in a garage. "It would have cost five hundred dollars to ship it to Paris," Irwin reminded his wife. "So . . . ," she replied airily, "what's five hundred dollars!"

The remark seemed to enrage Irwin. He accused Marian of being cavalier about money, and the exchange of words that followed became more acrimonious. "To hell with it, I'm leaving!" he finally exploded, got up from the table, and crossed the street in front of us to where the Hillman Minx was parked. Stunned by the suddenness of his actions, Marian and I sat for a moment in silence watching Irwin get into his car. "This is too silly," Marian said finally. "Go and stop him, Peter."

Within minutes I was at the side of the car. "Irwin! Come on . . . at least wait until we've had our bouillabaisse," I pleaded.

"You and Marian have it," he replied tensely and, without warning, he started off. I just had time to draw in my toes before I felt the rear tire cross the tip of my moccasins.

"Irwin!" I shouted, to no avail. The small black car with its broad-shouldered driver continued down the road.

I arrived back at the table at the same time as the steaming bowl of soup, complete with the thick sauce that is quite suitably known as "rust." Marian remained calm and seemingly undisturbed. We laughed briefly about the near mishap to my foot. Irwin's sudden fit of anger was a mystery to both of us and we expected him to reappear momentarily, but he didn't. It occurred to me that the financial discussion had merely been an excuse for his sudden revolt against well-ordered domesticity. Yet I knew that he enjoyed the bourgeois life, indeed needed it to do his work. A writer had to be married, he had told me on various occasions, or else he dissipated his energies in the search for amorous adventures and the boring details of everyday life. He also enjoyed the decorum of a well-ordered social regime. Even when the Shaws had people to dinner in Paris, he liked to be seated at a table and served by a maid. A buffet dinner, he had once remarked in Malibu, reminded him of his early days when he had been obliged to eat at the Automat, where you helped yourself to food on a tray.

Neither Marian nor I was able to sleep once we returned home, and

142

at two o'clock in the morning we set out in a taxi on a fruitless search of the roads near Antibes. The Hillman Minx was nowhere to be seen. Marian was afraid Irwin might have had an accident, but I convinced her that it would be a mistake to call the police. In the morning he turned up for breakfast, having recovered from his pique, and our days resumed their hedonistic pattern. That their quarrels could so easily be forgotten was proof of the strong bond that existed between them.

Upon my return to Paris I found several letters waiting for me at the offices of 20th Century-Fox, where my former French tutor Edward Leggewie was in charge. There was one from Papa informing me of the good progress he was making on his trilogy about the sea, one part of which was the story of his submarine hunting aboard the *Pilar*, the novel he had wanted me to collaborate on. He commented briefly on my trial separation from Jigee, saying that he "sensed you guys were headed for trouble." Despite the death of his ex-wife Pauline and a few more of his friends, he was working well, he wrote, and his health, after a nasty fall on the flying bridge of the *Pilar*, was "pretty good."

There was also a letter from Bob Parrish urging me to return to California. He had received the script of *The Brothers Rico* and had liked it, but as Bill Goetz still opposed a "downbeat" ending, he warned that the movie would be delayed. He had decided, somewhat reluctantly, to take another job, as "a director had to direct," a statement with which I couldn't argue. Disappointed that our project had been put on hold, I thought it best to take his advice and return to California. There was also the ever-present worry about money, as both Jigee and my mother still required my financial help.

Browsing in a bookshop on the Left Bank, I came upon a slim volume entitled *De l'amour* by Stendhal that I bought, along with a copy of *Time* magazine, to read on the plane. On the back cover of the magazine was an advertisement for a new fountain pen, endorsed by Ernest Hemingway. It was a most unusual appearance for a writer in those days. A single sentence in his familiar handwriting was included in the ad. War, he had written, is still the greatest crime that mankind can commit, or words to that effect. It was, to my knowledge, his only public statement on the conflict in Korea, a hidden reference to the tragic events thousands of miles away that were still uppermost in my mind, although the possibility of my being called back to active duty seemed to have faded.

. . . .

A QUICK WAY to make money in the motion picture business was to sell an original story. If the idea was startling enough and the screen-writer could gain access to an established producer, it was sometimes enough to tell the idea for the story he had in mind to make a sale and then be hired to write a treatment or even a screenplay. In the past I had been fortunate enough to make this procedure work for me and on several occasions had found it an easy way to secure an assignment. Stendhal's long essay on love was certainly not material for a movie story, but after I had spent the first two hours of my flight to New York reading it, an idea occurred to me, inspired by the great French writer's witty comments.

During most of the remainder of the thirteen-hour journey west, I developed my story idea, and by the time I landed I felt confident that I had constructed a salable vehicle for a musical comedy, a form that was still popular in Hollywood during the early fifties. In contrast to *The Brothers Rico* it was lightweight and frivolous and was meant to send audiences out of the theater in a good mood. A title occurred to me over the fields of Kansas, always a good omen. I decided to call my story *The Strategy of Love*.

I still remember the fairly simple plot. Two young writers share an apartment in Paris. One of them becomes enamored of a French girl who seems totally uninterested in him. The older writer comes upon a tattered book in one of the stalls that line the banks of the Seine—*The Strategy of Love*, a textbook of the stratagems required for an amorous conquest. To help his pal, the older writer divulges, step by step, the suggestions in the ancient guidebook. The younger writer is soon rewarded with increasing success. But then the older writer is introduced to the girl and becomes enamored of her himself. Diabolically he invents what he hopes will be a fatal mistake in his roommate's conquest. "If all fails, the book says to ask the girl to marry you," he tells his friend. The younger writer balks at using such an obvious ploy to get the girl in bed with him. Yet finally, in despair, he does just that, and to his amazement it works and the older writer is relegated to being the best man at his pal's wedding.

It was a flimsy premise, the sort of idea one is apt to forget after recovering from jet lag. But many musicals had been based on much less, I thought to myself, and soon after I arrived I cornered Lazar and outlined my idea to him. Swifty agreed that the story was no worse than the basis of many musicals that had already been made. He urged me to write a short treatment, and I agreed hesitantly to do so, thinking it was probably better to tell the story, as getting someone to read even twelve pages was usually more difficult than getting them to listen to an idea. Lazar was not the only person in Hollywood who was averse to reading.

To cut down on expenses I had moved back temporarily into my old room at my mother's house. She suggested I contact Jigee, who had rented an apartment in Westwood, but prior to doing so I called Frank McCarthy, who invited me to lunch with him at the studio. Having completed his apprenticeship, he informed me, he had been elevated to producer by Zanuck. During lunch we talked mostly about his "dangerous days" with Tola Litvak, and after we had eaten our chef's salads I accompanied him to his new, somewhat comfortable office, complete with secretary. He was looking for a story, he told me, "like everyone else in town," preferably a musical." It seemed a good opportunity for me to try out my yarn on a friendly listener, and I launched into my idea, embroidering the story effortlessly.

McCarthy was immediately enthusiastic about the possibilities. The studio had just signed Dan Dailey to a long-term contract, and Zanuck, Frank informed me, was hoping to make the young dancer a star to rival Gene Kelly, who was under contract to MGM. But as McCarthy was a very junior producer, he was not in a position to make me an offer without first consulting Darryl, who was vacationing in the south of France. Frank said he would send off a cable immediately and was confident that he would have a positive reply in a week or so.

Elated with this first, positive reaction, I drove to Lazar's office and gave him a full account of what had happened. Swifty was only mildly impressed and said that he doubted Zanuck would allow a neophyte producer like Frank to make such a costly movie. He put in a call to Arthur Freed, the dean of musicals at MGM, and arranged for me to tell my story to him the next day. I told Lazar that I would prefer to work with McCarthy, as he was a friend, but Lazar insisted that it was a mistake to put all of my eggs in one basket and that in any event it would be better to have two studios bidding against each other. He knew what he was doing, he assured me, and I had no reason to doubt his word.

I dined with my mother that night, still somewhat nervous about the outcome of my pending deal. Her financial status had not improved, but she had started giving drama lessons with which she hoped to make a little money. She feared that she was being blacklisted because of her membership in the Anti-Nazi League, which had been labeled a Communist-front organization by the Un-American Activities Committee. Coaching young actors and actresses, however, was outside the committee's realm of influence.

Freed's lavish suite of offices in the executive building at MGM was intimidating, all the more so as my audience included Kenneth Mac-Kenna, the head of the story department, and Margaret Booth, a film editor who had become Mayer's favorite Scheherazade and whose function it was to tell L.B. the stories that were being submitted to save his having to read them. Freed ultimately appeared, a pale, pudgy man I had met several times in Zuma Canyon, where he owned a large piece of land on which he grew orchids. He asked after my mother and then settled down in an armchair to listen to my story idea.

Somehow I managed to get through my performance, even though I had the distinct impression that my listeners were less than fascinated. Freed nodded quietly and said it was "an interesting idea," and after shaking hands all around I returned home thoroughly dispirited, determined not to put myself through that kind of ordeal again.

Not long after I arrived, my mother informed me that Jigee had called to say that it was most urgent I go to see her, and I drove at once to Westwood. I found Jigee in a more agitated state of mind than I had ever seen her before. Her sister, Ann Frank, had called early that morning to say that she had been subpoenaed by the committee and had testified as a "friendly witness," naming Jigee, among others, as having been a member of the Communist Party. Ann was a few years older than Jigee, considerably less attractive, and plagued by a stutter that had probably been provoked by the advent of her younger sister, who had become the darling of the family. Like Jigee, she had a sharp tongue and was intelligent. After a long and stormy courtship she had married Melvin Frank, a round, jovial young man who in collaboration with Norman Panama had become a successful screenwriter of comedies specializing in the wisecrack.

Through Jigee, Ann had come to know Budd Schulberg and the circle of young Hollywood intellectuals that included Maurice Rapf, Lester Koenig, Ring Lardner, and others. Jigee and Ann had joined the discussion groups that were sponsored by the Communist Party in the thirties and had ultimately joined the party. Ann, however, had abandoned all political activity after marrying Frank, who was a liberal and had never been attracted to radicalism of any kind and had been mainly interested in pursuing his career. As "joke writers," Panama and Frank had often been employed by Bob Hope, who was aggressive in his conservative views, another reason Ann had chosen to withdraw from left-wing activity. It did not surprise me in the least that she had decided to testify, as she undoubtedly felt that by refusing to do so she would be endangering her husband's blossoming career.

That she had named her sister was not particularly astonishing either. Many others in the same circumstances had named their closest friends, in some cases the people they had proselytized and converted. The conclusion Jigee had drawn from her sister's call was that she would soon be subpoenaed in turn, although for the time being the committee was still under the impression that she was residing in Europe. She then told me she had resumed a love affair with Ring Lardner, who had already taken the Fifth Amendment, and under no circumstances would she name him or any of her other friends who were defying the committee; in all likelihood, she would be sentenced to a year in prison.

I was upset by her admission that she had resumed her relationship with Lardner, even though we had decided on a trial separation. Yet I didn't want her to go to jail. She had already been fired from her job with Sam Goldwyn, undoubtedly because of her political views, and so we both decided that it would be best for her to return to Europe as soon as possible. I gave her a check to buy tickets for herself and Vicky and called Lazar, who insisted I join him for dinner. Jigee and I made no plans for how to arrange our lives when I too returned to Paris, but I promised that I would see her after I'd had dinner with Lazar.

Swifty insisted we go to Chasen's, probably to bolster my morale, and we were seated in one of the booths in the front room, a sure sign that Lazar was now a local celebrity. I told Swifty that Irwin and I had often dined there in the past and that old Louis, a gray-haired waiter with radical leanings, had never failed to ask us what "two liberal young fellows like yourselves" are doing in this place.

"They'll probably get to him, too," Lazar muttered darkly. He was pessimistic about the current witch-hunt and was sure it was bound to last for several more years. He also felt certain that Jigee's past would ultimately jeopardize my ability to get jobs and approved of my decision to send her back to Europe; he agreed it was vital to prevent Jigee from going to jail. He also sympathized with her firm resolve not to "sing," a bit of gangster terminology that was current. The most important thing, in his opinion, was for us to sell my original story, and he said that he would put pressure on both 20th Century-Fox and MGM to come to a quick decision.

Jigee was relieved to hear of Lazar's supportive attitude. Probably because of the three months we had spent living separate lives, we were, for the first time in many years, able to discuss our personal problems dispassionately. We were in agreement that as a married couple we had been a dismal failure. Jigee said that she had always known that her being five years older would ultimately lead to trouble. Holding down a job had helped her establish her identity, for she had never been satisfied to be "just a wife."

Late at night, drawn closer by our candid discussion, we both decided that there would be nothing wrong with my staying with her until morning. Returning to the status of lovers didn't seem particularly strange or dangerous to either one of us. We made no plans, exchanged no promises.

At ten o'clock in the morning Lazar called, an unusual hour for him to be on the telephone, even in those days. He had spoken to my mother and she had given him Jigee's number. Sounding pleased with himself, he told me that he had sold *The Strategy of Love* to MGM for fifteen thousand dollars, quite a feat, he thought, as he had managed to reach Arthur Freed at his home before the eminent producer had left for his office.

But his moment of triumph was short-lived. He called back half an hour later to inform me in an agitated voice that Lew Schreiber, the head of production at 20th Century-Fox, had just telephoned with the news that he had had a cable from Zanuck offering twenty-five thousand dollars for my story. As Lazar had demanded that Freed make a quick decision, he had had no alternative but to tell Schreiber that he had already sold the story to MGM. Schreiber had exploded in a rage.

"We're in big trouble, Pete," Lazar informed me. "Of course, I couldn't tell Lew the reason why we were in such a hurry. If I had, he might have called Metro and killed our deal. He wants to see us both in his office in half an hour."

We met in the studio parking lot, and I noticed that Lazar was more nervous than I had ever seen him. He said: "You've got to back me up. As it is, you'll have to sign some kind of loyalty oath in Nicky Nayfak's office at MGM. That's standard operating procedure in this town today."

I had never met Lew Schreiber, but having worked at the studio with Litvak I was aware of his reputation as being tough and aggressive. Nevertheless I was not prepared for the scene that followed. As soon as we had been ushered into Schreiber's office by a suitably alarmed-looking secretary, the then vice president of the company began to shout at us in his high, slightly hoarse voice. In all his years in the business, the small man behind the big desk informed us in shrill tones, he had never experienced such perfidy. "McCarthy is a friend of yours, and Darryl has always liked you, and now you've double-crossed both of them! And *you*," he continued, turning to Lazar, "you're barred from the lot! As long as I sit behind this desk you'll never do business with this company again. Now get the hell out of here, both of you!"

"I should be the one to take the blame," I said, starting for the door. "It was all my fault."

"I don't give a shit whose fault it was," Schreiber screamed, his voice rising even higher. "Just get out of my sight!"

We retreated into the carpeted hallway, decorated with large photographs of the stars under contract to Fox. Swifty looked a little shaken, but when I expressed my regret he shrugged and said that Lew would soon change his mind if he wanted to purchase a property Lazar was representing. "Anyway, this is not the only game in town. I do more business with Arthur Freed than with Zanuck!" he concluded.

He proved to be correct in his assessment, for less than two months later he sold Freed the services of Adolph Green and Betty Comden to write the screenplay of *The Strategy of Love*. They promptly discarded my story to substitute a plot line of their own, not because they disliked my idea but because that way they could get a higher price for their services at MGM, as Adolph explained a few years later after we had become friends. But even at that moment I realized I had been the victim of bad timing. Had Zanuck's cable arrived a few hours earlier, we would have sold my story for a higher price. Lazar's eagerness to close a deal had been prompted by the fear that was rampant in the town.

Afterward I was summoned to the office of Nicky Nayfak, where I signed a prepared statement that I was not and had never been a member of the Communist Party and was subjected to a lecture on loyalty to my country that made me slightly sick to my stomach. On the wall of Nayfak's office was his framed discharge certificate from the naval reserve, as well as a photograph or two of him in uniform. I made no mention of the fact that I had been on the U.S. Navy's payroll too. There was no point, I felt, in wrapping myself in the same flag. I wanted merely to get out of his office as quickly as possible. Hemingway was right, I remember thinking: It was better to say good-bye to the industry, although it occurred to me that Papa had not taken any kind of public stand against the current witch-hunt.

NOT LONG after I returned to Paris, Jigee informed me that she was pregnant, the unexpected result of the one night we had spent together in Westwood six weeks earlier. Although none of the problems between us that we had discussed so freely had in any way been resolved, we decided that we should resume our marriage. Mutual friends recommended a reliable physician, and Jigee made up her mind that she would have the child in Paris the following spring. We stayed at the May Fair for a month while I completed the treatment of the story I had sold to MGM. Then as winter was approaching, we moved on to Klosters, where Vicky joined us in the apartment Colette Harrison had occupied the previous season.

Coming back to the small Alpine village had always been a strangely reassuring experience, but it was even more so that year. Everything was easier in Switzerland, many of our old friends among the villagers were pleased to welcome us, and the snow came early, promising a good season. Colette had taken up with a handsome young Canadian fighter pilot who had seen active service in Korea, and she was delighted to resume her former role of family friend. At Christmastime many friends from the outside world arrived, among them Sam Spiegel who, although he didn't ski, seemed to enjoy the social life, which included gin rummy sessions with Tola Litvak and Georges Cravenne, a successful publicist from Paris. I set up my typewriter on the table of the dining alcove of our small flat and prepared once again to devote myself to my O.S.S. novel.

Then a strange thing happened. Following a long dinner with Sam that included a great deal of reminiscing about our African adventure, the idea entered my mind that my experiences with John Huston in London and British East Africa would make for an amusing novel. I had struggled too long with my O.S.S. novel, and taking on a new subject that was fresh in my mind seemed a good alternative, a way to cure my writer's block and start afresh on what I felt certain would turn out to be an amusing book about two Hollywood characters in darkest Africa. Apprehensive about how Huston would react to seeing our contretemps in print, I consulted Spiegel about the wisdom of my writing this kind of roman à clef, which was what the novel would obviously turn out to be.

To my astonishment, Spiegel was enthusiastic about the idea. "Give it to him," he said, chuckling. "Sure, write it. It will turn out to be a hell of a book."

"You'll be in it too, Sam," I warned him.

"I don't care," Spiegel said. "Just write what happened."

"I'm going to call it *White Hunter, Black Heart*," I told him.

"Wonderful, baby," he replied. "That's a great title!"

I started chapter one that same afternoon.

PRODUCING A NOVEL that writes itself, or at least seems to, is probably the most euphoric experience a writer can have. There are, I assume with a certain amount of envy, a good many authors who have had the experience repeatedly, but I am not one of them. That was why the rapid progress I found myself making that winter made me feel as if I were living in a dream from which I was afraid I would awake at any moment. I plunged ahead recklessly, not worrying about what I was writing, whether it was good or bad or whether anyone would be interested in reading or even publishing it. The scenes and the words came rushing into my mind with such speed that I found it necessary to pace myself, to stop working before I was completely exhausted and to save the scenes that I knew would follow for a fresh start the next day.

The snow-covered mountains outside my window no longer tempted me as they had in the past. I made myself go skiing on most afternoons merely to get out into the fresh air and leave the clouds of pipe smoke with which I filled our small living-dining room while I typed away. Jigee was less inclined to stay up late, and she drank only on occasion, although she still smoked almost two packs of cigarettes a day. At age thirty-seven, she seemed more at peace with herself. Her pregnancy had made her decide to give up skiing, partly because her physical strength had greatly diminished. She admitted that she was anxious to return to Paris as she had great faith in her doctor there and was less inclined to trust the gynecologist in Davos who had been recommended by one of our Swiss friends.

So I was conscious of an imposed time limit as I worked away. I was worried quite naturally that a change of locale might interrupt the flow of my novel. But I still had a month or six weeks ahead of me, and as I was averaging ten pages a day I calculated that I would be very

151

near the end of my novel before we would be packing up to leave Klosters. But the story seemed to be getting longer, as I found myself including episodes out of Huston's life that he had told me about long before the start of our African trip, such as his fistfight with Errol Flynn, which I transposed to Entebbe by making the racist head waiter at the Sabena Hotel my protagonist's opponent.

Huston's eagerness to go on safari was still the main theme of my novel. In fact, he could easily have arranged to go hunting for ten days as soon as we had finished our screenplay. But somehow that was too simple. He didn't want to settle for the kind of outing that was popular among millionaire sportsmen; he felt that being led by a white hunter was not adventurous enough, too easy. A white hunter drove his clients out into the hunting grounds in a Land Rover, found the lion or the buffalo or the elephant in its habitat, and then stood aside, backup gun at the ready, while his charges blazed away. John wanted to go big-game hunting in a less conventional way, not in Kenya, but in Uganda or the Belgian Congo, less organized terrain and therefore more perilous. His perhaps admirable wish to deviate from the norm, made me apprehensive, and in the end caused him to be frustrated in his efforts to shoot an elephant.

His plan had a touch of madness about it right from the start, but I did my best to include in my story the affection and admiration I felt for him. His drive to live out our adventure to the limit, as well as his charm and talent, was included in the portrait I was attempting to paint of him, as was the disenchantment I had felt for the ruthlessness that was a part of his character and that was revealed during his quest. In a way I felt I was writing a long letter to a close friend, using a roman à clef as a vehicle to explain what I had come to perceive as our troubled friendship.

I made no attempt to hide the identity of my protagonists, a decision that Irwin argued against and that Papa felt was a mistake, as he later said in a complimentary letter he sent me after the novel had been published. Now, many years later, I tend to think they were right and I was wrong; had I changed the names of my leading characters, my novel would probably have been judged on its own merits rather than as a scandalous "knock piece," which was how it was received by a majority of critics.

THE GROUND having been prepared by his loyal secretary Annie Selepeno, Litvak arrived in mid-February. He stepped off the con-

necting train from Paris on a bright, sunny day, accompanied by Sophie Malgat, his girlfriend of the moment, a handsome model at least
fifteen years his junior. A natural blonde, taller than her escort, with a
slim figure, Sophie was one of the top fashion and photo models,
much in demand in New York as well as Paris. Endowed with a good
sense of humor, although often cuttingly sarcastic, she was flirtatious
by nature, knowing that her hold on Tola was enhanced by her ability
to make him jealous, a situation that did not endear her to Jigee and
some of the other Klosters wives.

Tola and Sophie had decided to come to the mountains to escape
the Parisian winter, although neither of them was a skier. So while he
dedicated himself to gin rummy and long walks, I occasionally went
sledding with Sophie on the well-prepared but icy track that started
down from the middle station of the Gotschnabahn. Now that we
were no longer collaborators, Litvak proved to be an entertaining
companion, although when I told him about the novel I was writing
he made a disgruntled face.

Sophie and Tola returned to Paris, but after a few days he reappeared, this time in the company of Bettina Graziani, another Paris
model and allegedly Sophie's best friend. Whereas Sophie was pretty,
Bettina was beautiful, a shy, slim young woman with auburn hair and
freckles that gave evidence of her Breton heritage. Jigee and I, as well
as some of the other semipermanent residents of the village, were
puzzled by Litvak's apparent ability to change partners so quickly, but
the mystery was soon cleared up when both he and Bettina advised us
that they were merely friends and that he had invited her to come
along as she needed a rest from her routine of hard work as a mannequin and photo model. At Tola's suggestion I took Bettina skiing although she was little more than a beginner.

We became friends and skied together every afternoon for the remainder of her stay. On the long rides up the mountain she told me
about her life. Her mother was a schoolteacher in Laval and had been
abandoned by her husband when Bettina was five years old. Not surprisingly, in politics Madame Bodin belonged to the left, as she had
had a hard life, forced as she had been to provide for Bettina and her
older sister. Bettina had been married for a couple of years to Benno
Graziani, a young Italian journalist who worked for *Paris-Match*. Once
their marriage ended and after a brief romance with an Egyptian
movie producer of minor standing, she had become enamored of Guy
Schoeller, a wealthy French publisher to whom she was still romanti-

cally attached. Schoeller was at that moment vacationing in Brazil, as he had no taste for winter sports.

Even Jigee admitted that Bettina was an "enchanting young woman." As I was determined to be a good husband, and Bettina was equally determined to remain Schoeller's faithful mistress, we enjoyed a brief, intimate friendship, and on the eve of her departure for Paris with Tola she told me to be sure to call her as soon as I had returned to France, and I promised to do so. Once I had driven them both to Landquart and they had boarded the Arlberg Express, I went back to my novel without any further distractions.

But by the middle of March I realized that writing the ending of my novel was going to be the most difficult part of my task, and as Jigee was becoming more and more eager to leave the mountains, I agreed to pull up stakes and return to Paris. We had heard of a house in Neuilly that was for rent; the price was bearable, so we took a three-month lease on the place sight unseen. Vicky, we decided, would remain in her school in Klosters as a boarder until the end of the term, as she had no desire to change schools. She had made friends with many of the other pupils and seemed quite happy to remain alone in the village that had become her second home. I picked up my MG from the garage farther down the valley and we headed for the French border.

The change of address turned out to be disconcerting. The house in Neuilly, although grand in design, was run-down, drafty, and cold. The gray, melancholy light of Paris was no substitute for the clean white world we had left behind us. The room I chose to work in was large and unfamiliar; the pace of my writing decreased. Jigee, too, found herself longing for our small but warm apartment in Klosters, but she was reassured when her Parisian doctor told her that she was physically in quite good form.

We were invited to lunch soon after our arrival by Hélène Lazareff, whom we had befriended in Switzerland. The Berkeley was the restaurant favored by *le tout Paris* in the fifties, and we were somewhat intimidated by its elegant atmosphere. As we were leaving we ran into Bettina, and she asked why I hadn't called her. I told her that I was trying to get back to work and readjusting to living in Paris, and I thought no more of it.

Soon many of the tensions that had existed between Jigee and me began to surface again. She accused me of no longer being in love with her; our physical relationship had changed long before our separation, or I wouldn't have been attracted so often to other women, she said. It would be better, she hinted, that we ultimately go our separate ways. I told her that we should delay any decision about the future until after she had had our child. I realize now that she may have wanted me to say we would always be married. But as we had been frank with each other for quite some time, I felt that it was useless to lie.

Not many days later we dined with Litvak and another of his mannequin friends, Ghilaine du Boyssons, a vivacious and pretty young woman in her early twenties. Tola had purchased four tickets for a play that was said to be good movie material. Jigee decided that she would prefer to return home rather than sit watching a play she could not follow. She suggested that I accompany Litvak and Ghilaine and said that she would drive herself back to our house in Neuilly. A young Swiss woman we had hired to help look after Vicky when she joined us had recently arrived from Klosters, so I knew Jigee would not be alone for the remainder of the evening.

I demurred at first because I sensed that Jigee was suspicious of my friendship with Ghilaine. I had taken her to dinner a few times during the previous summer while Tola was out of town, but we had never been anything but casual friends. That Jigee was unable to accept my maintaining a friendly relationship with another woman without wanting to go to bed with her infuriated me, no doubt an insensitive reaction considering that she was pregnant.

The play turned out to be nothing more than a silly farce, and we left after the second act and went for a drink at the Brasserie Lipp, as Ghilaine professed to be hungry. As we stopped for a traffic light on the boulevard St. Germain, a black Simca convertible pulled up alongside of us, driven by Bettina. Tola tapped the horn of his Cadillac and, with Ghilaine's agreement, invited Bettina to join us.

Lipp's was as crowded as ever, but Tola soon persuaded M. Paul to give us a table. It was all innocent enough; Bettina and I recalled our skiing adventures, while Tola devoted his attention to Ghilaine and her many personal problems. After the women had eaten, Tola suggested we all go to a Russian nightclub for a quick drink. I said it was time for me to return home, but Tola replied that Jigee would probably be asleep and that I might as well enjoy my evening on the town.

At the *boîte de nuit* we ran into Evelyn Keyes, who joined us, saying that she had just had an unpleasant quarrel with her French escort, who had left the place in a fury. Tola ordered a bottle of champagne to celebrate this unexpected reunion with John Huston's ex-wife, who by that time was romantically involved with Mike Todd. Champagne was the only alcoholic beverage I was prone to in those days, and I drank several glasses, which apparently did little to improve my judgment, and I found myself enjoying a dizzy state of contentment. I wasn't drunk, or at least I didn't think I was. I was floating, floating just high enough so as to be able to forget the past and the future and dizzily enjoy the moment.

I danced with Bettina and was relieved to hear her admit that her dancing ability was limited to the fox-trot; the South American rhythms of the band were beyond both of us. Returning to our table I found myself seated between Bettina and Evelyn, who seemed amused by the whole scene. "Here you are, between your old love and your new," she said, which was an exaggeration, as ours had been the briefest of brief encounters after she had left Huston, or thought she had. I shrugged off her remark, not quite realizing that her feminine intuition was one step ahead of the game.

As I was without a car, Bettina volunteered to drive me home, and Tola said he would take Evelyn back to her hotel. I didn't want Bettina to drive me all the way to Neuilly, and we agreed that I would take a taxi from her apartment on the avenue Montaigne. I don't remember exactly what followed. I do recall that the champagne made me more forthright than usual and prompted me to tell her what I felt about her—not love, but complete adoration. As a result of my declarations, made in the dark interior of her car, Bettina asked me to come up for a final drink, and without a moment's hesitation I followed her up the single flight of stairs to her studio apartment.

It was six o'clock in the morning when the taxi I had managed to find on the Champs-Elysées dropped me off outside our garden gate in Neuilly. After forty years I am unable to recall my exact feelings at that moment. I do recall that instead of letting myself in with my key I walked down to the banks of the Seine one block away, not with any thought of throwing myself into the river, although later many of my friends said that might have been a good idea. Instead I stood for a long time in the cold early morning air, pondering where I should tell Jigee I had spent the night. There was no use telling her that I had stayed up all night with Tola, dancing and drinking and listening to old Russian folk songs. She knew me too well for that. Yet I was hard pressed to think of a more believable lie.

I knew that I had behaved in an irresponsible and selfish manner. I was tortured by the unhappiness I had caused Jigee, and yet was unable to control my feelings for Bettina. I cursed the bad timing of it all; if only I had met Bettina during the previous summer when I was alone in Paris, I found myself thinking. In a minor way it was the same sort of bad timing that had made Zanuck's cable from the south of France arrive a few hours too late. Everything might have turned out differently then.

Jigee was sure I had spent the night with another woman, and I knew that it was futile to pretend anything else. Later that day she asked me whether it was Bettina whom I had been with, and I admitted the truth. "I'm glad it wasn't Sophie," she said. "Bettina I can understand." Then she asked whether I was in love with her, and I replied that there was no point in discussing anything like that for the time being. "I'd like to know," she insisted, but I avoided her question. It would have been easy to pretend that it was a momentary infatuation. Instead I said nothing, and that confirmed Jigee's worst suspicions. She was deeply upset, although I tried to be as affectionate as possible and to reassure her that we could continue on as if nothing had happened. She knew better, she said; it was the end of our marriage.

Bettina and I had arranged to meet for lunch, and seeing her again did little to calm my turbulent feelings. She was no more composed than I was, had come to the conclusion that her relationship with Schoeller was in jeopardy, and was dreading his imminent return from Brazil. Fortunately, she was supposed to leave for New York in a matter of days on a two-week photographic assignment for American *Vogue*, and with any luck she could thus avoid a confrontation with Guy. "Wouldn't it be nice if you could come along?" she said with a wistful smile, and I agreed that it would be an ideal way for us to spend more time together, far from the complications that were facing us in Paris.

That same evening I received a telephone call from Lazar Wechsler, the Swiss movie producer I had worked for a few years earlier. Wechsler told me that he was preparing a film about Anton Pestalozzi, the Swiss philanthropist, and he wanted to know if I was interested in collaborating on the script of the movie with his son David. I told him that I was working on a novel and would not be available. But he insisted I consider his offer, which surprised me, as he had been glad to get rid of me after I had written the first draft of the movie he had made with Fred Zinnemann.

He called back an hour later and suggested that while I was finishing my novel I could act in an advisory capacity on his project. That way I would have to spend only a couple of hours a day three times a week, with whatever screenwriter he could find to collaborate with his son. He was going to New York in a few days to talk with some exhibitors, and he suggested I join him there to help choose a screenwriter and thus avoid any possible clash of personalities during the month of conferences that would precede the actual writing of the script, should I decide to accept this, his second offer. Someone had suggested he hire Nardo Berkovici to take my place, but as Berkovici spoke no German, hiring him would be a solution only if I were to join the team.

Under normal circumstances I would have told Wechsler to forget about my participation in any capacity, but spending a few days in New York while Bettina was working there was a seductive proposition. Beyond that, going to Switzerland alone for a month with all expenses paid seemed like a possible solution to my current dilemma. The fact that I would be able to finish my novel without having to worry about money was tempting in itself. Furthermore, helping construct a story was never as taxing as writing a script, and I felt fairly confident that three story conferences a week would not jeopardize my work on *White Hunter, Black Heart*. However, knowing Wechsler and his demanding personality, I was still hesitant. I told him that I'd call him back the next day, and my apparent indecision only made him more eager to hire me.

I discussed the matter with Jigee. Both of us were relieved to be talking about something that had nothing to do with our personal problems, and although she agreed that a story about a Swiss children's village was not really the sort of assignment I was suited for, she saw no harm in my accepting a job that would require only my giving advice. She knew that staying in Paris would probably make it difficult for me to work and urged me to tell Wechsler that if indeed my services would be required only three times a week, I would join him in New York in a few days.

I CHECKED INTO the Gotham on 55th Street, where Wechsler had reserved a room for me. Its windows gave out onto the roof of a church, and had I been of a religious nature I might well have had plenty of time to reflect on the sins of the flesh. As it was I had been plagued by guilt during the entire flight from Paris, but once I was three thousand miles removed from my responsibilities, I began to feel less tortured by my own duplicity. I called Bettina at the Waldorf, where she had been billeted by *Vogue*, and we made a date to meet for dinner. She was, of course, surprised and delighted that I had come. Then I called Wechsler, who sounded irritated that I couldn't have dinner with him. I invented a previous appointment with my publishers, an unconvincing lie that he was forced to accept. We agreed to have breakfast at eight o'clock the next morning.

The next problem I encountered was more complex. The Waldorf in those days was not the kind of hotel that approved of late visitors to any room that had been booked for single occupancy. There was a house detective on duty on every floor, seated at a desk near the elevators, and his presence, we both realized, would make it difficult for me to join Bettina in her quarters after dinner. I explained to her that if she had been occupying a suite no one would object to her entertaining a male visitor at any hour of the night. "Then I should take a suite, no?" she asked with a smile.

"A suite is more expensive."

"You mean to say you have to be rich to make love in New York?" she replied in disbelief.

"Rich or married . . . if you live in a hotel," I told her. "Or you have to make love in the afternoon."

But that, in her opinion, was not a practical solution, as she would be running from one photo session to the next during her entire stay, and at the fee she was being paid in dollars the photographers would object to a model *"avec des yeux cernés,"* unlike in Paris, where many girls had circles around their eyes.

As we were both feeling lightheaded after our long flights across the Atlantic, the problem solved itself that first night and we were content to say our affectionate goodbyes on the sidewalk in front of the suitably forbidding entrance of her hotel.

NARDO BERKOVICI turned out to be a quiet, friendly man of Armenian parentage a few years older than I. He was being hounded by the committee, and that was without a doubt the principal reason he was willing to work for Lazar Wechsler at a reduced salary. The language barrier between the two men resulted in a strange interview, all the more so as Wechsler had a slight speech impediment. Nardo had read the treatment David Wechsler had written, and he admitted hesitantly that it could serve as a "thematic basis" for a screenplay. I translated his less than enthusiastic opinions, and the Swiss producer

appeared to be favorably impressed. He asked no questions about
Nardo's political problems and promised to call his agent about financial arrangements. The entire matter of his employment was settled
that same day, and Wechsler returned to Zurich.

I moved from the Gotham to the Waldorf and called Ken McCormick, one of the senior editors at Doubleday, who at Oscar Levant's
recommendation had sent me packages of books during the last year
of the war. My contract with Harcourt, Brace had expired, and as both
Stanley Young and Frank Morley, my former editors, had left the
company, I felt no hesitation about going to a new publisher. McCormick suggested I send him as much of my novel as I saw fit, promising
a quick answer. All of my business in New York had been completed.

Nevertheless I decided to wait until Bettina and I could return to
Paris together. Neither of us had come to any conclusion about what
we would do with our lives once we were back in Europe. For the
moment we were absent without leave in Manhattan, and we decided,
perhaps unreasonably, that we might as well enjoy ourselves for another eight days and face the consequences later. "The heart has its
reasons that reason cannot conquer"—at the time I could readily testify to the truth of the well-known dictum.

Yet we were both relieved to find ourselves back on the avenue
Montaigne upon our return from New York. Fatigued by the long
flight home, we sat on the terrace of the Bar du Théâtre and watched
the magical evening activity of our favorite *quartier*. Then we carried
our bags upstairs and deposited hers in the small studio apartment she
had shared with Guy Schoeller. There was a message from him informing Bettina that he was in the south of France, and so we went to
bed and fell asleep as if we had not a worry in the world. In the
morning I collected my car from the garage where I had stored it and
drove to the villa in Neuilly.

Jigee received me calmly and told me that Wechsler had called from
Switzerland to ask when I would be reporting for my new job. It was
useless to lie, as she had been informed of Bettina's presence in New
York by a mutual friend. She said that she had guessed that we had
been together for the last ten days and had made up her mind that she
wanted me to move out then and there. I argued with her, told her
that it would be better for us to delay that decision until after the birth
of the baby, but to no avail. Maybe with time the hurt I had inflicted
on her would heal so that we could be friends, but she was certain, she

160

said, that I was hopelessly in love with Bettina and that things would never be the same between us.

Feeling guilty and generally miserable, I went to my room and packed up most of my belongings. Vicky returned from a visit with one of her girlfriends and witnessed our final parting. Jigee pulled herself together so as not to upset her daughter, and the brave face she put on only made me feel worse.

I drove back to the avenue Montaigne and waited for Bettina to return from Hubert de Givenchy's new shop. Sitting on the terrace of the Bar du Théâtre I felt more distracted than I had ever been. When Bettina at last arrived, she helped me carry my bags upstairs, and we sat for a long time in silence, like two criminals. The small studio, she informed me, belonged to Guy Schoeller, and the first thing we must do was find ourselves a place to live, not an easy task, as the financial means at our disposal were limited.

A week later, through the help of Cecile de Rothschild, I found a small one-room apartment on the rue Spontini. It was on the ground floor facing the street. Needless to say, sleep was out of the question for the next few nights. I found it impossible to work, and my depression increased. Bettina knew what I was going through and tried her best to counteract my morose mood. Fortunately for her, she was kept busy by her work, as the summer collections were just starting, while I sat alone facing my typewriter, trying to shut out the voices and the footsteps on the adjacent sidewalk. One bright Sunday morning, I recall, after we had breakfasted in silence, she rose from the table with a deep sigh. *"Si tu me quitte,"* she said, "if you leave me . . . I'll jump out the window!" Her remark caused one of our rare moments of hilarity during those early days of our liaison.

THAT WE WERE NOT the most popular couple in town came as no surprise. The "group" was appalled by my behavior. Irwin told me that he couldn't understand why I hadn't at least waited a few months before leaving Jigee. He knew Bettina and liked her, but he had little sympathy for our situation. I tried to explain to him that Jigee had insisted I go at once, but he only shook his head, maintaining that I should have stayed on nevertheless. Tola, too, felt I was wrong, but he was sympathetic. Bettina's friends, mostly fashion models and photographers, accepted me as her new escort without offering any moral judgment. Changing partners under all kinds of circumstances was pretty much the order of the day in their circles.

John Huston was in Paris shooting *Moulin Rouge*, and a strange account of his reaction was reported to me. He was on his way to Chantilly with a group of friends on a Saturday night when the subject of my defection was brought up by Grace, the wife of Anthony Veiller, a screenwriter who had collaborated with John on several movies. Seated next to the chauffeur of the limousine in which they were all riding, he remarked, "Pete has struck a blow for all members of the male sex!" It was high time that someone demonstrated that having children was not such a big deal, he added. The storm of protest that broke out in the back of the car continued throughout the evening, I was told.

It was, of course, a typical Huston reaction, intended to shock his listeners rather than to express his honest opinion. I also knew that he disliked gossip and always refrained from making moral judgments, but the anecdote made me suspect that he had forgiven me. It was also obvious to me that it was high time I showed him the manuscript of my novel, even though I had not yet finished it. I called Jeannie Sims, his production secretary since the making of *The African Queen* and, after checking, she asked me to visit John on the set the next day. The *Moulin Rouge* company was shooting in one of the big restaurants in the Bois de Boulogne, and I made my way there with a copy of my typescript in a manila folder.

On the set were scores of extras, a band, and a large crew, not an ideal locale for my visit, I thought as I was led by a uniformed guard to the center of all the activity. I greeted Jack Clayton, the unit manager, and Ozzie Morris, the cameraman, and then John appeared from behind the camera. "Well, kid, it's nice to see you," he said, chuckling to himself as he did whenever he was pleased to see an old friend. Hesitantly, I told him that I would like to have a word with him whenever he had a moment to spare, and he said: "What about right now?" He took my arm and walked with me to a quiet corner. "You're busy," I objected. "I'll wait until you break for lunch."

"They don't break for lunch in this country," he told me. "Go on. What's on your mind?"

"I've written a novel about you," I said. "About both of us, would be more accurate. . . ."

"You have, have you, kid?" he replied. "Well, that's interesting." He seemed flattered and amused.

"I want you to read it," I went on. "If there's anything in it you don't like, I'll change it. And if you hate the whole thing, I won't publish it. If it really bothers you, I'll just throw it away."

"Nothing anybody writes about me bothers me, kid," he said, grinning. "You want me to sign a release? I'll sign one right now."

"I want you to read it. Whenever you have time."

"I'll take time," came the reply. "I'll start reading it tonight."

Behind us I could see the worried face of an approaching assistant director. Jeannie Sims was a step or two behind the man. "I think they want you back," I said, but Huston was unperturbed.

"Everything else all right?" he asked.

"No. Everything else is not all right."

He laughed. "I know what you mean, kid" was his only pointed comment. "I'll call you tomorrow after I've read your novel."

"There's no hurry."

"I'll call you tomorrow," he insisted.

He did call, surprisingly enough, or rather Jeannie did, on his instructions. Again I was summoned to the set, and again he abandoned his duties as a director without a moment's hesitation. He was enthusiastic in his praise, more so than he had ever been about anything I had shown him. I knew him well enough to realize that he was sincere. I had witnessed several occasions when his praise for another writer's work was meant to be an encouragement and nothing more. But that day his comments gave proof of a personal involvement in what he had read that went far beyond mere approval. "It's the best thing you've ever done," he said. "I'm proud of you, kid."

"Did it bother you?" I asked lamely.

"Sure, it bothered me," he replied, "and that's added proof it's good."

"Are there things in the book you'd like me to change?"

He laughed. "Don't be a horse's ass. Of course not," he said. "How does the story end?"

In a few sentences I described the ending I had planned. He listened attentively. "The director shoots an elephant, a cow," I told him. "And the herd, led by three or four males, destroys a native village. The end is a total disaster for the natives that live in the village."

He shrugged. "Yeah . . . I suppose that's a pretty good ending," he said. "But I feel it would be better if there was a personal disaster, the death of someone close to your hero that results from the shooting of the elephant."

"The writer? The storyteller?"

He laughed. "Not a bad idea, but it won't work, as you well know. No, I was thinking that Kivu should die, the little black guy with the spear, the chief hunter. What do you think of that? It would have a greater effect on the hero of your piece, be more devastating for him."

It was an idea that had not occurred to me, but I knew immediately that he was right. "I'll try it," I said.

"You do that, kid. And then show it to me. Take your time. Don't be in a hurry to finish your novel. It's too good to foul up now."

"And you're sure you won't mind if I publish it?"

"That's a damn fool question if I ever heard one," he said. "Of course you're going to publish it. Why shouldn't you? That's why you wrote it, isn't it?" He gave me an affectionate hug. "Now I've got to get back to work, I suppose, although I'd rather spend the rest of the day talking to you about your book."

I drove back to the rue Spontini, and for the first time since we had moved into the small flat neither the noise from the passersby on the sidewalk outside my window nor the memory of the upsetting events of the past weeks disturbed my sleep.

CHRISTINE, OUR DAUGHTER, was born at the American Hospital in Neuilly on the thirtieth of April. I visited Jigee on the evening of the same day. She greeted me with a sad, rather distant smile, and we talked for a few minutes. She said she was feeling "all right," was glad that it was all over. I kissed her on the forehead, and a nurse came into the room. Jigee introduced me as her husband, and the young woman in white acknowledged the introduction with an icy nod that seemed to say everything about my late arrival. "*Il faut dormir maintenant, madame,*" she told Jigee, and gave her a sleeping pill accompanied by a glass of water. The hospital's sleeping pills were much too mild for her, she told the nurse. They were what her doctor had prescribed, the young woman answered and left the room. Jigee made a face. "Can't wait to get out of here," she said. "Be patient for a few days," I told her, and she promised she would. "You needn't come back," she added. "We can talk when you return from Switzerland."

I went out into the dimly lit hallway. The nurse was waiting for me. She wanted to know whether I wanted to see my daughter, and I followed her to stand outside a glass window and peer in at a score of babies that had been born that day. "If you come back tomorrow morning to visit your wife we'll bring your daughter to the room," the nurse said. I didn't tell her that I would be leaving for Zurich early in the morning, nor that my wife had asked me not to visit her again in the hospital.

I was waiting for my flight to be called at Orly when I saw a familiar figure approaching. It was John Huston. He looked drawn and tired. "Come over here for a minute, Pete," he said, indicating a quiet corner of the departure lounge. "I've got something to tell you."

He had had a harrowing experience, but under no circumstances was I to repeat what he was about to tell me. I assured him that I would be discreet. Several nights ago he had had dinner with Suzanne Flon, a well-known and attractive actress who was playing a minor role in *Moulin Rouge*. Around midnight he had taken her home in a taxi, and as he was seeing her to her front door a man he had never set eyes on before had come running out of the house with a gun. Shouting angrily in French, he had pointed the pistol at John and had pulled the trigger. Fortunately the round in the chamber had been a dud, or else, Huston said with a grim smile, he wouldn't be here now to tell the story. A brief struggle had ensued, during which the taxi driver had helped disarm the man, who, Suzanne explained a short time later, had been in love with her for years, although their relationship had never been more than platonic.

John had returned to his hotel to tend to the bruises he had received in the unprovoked assault. But then he had found himself getting angrier and angrier. The following evening he had gone back to the actress's apartment with a boxer friend who was working in *Moulin Rouge* as a stuntman. His second in this most irregular duel had strict instructions not to intervene unless a firearm was produced by John's opponent. Then Huston had administered a beating to his erstwhile assailant, who was taken to the hospital after the fight. "Not since the war in Italy have I come as close to leaving this world," Huston added with a grin. I congratulated him on his having survived such a close call with death, and he went off to board his flight to London, where he said he planned to stay for a couple of days "until things cooled down."

It was a disturbing story. He appeared to be proud of the beating he had administered in cold blood, and he had felt the need to tell me about the incident believing that I would approve of his behavior. I was amazed. Despite our fifteen years of friendship and collaboration, there were aspects of his character that puzzled me. I would never have suspected that he was capable of such a calculated desire for personal vengeance.

The loudspeakers were announcing the departure of my flight to Zurich, and I made my way through the crowded airport feeling puzzled and depressed, yet hoping, like John, that things would have "cooled down" before my return to Paris.

LAZAR WECHSLER met me at the airport in Zurich, an unexpected honor, and drove me to his baroque house overlooking the placid lake and the surrounding mountains. On the way he offered me a generous per diem and suggested I find a quiet hotel near the town where I could finish my novel. David Wechsler, his son and heir, a stocky young man in his early twenties, arrived for lunch, as did Berkovici. Our first story conference was not particularly productive, although everyone agreed that we wanted to make a meaningful and important movie, a familiar resolve.

During the past winter in Klosters I had made the acquaintance of Fritz and Irma Frey, who owned several hotels on the Bürgenstock in Lucerne. I telephoned them, and Frey suggested I make my headquarters in one of his hotels, offering me a daily rate that I could not refuse. Lucerne was only an hour away from Zurich by train, although staying on the Bürgenstock would involve a short boat ride to the railroad station on the far side of the lake. It also meant I would be far enough away from my producer to avoid constant interruptions.

My small suite was luxurious; the housekeeper furnished me with a straight chair and a card table, and I set up shop. Bettina, when I called her in Paris, told me that she would be able to join me in ten days, and all of my worries vanished into the clean, Swiss mountain air. Huston's ideas for a new ending to my novel led me to believe I would be able to finish it in a few weeks. Work provided a welcome escape, and sitting at the typewriter, as Irwin had often assured me, turned out to be the purest pleasure.

Not so our story conferences. David Wechsler was a stubborn young man with predetermined ideas that were mostly impractical, and our first few meetings were spent arguing without making any noticeable progress. Berkovici, who like myself had taken part in innumerable script meetings, did his best to convince his young Swiss collaborator that even if his treatment was based on fact, it was hardly the basic material for a dramatic movie. The title he had chosen was *If All the Children in the World Joined Hands*, not one to lure audiences into the theater, and it seemed likely at the outset of our work that we would spend the rest of our lives in Wechsler's library arguing with his son.

More than a week passed; then suddenly the Swiss Army intervened. David, who was a lieutenant in the artillery, was summoned to take his place in one of the underground bunkers of the defense force, inside a harmless-looking Alp. Progress on the preliminary work of the script quickened noticeably, as old man Wechsler turned out to be a more practical collaborator than his son, who could now only telephone his comments to us from inside his mountain fortress when he was off duty.

Bettina arrived at the Bürgenstock, and was delighted with our comfortable and luxurious quarters. The view of the lake and the green countryside, as well as the efficient room service were, she realized, a perfect setting in which she could rest from her exhausting work period in Paris. Although thoughts of Jigee were constantly returning to my mind once I was away from the typewriter, I found that I was more in love with Bettina than ever before. She too seemed quite content to wait in our suite while I worked, and then would join me in long walks around the hotel grounds. However, her status as my mistress was obviously troubling her. She never mentioned *la question*, as the French call it, yet I sensed that she didn't want to go on for too long in an unmarried state. I did my best to explain to her that our getting married in the near future would further damage Jigee, a conviction she halfheartedly agreed with, although it was quite apparently unconvincing as far as she was concerned. Nor am I, looking back, altogether certain that I was right. Bettina was a normal young woman who wanted children, and neither one of us was bohemian enough to think it possible to start a family without getting married.

More involved with finishing my novel than anything else, I put this problem out of mind and assumed, quite erroneously, that everything would ultimately work itself out. That she was occasionally melancholy bothered me, but I did not allow what was troubling her to distract me, and in less than a week I finished my work on *White Hunter, Black Heart*. Nardo Berkovici had gone off to write his screenplay, and as Wechsler was satisfied that I had contributed my share to the movie he was planning to put into production later that year, Bettina and I returned to Paris.

I sent off a letter to Papa in Cuba and informed him of everything we had been through. He replied at once with a long, cheerful, and rambling report on how well his work was going. He had finished, he said, a long section of the book I had declined to write with him, as well as a short piece about Santiago, a local fisherman, that he was thinking of publishing as a novella, perhaps in *Life* magazine. There was no direct mention of my final breakup with Jigee, only a brief sentence that read: "Try not to take life too seriously," strange advice from a man who was often deeply upset by small, daily problems and appeared to take life very seriously indeed.

IN SPITE OF EVERYTHING that had happened, Bettina and I were happy together. Her amiable disposition and her striking beauty made it possible for me to push my guilt temporarily out of my mind. She enjoyed her work, rushing cheerfully from one photographic session to the next, as much in demand for her reliability as for her unusual ability to present a hundred different faces to the camera and yet remain recognizable, either in an evening gown or a summer frock. The old Hollywood saw that "the camera loved her" was borne out by her repeated appearances on the cover of magazines as well as the inside pages of *Harper's Bazaar* and *Vogue*. Every weekday afternoon she performed as one of the three or four star mannequins presenting the new collection of Hubert de Givenchy, a rising power in the world of *la haute couture*.

I often went to see her strut up and down in front of the rich ladies who attended these sessions and was always amazed by the cheerful freshness of her performance, even after a late photographic session the previous night. It was a new scene for me, slightly similar to the theater: the same excitement prior to an opening night, the importance of good notices, and the approval of a handful of critics enough to assure financial success. Bettina's comrades-in-arms were all friendly young women, and there was an amazing absence of bitchery among them. I remember their names and faces as if it were yesterday: Sophie, Capucine, Gigi, Sylvie, and Nelly, each of them with a distinctive prettiness and a different set of problematic romances. They accepted me as a member of their small club that Paris summer.

Guy Schoeller, Bettina's ex-boyfriend, was finding it difficult to forget her, but he had moved out of the studio apartment at number 8, avenue Montaigne, and with an unusually generous and gentlemanly gesture he passed on the key to Bettina, as he knew we were having trouble finding a suitable place to live. Without regrets we gave up the rue Spontini apartment and moved back into our favorite *quartier*. The rent was lower, and we were delighted to be back on a more pleasant street, to sit on the terrace of the Bar du Théâtre and eat our breakfasts and lunches in the shade of the stately chestnut trees that still stand on the wide *trottoir*. Bob Capa was a frequent visitor, as his current girlfriend, Alla, a beautiful Chinese model, sporadically resided in the Hôtel du Théâtre next door.

Sydney Chaplin, one of the two sons the famous comedian had sired with Lita Grey, arrived in Paris about this time. Tall and athletic, with the good looks of a Latin leading man, he was outrageously funny and soon proved to be a valuable addition to our group. His mother had forced Chaplin to settle a flat amount of money on each of her sons, the modest income from which made it possible for Sydney to live frugally in Europe. He adored his elderly father but was well aware of Chaplin's overbearing ego. The two brothers, both in their twenties, had organized a small theatrical company in the suburbs of Los Angeles that put on plays by contemporary authors. Talent scouts from the major studios usually attended these performances, and Sydney was offered a five-year contract by Columbia at a starting salary of a thousand dollars a week. Chaplin Sr., who up to that point had paid little attention to the ambitions of his sons, now intervened and insisted that Sydney turn down this lucrative offer and wait to be launched by playing a role in a film the old man was still in the process of writing.

Sydney realized that working for his dictatorial father would not be easy yet was loath to pass up the opportunity of appearing in one of Chaplin's films. He had always lived with his mother, except when attending various military schools. The rather formal, upper-class atmosphere of the Chaplin household intimidated him, although he liked Oona, his young stepmother, and enjoyed the company of his half-brothers and -sisters, who looked upon him as a favorite bad-boy uncle.

Although nervous about his future acting job, he decided to wait for his father's call from London to play the romantic lead opposite Claire Bloom in *Limelight*, the movie Chaplin was preparing. It was a pleasant holding pattern that he knew was not particularly beneficial, and to keep in shape we both started playing tennis again at a small private club in St. Cloud. At last orders came through for Sydney to report to London, and he departed full of misgivings for what lay ahead. He returned to Paris two months later visibly shaken by the experience, as his father had bullied him mercilessly throughout the making of the film. The sponsorship of a hugely talented parent was a dangerous thing, I realized, and felt reassured that my decision not to collaborate with Hemingway had not been a mistake.

That summer, to be near Irwin and Marian Shaw, Jigee had rented a small house in St. Jean de Luz, and I went to see her there. She appeared to have recovered, although she looked thin and fragile despite her suntan. Our daughter, Christine, was an adorable child, healthy and cheerful, and Jigee said that she was as happy as could be expected under the circumstances, words that did not make me feel any better about my defection.

I had finished correcting the galley proofs of *White Hunter, Black Heart.* I knew money would soon be a problem again, so I planned a trip to the West Coast in search of another movie job, with a stop at Doubleday in New York to deliver my proofs. In St. Jean de Luz Irwin begged me once again to change the names of the characters in the novel, but I felt it was too late to alter the text in even such a minor way. Ken McCormick, my new editor, didn't seem particularly perturbed about the similarity of the names to living persons, especially as John Huston had signed a release after reading the final typescript.

NOW I WAS APPREHENSIVE about returning to the place I still somehow thought of as home. I had recently deserted my pregnant wife and had completed what many people would consider a vindictive roman à clef, actions not designed to ensure me a warm welcome. But I was somewhat reassured by the sight of Irving Lazar standing at the airport outside the arrivals gate. Traditionally an agent is supposed to be the last person to desert a man or a woman who is in trouble, but driving out to Burbank was proof of something more than professional loyalty. He stood there beaming fondly at me and said: "Hiya, kid. I'm glad to see you. Before I forget," he added, "don't make any plans for dinner. We're going to the Bogarts'."

I nodded, thinking it was fortunate I had not advised my mother of the exact day of my arrival, knowing that she always worried when one of her sons was flying. Bogie wanted to talk to me about "some project" he had in mind, Lazar said. He had read an advance copy of my novel and had been impressed by it, as had several other members of the community. A movie sale was out of the question, however, as most of the major studios were afraid of a possible libel suit, despite the clearance Huston had given me; there were too many other characters described in the book that might take it in their heads to sue. But in any event, Swifty said, the fact that I had written a novel that was about to appear at the bookstores had improved my status as a writer.

He dropped me off at the Bel Air Hotel and said he would pick me up in an hour and a half. If I felt tired I should lie down for twenty minutes. "You can sleep tonight," he added, leading the way to his illegally parked car.

The California sun was still shining brightly as we rang the doorbell at 232 Mapleton Drive. A maid admitted us, Betty Bacall standing directly behind her looking as glamorous as ever. She bestowed a kiss on Swifty's bald head and greeted me with a wan smile. Bogey was taking off his makeup, she informed us, and Lazar went upstairs to chat with our host. Betty led the way into the living room, commenting directly and acidly on the way I had ended my marriage with Jigee. "You could have waited, for God's sake," she said, echoing familiar words. She had never been close to Jigee, but she felt sorry for her now and told me that I had "behaved like a shit." Having gotten this off her chest, she declared that she was glad to see me, adding: "It's about time you showed your face around here."

Bogart and Lazar joined us a few minutes later. Although in his mid-fifties, Bogey looked spry and in good physical condition.

One is inclined, now that Bogart has become a legend, to look back at him more searchingly than at the time. That he had a remarkable presence was evident even in those days, however. His young wife was a more flamboyant character, but one was conscious of his being there, took notice of his approval or disapproval of whatever was being said. Bogey was the hub of the wheel, the King Rat who held court for the rat pack, which included Sinatra, Sid Luft, Judy Garland, and others.

The conversation soon turned to Huston and his reaction to my novel. Bogey was immensely fond of John, respecting his talent while being aware of the tomfoolery he was capable of as well as his occasional irresponsibility toward his profession that we all had witnessed in Africa. The reason for stating their misgivings about our mutual friend soon became evident. Bogey had recently signed a contract with Columbia Pictures to make several films for his own company, which was named after his yacht, *Santana*. Columbia would finance the movies, and Bogey's company would share in the profits. Until now he had merely been a salaried employee whose personal income had been heavily taxed by the government. Like many big stars in the business, he had never had to worry about money, but he was far from being a rich man.

The first movie he was planning to make was to be based on the novel *Beat the Devil*, purchased outright at Huston's recommendation. John had promised to direct the film, in which Bogey would star, and Bogart, now a producer, was concerned about the screenplay for this initial, all-important venture. I remembered seeing a copy of the novel on Huston's night table in London, knew that it had been written by Claude Cockburn under the pen name James Helvick. Although Cockburn had been John's houseguest at the time, I had never read the book.

Bogart admitted that *Beat the Devil* was not a masterpiece. He felt, however, that it might make a good movie on the lines of *The Maltese Falcon* if somehow a writer, working with John, could fashion a good screenplay. It had been agreed between Bogey and John that Anthony Veiller would do it, as Veiller had written the script for *The Killers* with Huston nearly ten years earlier. "I'd like you to read the novel," Bogart said. "Knowing John, he probably won't have much time to devote to writing right now, and Veiller could probably use some help."

Betty went upstairs to get the book, and I agreed to read it as soon as I had had a good night's sleep, although I warned Bogey that three collaborators were usually two too many.

Bogart said: "Well, you and Veiller will be doing most of the work," a statement that Lazar seconded. "Then, too, I reckon you can handle John," Bogey continued.

"What makes you think that?" I asked him.

"Well, you've worked with him a couple of times before." He lit a cigarette and then squinted at me through a cloud of smoke, very much the character out of *Casablanca*. "This one is my baby, you know," he said. "A chance to make some real money, and they don't come along every day."

"I'll read the book," I said and Lazar glanced over at me, puzzled by my lack of enthusiasm. I realized that for him to sell my services even before I had unpacked my bags would be a source of great satisfaction to him.

Sid Luft and Judy Garland dropped in, as was their habit on most evenings, I soon learned. Luft had read *White Hunter* and was interested to know how much of the novel was based on actual happenings. The fight with the headwaiter was uppermost in his mind. I told him that I had used Huston's fight with Flynn as my inspiration for the incident, and the discussion switched to the strange subject of Huston's pugilistic talents. Could Huston "really go?" Luft wanted to know. Was he a good "street fighter"? Or was he a "one-punch character," like David Selznick in his youth? I assured Luft and the others that John's physical courage was without limits when he was provoked, and whether he could "go" or not was immaterial.

"What about Hemingway?" Bogart asked, more interested in the man than his work.

I replied that I had no firsthand knowledge of Papa's ability as a brawler but reckoned that he could be a dangerous opponent. It was a juvenile discussion, I thought, and I noticed that Bogart appeared to be of the same opinion and was willing to continue the conversation only because it was vaguely amusing. He stated flatly that he was a coward and usually walked away from any fight he himself might have provoked in a drunken moment. It was anything but his wife's favorite topic of conversation; in her eyes the various alcoholic confrontations, some of which Bogey had taken part in, belonged to another era, part of Bogey's less than happy matrimonial past.

Lazar nodded to me, signaling that it was time for us to depart, and not much later he dropped me off at the Bel Air Hotel. "Read that book Bogey gave you" were his parting words. "I think we can make a deal for you to do it, and that way you can get back to Europe without wasting a lot of time." I told him that working with Huston again didn't seem like such a great idea, but he remained adamant about my accepting the assignment. "It's a movie that's going to be made," he told me, "and that's vitally important for you right now. I know what I'm talking about."

BOGART HAD SUGGESTED I come sailing with him on the following weekend so that we could talk undisturbed. Betty was not fond of the sea, and she urged me to keep her husband company aboard the *Santana*. I reported to Mapleton Drive early that Saturday morning as arranged, and Bogey was just finishing his breakfast. Once he had swallowed a final cup of coffee, he offered me a "phlegm cutter," a neat shot of whiskey that he helped himself to and that I declined. Then he reached out for a cigarette from the silver box on the table in front of his favorite armchair and lit it. "Another nail in my coffin," he murmured, a prophetic wisecrack that still haunts me today, for he was to die only a few years later from cancer of the throat. He was fifty-eight, much too early.

We drove to San Pedro in his convertible Jaguar and set sail for White's Landing, accompanied by one of his cronies. Bogey was quite a different man once he was seated in the stern of his beloved *Santana*. He spoke very little until we arrived at the small cove on Catalina Island. Then after we had anchored and he had accepted a drink from his crewman, he began to ruminate on his life. He had been married four times, he told me, had actually never been single for more than a few hours. But now, finally, he had found the right partner. "That gal," he said, "saved my life." And that was the reason, he gave me to understand, for his not wanting to throw away the chance to make some money with the movie. Betty was twenty-five years younger than he was, and he wanted to provide "a little financial security for her and our kids." He wasn't like Huston, he said: "John kind of sails along from one day to the next and isn't much concerned with putting something aside for a rainy day."

I told him that what worried me was that I had never been able to influence Huston. And aside from Henry Blanke, the producer at Warner's who had given John his first chance to direct and who had produced Huston's two best movies, nobody could really exert any pressure on him. *Beat the Devil* was an amusing novel, I went on to say, but it wasn't really in a class with Dashiell Hammett's *Maltese Falcon*. It lacked a central plot. The dialogue was good and the characters were unusual, but the structure was lacking.

"John probably got me to buy the thing in order to help his pal Cockburn," Bogey said, staring out across the sparkling water at the distant island.

"Could be," I said.

Bogey took a deep breath. "Well, I'd still like you to help out on the script," he said. "I'd feel a little safer knowing there was one more guy around trying to get John to go to work. Anyway, you and Veiller ought to be able to come up with something."

With the passage of time *Beat the Devil* has become a cult film, a tongue-in-cheek parody of Huston's earlier melodramas. That it should turn out that way was not John's intention. When Tony Veiller and I first met with him in London about the film, he told us that he planned to cast some of the actors he had used in *The Maltese Falcon*— Bogart, of course, and Peter Lorre, and one or two others. Sydney Greenstreet had recently retired from the screen, and to take his place in the cast John was thinking of using Robert Morley, a good actor but hardly a suitable replacement, as he lacked Greenstreet's menacing overtones. Morley's real talent was comedic, which perhaps influenced John to "send the whole thing up" once he realized that as a melodrama the story was sadly lacking.

For me it turned out to be a frustrating assignment. Veiller, a seasoned scriptwriter, and I struggled with the first draft of the screenplay for three months of 1953, doing our best to please the "monster," Tony's sobriquet for John, who seemed only vaguely interested in our efforts. Huston had for many years been intrigued with filming *Moby Dick*, with his father playing Ahab, but after Walter Huston's death a few years earlier he had abandoned the idea. Now he was again tempted to remake the Melville novel.

As a result his heart and mind were elsewhere. Left to our own devices Veiller and I worked relentlessly on the Cockburn story, but the longer we persisted in our efforts the more apparent it became to us that the material was flimsy despite its bright dialogue. Huston's apparent lack of interest made Veiller mutinous. He was a high-strung man in his early fifties, plagued by high blood pressure, a self-confessed Anglophile whose presence even in his beloved London did little to calm his growing irritability.

We finished a first draft, which Huston read with little enthusiasm. We both decided that we had gone as far as we could with *Beat the Devil* and told Huston so. He accepted our joint resignation with a tired shrug. By that time I began to suspect that John was having second thoughts about *White Hunter, Black Heart*. Many people had expressed their surprise to him that we were still friends. He declared that he was thinking of abandoning the project and was concerned only with the damage this might do to his friendship with Bogey.

A few weeks later, upon my return to Paris, I heard that he had persuaded Truman Capote to attempt a rewrite of our script, news that didn't upset me. Capote seemed a strange choice to me, for although I admired his talent, I didn't think a tough-guy melodrama was particularly suited to his abilities. As it turned out, he was clever enough to suggest making a farce out of the story, a stratagem that John was willing to accept as a way out of his dilemma, so as not to let his friend Bogart down, no matter how the film might turn out.

Nearly a year later I was invited by John to a private viewing of *Beat the Devil* a month before the movie was to be released. Along with Willy Wyler and a couple of other friends, I went to a theater in

Beverly Hills where John had arranged a morning showing of the film. We were all seated in the first row of the balcony of the empty theater, and when the house lights went up at the end, I recall that there was a long silence. "Well, John," Wyler said, scratching his head, "that's the kind of movie that when you've finished making it, you should make another one as quickly as possible."

John grinned, put his arm around Wyler's shoulders, and gave him an affectionate hug. "Thanks, Willy," was all he said as we made our way out of the darkened theater into the bright sunlight of Wilshire Boulevard. I was amazed at how philosophically Huston had accepted Wyler's words. He had in all probability realized that *Beat the Devil* was doomed early on to be a failure. The reviews confirmed Wyler's brief but honest opinion. At the time it was a disaster at the box office, as only a handful of critics accepted it as a gorgeous spoof—which during the making of it had become Huston's intention.

IN EARLY 1953 the witch-hunt was still rampant in Hollywood and was spreading to many other cultural institutions inside the United States: education and journalism and television. Only the New York theater seemed able to defend itself to some extent against the committee. More than a dozen of our acquaintances—actors and actresses, writers and directors—had fled to the French capital. Many of them, like Jules Dassin, were old friends who had left California when it became impossible for them to continue working there.

Sitting on the terrace of the Café Alexandre one evening with Bob Capa, we saw a small group of "exiles" moving down the sidewalk of the avenue George V. "Uh-oh," Capa said with a grin, "here come the North Koreans." Almost as if in retribution for his cruel joke, it was soon Bob's turn to run afoul of the witch-hunt. Although his passport was still valid for a few years, he received a letter from the U.S. embassy asking him to drop in at his earliest convenience and to bring his passport. It sounded like an innocuous request, but Capa suspected that there was an ominous purpose behind it.

Capa's back had been bothering him again, and thinking that the dry climate of the Swiss Alps might improve his condition, he had been thinking of going to Klosters for a few weeks of skiing early in December. Jigee, after spending the summer in St. Jean de Luz, was already in residence in the small village and I was planning to visit her and Christine while Bettina was busy with the January collections in Paris. Taking the night train to Klosters with Capa seemed like a good idea for both of us, so Noel Howard and I suggested that Bob disregard his summons from the embassy until after a two-week skiing vacation.

Capa agreed with our logic, but after lunch, once he was alone, he was unable to resist the temptation to put an end to the suspense and took a taxi to the American consulate. The clerk on duty asked to see his passport, and after Bob had handed over the little green booklet the man told him that his passport was being confiscated pending an investigation. Capa demanded to know the reason for his being deprived of this document that was vital for his work as a reporter, and the clerk told him that he was suspected of being a Communist and that a new State Department ruling made the passports of Communists and Communist sympathizers subject to revocation.

For the first time in the seven years that I had known Capa he seemed truly distressed. When Noel and I met with him again that evening, he told us that he had sent a cable to Morris Ernst, the co-counsel of the American Civil Liberties Union and a prestigious lawyer, asking him to file an urgent appeal to his case. As he had an assignment to go to Cortina d'Ampezzo in the Dolomites for *Holiday* magazine, a quick solution was essential.

My mother had had similar problems with the director of the Passport Division, a Mrs. Shipley, who was well known for her reactionary political views; in all probability, Capa's case was now in her hands. Knowing that Henry Hyde, my former O.S.S. boss, was acquainted with Mrs. Shipley, I offered to call and ask him to intercede on Capa's behalf. I felt that Hyde, a staunch Republican and a conservative, might do better with Mrs. Shipley than Morris Ernst, and Bob agreed. Our trip to Klosters, in any event, was out of the question, and we both decided to go to Val d'Isère instead, where Capa had skied on many occasions and where he would not even be obliged to present his passport to check into a hotel.

Capa's current girlfriend, Alla, a Eurasian model, appeared at the Bar du Théâtre that evening to dine with us. In the middle of dinner she suddenly announced that *she* had a Chinese Nationalist passport. "I wish I did," Capa said, chuckling gleefully.

Capa's passport was returned to him a month later as a result of Hyde's intervention. The reason for Bob's troubles, it turned out, was that he was rumored to have a Chinese girlfriend who was said to be a Soviet agent, a ridiculous accusation. Alla had had a White Russian boyfriend before Capa, a photographer who was equally uninterested in politics. Hyde never sent Bob a bill for his services, while Ernst later demanded and was paid five thousand dollars for whatever he had supposedly accomplished.

Yet the incident was disturbing. No one seemed safe from the malevolent influence of the Un-American Activities Committee. Capa was rightly considered to be a war hero with a record of courageous involvement in the fight against fascism from the early days of the Spanish Civil War through the battles of World War II. He had photographed the London Blitz, the air assault of Sicily, the Tunisian campaign, and the war in Italy, France, and Germany. He had covered the landings on Omaha Beach and had parachuted across the Rhine with the 82nd Airborne Division. Averell Harriman, General Matthew Ridgway, and General Gavin were among his faithful admirers. Yet all of his connections and friendships were of little help to him at that moment. He had never been a member of the Communist Party—he had been a journalist whose sympathies had been antifascist and nothing more.

IT WAS NOT A GOOD WINTER. A snowstorm in Val d'Isère made skiing impossible, and Capa, Bettina, and I spent ten days cooped up in an expensive hotel unable to venture out on the slopes. A bit later I went to Klosters to see Jigee, who was living with Flury Clavadetscher, our onetime ski instructor, in a small rented apartment on the main street. She was tense but friendly. Christine, our daughter, looked up from her toys on the carpeted floor and showed a child's normal curiosity at the presence of a stranger. I asked Jigee whether she had had any news from Papa, and she replied that she had not heard from him for some time, not since his novella *The Old Man and the Sea* had been published to glowing reviews. We discussed the book briefly and agreed that it was strange that Hemingway had chosen to write such a simple fable at that stage in his life. The story had a magic about it, an allegorical strength that its shrewd author had, of course, denied.

Curiously enough, Bogey had been impressed by *The Old Man and the Sea* and ventured later that he would like to try his hand at playing the role of Santiago, the old fisherman, should anyone attempt to bring the novella to the screen. As he was an experienced yachtsman, he felt that he would be better able to move around a small boat than any other Hollywood actor his age.

But that winter the idea of making a movie out of the Hemingway story was far from anyone's mind. It was a literary tour de force, a small masterpiece containing brief passages that read like a parody of Hemingway's style. Nearly all the action in the book was confined to Santiago's small craft, so as a movie it seemed to qualify as a one-man "lighthouse" story. It was rumored in the press that Spencer Tracy was going to travel across the country for a series of readings of the novella, just as Charles Laughton had done with Bernard Shaw's *Don Juan in Hell* and that later Vittorio De Sica would film the story with Tracy, using Cuban nonactors to play the other parts. This seemed like a practical solution. De Sica, I felt, was probably the only movie director who could bring off a feat of this kind and I wrote Papa to that effect.

Meanwhile I was looking forward nervously to the publication of *White Hunter, Black Heart,* and as is often the case with writers, my anxiety interfered with my getting down to work on a new novel. Then, too, I was rediscovering the wisdom of Papa's warning that getting over "whoring" on a movie" took some time. "You can't work for months for John and then expect to make love for love," he had written in an early letter.

The Old Man and the Sea won the Pulitzer Prize for 1952 and I wrote Papa congratulating him. He replied a few weeks later to say that he and Mary had decided to go to Africa to celebrate the enthusiastic critical reception accorded his short fable about "Santiago and the marlin." He would sail for Europe on the *Flandre*, stop briefly in Paris, and then motor down to Pamplona for the *feria* of San Fermín. It was to be his first visit to Spain since Franco had come to power, and he suggested I join him and Mary for the festival. He confessed that he was nervous about visiting Spain while so many of his former comrades-in-arms were still languishing in jail or, like some of the Americans who had fought for the Loyalist cause, were being persecuted for their political beliefs in their own country.

His was a familiar dilemma. That past summer during a visit to Biarritz and St. Jean de Luz, we had often gone for lunch at a restaurant in Biriatou, where from the terrace we could see a few of the Spanish soldiers guarding the frontier. They still wore German-style steel helmets—a vivid reminder that Franco had been Hitler's ally—but our curiosity about the bullfight tempted most of us to cross into Spain, proof that Papa's influence was still in evidence even among those of us, like Irwin, who were no longer his fans. Yet whenever we crossed the border it was as if we were betraying our own political beliefs, and we regretted having spent our dollars in a fascist country.

Not long after I received Papa's letter I heard from friends that Huston had returned to Paris, and when I called him at the Hotel Lancaster he sounded as friendly as ever. He said, "Come over right away, kid. I'm anxious to see you," apparently having dismissed from his mind Veiller's and my failed screenplay. He made no mention of *Beat the Devil* until he asked after my mother, Bettina, and Jigee. Then he merely noted in passing that the movie he had just completed was not as bad as he had feared it would be. "I think we got away with it," was all he said. "What about Bogey?" I asked him. "Oh, Bogey will be all right," he replied.

He suggested we go to Fouquet's for lunch. We sauntered down the rue de Berri, and he told me he was looking for a story, something along the lines of *Treasure of the Sierra Madre*, although he knew that such a property was almost impossible to find. *Treasure* and *The Maltese Falcon* were the two stories that had intrigued him more than any of the other movies he had made.

As we ate, I listened to him reminisce about the past and about how pleasurable it had been to work with his father. Then I ventured to say that I had read a story many years ago that had always haunted me, but the locale was a difficult one. Nothing I might have said could have intrigued him more. "What story is that?" he asked.

"It's a Kipling story called *The Man Who Would Be King*," I told him.

"Recall it for me," he said. "It's been years since I read it."

I told him the plot as well as I could remember it. He listened intently. "It just might be exactly what I'm looking for," he said.

"You don't have to hire me if you decide to do it," I told him.

"Oh sure, kid," he said, grinning. "I'll probably get somebody else."

"I mean it," I said.

"I'll read it this afternoon if I can get my hands on a copy," he told me.

He called me early the next morning and we arranged to meet. "I'm crazy about the Kipling story," he said. "In some ways it's better than *Treasure*, more challenging." He had already sent a cable to California, asking the Mirish brothers, his new employers, to purchase the rights from the Kipling estate. "I want to cast Bogey and Gable in the two leading roles. Wouldn't that be something? We'll shoot in India and Afghanistan. And we'll write the script together."

I had never seen him as excited about a project. He asked me where I was planning to spend the summer, and I told him that I was going to St. Jean de Luz and would probably be leaving in a few days. That, too, seemed like an excellent idea to him, as had heard from many French people that the climate on the Basque coast would be better for Ricki and the children. I should look around for a suitable villa near St. Jean and then telephone him so that he could come down and look the place over. After that he would fly to California and make all the financial arrangements for his next two movies, the Kipling story and *Moby Dick*, whichever would be ready to go first.

THE CHANTACO is a small hotel facing an eighteen-hole golf course of the same name two miles inland from St. Jean de Luz, known mainly in the history books as the place where Louis XIV married Beatrice, the Infanta of Spain. Modestly priced and staffed by a friendly crew of Basques, it was an ideal spring and early summer residence for an itinerant writer. Pierre Larramendy, its mild-mannered owner, was willing to keep me on as a semipermanent guest at a reduced rate, and before the season got under way he made himself available to play pelota with me on rainy days in a *trinquet* in St. Jean. He was surprisingly adept at the game considering his slight build and his thick glasses. He was more fond of playing the piano in his hotel's salon, was an aficionado of classical music rather than the bulls, and ultimately became the first and last culturally oriented mayor of St. Jean.

Larramendy helped me find a suitable villa for the Hustons, a spacious Spanish house in the hills overlooking the village of Urrugne. I called John in Paris, and he arrived a few days later to inspect his future summer residence. Prepared for a short stay, he was attired in a green velvet suit and had brought with him only a small canvas bag containing a change of shirts, some underwear, and his toilet articles. We visited the villa and he promptly made a down payment on the season's rental, venting his total charm on the aging Frenchwoman who owned the villa. He seemed pleased with everything else—the hotel, the mild spring climate, and the jai alai arena—which, despite the limits imposed on betting, reminded him pleasantly of our stay in Havana. He even ventured out on one of the tennis courts adjoining the Chantaco, still in his green velvet trousers, with the spare top of his lanky body sheathed in a khaki T-shirt. He didn't play well, but he enjoyed it and was content, after we had rallied for half an hour, to watch me play doubles with some of the locals.

He found the place relaxing and stayed on for more than a week, going to bed early and not drinking. We discussed the Kipling story for a scant half hour, as he felt that it was no use going into detail before the Mirish brothers had secured the rights. I had not known him to be as genial and relaxed since the early days of our friendship in California. He agreed that *le pays basque* would be an ideal place for us to work on our screenplay and regretted having to leave for California when the time came, saying that if he never had to set foot in Beverly Hills again he "would not die of a broken heart." I took him to the railroad station where he boarded the night train for Paris, and we said our good-byes like the old friends we were again.

Many years later, in the late seventies, when John wrote his autobiography, *An Open Book*, he chose to leave out everything that transpired that summer and fall, even our collaboration on the first draft of *The Man Who Would Be King*. When the movie was finally made in the mid-seventies, however, the Writers Guild sent me a copy of the shooting script, asking whether I wanted to enter my name in the credit arbitration, as the guild had been informed that I had written a first-draft screenplay. I waived any claim, as only one sequence of my script had been included in the final draft. I had been told that John wanted only his and Gladys Hill's names to appear on the screen, Gladys having been promoted from secretary to collaborator by her boss, undoubtedly as a reward for many years of faithful service.

It was a strange lapse of memory on his part that I can attribute only to a long-dormant bitterness about *White Hunter, Black Heart*. Nor does he make any mention of the novel, which I can only guess disturbed him more than he was willing to admit. Fair enough, I reckon, although his reminiscences turned out to be anything but an "open book."

On the fifth of July that summer Hemingway telephoned to say that he was arriving in St. Jean de Luz the next day and asked me to reserve rooms for him and his group, which included Mary, an Italian driver named Adamo, and Gianfranco Ivancich, the brother of Adriana, the Venetian girl who had served as the model for the heroine in *Across the River and into the Trees*. I looked forward to Papa's arrival with a mixture of anxiety and pleasure, as we hadn't met since the dissolution of my marriage with Jigee, and his complex personality had always created a certain amount of tension. I was also expecting Bob and Kathy Parrish, who were easygoing but nevertheless strangers to Papa.

My worries soon vanished. Papa and Mary were enthusiastic about the Chantaco and settled contentedly into their small suite. Gianfranco turned out to be an amiable young man my own age with a slight speech impediment, and he was interested only in having a good time. We became friends at once.

Not a word was said about Jigee during the first day of our reunion. Hemingway seemed more concerned about the *feria* in Pamplona, which was to begin in two days. He had received a call from Juanito Quintana, his closest friend in the Basque town, perhaps in all of Spain, who had been unable to find rooms for Papa's troupe in any of the local hotels and had made reservations at the Hotel Ayesterán in Lecumberri, a village thirty kilometers north of Pamplona. This seemed an agreeable solution to Hemingway, and he declared that we would all be able to sleep better in the quiet village, far enough removed from the all-night festivities. The hired Lancia would get his party to the early morning *encierro*, the running of the bulls, in half an hour, and in any case he wasn't planning to attend the *encierro* every day.

The Parrishes arrived and Hemingway accepted them immediately, assuring them that he was glad to have them "on board." I told him about my possible new job, and he appeared not to disapprove too much. *The Man Who Would Be King* was, in his opinion, one of the greatest short stories in the English language, and he felt confident that it would make a good movie. Still, he said, he regretted that I had turned down his offer to collaborate on his sea novel, the first section of which Leland Hayward had convinced him to publish first in *Life* magazine and then as a book. "You would have made enough monies to keep you going by now," he muttered. Then he went on to tell me about the plan to make *The Old Man and the Sea* into a movie with Spencer Tracy and Leland Hayward. "I think I can inflict you on the project," he said, "because I'd like you to write the screenplay." I told him that I had heard that Paul Greene, a well-known playwright, had been signed by Leland to do the adaptation, but he merely shrugged and said, "Let's wait and see."

I wasn't eager to get involved in a screenplay of a book whose magic was contained in the prose rather than its action, and I said so guardedly. He didn't reply, but the following day, in the presence of Bob and Kathy, he mentioned my working on the script. I restated my doubts, which Papa brushed aside, saying that he had agreed to over-see the making of the movie and couldn't go back on his word. "If I ask you to help out as a favor to me, would you do it?" he asked.

"Sure," I replied. "But as you said yesterday, Papa, let's wait and see. Maybe Paul Greene will do a good job."

"I doubt it," Hemingway said.

Bob Parrish was somewhat intimidated by Hemingway, just as I had been during our initial meeting, and I sensed once more the atmo-sphere of appraisal Hemingway exuded. Yet I could tell that both Bob and Kathy had met with Papa's approval. Bob did not kowtow to Hemingway, and Kathy was her usual, slightly flirtatious self.

Papa, like most self-declared leaders, was not displeased with the increase in the size of his command, and we set off in caravan the following morning for the Spanish border. There was no unusual de-lay on the Spanish side of the bridge across the Bidasoa, although the Guardia Civil in charge of customs were curious about Papa's copy of *For Whom the Bell Tolls*, which had been banned in Spain. But as the novel was in English, they made no objections, and we drove on to-ward the foothills of the Pyrenees.

The direct road to Pamplona was a small, winding passage through mountain scenery, one of the most beautiful drives in that part of Spain. After the Puerto de Velate, the highest pass on the road, the country changes visibly; the meadows turn yellow and golden in the early summer, and the valleys broaden, until finally you reach Pam-plona, a small city that has the look of a university town standing on a huge plain. It was not at all what I expected from having read *The Sun Also Rises* while I was still in high school.

Rupert Belleville, an old friend and admirer of Papa's, was there to meet us in the town square, as was Juanito Quintana. Belleville, a tall Englishman with an aristocratic bearing, more or less Hemingway's age, had fought on the Franco side during the Civil War, I soon discovered, while Quintana's sympathies had been with the Loyalists. The latter was a small man, nearly bald, somewhat impoverished-looking in his gray summer suit. His Loyalist convictions had cost him dearly, Papa explained, as he had lost his hotel once the Generalissimo had come to power and was now having a hard time making ends meet. His eyes filled with tears as he greeted Hemingway, their long embrace bringing back memories of better days.

Papa was delighted to be back in the atmosphere he had done much to immortalize in his earlier novel. He patiently explained just what was going on: the noisy arrival of the many brass bands, complete with Basque pipers, joined by hundreds of young men dressed in white, who danced around the square in their espadrilles. It was an impressive spectacle, and Hemingway pointed out that despite all the wine consumed by the locals and the visitors, there was hardly ever a fight, nor was a girl ever molested in the street.

Reluctant to diminish our enjoyment of the spectacle we were witnessing for the first time, Papa nevertheless complained about all the changes that had taken place since his initial visits to the *feria* in the twenties. The main plaza had been spoiled by an opening for a second main road, probably because of increased traffic. But the bars and the cafés were more or less the same, he admitted, with their white-jacketed waiters, harassed but still amiable, in their best *feria* mood. *Churros*, the indigestible Spanish version of the doughnut, were still served with hot chocolate early in the morning, and *tapas*, Spanish canapes in innumerable variety, were available in all of the bars. The gypsy horse fair down near the corrals where the bulls were kept before the fights was still a part of the *feria*, and we visited it and stood in the dust outside the paddocks admiring the livestock on sale.

Of course the bullfight was, as it had always been, the climax of the day, and Hemingway, Belleville, and Quintana looked forward to it with an almost religious sobriety. The Parrishes and I had been unable to secure tickets for the first *corrida* but had managed, with the affable Juanito's help, to find a scalper who sold us our *entradas* for the second bullfight, in which Antonio Ordóñez was scheduled to appear. Ordóñez was already reputed to be the up and coming star of the season, so we were quite content to tour the town and surrounding countryside and return early to our hotel.

That night at dinner in Lecumberri Papa confessed his disenchantment with the bullfight. The abuses of the picadors had increased since his time, and he told us that the introduction in 1928 of the *peto*, the protective mattress on the right flank and chest of the picadors' horses, had done more to cause the degeneration of the *fiesta brava* than anything else. Pic-ing the bull with comparative immunity had resulted from orders of the dictatorship of Primo de Rivera that had endured. "Also," he added, "the strict disciplinary actions of the police against anyone who threw a bottle into the ring had helped change things a lot." Yet it was a show of macho courage that distinguishes the *feria* of San Fermín and that he had always enjoyed.

After the bulls have been herded into the corrals behind the bullring, he explained, a *vaca brava*, a female of the breed, which is said to be fiercer than the male, is turned loose in the ring for the amusement of the local amateur bullfighters, the tip of the cow's horns covered with an object resembling a tennis ball. Papa recalled that in the "old days" a bullring servant had often given an additional blow with the flat of his hand to these round objects, with the desired result that the sharp tips of the horns were uncovered, to make the game "a little more serious" and to prevent too many amateur matadors ganging up on the animal.

We arrived in Pamplona at six-thirty the next morning to discover that most of the townspeople were already lined up along the route the bulls would run in pursuit of the young men sprinting ahead of them. Gianfranco had returned to Pamplona after dinner and had spent the night celebrating, intending to run with the locals at dawn, but he had fallen asleep on the sidewalk in front of a bar and had been awakened only when the cannon boomed to signal the start of the *encierro*.

But the spectacle turned out to be disappointing. We had managed to get inside the bullring a few minutes before the arrival of the runners, who numbered well over a hundred, and when the seven bulls that were being herded in that day appeared, they were quite docile and intimidated and crossed the ring without incident through the *puerta de chiqueros*. The *vaca brava* that was then let out into the ring looked thin and spindly and charged its tormentors only sporadically, although it did manage to scoop up one or two of the young men with its blunted horns, to the delight of the audience that had filled the stands of the arena. There were too many young men pretending to be valiant, and after a somewhat boring forty-five minutes the Parrishes and I decided we had had enough and went off in search of breakfast.

The day that followed was tedious, with much sitting around in the bars and cafés on the main square, and it wasn't until after lunch that the place came to life again. Then finally it was time to go to the bullfight, the much advertised climax long in coming, and I began to wonder if I would be able to last all six days of this sort of regime. A nondrinker, I reckoned, was a fish out of water in Pamplona, and I recalled the restlessness I had felt during the trip from Paris to Nice, which had also involved too much sitting around in bars and restaurants for my taste. But I was determined not to be a bore and to at least take in the local color.

With Papa in the lead we walked through the shade of the ancient trees that stand outside the bullring. Raising his deep voice above the half dozen bands that were all playing at the same time, Papa warned us sternly against the danger of pickpockets at the main entrance of the plaza, only to discover once we were inside that one of the local clip artists had made off with his wallet. But even this minor disaster didn't seem to upset him too much, as he was looking forward with anticipation to his first view of the artistry of Antonio Ordóñez.

Gianfranco and I sat together that day, in the shade, but more than fifteen rows up in the *tendido*, and even at that distance the young matador from Ronda had a charisma that made him stand out among the two other bullfighters appearing with him. Slim, yet solidly built, he had the good looks of a tango dancer, with piercing dark eyes and black hair, which he combed straight back from his forehead. He was twenty-two years old, the son of Niño de la Palma, who had served as the model for Hemingway's hero in *The Sun Also Rises*, and was already known to be the most promising young matador in Spain.

And when it came his turn to step out onto the grayish-brown sand of the arena and face the third bull of the afternoon, there was a buzz of excitement that culminated in deafening shouts of *olé* once he had made his first two *verónicas*. My recently acquired knowledge of the bullfight was rudimentary, but the grace of the young man's movements, the way he stood close to his adversary without changing the position of his feet, made an instantaneous impression on me. And once he had killed, the entire audience was on its feet, applauding and waving their white handkerchiefs. Even the drunkards and the foreigners like me were awestruck by his performance.

He was a star, or destined to be one, but just how good he was became apparent an hour after the *corrida*, when we joined Papa at the café that we had chosen as our meeting place. He had gone to see Ordóñez at the hotel where he was staying, and with narrowed eyes he said Antonio was probably one of the best bullfighters he had ever seen in action. He might turn out to be *the* best, Papa added, and despite the current abuses of the picadors, bullfighting was after all the most fascinating manmade spectacle you could pay to see. "Indefensible but irresistible," I had read somewhere, but I kept the quotation to myself that evening.

THE PEOPLE SING A DIRGE on the last day of the *feria*. "*Pobre de mi*," they chant, "*pobre de mi, ya se acaban las fiestas, de San Fermín*"—

Poor me, poor me, the fiestas of San Fermín are ending. The beat of the song is slow and the worn-looking dancers stagger around the square in the early morning light, hung over and dead tired. That day it was raining, the weather contributing to the forlorn mood. A week of drinking and dancing results in an inevitable crash, as does the prospect of having to go back to work or, as in the case of the *señoritos* from Madrid and Bilbao, having to endure the long wait for the next *feria*.

In our group only Rupert Belleville looked much the worse for wear. Rupert had had an "alcohol problem" in the past, Papa confided to me, but he was not a "rummy," and it was virtually impossible to stay on the wagon during the Pamplona *feria*. At Papa's request I agreed to drive Belleville back to Biarritz, with Gianfranco following us in my MG. Prior to our farewell lunch at Las Pocholas, the best restaurant in the town, a strange conversation took place. Who was and who was not a "gentleman" was the subject broached by Rupert in his half-drunken condition, and I was astonished that Papa, an artist and a bohemian, was willing to enter seriously in this absurd discussion.

I ventured to say that it all sounded fairly snobbish to me, and Papa was obviously annoyed by my remark. "Everybody's a snob, one way or another," he replied in defense of his English friend, and the discussion continued for another tedious half hour. By the middle of lunch Papa had gotten over his pique and was our "friendly leader" once again. He hated good-byes, but as he was going on to Africa from Madrid, he seemed less sad than in the past when saying farewell to his loyal troops.

He mumbled that he was going to "check out" some of the places in my novel, although he was going to avoid the Belgian Congo, "the West Coast champion's reserve," he added in a sarcastic reference to Huston. Then, as was so often his habit, his tone of voice changed. "Give my best to John," he said, "and wish him good luck with his new project." Mary asked me to give "dear John a big fat kiss," as he had apparently won her heart by listening more attentively to her than to Papa, from whom I received an affectionate *abrazo* before setting out with Belleville for the French border.

During the first part of the drive Rupert spoke nostalgically about all the good times he had shared with Papa, even though they had been on opposite sides during the Spanish Civil War. Hemingway was the man he most admired in his life, whose friendship he treasured above all others. He said that he was proud to be a member of the mystical club of which Hemingway was the founder, a cabal made up of carefully chosen men and women. Marlene Dietrich was a charter member, as was Gary Cooper, Max Perkins, and a few others. I knew that it was flattering to be accepted as the famous writer's friend, and yet the allegiances his strong personality provoked were puzzling. In Rupert's case the love of the bullfight supplied a common bond. But that was not a prerequisite for membership in Papa's club. Loyalty and adulation were important, as was physical courage in time of war, no matter what side one had chosen or been forced to serve. I was gratified to be a very junior member, and, as in the case of John Huston's friendship, I wondered if I had been accepted to some degree on a basis of mistaken identity.

Half an hour after leaving Pamplona, Rupert fell asleep. Then on a sharp turn, he lurched toward me, and our heads collided. I saw a galaxy of stars and only just managed to keep the car from going off the road. I drove on at a somewhat reduced speed, and soon after we crossed the French border I pulled off the road and allowed my by now sober companion to continue his journey on his own.

It was high time, I felt, for me to return to a more normal way of life, as well as to my typewriter, which I knew was waiting for me in the attic of the Hotel Chantaco.

WHEN I COLLECTED Ricki Huston at the railroad station in St. Jean de Luz she appeared to be a changed person, no longer the tense young woman I had first met. I hadn't seen very much of her in Paris, as John had installed her in a house near Chantilly during the making of *Moulin Rouge*. She had undoubtedly heard rumors of John's love affair with Suzanne Flon, as he did not indulge in deception, but she had chosen to ignore his philandering and was solely concerned with the welfare of her two small children, Tony and Anjelica, whom she adored. Motherhood had matured her and made her realize her own identity.

I helped her move into the villa overlooking the green countryside and, settled in with a cook and a nanny, she seemed quite content to spend the summer waiting for her husband to return from California. Irwin and Marian had moved back into the farmhouse near the Chantaco, a somewhat run-down place that Marian transformed into a pleasant seasonal residence, what with the nearby tennis courts and the beach at Socoa only a five-minute drive away. In an unguarded moment Irwin had invited Sydney Chaplin to spend a few weeks with them as a houseguest, and although Sydney was as charming and outrageously funny as ever, he soon turned out to be a less than ideal companion for a man accustomed to a disciplined existence that centered on his work.

Irwin rose at an early hour every morning, had his breakfast, and went to the typewriter. Sydney never appeared before eleven, an hour at which his host was in the habit of taking a brief break. Inevitably Irwin would then succumb to his houseguest's presence and be lured into a game of chess or, what proved to be worse, a few hands of gin rummy, a game that lent itself more readily to gambling for small stakes. This was followed by a swim, lunch on the terrace, and a nap for Irwin, after which Sydney would be waiting for him with the playing cards until it was cool enough for tennis.

Irwin lost in the beginning and then recouped his losses, which made a return to the card table inevitable. Marian enjoyed Sydney's company despite the additional household chores his presence entailed, but Irwin soon realized that his working hours were getting shorter and shorter, so he was relieved when at my suggestion Sydney moved to the Huston villa, where Ricki said she would be happy to have him. Her house was half empty, and Sydney had already proved himself to be an ideal beach companion for Tony and Anjelica, who enjoyed waking him around noon and joining whatever childish games he was in the mood to invent that day. Ricki was apparently attracted to the handsome young man as well, which worried me slightly in case John might suddenly return.

Adolph Green arrived from Paris and accepted Ricki's invitation to move in as well. A week later Capa appeared with Jemmy Hammond, his New York girlfriend, and they, too, joined the house party at Ricki's insistence. She had had no word from John for a long time and was short of cash, but that did not deter her from extending her hospitality to her equally impecunious friends, who frequently helped out with the marketing and saw to it, mainly in Capa's case, that the liquor supply was constantly replenished. As she was the temporary proprietress of an expensive villa, the grocery stores in St. Jean were not hesitant about extending her credit, knowing that ultimately her movie director husband was bound to return and settle the outstanding accounts.

In the summer of 1953 France was in the throes of a number of political crises, and for most of August the country was without a government. Even with a bank strike and a railroad strike, the nation continued to function, although it seemed to be sputtering along on two cylinders. Bettina arrived by car and moved into the Chantaco with me the first week of August, and we concentrated on the simple pleasures of a vacation. Lazar had cabled that he had made a deal with the Mirishes for me to work on the Kipling story, thus ensuring my immediate financial future.

Although Bob Capa's passport problems had been resolved, he had slipped a spinal disk, and it was causing him great discomfort. He had assisted Werner Bischof and Ernst Haas in covering the coronation of Queen Elizabeth II in London, but apart from taking a few shots of the patient crowds standing in the rain, he had done no photographic work to speak of, which concerned him almost as much as his back. A corset had been presented by a Harley Street specialist, but it gave him little or no relief. As a desperate therapy he would, on occasion, ask Ricki to walk barefoot on the small of his back while he lay groaning on the floor, not a treatment anyone in his right mind would have ordered.

It was distressing to see the once debonair Capa partially crippled by an injury that was in no way connected with the many wars he had been involved in; he was pale and overweight, his normal joie de vivre reduced to a minimum. We often discussed his future, but he said he was tired of going to the wars, tired of looking at horror through the finder of his Leica, tired of boarding airliners to places he really didn't want to go, tired of living in crummy hotels in godforsaken corners of the globe. Nor did working on the movie sets of his director friends Huston and Howard Hawks amuse him anymore, although it helped him earn a little money, most of it destined to pay the legal fees entailed in the loss of his passport. His personal life was equally unsettled. He was devoted to Jemmy Hammond, but he knew full well that he would never make any woman a good husband.

He still felt a great affection for Judy Thorne, a young American woman he had met in Klosters some years earlier. I reminded him that a year ago he had asked me to deliver a message to Judy to not join him in Paris because he was with another woman. I had declined to be the bearer of such tidings and had asked him which of the two young women he preferred. "Well," had come the answer, accompanied by a rueful grin, "when I'm with Judy, I like Jemmy better, and when I'm with Jemmy . . ." It was a funny but cynical remark of which he didn't like to be reminded. Having a girl in every port was all right while the bombs were falling; it was normal then to live for the moment. "It's all different now," he remarked ruefully. "Now it's worse to have two girlfriends than one." He chuckled thoughtfully and lit a cigarette, letting it hang from the corner of his mouth and squinting through the wisp of smoke.

Although I knew that his comments on the subject were not meant to be taken seriously, I was well aware of what was bothering him. The romantic role he had played for so many years was coming to an end. He had even grown tired of it himself. His disability and the fact that he had passed forty made him realize that he was facing middle age. Yet he knew he was incapable of settling down to a normal life with one woman, a regular job, and an apartment in Paris or New York instead of the pleasant impermanence of living in a hotel. He was such an incurable bohemian that he didn't even like going to someone's house for dinner, preferred restaurants and cafés and standing at a bar late at night chatting with strangers.

He spoke often of Hemingway and the difficult task he felt it was to be Papa's friend. He denied that their falling-out had been caused by an incident during the French campaign when, according to Papa, Bob had "cut and run" while Papa was lying under an overturned jeep, pinned down by German artillery fire. Hemingway had accused Capa of wanting to file the first report of his death, an accusation Bob ridiculed. The "real" reason their friendship had come to an end, he said, was that he had advised Hemingway not to rush into marriage with Mary Welsh. Bob still had a liking for the "old bastard," he admitted, but Papa was a dangerous friend, he warned me, because he took unnecessary risks at the front and was inclined to be treacherous when you were no longer a member of his entourage.

Their friendship dated back to the days of the Spanish Civil War, when they had first met. Spain was a mystical bond between all those who had been at the war, a lifelong character reference. It was Papa who had first told me of Capa's early love affair with Gerda Taro, which had ended tragically when Gerda was killed in a collision with a Loyalist tank that had sideswiped the car on whose running board she was riding. He had never gotten over the loss of her, and that perhaps kept him from committing himself completely in any other relationship.

THE AUTUMN is nearly always the most enjoyable time on the Basque coast. The south wind predominates, keeping the sea temperature at an agreeable level, most of the "invaders" from Paris have returned to their city, and the green hills of the *arrière-pays* rise above the meadows that have taken on a golden hue.

Capa and Adolph Green had departed, but Harry Kurnitz arrived to take their place. Irwin and Marian decided to stay on to benefit from the perfect weather, and as Ricki had still not received any word from John, Sydney prolonged his stay as well, making it possible for us to continue our afternoon tennis games, followed by a group dinner in one of the less expensive restaurants. At least three times a week Irwin would visit the local casino, as he was definitely on a roll, and he began to look upon the chemin de fer table rather than the bank as the place to go to replenish his household funds.

It was one of those magical periods that come along rarely and that you know in the back of your mind will soon come to an end, but while the skies over the Bay of Biscay were clear, we hardly bothered to look at the calendar and noticed only the shortening of the days and the cooler night air. Capa called from Paris to report that his back had improved and that he intended to return shortly as he had sold Ted Patrick, the editor of *Holiday* magazine, the idea of doing an illustrated article on the dove and wood pigeon season that was to begin in early October. The Shaws spoke vaguely of buying the farmhouse they had been renting for the second year and making it their main residence in Europe, thus joining Charles and Lael Wertembaker, their close friends, who lived in Ciboure.

Toward the end of September Huston finally telephoned from Paris to say that he was not coming down at all, telling Ricki to pack up all of their belongings as he had rented a big country house in Ireland for a couple of years, where he planned for her and the children to live. His movement orders included a brief message for me: I was to join him in County Kildare at my leisure, for once Ricki and he and the children had settled in, we would begin work on the script of *The Man Who Would Be King*. I was disappointed by his message, as I was hoping we would work in the Basque country where there would be fewer diversions in the off season. He was the boss, however, so after helping Ricki load up her car, Bettina and I began to talk about leaving for Paris.

Then a telegram arrived. It was from my mother in the States informing me of my father's sudden death in Vienna. The funeral would take place in three days. I called her at once, and in a voice heavy with sadness she told me that she had decided not to make the expensive trip to Europe and that Hans, my brother, who was living in Germany, would be joining me in the Austrian capital.

As clearly as I can recall names and places and even things people said, emotions are more difficult to remember accurately and to put into words. I was shocked by the news, although the last time I had seen my father I had noticed that his health was deteriorating. But the knowledge that I would never see him again was something I was unprepared for.

I drove off at once to Paris, with Bettina following in her small car. For the many hours behind the steering wheel I was plagued by the regret that I had not spent enough time with him. I should have stayed on in Vienna at the time of my trip with Litvak, and yet I remembered how busy my father had been during those days as he was preparing to rehearse a play at the Burgtheater.

He had often expressed his love for his three sons, and we had respected him for his intellect and the independence of his strong opinions, but he had always been a distant personage to me, a great man whose paternalism did not affect our relationship. He seemed to accept early on that my brothers and I were separate human beings whose lives he could not influence. He had never made any demands on me, had always been preoccupied with his own work; I recalled without bitterness that he had never commented on the novels I had written, and I could only surmise that this was because he belonged to a different culture and was more at home in his own language.

As a poet he had fulfilled his promise, although the theater and the movies had prevented him from finishing his reminiscences of the First World War and the story of his years as an exile in the United States. Like most writers, he felt that he had not written enough, but at least he was acknowledged as an important intellect in his own country. As a son I had been upset by his excesses, his addiction to cigarettes and rich food, but it would never have occurred to me to say anything because of the respectful distance between us. Now he was gone, and I discovered that I felt a great void, an emptiness that was numbing and that cast a great sadness.

My older brother, Hans, had already arrived at the small apartment in the Zedlitzgasse when I at last got there. We shook hands, both deeply affected by the moment. We had not seen each other for many years for Hans lived in Wellesley, where he was a professor of linguistics. My younger brother, Thomas, lived in Los Angeles, where he worked for the county, but as he had seen my father quite recently he had remained at home because of the expense of the trip.

Liesel, my stepmother, hugged me, fighting back tears. Other members of the family were present, aunts and uncles and cousins who introduced themselves, realizing that I would not have recognized them otherwise. It made me recall the dedication of my first novel: "To the foreign family up the street." The unfortunate phrase, suggested by Oliver Garrett, my American surrogate father, was meant to be humorous, but it had offended my parents. My family had always seemed foreign to me, and even more so on that gray afternoon in Vienna.

The next day, after a religious service in a synagogue, Hans and I, my uncle Joseph Gielen, and several of my father's younger friends from the Burgtheater carried his casket to his grave in the Ehrenreihe, the "row of honor" in the Vienna cemetery, where he was buried next to Karl Kraus, Peter Altenberg, and Theodor Loos, the three men he had admired most in his youth; they were all prominent citizens of the city they had both loved and hated, a city from which my father had been exiled for the most productive years of his life. He was sixty-nine, a year younger than I am now as I write these lines.

Part Two

DURING THE MANY YEARS of our friendship Huston had mentioned that his father was only half Irish—his great-grandfather had left County Armagh for Canada at an early age, and the greater part of his blood was Scottish and English. In fact, he had always seemed proud of his genuine American heritage and of the fact that ancestors on both sides of his family had fought in the Civil War. So I was puzzled that John had suddenly decided to move his family to Ireland, a country famous for its poor climate.

I flew with my car on an air service that no longer exists to Lydd airport in England and drove to Wales, where I boarded a ferry to Cork, so my first view of the green, rain-soaked countryside only increased my bewilderment at why anyone in his right mind could have chosen to abandon the sunshine of the *pays basque* for this wet and windy island. But knowing John, I was certain that there was some strange, ulterior motive for his decision. Instinctively I felt that I was on my way to a new version of our African adventure.

After being misdirected several times in a most amiable manner, a specialty of the country, I was to learn later, I arrived at the village of Kilcock, which consisted of a pub and a small church. The publican, a stout, cheerful man with a red face, assured me that Courtown House, the new residence of "Mr. Hoosten" was just down the road, and minutes later I drove through an imposing gate complete with a dilapidated gatehouse, which stood at the end of a long tree-lined drive leading to an imposing residence that had the look of a correction center for juvenile delinquents. Large paddocks of green pasture lay facing it, I noticed as I brought my car to a halt on the uneven gravel of a large parking area.

The front door opened and John appeared, dressed in fawn-colored cavalry-twill trousers and a tweed hacking jacket befitting the newly established lord of the manor. He was followed by a butler and two maids who took charge of my luggage. "Welcome to Ireland, kid," he said, as affable as ever.

The house was a monstrosity, he explained, leading me inside, but unlike most Irish country houses, it was warm and comfortable, as well as being maintained by an excellent staff, headed by Mr. Creagh, the butler, who nodded politely once we had been introduced and took charge of my hand luggage. We entered a well-furnished reception room where a peat fire was blazing, and John insisted on my having an Irish whiskey laced with bottled water to celebrate my arrival. Of all the countries he had lived in, he told me enthusiastically, this was his favorite, and he had already decided to settle there for many years to come. He planned to buy a house, he announced, so that he could have "a place to crawl back to, and lick my wounds."

"Does Ricki like it here?" I asked, hiding my own misgivings.

"Not yet, but she will," he assured me. Then he went on to brief me on what had transpired in California. He had made a deal for two films with the Mirish brothers—the Kipling story and *Moby Dick*, the screenplays of which he intended to complete during the next few months. Knowing how difficult it had been for him to concentrate on merely one script, I stated my doubts, but he assured me that he would be available to discuss my work on the Kipling story on a day-to-day basis and that he felt certain that together we would be able to "lick the screenplay quite easily."

I asked him if he had chosen a collaborator for *Moby Dick*, and he told me that he had decided on Ray Bradbury, whose work he greatly admired, although he had never written a screenplay. I expressed surprise. "You'll see, kid, he'll do an interesting job," John said. "He's arriving here in a week or so, and then we'll all get down to work."

In the meantime he was eager to introduce me to the pleasures of Irish country life, among them fox hunting. Quoting the nineteenth-century sporting character Jorrocks, he added that "fox hunting is the very image of war, with none of the guilt and only seventy percent of the danger." He had already purchased a hunter, he told me, and the animal was to be delivered the next day.

"Wait till you see him, kid," he said, sounding very pleased with himself. At that moment there was the sound of hoofbeats, and through the tall windows of the room I could see that a tweed-hatted rider on a bay mare had pulled up next to my car. "That'll be Betty O'Kelly," John explained. "She's our nearest neighbor, and she's quite a gal."

I followed my host outside and was introduced to Miss O'Kelly, a pleasant-looking young woman with a squarish face, dressed in an old pair of corduroys and rubber boots. She had come by to ask John at what time his hunter was to be delivered. John invited her to lunch the next day to await the arrival of his new acquisition, and then he and I went back into the house to finish our drinks.

"I'd better go upstairs and unpack," I said hesitantly after my second Irish whiskey and water.

"Creagh and the girls will take care of all that," Huston said matter-of-factly, as if we had both lived in grand style all of our lives. After my long trip, the pleasant smell of peat glowing in the grate and the foreign taste of Irish whiskey was making me feel decidedly drowsy.

"You don't, by any chance, dress for dinner?" I asked warily.

"We won't tonight, seeing as how you've been traveling," John said with a straight face and a slightly Irish lilt to his speech. Then as I got slowly to my feet he gave me a quick hug with his left arm and grinned happily. "It's wonderful to have you here, Pete," he said affectionately. "We're going to have a great time."

I made my way up the carpeted stairway and on the first landing was met by Ricki. Her striking Renaissance looks were all the more stunning in the somber decor of the old house, and her greeting was enthusiastic. Leading me into a comfortable bedroom, she asked anxiously for news of all "the gang" in St. Jean de Luz, especially Sydney. I asked whether she was happy to be in Ireland, and she made a face. "It's comfortable enough," she said, "and John seems delighted to be here."

"It's not forever," I replied consolingly.

"No, I suppose not," she said with a sigh. "But then nothing is, is it?"

"THE CHASE" was his new passion, the ultimate test of horsemanship, as John informed me during dinner, "for nonprofessionals" more exciting than polo or show jumping, only one step removed from steeplechasing and perhaps even more difficult, as a rider had to choose his own route over the natural obstacles of the Irish countryside. It seemed at first blush to be an obsession I would find easier to live with than some of his others, for I would be able to remain on the sidelines, write my screenplay as quickly as possible, and return to Klosters that winter.

The following afternoon John's hunter was unloaded and paraded across the cobblestones by the new groom, Paddy Lynch, who was to be a member of our large household. Naso was the frisky bay gelding's name, and after admiring the animal's conformation his new owner tried to lead him around the yard himself. Naso reared and struck out with his front hoofs, an ominous beginning, which led Miss O'Kelly to mutter to me that he looked to be "a dirty brute." I agreed with her but said that John had always favored difficult horses.

Despite my initially negative impression, I soon found that I was quite happy in my new surroundings. The well-heated house and the rich farmland around it provided a rural environment that was peaceful and pleasing. Unlike their Irish-American counterparts, the people were anything but boisterous. Their conversation was rich and amusing, and many of them often expressed their wonder at the change the Irish seemed to undergo once they landed in the New World. "I don't know what you feed them over there to make them the way they are, your American Irish," I heard it said over and over again. "The United States is a very special place," I would reply, and invariably the answer would be: "Ah, it must be, it must be," this accompanied by a puzzled shaking of the head.

John was an impeccable host, generous and thoughtful, and I even eventually agreed with him that the damp weather was soothing, as were the views of the fields and trees in the mistlike rain and the sudden changes of climate that would cause one half of a paddock to be bathed in sunshine, while the other half was still obscured by a low cloud. "It's like living on a ship," John said, "and plowing through a sudden squall."

After a few days he suggested I send for Bettina, saying that a large household was an essential part of country living. I realized that he enjoyed a crowded table at lunch and dinner, that it was a desired element in his new role of country squire. Courtown, he informed me, was the property of a Captain Drummond, who had a title he never used and who had been "the riding master to the royal family" until one day, early in the war, he had stood up in the Cavalry Club to announce that he agreed with Hitler's plan for the Jews, a statement for which Churchill had banned him to Ireland. It was a revelation that made me feel slightly uncomfortable to be sleeping in one of the captain's beds.

I informed Bettina of John's invitation, and she arrived a few days later. Ricki thought it best she tell the servants that we were married so as not to offend their Catholic sensibilities, and I agreed reluctantly. However, Ricki informed Betty O'Kelly of our true status, so of course the secret was soon divulged to most of our other neighbors, which caused some friction between the two women that was soon healed when at John's suggestion they both enrolled in Colonel Dudgeon's riding school outside Dublin, where they went three mornings a week for their lessons in equitation and became friends again. Bettina was a less determined pupil than her hostess, which made Ricki feel superior and protective toward her.

It was the cub hunting season, that rather cruel period that precedes fox hunting and is meant to decrease the number of foxes in the domain of the hunt, partly to please the farmers and partly to increase the possibilities of longer runs once the formal hunting of foxes would begin. Foxes that went to ground were often dug out and killed by the hounds to "blood" them. It was, John explained, a good time to get horses used to working in the field again, which was why he now started taking Naso to the cub hunting meets and suggested I join him by hiring a hunter from Mr. Cash, the local horse dealer.

I was reluctant to get involved in the local madness. I hadn't been on the back of a horse for more than four years and had left all of my riding gear at my mother's house in California. But John insisted that as I was in Ireland and had ridden most of my life, it would be a sin to forgo the pleasure of riding with an Irish pack. Finally I went into town with Ricki and Bettina to get equipped. Tyson's was in those days the leading horsey haberdasher, and I purchased riding breeches, a pair of black jackboots, and a bowler hat in which I looked like a movie gangster.

Betty O'Kelly arranged for a hireling through Colonel Dudgeon, and early on a Saturday morning a horsebox delivered my steed to the stableyard at Courtown. Standfast was the chestnut gelding's name, Paddy informed me, and Mr. Cash, who had come along with two other horses for the meet, assured me that Standfast would "never put a foot wrong for yez" and that although the animal had seen better days, "he was as safe as a choich." I noticed that Standfast was "over at the knees," which meant that the poor old thing's forelegs trembled slightly as he stood waiting for me to mount him. John appeared looking suitably elegant in a brown hacking jacket and a stock tie that made me feel more like an interloper in my tweed jacket, the visiting American tourist out for a day with the hounds. Apparently quite confident that Naso would not make a protective headgear a necessity, Huston wore a tweed cap, while Betty O'Kelly was in boots and breeches and a proper hunting cap that made her look the professional that indeed she was.

It was like stepping into the pages of Siegfried Sassoon's *Memoirs of a Fox-Hunting Man*, a book I had read during the first year of the war when my Anglophilia was at its most intense. The atmosphere on that October afternoon was a replica of Sassoon's descriptions of his youth: the long preliminary hack to the meet through the autumn countryside and the short gallops that ensued. My hireling proved to be everything Paddy and Mr. Cash had promised he would be. We crossed the fields and ditches of County Kildare without a mishap, and I was even able to give John a lead over one of the more daunting obstacles that his Naso refused to take on.

My seduction to the chase was immediate. Two days later I bought Standfast for a hundred and thirty pounds, and he too moved into Courtown House. I also purchased a secondhand saddle and bridle and a week later completed my equipment by acquiring a black hunting coat and a top hat, as well as two stock ties and two hunting shirts. John was ecstatic that I had been won over to his cause so quickly. Our original purpose for coming to Ireland had not even been mentioned up to that moment, and only when Ray Bradbury's arrival was announced at the beginning of November did John allow that we would be "having to get down to work pretty soon."

Thereafter we adopted a routine based on our personal habits; John was not an early riser and enjoyed having breakfast in bed while reading the day-old Paris *Herald Tribune*. On weekends he would spend an hour with his children, Tony and Anjelica. I liked to get up long before the rest of the household, have my boiled egg and brown bread toast with my coffee, and then go for a morning ride with Paddy no matter what the weather. Naso was more in need of exercising than Standfast, but Paddy, although he was a naturally accomplished horseman, didn't like to venture out on the roads with John's spirited animal by himself. Then feeling relaxed after an hour's ride, I would join John in one of the back reception rooms for a work session that usually lasted until lunchtime.

In our initial discussions of the Kipling story we circled the subject like wary dogs, concentrating on the basic theme of *The Man Who Would Be King* rather than starting to plot the actual scenes I was to write. John advised me that it would be best if I wrote a first draft unassisted based on our talks, a new work plan I was not enthusiastic about, as setting out to write the screenplay without Huston's help filled me with trepidation. The characters in the story were foreign to my experience, but John assured me that I shouldn't worry too much about the dialogue and should concentrate on putting down the continuity of the piece that was indicated in the original material. In his opinion, writing the required scenes together would be too slow and laborious a job; there would be plenty of time for us to go into detail once a first draft was complete. So I agreed reluctantly.

Then Ray Bradbury and his wife, Maggie, arrived. Bradbury turned out to be a stocky young man in his early thirties, with a crewcut, and Maggie had the look of his female counterpart, physically robust but equally timid in manner. Neither had ever been to Europe—they were young Californians, or at least had lived in Los Angeles for most of their lives—so that their new surroundings were a culture shock to say the least. They appeared to be a devoted young couple, protective of each other, and doubtful at the prospect of joining a house party made up of strangers. They had hoped, Ray confided in me, to live in Dublin so that he could commute to work by taxi, an impractical plan that would be expensive and time-consuming, John had informed him. Not too happily the Bradburys moved into one of the many upstairs bedrooms of Courtown House and accepted their fate.

Ray had read and enjoyed *White Hunter, Black Heart,* but the novel had made him somewhat dubious about accepting an assignment to work with Huston. I assured him that coming to Ireland was nothing like setting out with our mutual boss on an African safari and that as John was a great admirer of his talent, he needn't worry too much about the months ahead. If he and Maggie needed to relax, they could easily take a taxi to Dublin and see a movie, a simple suggestion that reassured both of them.

It became immediately apparent that John was more eager to get to work on *Moby Dick* than on the Kipling story, and he admitted to me that he would probably film the Melville classic first. He and Bradbury soon began to work in earnest, and although I felt neglected, I was pleased that the Bradburys had become a part of the household. Conversation at the luncheon and dinner table would on occasion veer off into the subject of writing, which was a relief from the constant talk of horses and hunting, which initially, Ray confessed to me once we had become friends, had made him and Maggie feel that they had been interned in a madhouse.

·   ·   ·   ·

I HAD READ *Moby Dick* in high school, and now I decided to read it again, as I was puzzled by the fact that John had started so much more readily to adapt it rather than get to work on *The Man Who Would Be King*. My initial suspicion had been that because he admired Bradbury's literary talent more than mine he didn't want to keep him waiting; Ray was also a new person to charm and impress. Then as I plowed through the pages of Melville's novel, I realized that there was another factor involved. *Moby Dick* was an account of a man's obsession, a character trait that fascinated Huston because he recognized a similar strain in himself. His wanting to kill an African elephant was in a small way similar to Ahab's insane desire to kill the white whale that had bitten off his leg. Long ago John had told me about a childhood illness that had caused a doctor to warn his mother that her son would always be an invalid. That prognostication had made him decide early in his youth to live each day as if it might well be his last.

His discussions with Bradbury occasionally lingered on through lunch, and I took note that both of them had come to the conclusion that Starbuck, the *Pequod*'s first mate, was essentially the quiet hero of the novel and that the key to his relationship with Ahab was his warning that "vengeance on a wild beast" was a madness Ahab should resist before it destroyed them all. I had been John's Starbuck in the Belgian Congo, I realized, as I had warned him repeatedly that his obsessive desire to shoot an elephant might well jeopardize the completion of *The African Queen* as well as endanger his companions. It was perhaps a fanciful theory, but it seemed to me fairly valid.

I was also becoming aware that here in Ireland I was beginning to play the same role, aided and abetted by Betty O'Kelly. For Naso, John's unruly hunter, was fast becoming his white whale. John had already had two bad falls while out hunting with the Kildare hounds. He was able to exercise the bay gelding without any great difficulty whenever he rode out with us on the roads, but once Naso was surrounded by fifty other horses galloping across the green meadows, his wild temperament reasserted itself. The Saturday country adjacent to Courtown where we hunted was known for its treacherously wide ditches, and the normal way to approach these obstacles was to slow your mount to a walk, or a trot at best, and then leap the fences from almost a standstill. Naso, once his blood was up, came at the slippery takeoff points at what amounted to a gallop, as John was unable to slow him down sufficiently and make a safe leap.

Betty suggested politely that it might be best to sell the animal and

206

buy a "more suitable horse," but John brushed her suggestion aside. In his opinion it was only a matter of schooling the horse and, with time, he would "settle down." John asserted that his two crashing falls had been his own fault rather than that of his mount, and so we began to look forward to our hunting weekends with abnormal trepidation. John was possessed of "good hands," but he had always had a "loose seat," which made the wild lunges of Naso especially "unseating."

At this point Tim Durant appeared on the scene. Durant was a lithe, athletic man in his early fifties, an excellent tennis player I had often met at Charlie Chaplin's house in Beverly Hills. He was also a fine horseman whose ambition, he declared shortly after his arrival, was to ride as a gentleman jockey in the Grand National. It was an ambition Huston shared, but he was obliged to work for a living, a failing that was in no way a part of Durant's lifestyle, as he had enough money to continue on as a "gamesman" for as long as he was sound in mind and limb.

He joined the household as a semipermanent guest and spent most weekdays roaming County Kildare and County Meath in search of a suitable horse to buy, which made it possible for him to secure mounts on a tryout basis, thus avoiding having to pay for a hireling. Durant had an agreeable personality and was still quite handsome, with graying hair and a ready smile, and he was immediately accepted in the horsey circles of the two counties.

John enjoyed his company and admired his horsemanship. Betty and I were less pleased by Tim's presence, as he brought with him a spirit of competitiveness that had not previously existed among us. Mounted on wily Standfast, I was a cautious rider who kept well back during the chase, and as Betty was virtually a professional, John was not inclined to compete with her.

John's work with Ray Bradbury seemed to be progressing, and he now imported an American secretary from California to type the screenplay of *Moby Dick* and to help him with his correspondence. Laurie was a plump, vaguely attractive young woman who had worked for John in the past and, like all of his former secretaries, was obviously a little in love with him, a complication John appeared not to mind. A few years earlier, while between marriages, he had confided in me that it was never a bad idea to bed down with a secretary, as that ensured a fierce loyalty that he believed was beneficial. It was one of his half-serious statements I hadn't bothered to dispute at the time, although I considered it a dangerous operational procedure that could only lead to trouble.

And trouble was not long in arriving in the large household that also included a self-effacing Irish nanny who was in charge of Tony and Anjelica. The hunting season was in full swing in December. Bettina returned to Paris, and Ricki flew to London to do some Christmas shopping. She came back unannounced late one night to discover that John was not in their bedroom; when she went down the darkened hallway to Laurie's quarters, she found her husband asleep on his secretary's bed, fortunately still fully clothed. His explanation, either truthful or inspired by a lightning stroke of genius, was that he had had too much to drink and had gone to Laurie's room to obtain her help in untying his shoelaces. Once there, he had fallen asleep on the empty bed next to Laurie's. It was not an entirely convincing alibi in Ricki's angry view, but she decided to accept it. Somehow the two women made their peace in the week that followed, although Ricki continued to be somewhat hostile toward Laurie, which made for a tense atmosphere at meals. John pretended not to notice the barbed phrases that his young wife launched across the dinner table, and Durant agreed with me that our host was probably the only man in the world who could survive this kind of a situation apparently un-damaged.

My mother wrote from California that she had finally sold the house on Mabery Road to Joan and John Houseman, who at least were friends, which made her feel less upset at having to give up her home. She had decided to move to Klosters for a while to be near Jigee and her granddaughter. John, with his customary generosity, insisted that she stop in Ireland on her way, and I telephoned her and suggested she stop in Shannon so that she could spend the weekend at Courtown, a not too complicated detour that would enable her to get a good night's rest before continuing on to Switzerland. She accepted the invitation, and John arranged for a limousine to collect her at the Limerick airport.

The big, slightly run-down house filled with children, guests, and servants, complete with a stableyard of horses, reminded her of her youth in the Ukraine in the years before the First World War, as did the bucolic countryside; even the Irish peasants brought back memories of what had been a golden youth. She had never felt completely at ease with John, had always found him a little too "theatrical," but she was charmed by him during her brief visit, as he made a great fuss over her. She could well understand, she told me, that I had fallen in love with this country that appeared not to have succumbed to the twentieth century, and only the fact that she was eager to celebrate Christmas with her granddaughter made her refuse Huston's invitation to stay until the end of the holidays.

Christmas Day turned out to be bright and sunny, with a light covering of frost on the green fields. There was a pile of presents under the tree that were opened ceremoniously by all hands, but the high point of the occasion came when John announced that we should all move outside into the yard for Ricki's present. After a brief wait, Paddy appeared leading a pretty bay mare onto the graveled drive, a secret gift that only Betty O'Kelly had known about. Tears of pleasure filled Ricki's eyes, and she rushed upstairs to put on her jodhpurs, insisting that she had to try out the mare before she did anything else.

John warned her that the animal had only one bad habit, a tendency to roll once it was saddled, but Ricki was too excited to listen, and so after trotting around the field directly in front of the house, she pulled up to pose for a photograph. The mare and her new mistress did look their best, until suddenly the animal began to paw the grass under her forefeet. "Kick her on!" John shouted, repeating his command several times. Instead of obeying, Ricki pulled on the reins in an attempt to stop the mare from nibbling at the frozen grass; an instant later, the animal dropped to its knees and rolled over on its side, projecting Ricki to the moist ground. No harm was done except for a smudge on Ricki's new jodhpurs, and Paddy rushed out to urge the mare back onto its four feet.

"I knew she was going to roll," John said. "That's why I shouted for you to kick her on."

"I tried to do just that," Ricki replied angrily. "So for God's sake stop repeating yourself!"

The incident was soon forgotten, however, and we all trooped back into the study, where Tom and Jerrys were served by Mr. Creagh and his wife, with the entire staff taking part in the celebration. My mother was correct, I thought to myself, when she had confided that the Huston family was enacting a modern version of a Tolstoy novel.

OSCAR WILDE was said to have described fox hunting as "the unspeakable in pursuit of the inedible," a witticism that was inaccurate when applied to the followers of the Kildare hunt, for the people I rode with that winter were polite and friendly, quite unlike their British counterparts who had inspired Wilde's comment. That most of them had chosen to live in the Irish countryside to hunt the fox seemed perfectly reasonable to me.

Yet Ireland had more to offer than just the chase, I soon discovered. The rich speech of the locals that was to be found in any pub had a special charm. With Betty O'Kelly as my guide, I often went out shooting in the fields and bogs adjoining Courtown. Bettina had given me a shotgun for Christmas, a generous present I made frequent use of during the late afternoons. We also drove to Galway, a wilder countryside that was well stocked with snipe and woodcock and where our gillies spoke a poetic language that was different from that of the people in the counties surrounding Dublin.

Because of John's waning interest, my work on the screenplay of the Kipling story proceeded slowly, but by the middle of January 1954 the end of the first draft was in sight. John read what I had written and was dutifully complimentary. There were some good sequences, he said, but the beginning was weak; however, before he could devote any time to the project he would have to "go ahead and shoot *Moby Dick.*" He had decided on Gregory Peck to play the role of Captain Ahab, and the Mirish brothers had signed Peck and had given him a starting date. He had chosen Fishguard in Wales for his principal location, as shooting the film in New England, the arena of the novel, would endanger his and Peck's income tax status—they were both trying to qualify under the tax law that would exempt them from full payment, provided they remained outside the United States for seventeen out of eighteen months.

The *Pequod* was being built in a shipyard "somewhere" and would be ready in the spring. John had decided to cast Friedrich Ledebur in the role of Queequeg, a strange choice as Ledebur, an Austrian aristocrat, was certainly not a "magnificent savage." It was the kind of wild miscasting that occasionally amused John. Friedrich was a handsome six feet eight inches tall, and although he was desperately in need of work, he was taken aback when John told him he would have to shave his head to play the part, a prospect that made Ledebur waver briefly. Ultimately the makeup department in London devised a way to avoid this radical threat to Friedrich's appearance, and he signed on for the movie.

Winter had closed in on Europe. A thick blanket of early snow covered the Swiss Alps, and Bettina and I made plans to leave Ireland. My job had been temporarily suspended, and Bettina and I were eager to stop living as houseguests, despite John's urging that we stay on as long as we liked. Our last weeks in County Kildare were marked by feverish hunting activity. Bettina's single sortie into the hunting fields had been brief and unsatisfactory, as she had fallen at the first ditch she encountered on her quiet hireling, a "harse a baby could ride in purrfickt safety," as Mr. Cash had assured her. She returned to Paris ahead of me, having decided that she had had enough of any four-legged animal larger than a dog.

Jack Dunfee, an English theatrical agent and another of Huston's horsey friends, arrived at Courtown for a hunting weekend. Dunfee was a tall Englishman, very much the country squire, a rarity in his profession. He spoke in a slow, cultured drawl that accentuated his very special sense of humor. He was reputed to be an excellent rider and had also made a name for himself as a race car driver at Le Mans and various other circuits. He was the surviving brother of one of those dauntless British upper-class families that in time of war provide good soldiers for King and Country. One of his brothers had been killed while serving as a fighter pilot of the RAF. His other brother had been a fatality during a race at Brooklands.

Dunfee's good-natured presence increased the festive atmosphere at Courtown. The breakfast table had the look of a cavalry officers' mess, with Tim Durant, Ricki, Betty O'Kelly, Dunfee, and me all booted and spurred. John joined us the Saturday of Dunfee's visit, impressively elegant in his pink coat, white breeches, yellow waistcoat, and white stock tie. The rest of us were not quite as fashionable in the black hunting jackets that were considered the proper dress for non-members of the hunt.

It was to be Ricki's first day as an independent thruster, as in the past Paddy had been detailed to accompany her; she was nervous and slightly apprehensive about her hunting debut, for she had made up her mind to show her husband that she was as fearless as he was once the huntsman had blown "Gone away!"

Dunne, the steward, had outdone himself at stopping the earths, and a fast gallop away from the main house was the result of his efforts. Keeping Standfast back with the main body, I saw that Ricki and John were galloping ahead with the leaders. She was jubilant, her face shining with pleasure once the fox had gone to ground. John was suitably proud of her, amazed at her recklessness, as it was apparent to us all that she was not really in control of her mount.

Then, galloping away from the second covert, she had a fall when her mare refused a ditch. She chipped a front tooth, but she re-mounted immediately, intent on continuing despite her bloodied lips. John suggested she go back to the house, but she wouldn't hear of it—replied angrily that she was "quite all right" and rode off to join the field a few miles down the road. Her blind valor was rewarded half an hour later when Naso jumped into the bottom of a wide ditch, unseating John. Both members of the family were now muddied but un-bowed, and it was quite apparent that a duel was on between John and his young wife that might well end with broken bones or worse.

Seated at his normal place at the head of the dinner table that evening, John asked Ricki with unusual concern in his voice if she wanted to fly to London to see a dentist, and she replied rather flip-pantly that she might as well wait until the end of the hunting season in case there might be "more work for him to do."

The Bradburys listened to all of this sporting talk in silence, al-though I could tell by the expression on Ray's face that he felt once again like a prisoner in a very special kind of madhouse. "Certainly," he ventured in a low voice, "seeking out and killing the fox is not an obsession comparable to that of Captain Ahab's search for the white whale," a mild barb that did not go unnoticed by John, who smiled dangerously but did not reply.

"I don't think most of the followers of the Kildare care much about whether the hounds kill or not," I said, partly to avert an unpleasant argument between Huston and Bradbury, as I had already noticed that Ray had been getting more and more on John's nerves, which was not surprising considering the huge difference in their personalities.

Ricki, the latest convert to the chase, put in that "it is the gallop that is so exhilarating, not the hunting of the poor little fox," a com-ment her husband advised her never to make in the presence of the master, Major Beaumont, or the huntsman, Jack Hartigan.

"Killing foxes is, of course, only an excuse for the whole exercise," John explained. "There would probably be a good many more hu-mane ways of getting rid of them."

"Well, trapping foxes would not be more humane," Betty O'Kelly argued, "nor would poisoning them be any better."

For once Ray persisted. Being chased by a pack of yelping hounds and fifty mounted maniacs, he observed, must be a harrowing experi-ence for the poor little animal. Recalling my objections to the killing of elephants, he turned to me for support. I said that I felt sure that our hunt didn't kill many foxes and was more apt to chase them from one part of the county to another.

Ray seemed disinclined to continue the argument. Country life, he sighed, was probably not for him, which statement prompted John to suggest he take a weekend off and fly to London now that their script was almost finished.

"I would," Bradbury said, "if I didn't hate the airplane as much as I do." Both he and Maggie were terrified of flying, he added, and went by bus or train whenever they could. It was a strange admission for a man who had written endlessly about men flying in spacecraft, John remarked.

Fortunately, for the moment at least, the discussion was brought to an end by Tim Durant, who suggested that we all go to Tipperary during the coming week and "have a day out with the Scarteen Black and Tans," the most famous pack of hounds in Ireland. John agreed that this would be "a fine way for us to end the hunting season." We would ship our horses in a van, a long and expensive trip of three hours, and then join the field led by Thady Ryan and his hounds, an experience John promised we would remember for the rest of our lives.

LOOKING BACK, I am astonished that John and I could have been caught up so completely in a time-consuming activity that had nothing to do with our work. Rain or shine, we spent every Saturday in the hunting field and then needed Sundays to recover from our strenuous exertions.

Betty O'Kelly was apprehensive about our hunting with the Scarteen Black and Tans. Our horses, she warned John, would have to leave Courtown at six-thirty in the morning and after a long, tiring journey would then be faced with much more difficult fences than they had ever encountered. In private she informed me that the followers of the hunt in Tipperary were "a hard-riding, hard-drinking lot" of semiprofessionals who would not be as polite as our companions in Kildare, and for John to ride Naso in the company of these people was "madness."

As worried about Standfast's welfare as my own, I told John that I would gladly come along as a spectator but that I didn't think I would participate as a thruster. "So you think you'll just come along and pick up the pieces? Is that it, kid?" he said with a grin. "Well, Betty thinks that would be wiser," I replied. "Betty's an alarmist," he said. "And just think. . . . Tim will be riding a nag he's never even seen before. Doesn't that embarrass you? No, you're going kid," he concluded. "I've already ordered the box for our three horses."

The water in the ditches along the main road was frozen hard that Friday morning, making our trip south in the Hustons' Jaguar quite perilous enough for my taste. John complimented me for my driving ability and seemed generally amiable. Betty, my copilot, smoked incessantly and warned that there would probably be no meet because of the frost. But when we arrived at the small pub in County Tipperary where nearly thirty horses and their riders were already assembled, the winter sun was poking its weak rays through the scattered clouds. Our horsebox had arrived safely, and the drivers were waiting to unload once the welcoming drinks inside the public bar had been dispensed with and the hounds had arrived. This in itself was quite an event. Thady Ryan, a tall, exceedingly handsome man in his early thirties, dressed stylishly in a dark green coat, pale breeches, and a black hunting cap, stopped a few hundred feet up the road in a van and, without a word to his followers, began unloading his tall black and tan dogs.

By that time I had had several glasses of port at Betty's urging and had been introduced to a number of cheerful hunt members, all booted and spurred and vociferously friendly to the "visiting Americans." Standfast's knees, I noticed as I mounted him, were trembling almost as much as my own, and we set off at a smart trot to the first covert. Jamming her horse in close to mine, Betty pointed out all of the professional jockeys present and warned me that under no circumstances was I to follow their lead.

Her words did not fall on deaf ears. I selected a stocky woman in a black bowler hat whose broad behind, encased in tight riding breeches, was rising to the trot of her mount directly in front of me, and advised Betty that I had found my leader, a confidence that was accepted with a grin. "Ye niver can tell by looks," she chuckled, assuming a broad brogue that was not natural to her speech.

She was right, as usual. The woman in the black bowler hat, though plump, was all heart, and abandoning my normal caution I shoved Standfast in behind the equally broad rump of her horse as soon as Thady Ryan's hounds had flushed out a fox a quarter of an hour later. The country the fox led us across was fairly flat, and only occasionally could I catch a glimpse of Thady Ryan's green coat in the distance. He was an expert rider as well as a fine huntsman, but my appreciation of his talents was short-lived, as at the third double bank Standfast's rear

The novelist Irwin Shaw was one of my closest friends and a one-time collaborator (on a Broadway play in 1946). He's shown here with Jigee in 1952, during Irwin's first visit to Klosters, which would later become his home.

At a dinner party in Klosters, mid-1950s. The hosts are Irwin Shaw and his wife, Marian; seated between them and me is the guest of honor, twelve-year-old Winston Churchill, grandson of the statesman.

The Shaws lounge on the terrace of their chalet in Klosters during a winter in the late 1950s. The woman between Irwin and Marian is Zeusel de Dietrich, one of our closest Swiss friends and skiing companions. Irwin had just finished his novel *Lucy Crown*.

Ishmael, "the best harse in Kildare," photographed with his adoring jockey and owner in the stable yard of Courtown House, the Hustons' residence, autumn 1954.

I worked on several scripts with the film director John Huston, a
larger-than-life personality who loved (among other things) horses,
exotic places, travel—in short, adventure. In the 1950s Huston took
up residence in Ireland, where this photo was taken. Here Betty
O'Kelly and I arrive at a meet of the Kildare Hunt in 1954. John and
I were working on the script for *The Man Who Would Be King* (a movie
John didn't film until twenty years later). Betty had installed herself
as guide and counsellor to the Huston household.

Working with the irrepressible Huston—in particular, on the script
of *The African Queen*—gave me the background for my roman à clef,
White Hunter, Black Heart, which was published in 1953. Thirty-five
years later Clint Eastwood directed and starred (playing the role of
the character inspired by Huston) in a screen version of my novel;
here Eastwood and I chat during location shooting in Zimbabwe.

Hemingway shows Huston and me some photographs he had
brought with him from Africa, after having survived the two plane
crashes that almost cost him his life. The man in the back is Papa's
Italian driver. We were staying at the Hotel Chantaco in St-Jean-de-
Luz, in 1954.

The producer Leland Hayward and I visited Papa in Cuba in 1954 to consult with him on the screen adaptation of *The Old Man and the Sea*. Here we are, with our marlins, on board Papa's craft, the *Pilar*, on our first and last successful day of fishing in the Gulf Stream. Gregorio, Papa's second-in-command (and the inspiration for the fisherman in *The Old Man and the Sea*), is at right.

Slim (Hawks Hayward) Keith, one of the most scintillating personalities I've ever encountered, captured in a candid shot by her (at the time) husband, Leland Hayward, during a trip we took to Tijuana in the late 1950s to watch the legendary matador Luis Miguel Dominguín perform his art.

Irving Lazar, affectionately known as "Swifty," became my literary agent in 1953. Here he is after our long weekend in Tijuana to watch Dominguín. The straw hat was the property of the filmmaker Billy Wilder.

Bettina Graziani, one of the most sought-after fashion models during the 1950s, when I knew her. (Gordon Parks)

legs became entangled in a strand of wire and we both came down on the far side. I landed on one knee and one shoulder but managed to get quickly back to my feet, the reins still in my left hand. My horse, wise old thing that he was, stood still once he had regained *his* footing and, with nostrils flaring, waited for me to free his rear legs. The black bowler hatted lady proved to be just that, for she turned back to offer help and sympathy instead of relentlessly galloping on.

My rescuer and I rejoined the field half an hour later, as the fox had gone to ground and Thady Ryan had called for the terriers to be put down the hole. After some fruitless digging by some of the rubber-booted infantry who had followed along in cars, the task of killing the fox was abandoned, and we were off again down a slippery road to the next covert. A dark green station wagon pulled up alongside of me, and an elderly woman in a tweed hat and raincoat commanded me to give Standfast's reins to a young farmer in rubber boots and corduroy trousers who was mounted on a sweating chestnut, saying that he would lead my horse to where the hounds were going four miles down the narrow highway. Once inside the station wagon, I was given a slug of Irish whiskey and a digestive cookie to chew on during our short trip. The members of the Scarteen were human after all, I reckoned as I felt pampered and consoled after my first mishap.

Another hunt ensued as soon as I remounted. Standfast, I discovered, was unharmed except for a trickle of blood above one hoof. "It's a long way from his heart," one of the other riders assured me, and, true enough, Standfast seemed more anxious than ever to continue the chase. It started to rain half an hour later, but that didn't appear to matter to anyone. I had another fall as the afternoon wore on, this time at a drop fence at which Standfast pecked badly upon landing, depositing me on the muddy ground. I remounted again, but my blood was up, as the saying goes, and despite my soiled trousers and muddy top hat, I managed to finish the day.

Paddy was there to load my tired steed into the horsebox, which already had Naso on board. I asked about John and the others of our party, as I hadn't seen them since the start of the second hunt. A friendly Irishman took me in his car to a small, badly lit pub where, next to a glowing peat fire, I found my friend "Hoosten." He had removed his pink coat and was sitting on a rickety chair, his long legs stretched out in front of him. He seemed to be in pain and explained that he had had a "nasty fall" during the last three-mile point. Although his back was giving him "hell," he disregarded my expressions of concern. "You don't look as tidy as when we started, kid," he said, chuckling. I explained that I had had two falls, which news seemed to please him. He said, "It was quite a day, wasn't it, Pete?" "Fantastic," I agreed, "although I wonder how long we'd last if we went out with these people every week."

Betty and Tim appeared, wet but not nearly as disarrayed as John and I. More drinks were ordered. I chose to have a large cup of strong tea, as I was not looking forward to the long drive home. Despite his injury, John was in a triumphant mood. Standing in my wet clothes at the small bar and surveying the scene in front of me, I could only marvel at his mad, indomitable spirit. Here he was, one of Hollywood's most successful movie directors, seated in a grimy Irish pub, as pleased as if he had just won an Oscar; probably even more so, as the movie business, I realized once again, was mainly a means to an end for him, a way to make enough money so that he could satisfy his longing for adventure. In Ireland he was like a character in a movie he might have been tempted to make—the story of a slightly mad country squire in love with horses and the chase. He seemed to regret that he was stuck in another world that was solely concerned with money and power, box office returns and big deals.

THE HOUSE PARTY BROKE UP. Only Tim Durant stayed on, unhampered as he was by a profession. John and I flew to London, while Bradbury took the boat-train. We met that night in one of the better restaurants of Mayfair to celebrate the quasi-completion of our two screenplays, for Bradbury would soon be returning to California to rejoin Maggie, who had left several weeks earlier. During the last few days I had noticed that Ray seemed tense and unhappy, and he had admitted to me that not only did he not like being on his own, but he had come to detest Ireland.

Nor was Huston in particularly fine spirits. His disaffection for Ray was even more apparent, but it was equally apparent that he was also still suffering from his fall. On our flight to London he had sought relief from the pain in his back by drinking a little more heavily than usual, so by the time we arrived at the restaurant he was not in a genial mood. I don't know how the subject of our traveling in different modes of conveyance was first brought up, but Huston began to bait Bradbury about his fear of airplanes, humorously at first and then somewhat cruelly. "How can you send those boys up in their spaceships to the moon and other planets when you won't even fly BEA?" he asked.

Bradbury did his best to explain his anxieties about air travel, but Huston continued his questioning more or less in the same vein, and Ray's replies became less gentle and less respectful. The meal was almost over when Mary Anita Loos and her husband, two Hollywood screenwriters who were friends of Bradbury's, stopped at our table on their way out of the restaurant. They greeted us and then engaged Bradbury briefly in conversation. As they left Bradbury said, "Bless you, bless you both," words that seemed to increase John's irritation. "Who the hell are you to bless people, Ray?" he asked drily. "The Pope?" Ray, losing his temper entirely, replied with an insult, something on the order of "Why don't you go and fuck yourself!"

Huston's anger increased, but he controlled himself. He signed the check and we made our way outside. Standing on the sidewalk, they exchanged more insults and John's fury soon got the better of him. He threatened to hit Ray, who stood his ground fearlessly. I did my best to keep them apart and, taking John by the arm, steered him to a waiting taxi. An old lady had stopped near us and had witnessed the scene. "But there's no need to fight over a taxi," she said. "There are plenty of them available tonight."

This comical intervention went unnoticed by the two adversaries, and with a final insult John stepped painfully into the waiting cab and was driven off. I took Ray by the arm and walked with him in the direction of Piccadilly. He wanted to leave England immediately, never wanted to see "that bastard Huston again," and was ready to abdicate his screen credit on *Moby Dick*. I urged him to forget the incident and finish the two or three scenes he had still to rewrite before leaving. After half an hour or so, Bradbury's outrage subsided and he promised to apologize to Huston if John would agree to apologize to him.

We had coffee in a garish little café facing Hyde Park Corner, and Ray went off to his hotel somewhat appeased. It was an unpleasant ending to what had been an enjoyable, if not particularly productive, four months as far as I was concerned. Somewhat shaken by the events of the evening, I walked back to my hotel and went to bed. I dreamed that night of taking part in a long hunt that seemed never to end, with the fences getting bigger and bigger and John always out in front of the pack as if he were the fox, and it was no fun at all.

.   .   .   .

I HAD LEFT MY CAR in a garage in Dublin, as I planned to return to Ireland in the spring and then make the journey by road back to the Continent in milder weather. Seated now in a taxi, the boulevard des Italiens looked gray and dreary after the green fields of County Kildare, and I was not at all sure that I had been wise to turn down Ricki Huston's offer to stay on at Courtown House. Even Bettina, eternally in love with Paris, admitted to me that she had felt *dépaysé* once I rejoined her at number 8, avenue Montaigne. We had both become accustomed to living as members of a large, if occasionally unhappy, family, and the small studio apartment seemed suddenly confining and even lonely, especially during the long, gray days when Bettina was involved in a modeling job. We planned to leave for Switzerland as soon as the collections were over.

We made reservations in Zermatt, one of the few winter resorts where automobiles were not permitted, and after buying our train tickets, I went on to the 20th Century-Fox production office to collect my mail. There was a handwritten letter from Hemingway giving his return address as "Barclay's Nairobi until 1 March."

He was writing to say that he was sorry to hear about the death of my father, adding that "anyway he didn't shoot himself." He was flying to the Congo later that day after finishing a "temporary hitch as a game ranger in Eermalni," which he had enjoyed. The letter included a message for Jigee: "I don't write because too plunked. She will understand." He was a country boy and a northern Cheyenne, "and how the hell can I love you as my best son and her too." That was too rough on a guy with one heart, two balls, and sometimes "the gleet." After the Belgian Congo he was flying on to make an elephant survey for the local game authorities and then returning via Mombasa. They were using a Cessna 180 that he thought was a "lovely plane." Roy Marsh was their pilot, the same ex–RAF officer who had often flown Huston in Uganda.

I walked back to the avenue Montaigne feeling gratified that he had written while on safari and turned on the small radio we kept in our studio. A news flash interrupted the program. Hemingway and his wife had been killed in an airplane accident somewhere in Africa, the commentator announced tersely. I sat for a long time without turning on the lights, staring at my familiar surroundings.

My first reaction was one of disbelief. After all the dangers Papa had survived, the three major wars he had gone to, it seemed incredible that he had become the victim of a crash in a light aircraft. Yet I could remember my own nervousness while flying over the rain forest of the Belgian Congo in a de Havilland Rapide, exactly the same kind of antiquated machine in which it was reported Hemingway and Mary had been traveling. Capa was in Klosters, as was Irwin Shaw, and Harry Kurnitz was in Rome working with Howard Hawks, so the only person I could call was Tola Litvak who, although he was stunned by the news, was not particularly upset. He had never met Hemingway, but realizing that I was upset and on my own, he invited me to join him and Sophie for dinner that night.

We went to a small bistro near the central wine market that was very much in fashion. Tola did his best to comfort me, although in spite of his empathy he launched into a long discourse on the foolishness of all the "he-man" pursuits Huston and Hemingway were prone to. Hemingway was a writer and Huston was a movie director, so why did they insist on risking their lives in activities that had nothing to do with their work? He seemed to be oblivious of his personal taste for fast cars and gambling for high stakes, but I was too stunned to remind him of his own self-destructive bent.

Then while we were in the midst of our meal, the *patronne* of the bistro stopped by our table to inform us that a second news flash had corrected the previous announcement of Papa's death. Hemingway and his wife had sustained serious injuries, but at least they were alive. I hurried home, where Bettina had just arrived, and we celebrated Papa's survival in the small café next to our apartment. I reread his letter and realized that there was no use cabling him, as he had written that he was returning to Venice on the twenty-sixth of March.

ZERMATT WAS OVERCROWDED in February, and I missed the familiar runs of Klosters and Davos. After ten days we went on to Mürren, but the staid, British atmosphere of the hotel we had chosen proved to be depressing. Bettina had to go back to work in Paris, so I returned to Ireland. But hunting in March was less than satisfactory, as many of the fields we had crossed during the winter had been planted in spring wheat, and even some of the pastureland had been posted out of bounds by the local farmers.

I turned Standfast out to summer pasture at the O'Kelly farm near Courtown and began the drive back to Paris in my small car. On the way I stopped in at Fishguard to visit Huston on the location of *Moby Dick*. The rain had fallen steadily for the last three weeks in Wales, and John's film company was holed up in a small hotel waiting for the weather to clear. To kill time he had organized a poker game that had gone on most nights for more than two weeks. Yet he was more stoical about the foul weather than most of the other members of his cast and crew, especially Friedrich Ledebur, who was obliged to get up at five o'clock every morning to put on his complicated makeup in case the sky cleared. Gregory Peck was finding the role of Ahab difficult, all the more so as work had been virtually suspended. His admiration and affection for Huston was being tried sorely by the unfortunate circumstances surrounding the filming, and I found him to be tense and disenchanted with his director, who, it seemed to Peck, was accepting the endless rain too philosophically.

When I arrived in Paris, another letter from Hemingway was waiting for me. It was dated 18/3/54, and had been written on board S.S. *Africa*, "coming into Suez." In it he announced that he had gotten "the delayed action thing" on his internal injuries and that "Miss Mary was OK," although she had a couple of broken ribs. He had a ruptured kidney, he reported, major concussions, a busted liver, collapsed intestines, and a "paralyzed sphincter," and he had lost the three-quarters sight of his left eye. Mary, once they had started flying, "had longed for the deck." But "you died on the deck," he wrote. "Viva le deck!" But she was probably the only woman in the world who had walked away from two crashes in twenty-four hours. He promised to tell me all about it once we met.

There was more about his hunting with a spear—he would like to see John and Irwin out hunting with spears, he wrote, a strange fantasy that he found amusing. There was also a reference to our Pamplona tiff, an apology of sorts. His last postscript read: "Got good obituaries in Spain. Much love, Papa!"

From the description of his injuries, it sounded as if he would need a considerable amount of time to recuperate, but he seemed to be in a good frame of mind considering that he and Mary had had a close brush with death. That he enjoyed hardship and disaster had been evident to me for some time. It suited the role he saw himself playing in life. The last paragraph of his letter confirmed this. The detailed list of his wounds was typical of his penchant for accuracy and proved his sense of invincibility, as he claimed that he was well on the way to recovery. The long automobile trip across southern Europe that he was planning was certainly not what his doctor, or whatever doctor had treated him in Africa, could have prescribed. But he seemed determined not to let his misadventures interfere with his schedule, and I soon received a wire from the Italian port where he and Mary had landed that proposed we should all meet at the Chantaco in St. Jean de Luz and then proceed on to Madrid.

Working in the one-room apartment I shared with Bettina had again proved to be difficult, and so I set out for the Basque coast in my car, intending to stay for the rest of the summer. Bettina was to join me as soon as she had finished her various photo contracts.

Papa arrived on the day I was expecting him, with Adamo, his Italian driver, and Hotchner, his loyal companion. Despite his injuries, which he barely mentioned, he did not appear too changed. He had cut his hair short on top and wore a beard to protect the skin on the sides of his face. Mary had flown to Seville, where she had attended the spring *feria* with Rupert Belleville as her guide, and would "rejoin the unit" in Madrid around the eleventh or twelfth of May for the start of the *feria* of San Isidro. Taking advantage of her absence, Papa gave an account of his romance with his "Wakamba bride," a black beauty named Debba, which, although explicit, sounded like a product of his imagination.

The following evening Papa and Hotchner, with Adamo behind the steering wheel, set out for Madrid in the Lancia, and I took the night train from Irun. It was a long, bumpy journey and I slept very little, but arriving in Madrid for the first time provided a feeling of excitement mixed with doubt. Going to Madrid seemed like an even greater betrayal of my political convictions than spending a few days in Pamplona had. Papa had suggested I stay at the Hotel Victoria, which in his day had been the favorite of most of the bullfighters he had known. But the hotel had deteriorated since then, and the only room available had no bath, so I decided to go to the Castellano-Hilton instead, the new American hotel on Madrid's main artery.

It was a warm, sunny day, and I was surprised to find that the city had the appearance of a modern metropolis, unlike the newsreel shots I remembered from the time of the Civil War. When I reported to the Hemingways' suite at the Palace, Papa seemed exceedingly nervous. Several well-dressed elderly Spaniards had come to call on him, and Papa mumbled to me that the only people who were there to welcome him were "all characters who had fought on the other side." His back was still bothering him, he admitted once his Spanish guests had departed, and he showed me a clipping from the Royalist newspaper, *ABC*, a small paragraph that stated "an enemy of Spain has arrived in our city." We lunched in the suite, and after Mary left for the hotel's beauty salon, I sat with Papa while he rested in an armchair.

He told me that during the three days after his airplane crash at Butiaba he had found that he had a permanent erection, which the doctor who had attended him had diagnosed as being due to the twelfth vertebra in his back being pinched during the landing shock. I suggested that this was valuable information indeed, and we made a humorous pact that whenever necessary we would ask each other for a blow on the back at this very spot, a joke that improved his mood. Hotchner appeared a few minutes later in the company of Ralph Forté, a heavyset American newspaperman who was stationed in Madrid and was anxious to interview Papa.

Forté mentioned that Ava Gardner was one of the few Americans residing in the city at the time, which was welcome news, as I was anxious to find someone who spoke English to show me around the town. I had met Ava in 1946 while she was married to Artie Shaw. Shaw had passed through New Caledonia during the war, and we had spent a week together in Nouméa, a bond that had continued through the years he and Ava had lived in Beverly Hills. Artie had literary ambitions and had enjoyed talking to Jigee while Ava and I swam in the pool of their house.

Forté told me that Ava was staying at the Castellano-Hilton while the apartment she had bought was being readied for occupancy, so when I returned to the hotel I called her room. There was no reply, but ultimately the concierge informed me that Señorita Gardner had been taken to a nearby clinic after suffering an attack of kidney stones. Trying to reach her by telephone proved to be hopeless, so I got into a taxi and went directly to the hospital. The man on duty gave me her room number after I told him I was a friend, and I went upstairs to her floor and knocked hesitantly on her door.

"What the hell are you doing here?" she asked, sitting up in bed. Her pains had subsided somewhat, and she asked me to sit down and chat for a while. It was a nightmare, she informed me, to get sick in a foreign country where she barely spoke the language, and she was thinking of getting up and catching the next plane to London. But she admitted she preferred living in Spain to living in California.

As she spoke I found myself admiring her beauty more than ever. Only Garbo had the same hypnotic appearance that made you stare at her face as if you had never seen her before. Ava's southern accent was less noticeable than it had been, and only her lapsing occasionally into the slang of her native South Carolina betrayed her background. She had come to Europe "like everyone else," she said, to take advantage of the income tax laws, and everything had been fine until she got sick.

After a few minutes there was a knock on the door, and a nurse appeared, followed by a handsome young Spaniard, who took the syringe the nurse was carrying on a tray and, rising on his toes, approached Ava with the needle as if he were preparing to plant a pair of banderillas. Ava screamed with laughter and introduced the young man as Luis Miguel Dominguín. I of course knew who he was—at the time the most famous bullfighter in Spain, almost as well known to the American public as General Franco.

Once the nurse had recovered the syringe, Dominguín and I stepped outside in the hall while the shot was being administered. Then we returned to Ava's bedside and with a mixture of French and pidgin Spanish did our best to entertain her. Dominguín asked if I had been able to buy an *entrada* for the *corrida* that afternoon, and when I said no he suggested I join him as Ava, despite her protestations, would be forced to stay in her sickbed. I glanced at my watch. It was quarter past five, but Luis Miguel assured me that we would arrive in plenty of time in spite of the heavy late-afternoon traffic.

We said good-bye and went downstairs where his car and chauffeur were waiting, double-parked in the narrow street. Luis Miguel got behind the steering wheel, and we went off at high speed, zigzagging through the traffic and disregarding an occasional red light. I sat tensely beside him until we arrived at the back entrance of the bullring, which was cordoned off by the police. He raised his hand to the officer blocking our way, and as soon as he was recognized, we drove on to the gate through which we were to enter.

He seemed to know everyone, and people made way for us and helped us to our seats; a dark-haired woman selling carnations kissed each of us in turn and pinned a flower in our lapels, and after shaking hands with countless Spaniards of all ages, I settled down next to Dominguín in the front row, directly above the place where the toreros who were to perform were making practice veronicas with their capes. "You see," Dominguín said with a pleased grin, "we arrive in plenty of time." Then as the first bull came charging out into the arena, he fell silent, concentrating on the action in front of us as if he himself were fighting that afternoon. A hundred or more seats to my right I caught sight of Mary and Papa. He looked amazed to see me there, in one of the best seats and in the company of Luis Miguel Dominguín. I waved to him, one aficionado to another.

LESS THAN HALF A MINUTE after the death of the last bull, Dominguín touched my arm and jerked his head in the direction of the nearest exit. "We go now," he said. And as quickly as we had arrived, we made our way out of the bullring. On our way to the place Luis Miguel had told his chauffeur to wait for us, we encountered a young couple hurrying in the opposite direction. They stopped in front of us, and I recognized Antonio Ordóñez. The young woman with him was introduced as Luis Miguel's sister, Carmina. Strikingly pretty, she had her brother's dark complexion and brown eyes, as well as his prominent nose. Ordóñez was as handsome in a well-cut gray suit as he had been when I had last seen him dressed in a suit-of-lights. Dominguín kissed his sister affectionately, and we hurried through the crowd to where Mariano, the driver, was waiting.

"When is Ordóñez scheduled to fight?" I asked Luis Miguel.

"Please?"

He spoke English better than he understood it, and I translated my question into French. Dominguín said that he wasn't certain; he thought it was the day after tomorrow.

"Will you go to see him?"

"Perhaps. I'm not sure." He was intent on steering the big Cadillac through traffic. Any mention of bullfighting seemed to cause a reticence in him, as if it were the subject he was least anxious to discuss. Because of my halting Spanish, conversation between us was not easy, yet we managed to communicate in a mixture of French, English, and Spanish. He turned on the car radio and joined in with the voice of a flamenco singer who was bewailing a lost love, tapping out the complicated rhythms on the Cadillac's steering wheel.

His good mood, he told me, was mainly due to his having decided to retire from his profession. The English were right, he said, "it was a cruel and dirty business," a facetious remark that he corrected a few minutes later by saying that if bullfighting were abolished, that strange animal *el toro bravo* would become extinct. Nobody would be willing to breed those dangerous beasts if there was no way to make money out of them. But he had had enough. He had been involved in the business since the age of eleven. Now all he wanted to do was enjoy himself, eat and drink as much as he wanted and travel to any place in the world where there were no bullfights.

Inevitably we got around to Spanish politics. He was a supporter of General Franco, he told me, had even met the Generalissimo on quite a few occasions, at partridge shoots and at the bullfights Franco had attended. I ventured my own political views: Franco, to us Americans, was unforgettably Hitler's ally, had been helped to power by the Luft-waffe, and if Germany had won the war would undoubtedly have re-mained Hitler's friend. Luis Miguel shrugged. Politics didn't really interest him, he said. It was all *mierda*. To get to the top of the heap, you had to be a son of a bitch. But he had made what money he had by hard work and by risking his life. He was twenty-eight years old and had been a bullfighter since the age of twelve, and he was going to make damn sure no one would take what he had earned away from him. That was why he was going to stay on good terms with the man who ran the country.

We arrived at the clinic. On the way to Ava's room he asked me what plans I had for the next day, adding that if I had nothing special to do, I could drive with him to a nearby bull ranch for a *tienta*, the testing of the brave cows that was an integral part of the breeding of bulls destined for the ring. He would ask the Hemingways to come along, Domingu\u00edn said, and Ava, who was eager to meet "that old bastard Papa," assured me that she was already on the mend and that all she needed was to get out of "this poor excuse for a hospital," a statement about which her nurse seemed a little dubious.

Luis Miguel called his secretary and instructed him to invite Hem-ingway and whomever he wanted to bring along and then insisted on dropping me off at my hotel. Would I excuse him if he went to bed early, he asked with a politeness that was astonishing, but the *corrida* had tired him out more than if he had had to kill a dozen bulls himself. He would pick me up promptly at nine-thirty in the morning, as it was best to get an early start for our trip to the *campo*.

THEY MADE A HANDSOME COUPLE, the young movie queen and her bullfighter. Yet I had the suspicion that they were acting out a storybook romance that was expected of them as mythical figures, an expectation that was certain to complicate their relationship in the long run. For the moment they were amused by the language barrier between them—Luis Miguel said that he enjoyed their frequent mis-understandings—but how long this would last seemed questionable to me.

Seated in the back of his Cadillac coupe with Mariano, his driver and valet, next to me (in case it became necessary to change a tire, Miguel had explained), I did my best to translate Ava's remarks into French, of which Luis Miguel could understand a smattering because of his recent liaison with Annabella Power, a French movie actress who had been married to Tyrone Power before her involvement with Dominguín.

Papa, Mary, Rupert Belleville, and Hotchner were following us in the Lancia, and after a forty-five-minute drive we turned off the main highway to El Escorial and drove through the imposing main gate of a bull ranch. The fields were covered with lush grass, and behind the barbed wire fences on both sides of the dirt track we were following we could see large herds of black bulls that looked deceptively harmless. We arrived at a miniature bullring, complete with a covered pavilion, and were greeted by the owner of the ranch, a well-groomed man in his early forties. Ava, Mary, Hotchner, and I took our places under the tiled roof of the pavilion, while Papa and Rupert elected to stand behind a *burladero*, a small shelter that is meant as a refuge for the men taking part in the proceedings. Hemingway was wearing a beret, a checkered woolen shirt, and a leather vest that failed to hide the bulge of his stomach, and I noticed that he had some difficulty squeezing in behind the painted wooden planks that were meant to be used by slimmer and younger men.

A picador in a tweed cap and the buckskin breeches normally worn over one armor-encased leg took his place on the far side of the white-washed enclosure, and the first small cow that was to be tested came charging out onto the packed earth. It made straight for the mounted rider and was pic-ed with the small pointed *vara* that is smaller than the ones used in a formal *corrida*. Luis Miguel caped the animal and then turned it back to face the padded horse, repeating the maneuver over and over again. The heifer seemed in a wild fury and, despite the wounds inflicted on its hump by the rider's lance, continued its angry charges, bellowing fiercely.

I noticed that the owner of the ranch was making notes on how many times the heifer went for the horse, obviously an important guide used in breeding. Dominguín executed a series of graceful *verónicas*, then exchanged his cape for a muleta, and continued provoking the heifer's charges, passing the animal with complete control and ease. After a quarter of an hour he handed the muleta to one of the men assisting him and walked slowly over to the pavilion. I noticed that he was short of breath and heard him complain to the *ganadero* of his lack of conditioning. Three of the ranch hands in attendance ran out into the ring and wrestled the heifer to the ground, while another man administered penicillin powder to the animal's wounds.

Once the heifer's wounds had been treated, another cow came galloping out into the ring, and the entire procedure was repeated. At least five animals were tested in rapid succession, a rather tedious process that Hemingway and Belleville endured without moving from their place in the hot sun. Undoubtedly their interest in bullfighting was greater than mine, I thought to myself, for neither of the middle-aged men showed any inclination to join the rest of us in the shade, where refreshments were soon served—cold drinks and slices of cured ham. A boy of about fifteen who had climbed over the wall of the plaza was given a chance to confront one of the cows with the torn muleta he had brought with him, and once he had performed for a few minutes, Luis Miguel suggested I try my skill. Not wanting to make a fool of myself, I refused his offer.

Then he called Ava down to join him, and although she protested that she was in no shape for such "high jinks," she ultimately gave way to his urging and together they made several passes with Ava holding one end of a cape and her matador-boyfriend holding the other. She shrieked with excitement and terror, but Dominguín controlled the animal and kept it from charging her. Then finally it was decided that we had all had enough. It was nearly two o'clock in the afternoon, and Papa announced that he would have to be going back to Madrid, as he had tickets for the *corrida*. Dominguín suggested that we all have lunch in a restaurant outside the city limits, but Papa refused the invitation, saying he wanted to rest for an hour or two before the bullfight. He had been on his feet for nearly two hours without a hat to protect his face against the sun, but he seemed in good form. "You learn more by watching this kind of thing than by going to a dozen fights," he told me, "especially if you want to write about it someday."

"I doubt I'll ever be tempted to do that," I told him.

"You never know," he replied with a faint smile. He thanked our host for his hospitality, and he and his friends drove off in the Lancia.

We were a large group at lunch, as everyone who had taken part in the *tienta* joined us, but it didn't seem to bother Luis Miguel, who paid the check with complete indifference. Hangers-on were a part of a bullfighter's life, I realized, even after he retired. Money was no problem for the moment, Luis Miguel told me when we were on our way back to the city. He was curious about Hemingway and asked how we had become friends. He liked Papa, he said, but didn't trust him, a remark that astonished me. "He has a good eye and a bad one," he said, "like a painting by Picasso."

"He's a great writer," I said.

"*Quizás*," he said, perhaps. He hadn't read any of Hemingway's books, not even *Death in the Afternoon*. Why should he read about the bullfight? It was the man he was interested in, and, instinctively, he had his doubts about Hemingway's character. Then he explained that he had asked Papa about me, and Hemingway had replied that I had talent, but that I probably wouldn't write anything important. "Even if this is true," Dominguín went on to say, "it is not a remark you make about a friend."

"But maybe he's right," I said.

Dominguín shrugged. He didn't care about his friends' accomplishments, he told me—he was interested in them solely as people. Then he changed the subject, and we drove back together to Madrid, where I dined with Ava and her torero, feeling somewhat subdued.

MIGUEL'S REACTION to Hemingway's remark was not surprising, yet I wondered why he had decided to repeat Papa's statement to me, for he must have known it would be upsetting. A few days later, when we had gotten to know each other better, I questioned him about it, and he replied that he had done so unthinkingly. Bullfighters sometimes made the same sort of ungracious remark about a younger member of their profession. Papa's statement, coming as it did from an eminent author, had disillusioned him, made him suspect that *el viejo* had a mean streak, which put Dominguín on his guard.

The thing that disturbed me most was Papa's duplicity, a trait I had first become aware of in Paris when Hemingway had denigrated so many of his old friends. In this instance I sensed that his backbiting had been caused by his proprietary attitude toward bullfighting. The *corrida* was his domain, and he wanted no intrusions, not even vaguely potential ones. If I was correct in my assumption, it was proof of the ever increasing symptoms of his paranoia, for how could he, the greatest Anglo-Saxon expert on the *fiesta brava*, be at all concerned about a challenge from a neophyte like me?

That night at dinner, in my halting Spanish laced with French, I tried to explain Hemingway's character in simpler terms. He was a man who was finding it difficult to accept old age, a not uncommon phenomena. I went on to say that whenever I had been alone with him he had always been affectionate and sensitive to my feelings, but confronted with strangers in a new environment, his oversized ego had prompted him to assert himself, establish his dominance. Dominguín listened in silence to my explanation. Then he shrugged. In his experience, he said, people never changed. If you were born *"un hijo de puta,"* a son of a bitch, you remained *un hijo de puta* for life, a statement that I found to be oversimplified.

During the week that followed, I accompanied Luis Miguel to several more *tientas* at which he performed. At his insistence I even ventured out a couple of times, muleta in hand, to face the charges of the small, aggressive animals and learned for myself how difficult it was to remain calm and not move my feet to keep the heifers from buffeting my legs. A part of the fear a bullfighter encountered in the ring, Dominguín explained, was appearing to be ridiculous. He had always been more frightened of the crowd than of the bulls; perhaps, he added with a grin, that was the reason he had been successful.

I enjoyed our days in the country. Everywhere we went the hospitality of the people was extraordinary. In the early fifties, Spain was emerging from many years of isolation, probably one of the reasons that a foreigner was so well received. Then, too, Luis Miguel's fame encouraged people to give me a friendly reception. I made no secret of my origins whenever the subject came up and was told repeatedly that almost everyone in Spain had Jewish blood, even El Caudillo, and that during the war Franco had given refuge to a number of Jews. Unlike Mussolini, he had sent no one back to Germany.

As the end of that week approached, I went with Luis Miguel to his ranch near Saelices. He seemed pleased to share with me his great knowledge of Spain. I remember that as we approached a small village half an hour outside Madrid that day, he pointed to a large stone church that towered over the tiled roofs of the adjoining small houses. "That's what is wrong with this country," he exclaimed. "The church! There are more priests in Spain than soldiers and flies!"

He was a Catholic, but he didn't believe in all of the mystical nonsense he had been taught as a boy. The women in his family, his mother and his sisters, were all devout. His oldest brother, Domingo, was a Communist, and Pepe, his middle brother, was equally skeptical in his religious views. The three of them had all been toreros and had fought all over South America during the Civil War. He was eleven years old when he had started in "the business of the bulls," a child prodigy who, because of his age, had not been permitted to fight in

Spain. For twenty-five years he had lived the life of a monk, always in training, working to excel at his craft, so that he had never enjoyed a normal childhood. "Now I am finished," he said. "Forever."

The name of the ranch he owned then was Villa Paz. The main residence was a big whitewashed mansion that reminded me of the homes of Hollywood movie stars in the twenties. It looked out over the plains of Castilla la Nueva. Luis Miguel introduced me to his aunt and her husband, whom he had appointed caretaker of the *finca*. Their daughter, Maridi, an eleven-year-old in pigtails, spoke fluent French and appointed herself as my translator. Miguel insisted I accompany him to the kitchen to meet his grandmother, an eighty-year-old matriarch who he said ruled the hired help with an iron hand. "She has never seen a Jew," he informed me with a wicked grin. "To her they are the people who killed Christ." After he introduced me to the old woman dressed in black, he disclosed what he hoped would be a shocking revelation. The old lady stared at me with watery eyes and shrugged. "There are good people and bad people among the Jews," she said, "like everybody else."

Realizing that his joke had misfired, Miguel spun me around and pointed to the bald spot that was already in evidence on the back of my head. "He's also a priest," he said, "a priest who has been defrocked because he's fond of women." But by that time his grandmother had realized she was being provoked, and when he next made a blasphemous remark about the religious picture hanging on the kitchen wall, she picked up a dangerous-looking knife and threatened to chase her grandson out of the kitchen.

Lunch was served, and among those seated was a gray-haired man in his forties who was introduced as Dr. Manolo Tamames. Maridi whispered to me that he was Miguel's doctor as well as a close friend. A surgeon who was an expert in treating horn wounds, he had often accompanied Domínguín during his summer campaigns. Tamames had served as a doctor in the Army of the Spanish Republic during the Civil War and was still violently opposed to the regime of the Generalissimo. He had never met "Don Ernesto," he said, although he had spent time on the Madrid front while Hemingway was there.

He didn't criticize Papa for returning while Franco was still in power but said it was high time that foreigners should again visit Spain, for their presence would have a positive influence on its political life.

Luis Miguel paid little attention to our conversation; nor did

Maridi's father, who had served as an officer on the Nationalist side, take exception to Tamames's openly seditious remarks. The everyday problems of running the ranch seemed to be uppermost in both their minds, for the *finca* was costing Dominguín a considerable amount of money to maintain.

"There is no farm in Spain small enough not to ruin its owner," Tamames told me, translating into French a well-known Spanish saying, adding that Miguel would someday be forced to return to the bullring because his lifestyle was that of a dollar-millionaire. "All toreros want to retire to the country and raise bulls," Tamames said, "and not one of them has ever succeeded." Luis Miguel shrugged. *"Vamos a ver,"* he said, let's wait and see.

THE MADRID *feria* in those days featured ten fights, in contrast to the thirty or more that are scheduled now; partly because of the bad weather, they had been disappointing. It was therefore with the greatest expectation that Antonio Ordóñez made his appearance only a few days before the *feria* was to end.

A cold rain again threatened to spoil the afternoon, and Papa, in his most paternal mood, counseled us to take our raincoats and umbrellas along. Luis Miguel had secured an extra ticket for me not too far removed from his and Ava's front row seats. Ordóñez, as the junior matador on the card, was scheduled to fight the third and the last bulls.

His first bull was a reluctant and dangerous animal, and his performance with it was, of necessity, brief. A light rain began to fall as the last bull entered the ring, making the footing dangerous. Ordóñez kicked off his black slippers and, with complete disregard of the rain, performed with all the elegance and grace of which he was capable and with an artistry that was overwhelming compared with the performances the crowd had witnessed all week. His *faena* drew to a close amid shouts of *Bravo*, and I was amazed to see that some of the middle-aged men near us actually had tears in their eyes as Antonio profiled for the kill. He failed in his first attempt with the sword, which deprived him of cutting the ears he would have been entitled to, but the ovation after he had killed the bull was deafening, and the talk of the spectators as they left the ring was solely concerned with exuberant praise for the young matador from Ronda in Andalucía.

I had noticed that Luis Miguel had not joined in the applause for his future brother-in-law, but I soon learned that his restraint was customary among bullfighters watching a colleague perform. As we made our way back to his car, he remarked that with the last bull Antonio had established himself as the outstanding matador of the *feria*. His contracts for the entire season were now assured and would make it possible for him to earn a considerable amount of money that year and probably the next.

Luis Miguel dropped me off at the Palace Hotel, saying that he was too tired to go up and see Papa. I had noticed his extreme nervousness during the last few hours; he had jerked his head to one side as if he were wearing too tight a collar, a tic I had only been vaguely conscious of before. I had told him that I was leaving Madrid the next day, and sitting in front of the hotel in the car, he urged me to return to Spain whenever I wished and to stay at his ranch for as long as I liked. "You can work there," he told me, "and nobody will bother you, and if you get bored, you can always come to my house in Madrid for an evening in town." I thanked him and we exchanged addresses and said good-bye. Ava told me that she would probably be making her next movie in India but asked me to call her if I returned to Spain in the near future. I left them both with a feeling of regret.

I found Papa seated alone in the living room of his suite. He seemed pleased with Antonio's success but was not nearly as euphoric as I had expected him to be. His back was bothering him. The two hours he had spent seated in the cold damp of the plaza had aggravated his injuries. He seemed depressed, worn out, yet he reiterated that Ordóñez, with his last bull, had revived his interest in the bullfight. He still felt, however, that the business was being corrupted by the big fees toreros were being paid. The excessive pic-ing of the bulls was a manifestation of this unfortunate trend, as bullfighters stood to lose too much money if they got caught and put out of action for a part of the season.

He then went on to ask what Luis Miguel had thought of Antonio's performance, and I repeated my conversation with Dominguín. "Bull-fighters are even more jealous of each other than writers," he re-marked. Had I seen the bronze statue of Luis Miguel during my visit to the ranch? he asked. When I replied that I had, he commented that he thought it strange for a man to have a statue of himself in his own garden. "I don't think he posed for it," I said. "Somebody gave it to him, I guess, and he didn't know what else to do with it." Papa shrugged and made no further comment.

To change the subject I told him that I had met Manolo Tamames at the ranch, and Hemingway nodded. "He's a good man," he said. "He put in some time at the best university of them all," he added, explaining that Tamames had been in jail for two years because of his Loyalist past. Dominguín had made him a member of his entourage as an insurance policy after Manolete died as a result of inadequate medical attention after his goring in Linares. Luis Miguel had witnessed the tragedy as he had fought on the same card that fateful August afternoon in 1947. It was better not to make friends with bullfighters, Papa added thoughtfully.

Papa's "black-ass" mood seemed somewhat diminished the next day. He was looking forward to his return to Cuba and the warm weather, a sentiment Mary seconded. "We're getting too old for a harsh climate," she said. Hemingway again mentioned my working with him on the screenplay of The Old Man and the Sea, and I told him that I had not yet heard anything from Leland Hayward, whom Hemingway referred to as a "hero of noncombat aviation." "You'll hear from him," Papa said. "And I'm counting on you. Nothing will happen until next year. The word is wait and see."

Ava Gardner appeared a few minutes later to say good-bye. Her kidney stones were no longer bothering her, and she was in an excellent mood. She brought greetings from Luis Miguel, who had returned to his ranch. She said that she had decided to settle in Spain and would be returning to the United States only to obtain her divorce from Frank Sinatra. She was happier living abroad than in her own country, she explained, especially Hollywood. The remark caused Papa to grit his teeth, always a sign of displeasure. "There is nothing wrong with our country except the goddamn shanty Irish," he growled. Ava laughed. "You're talking to one of them right now!" she said. Papa apologized at once and asked her to forgive his surly mood. A waiter arrived with the drinks that had been ordered, and the incident was passed over without any further comment.

Mary had decided to fly to Paris to do some shopping, while the rest of us, with the exception of Hotchner, were all returning to St. Jean de Luz by road. I informed Hemingway that John Huston was anxious to meet with him and repeated the conversation I had had with John about him and Willy Wyler making a film based on three of Hemingway's short stories.

"Be glad to see John again anytime," Hemingway said.

His attitude toward Huston had quite obviously undergone a radical change, and he later welcomed him like an old friend when John arrived in St. Jean de Luz. Huston had brought along Paul Kohner, his Hollywood agent and closest adviser. Kohner, whom my father had always characterized with good-natured distrust as "the comparative of Kohn," was greatly impressed to be meeting Hemingway, and Papa, mistakenly assuming that Paul was Huston's producer, treated him with great respect. As Papa later explained, he didn't want to spoil Huston's chances of getting financing for his next movie. He signed a copy of *Men Without Women* that Paul had brought and was generally on his best behavior.

We all inspected a collection of photographs that had been taken by Earl Theissen of *Look* magazine during the early part of Hemingway's safari. Papa told us that he had lost interest in hunting big game and that his happiest time in Africa had been his brief tour of duty as a temporary game warden in Uganda. Huston asked Hemingway whether he had ever been to India on a tiger shoot. He hadn't, came the reply. "But I'll tell you how that works," Papa continued in a humorous vein, quoting Winston Guest as his source. "They take you out to your stand on elephants, and the highest ranked polo players get the choice spots. So if you're merely a visiting celebrity, it's doubtful you'll ever see a live tiger."

Concerning the project Huston had come to discuss, Papa explained that, unfortunately, he had already sold most of the short stories that were potential movies—"My Old Man," "The Short and Happy Life of Francis Macomber," and "The Snows of Kilimanjaro," which he still referred to as "The Snows of Darryl Zanuck." John asked him about "The Undefeated," and Papa said that he was skeptical about anything to do with bulls as the subject of a Hollywood movie because of the existing rules of censorship, an opinion that Paul Kohner seconded.

Kohner and Huston returned to London that evening, and the next day Papa and his Italian driver set off by road for Paris, where Mary was to join her husband for their return to Cuba. The Chantaco seemed deserted after they had all left, and I set about going back to work again.

ON THE MORNING of the twenty-sixth of May I was sitting at my typewriter, staring out at the rain that was falling on the fairways of the golf course outside my window. The telephone rang, and the man at the desk downstairs informed me that he was putting through a call from Paris. It was Sophie Litvak. She sounded strained. Bob Capa, she informed me, had been killed in Vietnam while covering the French Indochina War for *Life* magazine. There were no details available yet, but she had verified the report with Charles Gombault, the editor of *France Soir.*

I couldn't quite believe it at first, and yet there was somehow a terrible logic to Capa's death. He had risked his life so often that with hindsight it seemed obvious that he would ultimately wind up as a casualty of war. I located Bettina an hour later; she was in tears and promised to call me as soon as more news came through. When later in the day the full account of the story was broadcast by French radio, it seemed even more incredible to all of us who had known Capa. He had been riding in a jeep with John Mecklin and Jim Lucas, the latter an old Marine Corps comrade of mine who had become a professional war correspondent after his discharge from the Corps. The jeep had been part of a convoy stalled on a road in the mountains because of the deep trenches guerrillas had dug across the road. Capa had suddenly decided to take pictures of the convoy from an adjacent hillside. Less than a hundred yards from the jeep Bob stepped on a mine that blew off his leg, and he bled to death before help could arrive.

For a seasoned campaigner like Capa it seemed such a careless error, an inexplicable lack of caution that made his death even more tragic than if he had been killed in battle. I remembered all of our conversations of the previous summer. He didn't want to go back to war, he said, was sick and tired of focusing his camera on the dead and dying. He had accepted the *Life* assignment because he needed money to pay his lawyer's bills and the debts he had accrued in the period when his passport had been confiscated. Hemingway, who was asked for a comment about Capa's death, was quoted as saying that "Capa's luck had finally run out," a statement that sounded heartless and uncharacteristically lacking in feeling. I could only think that the press had failed to print his entire comment or that perhaps he had never forgiven Bob for their past differences.

For the rest of us, Capa's closest friends, Irwin Shaw and Art Buchwald and the Stantons, and many of the others in our group of which Bob had been such an integral part, his death was an irreparable loss. Klosters and Paris and London would never be the same without him. Time and time again in the weeks that followed, after I returned to Paris, I would look up and expect to see him ambling down avenue Montaigne with his trench coat draped over his shoulders, a cigarette hanging from his smiling lips, and then the harsh truth that I would never see him again would descend with a final feeling of gloom. He was mourned by everyone—waiters and bellboys and barmen, people whose lives he had come in contact with only briefly. On the same day as the announcement of Capa's death, news reached Paris that Werner Bischof, another Magnum photographer and friend, had been killed in an automobile accident in Peru. It was as if the war had never ended.

Huston called to commiserate with me. Someone had suggested that Capa's life would make a good movie he might want to direct and that I would be the logical person to write it.

"What do you think, kid?" he asked.

"I certainly don't feel like doing that right now," I told him.

He said: "You're right, Pete. Even if the movie turned out to be a pretty good one, we'd wind up remembering some goddamn actor's face instead of remembering Bob." He paused. "So what are your plans, kid?"

"I don't know," I said. "But I think I'll go back to California and look for a job. Get the hell out of here."

"Yeah, that sounds like a good idea," he said. "A change of scenery never hurt anyone. I may see you there."

IN A LONG LIFE, of all the friends I was fortunate to make, the one who invariably made me feel better whenever we were to meet again was Irving Lazar. There was something about his optimistic nature, his iron will, his combativeness in the face of any misfortune, that was and is unique. Lazar's energetic effervescence was unfailing, and it was probably that one characteristic that contributed most to his success. He was very much himself when I returned again to California.

The movie business was in a crisis, he informed me, but that was nothing new. A lot of writers were out of work, yet he admitted that his own personal fortunes were flourishing. As was his habit, he told me of all the fabulous deals he had made recently; I listened, as I had learned to do long ago, with patience. Then he went on to brief me on the efforts he had made on my behalf. Jerry Wald had left Warner Brothers and had moved to Columbia Pictures, thus exchanging one dictatorial boss for another, possibly even more unpleasant one, Harry Cohn. Wald had persuaded Cohn to buy the rights to Frank Harris's *Reminiscences of a Cowboy*, recalling Huston's enthusiasm for the book, and he was eager to discuss my doing a screenplay based on this property.

"Jerry loves you," Lazar assured me, "so I feel sure that if you want the job you'll get it."

Declarations of love were as much in vogue in the movie business then as they are now, and they meant just as little. I recalled that Wald, frustrated by my decision not to sell the idea of *The Survivors* to Warner's seven years earlier, had concocted a similar story with Collier Young, who was the story editor at the studio at the time. Many of my acquaintances had urged me to bring a suit for plagiarism against Wald, Young, and MGM, the studio that had ultimately acquired the story and made the movie, but I had not done so. Neither Irwin nor I had been damaged by Wald and Young's helping themselves to the plot of our play.

Wald was a genial and hardworking man whose enthusiasm had often carried him away in the same manner in the past. He was rumored to be the model for Budd Schulberg's hero in his novel *What Makes Sammy Run*, as was Norman Krasna. Both Wald and Krasna had made up for their sins of youth, Wald by becoming a prolific producer, Krasna by excelling as a playwright of gentle and amusing comedies.

During the "job interview" that took place the following day with Wald, I mentioned his and Collier Young's larceny and he paled and feigned ignorance, so I dropped the subject as I didn't enjoy his discomfort. That same day Swifty informed me that he had made a deal with Columbia for me to write the screenplay based on the Harris book, and I cabled Bettina, asking her to join me. Then after renting an apartment in Westwood, I reported to the studio on Gower Street.

The procedure for "reporting aboard" in those days was fairly simple. You were issued a pass that the policeman on duty at the front door glanced at once, and from that day until you either were fired or had finished your assignment, he waved you through. I was issued a stack of yellow paper, a typewriter, and a big handful of pencils, which were all delivered to my new office. Hardly anyone was permitted to work at home—Harry Cohn was the kind of boss who wanted to know at what time his high-priced help arrived in the morning and at what time they left for the day. Wald was always the first producer to arrive, and as I was an early riser, our story conferences took place undisturbed during the first few weeks.

Working with Jerry was both stimulating and pleasant; we made good progress, and after a month I had completed half of the screenplay. We both felt it was turning out to be a most original western, and we both had high hopes for it; my only regret was that John Huston would not be able to direct it, as it would have to be shot in the United States, and Huston was still intent on maintaining his foreign residency.

Bettina had joined me, and we found ourselves enjoying the California summer. I played tennis at the Bogarts' and was soon accepted again as a temporary member of the "rat pack." Betty Bacall liked Bettina, as did the other members of the group—Judy Garland and Sid Luft, Sinatra and Irving Lazar, as well as Spencer Tracy, who dropped in occasionally. Bogart and Tracy had a special rapport based on their mutual admiration and strikingly devoid of professional jealousy.

Tracy, it seemed to me, would be the ideal man to play the elderly cattle baron in the script I was working on, as he had the authority and elegance of the character in the Frank Harris book, who is in love with opera, and dreams of arriving in Chicago with his herd only so that he can sit and listen to "a bunch of Eyetalians sing." I mentioned the project to Spence, and he seemed vaguely interested, although he confessed that he didn't care much for horses and would certainly not enjoy sitting on one in front of the camera. He was also under contract to MGM, and Louis B. Mayer was adamantly opposed to loaning out any of his stars to another studio.

Wald agreed that Tracy would be ideal for the role, but he seemed doubtful that we would be able to persuade Harry Cohn to attempt to secure his services. Once the script was finished we could broach the idea to Harry, he said; the worst that could happen was that he would throw us out of his office.

We got a call to report to Cohn's office a week later. Los Angeles was sweltering in a heat wave when we were ushered into his presence. He was seated behind his desk in shirt sleeves, scowling at the notes he had taken after reading eighty pages of our script. He didn't look up but began at once with the business at hand. His secretary was told not to put through any calls, an order that was not immediately heeded, for a few minutes later she announced that Joan Crawford was on the line asking to borrow a print of *The Long Gray Line*, which she wanted to run in her private projection room. "Fuck Miss Crawford!" Cohn bellowed. "I told you no more calls!" Then he went on to state that our story had no plot, that it was interesting, but that he didn't want to make a movie "for matinee audiences only."

Wald defended our script rather timidly and explained that the plot of our story was the cattle drive, the success of which was threatened by the heart condition of the cattle baron in command. "Is he going to die before they get to Chicago?" Cohn asked pugnaciously. I explained that that was exactly what was going to happen, and Cohn shook his head. "Like I said, it's a movie for a matinee audience," he repeated, frowning.

"Why don't we wait until you get the end of the script, Harry, and then we'll meet again," Wald suggested and, reluctantly, Cohn agreed. I said, "I was thinking that maybe we could get Spencer Tracy to play the lead." Harry Cohn glared at me over the top of his reading glasses. "For Chrissake, why Tracy?" he asked. I replied that we needed an actor who could play the part of a gentleman, a lover of opera. "We've got Bogart under contract," Cohn roared. "Why the hell should we go for Tracy? Bogart can play it. And a most gentlemanly cocksucker he is, too!" A few minutes later Jerry and I were ushered out of the office.

Once in the hallway, Wald joined me in bitter laughter. "Good old Harry," he said. "Well, it could have been worse. At least he's accepted our story line."

"I'll suggest his words to Bogey as the title of his autobiography," I said. "*A Most Gentlemanly Cocksucker!* It should sell millions of copies."

A FEW DAYS LATER I was seated in Wald's office when his secretary announced a call for me from Harrison Carroll, the movie columnist of the *Herald Express*, the Los Angeles afternoon paper. Carroll was the least objectionable columnist in town, not given to the vicious gossipmongering of Hedda Hopper and Louella Parsons, and so I said I would call him back, but Wald told me to take the call. After apologizing for interrupting our work, Carroll informed me that he was checking on a story that had appeared in the *New York Post* that alleged I was thinking of taking up the career of bullfighting, for which I had shown great talent during a trip to Spain. The source of the story was an item in Jinx Falkenberg's column that quoted Luis Miguel Dominguín, who was visiting Jinx in the East.

I laughed and told Carroll it was a joke and advised him not to pay any attention to it. He seemed satisfied, asked after my mother and Garbo, and hung up. The following Sunday morning at six o'clock the telephone rang in the small apartment I shared with Bettina, and I heard a series of coins being deposited, after which Luis Miguel's voice came on the line. He was calling from a phone booth in Reno,

Nevada, and asked me to pick him up in two hours at the Los Angeles airport. He said that he would explain everything as soon as he arrived.

Luis Miguel looked pale and exhausted as he stepped off the plane. He had gone to Reno to visit Ava, who was in the process of getting a Nevada divorce from Sinatra, and they had had a violent quarrel at three A.M. He had decided then and there that it was time to put an end to their romance, but having traveled this far, he had decided that he might as well pay me a visit in Hollywood, as he didn't want to return to Spain until the bullfighting season had ended. His explanation of the story that had appeared in the *Post* was equally simple. Rather than admit that he was on his way to visit Ava in Reno, he had told a reporter in New York that he was coming to see me to discuss my career as a torero. Of course it was a joke, but it had served his purpose at the time.

I was pleased to see him and we drove back to Westwood, where after Bettina had cooked breakfast for the three of us, he promptly went to sleep in our bedroom. Our apartment was not big enough to house our guest, so I rented a small studio downstairs in the same building. That night I took him to dinner at Chasen's with Bob and Kathy Parrish. We had just ordered drinks when I caught sight of Sinatra entering the restaurant. He glanced at our table as he passed by, looked grimly at Domínguín, and nodded coldly to me. "The world is much too small," Miguel said in Spanish. Although Sinatra had agreed to a divorce, he was still inexplicably possessive of his ex-wife.

Lazar joined us for coffee and was charmed immediately by Luis Miguel, although their conversation was limited to Swifty's five words of French and Domínguín's fifty words of hesitant English. Relying on his instinct, Miguel was amused by the small, energetic man and treated him with an affectionate respect that endeared him to Swifty. Miguel christened Lazar "El Macaco," a not very polite nickname that translates as "small monkey." However, Lazar accepted his sobriquet with good grace, knowing that it was not meant to be hurtful.

At first I worried that Luis Miguel's presence would be distracting, as I still had to go to the studio every morning. But after the first two days I discovered that Domínguín was socially much in demand and that there were a good many volunteers willing to look after him, nearly all of them female. Ricki Huston, who was staying in California that summer, had always expressed her preference for Antonio

Ordóñez, but she changed her mind as soon as she met Luis Miguel. Annabella Power heard that her former boyfriend was in town, and as she was still very fond of him, she joined Ricki in showing him the sights.

On his first sortie with a rented car, Luis Miguel had been arrested for dangerous driving, so I was thankful that he now had two women to chauffeur him wherever he wanted to go. There was a bullfight in Tijuana the following weekend, and the strange threesome chose to drive down to Baja California for the fight. Once they returned they reported that after the three matadors had dedicated their bulls to their Spanish comrade, Luis Miguel was arrested by the Mexican police for entering the country without a visa and locked up in the local jail. After a few hours he secured his release by threatening to call his "close friend" Miguel Alemán, the president of Mexico, a threat that obviously had worked.

Stewart Granger and his wife Jean Simmons were eager to meet Dominguín, and after I introduced them, he was taken up as well by Elizabeth Taylor and Michael Wilding, close friends of the Grangers. Both Jean Simmons and Liz Taylor were between pictures, so they had plenty of free time to take Miguel to the beach or sit with him at the side of the Grangers' swimming pool. The invitations poured in. Merle Oberon invited him to lunch, Budd Boetticher tried to hire him for a bullfight sequence in a movie he was making, and a young Czech actress appeared out of his past to claim his attentions for a couple of nights.

He was conscious of his Don Juanism, explaining that it had always been an integral part of a bullfighter's life. But it was not really sex that prompted him to seek out the company of women, he stated. As the youngest son in a large family, he had always been surrounded by females, had been pampered and adored in early youth before his profession took him away to a world of men. Now he was discovering once again that he preferred women to men, was more at ease with them as they didn't ask him endlessly about the bullfight.

My Spanish was improving rapidly, and I was amazed to discover what an articulate man Miguel was about himself. He had never learned to read for pleasure, which made him dislike being on his own. He had bought a couple of English grammar books and a record to learn English, but he admitted that his attention span was limited. "I feel stupid sitting in a room without understanding what people are saying," he complained. He was thinking of visiting Papa for a couple

241

of weeks before returning to Spain—obviously having put aside his reservations about Hemingway's character—and called Hemingway in Havana.

A few days passed, and Papa telephoned to suggest I persuade Luis Miguel to postpone his visit. "I wish you could ask him to come here after I get my work done and the weather is decent," he said. He was fond of Miguel, but the visits of friends were making it hard for him to concentrate. "I have to work, Pete," he told me, "or I have to pull out of here."

But Miguel's restlessness increased, and he left finally, saying that he planned to stay in New York for a week before going on to Havana. I warned him that Papa was in the middle of a book, and he replied that he would not disturb him. Two weeks later a letter from Papa arrived. Luis Miguel had visited and had immediately approved of their simple way of life, which he had combined with a good many long-distance telephone calls and staying out all night in Havana. Hemingway went on to state that Miguel was the most articulate to-rero he had ever met, but that he was attempting to cure Papa of wanting to work, which Luis Miguel considered to be an obsession. He was also fond of Bettina and me, which endeared him to Papa. The letter ended somewhat ominously. I had asked Papa in a previous letter where he would go if he decided to leave Cuba, and now he wrote that he would probably choose to jump off the stern of the *Pilar* into eight hundred fathoms of still water. At the moment, he stated, that seemed like a preferable place.

DURING THE LAST WEEKS of my stay in California, I often ran into Spencer Tracy at Chester and Sally Erskine's beach house at Trancas. One evening he began to question me rather warily about Hemingway. He was apparently worried about doing *The Old Man and the Sea*, the production of which was scheduled to begin the following year. He had never met Papa, although he was now his partner, and was concerned because of Leland Hayward's description of Heming-way's character. I did my best to reassure him. Hemingway was now well into middle age, I told Spence, and was no longer the aggressive and, on occasion, bullying man he might have been in his early years. "I know that Leland won't be able to cope with him," Tracy insisted. "That's why I'm kind of worried about doing the movie." Nor did he look forward to the many hours of sitting in an open boat that would be required of him. "Why don't you get Bogey to do it?" he asked. "Bogey's a sailor. I'm a landlubber."

It was a half-serious comment, and I replied that I certainly had no voice in the matter, was not even sure that I would be given the assignment of adapting the novella. "Yeah, well, we'll see what happens," Tracy said, laconically.

He invited me to dinner a few days later and suggested we go to Chasen's, a restaurant he preferred to Romanoff's. Once we were seated at his favorite table and he had ordered a tomato juice with lemon, as he was conscientiously on the wagon, he began to talk slowly and thoughtfully about the strong reaction he had had when he had first read *The Old Man and the Sea*. He was a year younger than Papa, and he marveled at the creative impulse that had prompted a man that age to write such a simple and yet moving story; the ending had made him cry on first reading. That was why he had accepted Leland Hayward's proposition that they both buy the movie rights and somehow bring it to the screen.

Quite obviously the words had affected millions of readers in the same way, I replied, mentioning that the role of the old Cuban fisherman was in some ways similar to the role of the Portuguese sailor he had played in *Captains Courageous*, which had won him an Oscar for 1937. He nodded in agreement. But this time he was embarking on what was virtually a solo piece, he said, and was not at all sure an audience would sit there for seven reels watching an old man in an open boat. It was a concern that should have occurred to him before agreeing to play the role, it seemed to me, but I said nothing.

James Cagney and Pat O'Brien were dining at a nearby table, and Spence suggested we join them for coffee, apparently having decided that there was not much more to be said on the subject of Hemingway or the movie. And he appeared to relax once he was in the company of the two other Irish actors. Cagney had been one of my boyhood idols, partly because of his talent and partly because he had been known for his liberal political opinions, which he abandoned later in life. Before becoming a hoofer and movie actor, Cagney had been brought up in Hell's Kitchen and spoke fluent Yiddish, an amusing sideline to his varied talents. That he had played Bottom the Weaver in Max Reinhardt's film version of *A Midsummer Night's Dream*, a radical departure from his other film roles, had demonstrated his versatility.

The conversation was brilliantly amusing, and I sat enthralled as I listened to the three old troupers talk about their early days in vaudeville and the theater. O'Brien spoke with a marked Irish brogue that made me homesick for County Kildare, and I was surprised to learn that Tracy had never visited Ireland and seemed only vaguely interested to hear that I was returning there. He wished me a safe journey and assured me that we would be "seeing each other soon, probably in Havana."

TO LIVE IN PARIS and to write had been one of my romantic fantasies that I had discovered was not for me. While I still enjoyed the beauty of the city and the varied enjoyments it had to offer, I began to look upon it as "one big tourist trap," as did some of my fellow American expatriates, "expensive and uncomfortable, unless you're fabulously wealthy." For considerably less money I could live in Ireland and enjoy a way of life that my stay in the Huston household had revealed to me.

Betty O'Kelly had found a place for me to rent only a few miles down the road from Courtown—a working farm, the main residence of which the owners were happy to let for a minimal sum. An elderly woman caretaker came with the place, and a day after I moved in she suggested I hire a friend of hers to help clean and make the fires, as the small Georgian house had no central heating. The name of the farm was Mount Armstrong; it consisted of about two hundred acres of land, the main residence, and a courtyard, which included a dozen loose boxes. The living room and the bedrooms were pleasantly furnished, and nearly all of the windows looked out on the green countryside. The rent was forty pounds a month, about a hundred and twenty dollars in those days, and my "staff," incredibly enough, would cost me about the same sum. There was also a gun dog named Sam, a sturdy spaniel, who was soon to spend his days looking mournfully up at me while I sat at my typewriter, hoping I would take him out for a little rough shooting, his only passion in life.

October was dry and sunny, and Bettina's brief return to Paris proved beneficial for my work. In two weeks I completed a long short story I had promised Hélène Lazareff, the editor of *Elle*, and I sent it off to Paris for her approval. She wired me that she liked the story and was having it translated into French. A week or so later a check for four thousand dollars arrived, more than I could have earned in Hollywood during the same period. The title of the story was "You Don't Love Me Anymore," and it was serialized in four installments under the title "Alors tu ne m'aime plus." It proved Papa's theory that I was better off writing my own stuff than working in Hollywood.

John Huston was in California and Ricki, my nearest neighbor, was alone with her children in Courtown House. I drove there every morning and we took our horses out for their daily two hours of trotting along the deserted roads. Standfast, my old hunter, had been brought in from pasture, and although he was as frisky as a colt, his legs were showing signs of age. Betty suggested I buy a young horse for the hunting season ahead and promised to help me find one.

In the late afternoons, after work, I would take Sam out for a walk around the farm, often accompanied by Betty, who enjoyed potting away at the local pheasant and snipe, which were not too plentiful. In the evenings I would return regularly to Courtown and dine with Ricki and some of her Irish friends, although as a rule the three of us, Ricki, Betty, and I, dined alone. It was a simple routine, but a most enjoyable one, as I found Ricki to be a rewarding companion, relaxed and talkative in John's absence. Her earliest ambition had been to be a ballet dancer, and she had been totally engrossed in preparing herself for that demanding profession until she met Huston. Although she was aware of John's infidelities, she was still deeply involved with him and, come what may, had decided to be a good wife.

Betty had become Ricki's confidante, a dangerous role for her to play, as she adored John even while she disapproved of his need to charm any fairly attractive woman he might encounter. Betty was a devout Catholic and admittedly still a virgin at thirty-five. As she had to please both John and Ricki, she had a tendency to be two-faced, "an Irish weakness," Ricki stated with a tolerant shrug. Betty had a great eye for a horse and soon found a young gelding for sale. Egged on by Ricki and Paddy Lynch, the Hustons' groom, I bought the animal from Pat Taafe, a steeplechase jockey who was one of my neighbors. At Ricki's suggestion I named him Ishmael, the sole survivor of the *Pequod*. He was a handsome animal, stood more than sixteen hands tall, and, although frisky and fleet of foot, had a perfect disposition, rare in a horse that was three-quarters thoroughbred. In the lingo of Irish horse copers, expressed by Pat Taafe after I had paid him a hundred and thirty Irish pounds, "he was not in the book, but his picture was on the cover." As I didn't want to sell old Standfast to someone who might hunt him into the ground, I gave him to Colonel Dudgeon, to be used solely as a school horse at his riding academy.

By the time Bettina rejoined me at Mount Armstrong, Ishmael's virtues and exploits had taken over as the main topic of conversation at mealtimes, and she stated with a wistful smile that she never thought a horse would turn out to be her principal rival. Thirty-four is an advanced age for a young man to fall in love with his horse, but it's not an uncommon weakness in Ireland. I was also under the illusion that I had unlimited time ahead of me to do my work, and fox hunting had become an overwhelming passion. Ishmael, Pat Taafe had informed me, was "as safe as a church—even a child could ride him," to which statement Bettina replied: "Yes, an Irish child, but not a grown-up French woman."

She had always enjoyed dabbling with paint, and now that she had time she decided to pursue her hobby. We drove to Dublin and bought the materials she would need, and in the mornings Bettina would set up her easel in front of the living room fire to paint still lifes while I exercised Ishmael. After lunch I confronted my typewriter, and in the late afternoons Bettina often accompanied me and Sam for our walk around the nearby bogs and cornfields. We were happier than we had ever been, far away from the problems of Paris and Hollywood.

JOHN HUSTON returned to Courtown, and the hunting season started in earnest. He approved of my purchase of Ishmael and insisted that now that I was the owner of a fine hunter, I should order a pink coat, decorated with the Kildare Hunt buttons.

For the mid-November lawn meet at Courtown he invited a pretty American girl he had met at a cocktail party in London, who he said was an excellent rider, a description that was accepted with some skepticism by Betty and Ricki. When the young woman arrived, she was greeted rather coolly by her hostess, but Ricki's good mood was soon restored when her husband's guest fell off her hireling at the first fence and decided to turn her mount over to Paddy for the remainder of the day. As a result, John appeared to have lost all interest in her, and she returned to London the next day.

Huston had now decided to settle permanently in Ireland, and Ricki was detailed to find a suitable house to buy. During the week she toured the country, returning each night to describe what she had seen. Betty urged her to find a place in Kildare with enough land to pay for the family's living expenses, but neither John nor Ricki listened to this practical advice. Ultimately she found a half-destroyed Georgian manor house in County Galway, and we all drove out to look at the place. The surrounding countryside was flat, very little land went with the ruin, and it was apparent that a great deal of money would be needed to restore it. There was an extensive stableyard and a pretty stone cottage in one corner of it, but that was the only asset the entire estate had to offer.

John was nevertheless enchanted with the property. "Isn't this some place!" he said over and over, striding around the ruin in the gusty wind, carried away with his own vision of what he could do with it. Betty and I exchanged baffled glances. Ricki seemed to be delighted that she had found a property John approved of and, more important, that he had complimented her on the diligent search that had led her to St. Clerans. Betty warned John that there was not enough land and that it might be difficult to acquire more from the Land Commission. But he paid no attention to her, nor did he seem even vaguely interested when I suggested he ask Betty's father, who was a professional farm manager, to make a quick survey.

Not much later he bought St. Clerans at an auction for a low price. It took two years to rebuild the main house at a prohibitive cost, but in the end John felt he had realized his dream. Later, inspired by his visit to Japan to shoot *The Barbarian and the Geisha*, he would install a Japanese bath, a luxury that alone cost nine pounds a day to maintain. His collection of pre-Columbian art arrived and took its place with many of the valuable objects he had acquired over the years. Like the house he had built in Tarzana before the war, St. Clerans had the unusual quality of a Huston residence, beautiful and impractical, but a testimonial to his special taste, as well as proof of his remarkable eye. As Betty had warned him, there was not enough land to help defray the enormous running expenses of the main residence, and after living there for several years, he would be forced to sell it. Like his Tarzana house, St. Clerans was bought for a price far below its value.

But long before the house had been completed it was evident that he had surpassed his original intention of finding a place he could return to and lick his wounds. He had to make several movies that he wasn't really enthusiastic about in order to maintain his castle, but he didn't seem to care. He became the Joint-Master of the Galway Blazers, an honorary position that cost him some money. He entertained the local gentry and hunted with them whenever possible. He fished the nearby trout streams with his son and appeared to be more at peace with himself than ever before, oblivious of the financial drain the place was imposing on him.

During the early years of his tenure at St. Clerans he decided to make a film about Freud, having read and been fascinated by Ernest Jones's biography of the great man. He enlisted Wolfgang Reinhardt as his coproducer and then chose Jean-Paul Sartre to work as his collaborator on the screenplay. Surprisingly enough, Sartre agreed to accept the job, although he had never written a screenplay before. Reinhardt told me that when Sartre arrived at St. Clerans in the taxi that had been sent to pick him up at Dublin airport, John was waiting inside the main gate mounted on one of his horses. It was a strange way to welcome the originator of existentialism, a man who frowned upon all personal possessions, especially those of the upper classes. Booted and spurred, Huston greeted the small, homely intellectual whose work he had always admired. Sartre was not impressed. To show his distaste for all the splendor, Reinhardt informed me, Sartre entered the house and made no comment whatsoever about the architecture, the artwork on the walls, the lavish comfort of his host's residence. If Huston was surprised or disappointed, he didn't show it.

AN UNUSUAL SNOWFALL put an end to the fox hunting in mid-January. Even the road to Courtown from Mount Armstrong became impassable, and after bidding Ishmael a fond farewell I returned to Klosters. Partly because of tax benefits under U.S. income tax laws that required seventeen out of eighteen months of foreign residence, the village had become a winter gathering place for quite a few members of the movie colony, and it was often referred to as "Hollywood on the Rocks." Gene Kelly was there with his family, as was Kirk Douglas, Stanley Donen, Alain Bernheim and his wife, the Parrishes, Tola and Sophie Litvak, Sam Spiegel, as well as the original settlers—myself and the Shaws. Lex Barker, my old tennis partner, ultimately appeared, as he had become a German movie star in the role of Old Shatterhand, the hero of the western novels of Karl May that I had been addicted to as a boy.

And it was there that Leland Hayward telephoned me in February and suggested we meet in Paris to discuss my getting started on the screenplay of *The Old Man and the Sea.* Lazar had written me that the script Paul Greene had turned in had not been satisfactory and that Hayward was ready "to make us an offer." His reputation in the theater, where he had produced several successful plays, was that of a competent and intelligent executive, and as I knew him only slightly from the days when he was Garbo's agent, I was anxious to hear what ideas he had to make the novella into a motion picture.

I soon learned that Hayward had come to Paris on an equally important mission. With Billy Wilder as a partner, he had acquired the rights to Charles Lindbergh's book *The Spirit of St. Louis*, which he was planning to make as a movie, and he was seeking the cooperation of the French government for the scenes to be shot at Le Bourget airport. I went to see him at his hotel, and the moment I set foot in his suite he informed me that he was already late for an appointment at the Air Ministry and suggested I accompany him so that we could talk in the car, a Hillman Minx he had just purchased for his stay in Europe.

At the first intersection the driver ran into a small van that had gone through a red light, and I was propelled forward by the collision, slightly cutting my hand. Leland was unhurt, so we hailed a taxi and continued on our way. Seemingly unruffled by the mishap, Hayward suggested I fly to New York at the end of the week, have dinner with him there, and then proceed to Havana with him and his wife, Slim, for an initial meeting with Hemingway.

He confessed that he had found Papa quite difficult to deal with and was counting on my help to calm Hemingway's fears about the ultimate outcome of the movie, especially as he, Hayward, would be fully occupied with the production of the Lindbergh story. He had already signed James Stewart to play the role of the Lone Eagle, although Stewart was almost twice as old as Lindbergh had been at the time of his historic flight. But once again the fact that a big star was required by Warner Brothers had made Hayward and Wilder decide on this strange bit of casting.

It all had a familiar ring. Leland was suggesting a similar tactical plan to Sam Spiegel's on the two occasions he had hired me to work with Huston, and I mentioned to Hayward that trying to pacify a partner via a third party was a doubtful procedure. If he and Papa had differences, it was better to battle them out now before he hired a director and a large crew. Unlike Sam, my new employer was more direct in his reply. He said that he had made a deal with Warner's for the two films, and one way or another he had to get them made. I then brought up the difficulties facing us in regard to the screenplay and mentioned all of my misgivings about sustaining an audience's interest in Santiago's battle with the marlin, but by that time we had arrived at the Air Ministry, and we adjourned our meeting. Hayward was returning to New York the next day, and he asked me to join him there as soon as possible. His secretary would furnish me a ticket, he told me, assuming that I wouldn't mind leaving on the spur of the moment. From New York we would go on to Cuba, he said, without inquiring if this would fit in with my plans. He was accustomed to catching airplanes as if they were taxis and appeared certain I wouldn't mind joining him. Overwhelmed by his energy, I agreed.

It had occurred to me that it might be possible to invent a first act for the story. After going eighty-four days without landing a fish, Santiago might try to get a job in Havana, and after a fruitless search for a minor job in a picturesque background, we could then have the old fisherman return to the sea. The Havana sequence would be beneficial, I thought; the entire film would thus not take place in an open boat. I left for New York on the weekend and dined with the Haywards as soon as I arrived. I mentioned my idea about the Havana sequence and both Slim and Leland agreed that it might have some merit. Of course Papa would have to agree to my trying to write an addition to his novel, Hayward said, and he suggested we discuss the idea with his partner once we arrived in Havana.

He went on to say that he faced a similar problem with his other movie, in that much of it would have to show Lindbergh alone in his airplane crossing the Atlantic. With an attempt at humor I suggested that Leland combine the two stories, cutting from Santiago in his open boat to the Lone Eagle at the controls of his aircraft. Although Slim laughed, Hayward only managed a wan smile. He informed me that Charlie Lederer, whom Wilder had chosen to be his collaborator, had already made light of their project. When asked by friends why he and Billy, both Jewish, had agreed to make a movie about a man who was known to be an anti-Semite, Charlie had replied: "Oh, but you don't know . . . in our version he crashes," a wisecrack Hayward declared was entertaining but less than helpful.

As the conversation continued, I gathered that it was Slim, more than anyone else, who had championed her husband's buying the Hemingway novella. An attractive woman with a willowy figure that had earned her her nickname, she had met Papa in Sun Valley while she was still married to Howard Hawks. Hemingway, who at the time was married to Martha Gellhorn, soon fell under her spell. The phrase has a Victorian ring, but I can think of no better way to put it. Slim had the ability to involve any man who interested her in a conspiratorial friendship based on mutual admiration that was akin to a sexual flirtation but that as a rule she never allowed to get out of hand.

While Leland went off to call Wilder in Hollywood, she informed me that she had decided not to accompany us to Havana on our first trip. She was eager to see Papa again, she told me, but she thought it was better for our "venture" if she stayed behind and postponed her visit, a decision I seconded, as wives were usually excess baggage during the maneuvers that preceded making any movie.

A limousine called for me at the Gotham Hotel the next morning and then crossed Fifth Avenue to pick up Leland at the St. Regis. An airplane journey, I had learned long ago, usually provided Hollywood executives with a much-needed rest period, out of reach of the telephone and their pressing daily problems, and Leland was no exception. He slept peacefully throughout the three-hour trip and seemed rested and relaxed when we arrived at our destination. We checked into the Hotel Nacional, and Hayward asked me to call Papa and inform him of our presence. The line to the Finca Vigía had not improved during the seven years that had passed since my first visit, so Hemingway's greeting was of necessity brief, though cordial. He would send Juan, his chauffeur, to pick us up later that afternoon, he said, and we would have dinner at his house, where it would be easier to talk. I took a swim in the pool and changed for dinner in my air-conditioned room. It was only mid-May, yet the heat outside was already quite oppressive from the extreme humidity.

Papa was waiting for us on the front steps as we pulled up, just as he had on my previous visits, and he welcomed us with a broad smile on his bearded face. He thanked Leland for putting off our meeting long enough for him to complete the section of the long novel he was working on and led the way into the house. Black Dog was still alive, he pointed out to me, although the tropical climate had proved to be hard on his coat and eyes. Mary, when she joined us, looked somewhat worn, too, the skin on her face prematurely wrinkled from exposure to the strong sun. I mixed the dry martinis, remembering that Papa liked them with only a drop of vermouth, hardly enough to alter the transparent color of the gin. He asked after Slim and Bettina, and the evening started out in a friendly atmosphere.

The conversation at dinner was mostly about fishing; it seemed that the marlin were not as plentiful as they had been in the past; nevertheless, Papa proposed that we all go out on the *Pilar* in the morning, a plan to which Leland agreed. Mary said that she would not accompany us, as she had a lot of household chores to attend to as well as needing a rest from the sea. After dinner Leland and Papa began a discussion about a suitable director for their movie. Leland mentioned Elia Kazan as a possibility, but Papa vetoed him, saying that he didn't want to work with a "stool pigeon," a reference to Kazan's having testified in front of the Un-American Activities Committee, and Leland did not insist.

I suggested Fred Zinnemann, who, I told Papa and Hayward, had made a little-known film about a Mexican fishing village in his youth, a documentary that had shown considerable talent although it had never been widely released. Hayward agreed that Freddy would be an ideal choice. He had directed Tracy in a movie called *The Seventh Cross* during the war, and it was Tracy who had given the young Austrian a chance to make his first big feature at MGM by accepting him as a director. We agreed that Papa should meet Zinnemann, and that concluded the discussion.

THE SEA WAS CALM as the *Pilar* moved out of Havana harbor and headed out toward the Gulf Stream. It was pleasantly cool once we were under way. I joined Papa on the flying bridge, leaving Leland to sit in the shade of the afterdeck so that he could read the morning papers that were already a day old. Gregorio, Papa's first mate and deckhand, was preparing the lines to be attached to the outriggers. The broad "teaser" tied to the center of the fantail was already in the water. Hemingway was at the wheel, naked to the waist, his muscular legs spread wide apart to steady himself against the slight roll of the boat as we reached the open sea. He wore a white tennis visor to protect his eyes against the glare, as he never used sunglasses. He appeared to be in an excellent mood with the sun beating down on his broad, tanned back.

We fished his favorite holes without success, and it seemed for a while that we would return empty-handed, like the hero of his novella. Then at two o'clock we had our first strike, a smallish marlin that Papa hooked and turned over to Leland to play and land in less than ten minutes. Almost simultaneously a second marlin struck, a larger fish that Papa landed with quick expertise, after I had declined to take the rod, pleading inexperience. Then a third fish attacked the lure on the starboard line, and Papa insisted I take the rod Leland had used. Although I followed Hemingway's instructions, I was slow in taking in the slack, and the fish sounded.

It was the smallest marlin of the three, and yet it took me over half an hour to bring it alongside for Gregorio to gaff and haul on board. Despite the inferior size of our catch, Papa was pleased. His fish weighed more than two hundred fifty pounds by his estimate, Leland's a scant two hundred, and mine a hundred twenty-five. The rods were secured, and we motored on to a small cove for lunch, which Gregorio had already started to prepare while we were sailing. It consisted of turtle steaks that had been stored on ice, and I watched him rather apprehensively as he cut them into slices and marinated them in a plate filled with olive oil and sliced onions. I recalled how years ago Jigee and I had watched Gregorio trim his toenails with the same knife he used for cooking, which did little to whet my appetite.

Papa cautioned us to chew the meat well before swallowing, thereby getting the most out of its "delicious flavor," instructions I found difficult to heed. I concentrated on the salad of tomatoes and onions but was forced to eat my ration of turtle steak so as not to offend my host. Even in the shade it was hot and humid now that we were riding at anchor, and I asked Papa if it was all right to take a swim. He agreed hesitantly and went down into the cabin to get his .22-caliber rifle in case a shark appeared while I was in the water. Slightly reassured by this precaution, I dove off the side of the *Pilar*. The warm ocean was only mildly refreshing, and after a brief swim I crawled up the swimming ladder. As Gregorio was doing the dishes, I volunteered to pull the ladder up, which proved to be more difficult than I had anticipated. For the first time in my life I felt myself getting seasick.

Papa recognized the symptoms immediately. I assured him that I would be all right in a while, that I had never been seasick before, and that it would not be necessary to pull up the anchor and get under way so as to decrease the roll of the boat. I hadn't chewed my turtle steak sufficiently, I explained, or had eaten too many onions. "And the fish didn't leave you unmoved, Pete," Hemingway added.

Gregorio had a remedy. He poured a bucket of seawater over my head and body, and the cold chills I had been experiencing went away. I was the youngest and, with the exception of Gregorio, certainly the most physically fit man on board, and I felt embarrassed at having gotten seasick. Even Leland had survived the rigors of the day better than I had. Less than six months ago he had been hospitalized after an attack of internal bleeding, and Billy Wilder and I had driven to the hospital in downtown Los Angeles to donate blood, yet now he appeared to be the picture of health, pleased to have landed his marlin with a surprising degree of expertise.

After an hour's rest we resumed our fishing. But throughout the long afternoon there was no further strike, and we returned to Havana in the early evening, where we were photographed with our catch. The script we had come to discuss had not been mentioned, and Leland and I were driven back in a taxi to the air-conditioned comfort of the Hotel Nacional. "Tomorrow morning we'll go to work," Leland assured me. "Papa's in the right frame of mind for it now."

The photograph taken from the dock at the yacht harbor still stands on the mantel in my study in Klosters, the three sportsmen with their catch, along with Gregorio, who had done much of the work. When I glance at it, as I do occasionally, I am always amazed by Papa's appearance. He was only in his mid-fifties when the photograph was taken, and yet he appears twenty years older. Despite his sturdy legs and arms, his eyes already have the detached look that people acquire as they near the end of their lives, and although Papa is grinning happily for the benefit of the photographer, his gray hair and his stooped posture are that of a much older man.

He called the next morning and asked me to explain to Leland that he needed to work by himself most of the day and would expect us at the *finca* in the late afternoon, a message Hayward accepted with relief, as he preferred lunching at the hotel where it was easier for him to keep to his strict diet. The turtle steaks had given him a restless night. Although he never complained, he was obviously not a well man. He also needed to telephone New York and California, not an easy task considering the Cuban telephone service.

Our story conference took place in a small, dark room that gave out onto the garden and was relatively cool. Leland began our meeting by saying that I had an idea for the screenplay that was worth considering, and I launched myself hesitantly into a description of the first act I had in mind, prefacing it with the problems I envisaged at having most of the film take place in an open boat. Hemingway listened carefully and then shook his head. There was perhaps some merit in the idea, he admitted, but it wouldn't work. A man like Santiago would never go to Havana to seek employment. He was a fisherman, and it would never occur to him to try his hand at anything other than his trade. He added that this was the only movie he would ever have anything to do with, and he wanted it to remain faithful to the original.

Both Leland and I realized that it was pointless to go any further with my suggestion. In a foolish attempt to inject a little humor into the proceedings, I made the remark that maybe Santiago should go out on the eighty-fifth day and still not make a catch. Hemingway clenched his teeth, displeased by my joke. "The Jews," he said, "have always had a superior attitude toward fishing, probably because fish has never been a part of their diet." I flushed angrily. "I thought you'd gotten over all of your anti-Semitism with *The Sun Also Rises*," I replied. I don't know why I said it, but I did.

The atmosphere in the small room turned into one of open hostility. Leland, even more nervous than he had been at the start, said that my remark was uncalled for, and Papa's anger subsided immediately. "I wasn't being anti-Semitic, Pete," he told me. "If it sounded that way, I'm sorry." Embarrassed, I agreed with Leland that mine had been a dumb joke, and peace was restored. Papa went on to say that the characters in his earlier novel, Jake Barnes and Mike Campbell, reflected and expressed the views that were current at that time and had little to do with his own opinions. He had never been an anti-Semite, and it was too late for him to start being one now.

The remainder of the meeting concerned itself with the physical problems of the planned production. Papa wanted the film shot in Cuba, but he agreed with Leland that the company might have to look elsewhere for a fish the size of the one in the book. Leland told Hemingway that he had seen footage of a huge marlin that had been caught in Peru that had weighed out at more than seventeen hundred pounds. He was looking into the possibility of buying the footage from a man called Glassel who had shot it in sixteen millimeters, and he said it might be possible to blow it up to thirty-five. If this turned out to be impossible because of the change in quality of the footage, he suggested that Papa might go to Peru with a film crew.

Hemingway approved of this idea, as long as the trip took place the following year so as not to interrupt his present work. There was also the possibility of making a fish at the studio, Leland went on to say, and of using it for the shark sequence in the movie. Papa's eyes narrowed again. "I just want to tell you one thing, Leland," he said. "No movie made with a goddamn rubber fish ever made a goddamn dime." This remark ended our discussion, and we adjourned for dry martinis followed by a relaxed dinner of marlin steaks and salad. As we entered the dining room, Hemingway put his right arm around my shoulders and gave me a quick hug. "Whatever happens on this venture, I want us to stay friends," he mumbled.

LELAND DEPARTED, and my period of "indoctrination" began. I moved from the Hotel Nacional to the "guest house" at the *finca* so as to avoid the long taxi rides. Papa wanted me to become acquainted with the daily hardships of Cuban fishermen, the first step of which involved my being put out in a small open boat after being towed out to sea for that purpose by the *Pilar*. Gregorio was mystified by this procedure, and he watched dubiously while I rowed a few hundred yards out into the Gulf Stream. After an hour of watching me sit in the hot sun, Papa relented, and the *Pilar* returned to pick me up. Aside from a sunburn, I got very little from the exercise.

As a next step Papa booked a room for me above a bar in Cojimar, the small fishing village from which Santiago sailed during the eighty-five days of his calvary. The presence of a squadron of mosquitoes made sleep impossible, as did the heat in the airless room, but rising at five o'clock in the morning I was able to witness the daily walk of the local fishermen to the small port at which they boarded their boats. It made my stay worthwhile, as the spectacle of the dozen or so men carrying lanterns down the dusty road was remarkable.

I told Papa that since "visiting" Guadalcanal in 1943, I had never encountered the same mixture of heat and insects. Standing with him on the flying bridge of the *Pilar* the next day, I began to reminisce about my year's service in the South Pacific, which delighted Papa, although mine were not stories about combat, but comical descriptions of the strange characters I had lived among in New Caledonia and the Solomon Islands. He loved hearing about the police sergeant in my outfit, one Halloween Bags, who had the habit of drinking after-shave lotion as an aperitif and often complained that Aqua Velva was too sweet and that Mennen's had to be filtered through half a loaf of bread to make it drinkable. Hemingway was a wonderful listener, I discovered again. "The Corps," he said, must have been fun, but I assured him that it was much more "fun" in retrospect. Still, the comical side of war, he said, had been overlooked in all of the war books he had read, and he urged me to write my own book about the South Pacific.

Strangely enough, as I look back on my fortnight at the Finca Vigía, I realize that we never discussed the actual writing of the screenplay. Near the end of my stay a letter from a taxi driver in Chicago arrived for Papa. The man recounted how a preacher had taken his taxi one day, a Protestant minister stationed in Havana. The clergyman had complained at length about Hemingway, had asserted that Papa was a foul-mouthed, despicable character who frequented whores and other riffraff and had never made a contribution to his parish. Even as we were laughing about the letter, the same minister called from Havana to ask for a donation, and Papa amused himself by telling the caller that they had "mutual friends" in Chicago and that he had just heard from one of them. The telephone call ended abruptly, and Papa roared with laughter at the man's discomfort.

Hemingway suggested I stay on for a month or two and write my screenplay at the *finca*. I explained that I had to get back to Europe and would prefer to work in familiar surroundings, to which Papa agreed reluctantly. I then put in a call to Fred Zinnemann in California and was told that he was in New York, so I called him at his hotel and suggested that he fly to Havana to meet Papa as well as to discuss directing our movie. He arrived three days later, and we had dinner together in Havana.

I remember that the two of us sat on the terrace of a small fish restaurant and that Freddy was delighted with the atmosphere of the city, which reminded him of his long stay in Mexico many years earlier. He had read *The Old Man and the Sea* and had enjoyed it immensely, but he was rather skeptical about its film possibilities. He did say, however, that he wouldn't mind making a small movie as a change of pace from the big production of the James Jones novel he had recently completed. As a first step he wanted to meet Hemingway, as it was most important for him to find congenial people to work with. "It would be nice if we finally did something together," he told me, referring to the job I had abandoned in Switzerland in 1946.

Zinnemann had been my father's assistant when he had first come to California, long before the war, and he had often come to our house when I was a boy. Although he was now in his late forties, he had changed very little since those early days. His dark hair was only slightly sprinkled with gray, and his slim body was still that of a young man. His English was fluent, with a marked accent, but his mild, polite Viennese manners were unchanged, despite the fact that he was currently one of the most sought after directors in Hollywood. He had always been cautious about choosing his movies from among those he was offered, one of the few Hollywood moviemakers who was less interested in money than in the chance to make an outstanding film. I knew that it would be useless to urge him to take on our project, as he was much too much his own man to be persuaded by others. He said that Renée, his wife, had liked the book, which was a good omen, as she was the only person whose opinion mattered to him.

The encounter between the two men went far better than I had imagined it would. Papa was impressed with Zinnemann's modest manner, which was so different from the other "Hollywood characters" he had met, while Freddy was surprised and intrigued by Hemingway's outward gentleness, his slow, measured speech, as well as the tentative venturing of most of his opinions.

Then Zinnemann asked Papa about Hayward. Producers, in Freddy's opinion, were a breed one could do without, although he admitted that Harry Cohn had been of some help during the making of *From Here to Eternity*. Hemingway refrained from his usual negative comments whenever the James Jones novel was mentioned and merely accepted Freddy's statement that in his opinion the movie had turned out to be "just as good as the novel." "Maybe even better," was all Papa said. As for Hayward, Hemingway assured Zinnemann that he would not interfere in the actual making of our movie, as he would be "up to his ears in problems connected with the shooting of the Lindbergh story."

The following day, when Zinnemann arrived at the *finca* to say good-bye, he seemed to have decided to accept the assignment. Papa was delighted. He was seated at the side of his swimming pool, preparing to listen to a radio broadcast of a baseball game from New York. He and Freddy shook hands, and as Freddy was about to depart, a beggar appeared asking for a handout. Hemingway asked the beggar to leave, but as the man persisted, Papa suddenly flew into a rage. "*¡Qué se vaya!*" he shouted and then grew immediately calm once the intruder had departed.

I walked back to the house with Zinnemann, who was disturbed by the scene. "He reminded me of your father," he told me. "Berthold was apt to fly off the handle like that from time to time." I agreed. "But never because he wanted to listen to a baseball game," I told him, and he laughed quietly.

UPON MY RETURN to New York I found the normally restrained Hayward in a state of euphoria. Bert Allenberg, who represented Zinnemann as well as Spencer Tracy, had telephoned to inform Leland of Freddy's decision and, equally important, Tracy's approval of it. He now had two of the best directors in Hollywood under contract to direct two of the leading stars in the business, not to mention that the two literary properties he had acquired were on the best-seller list. It was a promising start for his initial efforts as a movie producer, an ambition he had nurtured since his early days as a theatrical agent.

The difficulties that lay ahead were temporarily forgotten and, partly to please Slim, he announced that we would all go to Madrid for a week's vacation to celebrate.

I flew to Paris the next day to collect Bettina, and together we traveled on to Madrid. Luis Miguel Dominguín had recently married Lucia Bosé, a young Italian movie actress, and he insisted we stay with him in his small house on the Calle Nervion so that we could get to know his bride. Lucia was in her early twenties, a classical beauty with dark hair and a pale complexion that Miguel explained was due to her frail health for she had had a mild case of tuberculosis as a child.

She had never been to Spain before her marriage, and the world of the bullfight was even more foreign to her than the surroundings in which she now found herself. Miguel had persuaded her to give up her career and she, in turn, had made him promise that his retirement from the bullring would be permanent. They appeared to be very much in love, given to constant touching and embracing. Once again Miguel had chosen a *novia* with whom verbal communications were difficult, although Lucia was making rapid progress with her Spanish.

They had known each other for only a week before Miguel had asked her to become his wife. He was seldom wrong about women and bulls, he informed me with a sly grin, but I suspected that he had also been motivated by his need to shock the society in which he lived. In choosing an Italian woman to be his wife, he had done just that. Toreros were expected to marry girls from their own hometown.

The Haywards arrived a few days later, with Truman Capote and Irving Lazar as members of their retinue. Capote was one of Slim Hayward's closest friends, just as he was Babe Paley's favorite confidant and companion. Small in stature and effeminate in manner, he was known to be talented and clever, qualities that endeared him to both of these famous ladies. I found him to be both perceptive and agreeable, and it astonished me, as soon as we had become acquainted, that Papa had taken such an instant dislike to a young man he had never met. Papa's negative public statements had wounded Truman, although he only mentioned Hemingway very briefly in our initial conversations.

Whenever Truman was introduced to Spaniards, his name and physical appearance provoked an immediate comical reaction. "*¡Capote!*" they invariably replied. "*¡Olé!*" This because his name was identical with the Spanish word for the fighting cape used in the bullfight. Truman ignored their reaction. He smiled and shook hands, as polite as ever. Luis Miguel accepted him at once, as he had a penchant for originals, and at the first *tienta* we were invited to as a group, he urged Truman to join him in the ring. To everyone's surprise, Capote complied with Miguel's instructions and stood his ground in his beige summer suit while the horned heifer charged past his diminitive form. Slim was delighted. "Trueheart," she said, using her nickname for him, "you were wonderful out there."

Capote was equally devoted to Slim; his affectionate name for her was "Big Mama," and he appeared to bask in her maternal affections. In retrospect it seems amazing that he turned on her late in life and wrote less than favorably about her in an ill-concealed nonfiction novel some years later. Apparently he came to resent his role of an oddity and felt that he was being used by Slim and Babe Paley, a rancor that only surfaced once alcohol and drugs had taken their toll. By that time he had tired of his role of the adorable urchin, although in Madrid he was still playing the part to the hilt.

So as not to be outdone by the other members of our group, Irving Lazar took his turn in the small bullring that morning as well, shedding the jacket of his elegant suit. The Spanish ranch hands watched the spectacle with amazement but refrained from comment. The next day we all drove out to Luis Miguel's ranch to spend the night and the following day. I recall that at dinner Lazar was seated next to Lucia Bosé, and in an effort to make conversation he asked his hostess what political party she had belonged to in Italy. "The Communist Party," Lucia replied, once the question had been translated. Thinking she was being funny, Lazar burst into appreciative laughter. She stared at him with annoyance. "What is he laughing at?" she demanded. "If he doesn't stop, I'll smack him in the face."

I hastened to explain that Lazar had thought she was joking. "It's not a joke," she said. "My father is a member of the party and so is my brother. Everyone who is poor in northern Italy is a Communist. What else do you expect them to be?"

Lazar made up for his gaffe the next morning. Our host had arranged for us to do some trap shooting on the terrace outside the main house. Luis Miguel was an excellent wing shot, and after he had blasted away at half a dozen saucers I took my turn with only very limited success. Then Swifty demanded that I hand him the shotgun. "Have you ever done this before?" I asked him, fearing that the kick of the 12-gauge gun would hurt him. "Of course I have," he replied haughtily, so I handed him the weapon. Miguel's chauffeur released the first disk and Lazar fired once and scored a direct hit. "That's it," he declared, smiling broadly. I urged him to have another go, certain that it had been a lucky accident. A second disk was sent off into the clear air with the same surprising result. "Let's have lunch," Swifty said, "or do you want me to embarrass you some more?"

Luis Miguel roared with laughter. Swifty had established himself firmly in his affections. "I don' unnerstan' one fockin' thing he say, El Macaco," he announced in English for Irving's benefit, "but I think he is very, very clever."

THE HAYWARDS and their troupe departed for New York. Bettina and I returned to Paris only to discover that Guy Schoeller had decided he wanted to move back to number 8, avenue Montaigne. The housing problem was ever present in Paris in those days, just as it is now, and the café downstairs and the Relais Plaza across the street provided an atmosphere that Guy admitted he missed.

He had been generous enough to allow us to reside there for almost two years, but we were forced to look for new quarters, not an easy task in Paris in the month of May. We moved temporarily into the Hôtel du Théâtre next door until a friend of ours, Paul Chadourne, suggested we rent his small villa in Garches near St. Cloud. But despite the bucolic surroundings of the village, I found it less than a satisfactory solution. The traffic, even in the mid-fifties, was heavy throughout the day, and I discovered that I was spending a good part of every day on the road to and from the city, either to meet Bettina for dinner or to go out to lunch with friends.

One night at a dinner party I was introduced to Carmen Baron, an interesting and charming woman who worked for Dior, and she suggested I rent her family's villa near Biarritz for the summer. It was unoccupied and she was willing to let me have it for a nominal sum. Summer was nearly upon us, and Bettina and I agreed that we should take her up on her generous offer. Le Chapelet was the name of the property, and it turned out to be a run-down mansion with a large park of more than twenty acres on the main road between Bayonne and St. Jean de Luz. The reason it had not been rented was immediately apparent, as the noise from the traffic was overwhelming. In order to sleep I moved into one of the smaller bedrooms that gave out onto the park.

Writing the screenplay of *The Old Man and the Sea* was a strange assignment, as it had been decided by Papa and Leland that I should stick almost verbatim to the novella. To preserve the poetry of Hemingway's prose, I adopted the simple device of an unseen narrator who tells the story that is acted out in front of the cameras, a job an intelligent, movie-wise secretary could have done equally well.

The short novel covers a little more than a hundred pages, and after I broke it down into scenes, my first-draft screenplay turned out to be thirty pages too long. My main task then was to eliminate some of the passages in the book, which I did as judiciously as possible. In less than a month I had completed a second draft and set about retyping it. Feeling confident that Zinnemann would be able to add the visual effects that would bring the story to life, I was nevertheless worried about how the film would turn out: almost one half of it would be shot at sea with Tracy the only live actor in front of the camera. Provided the entire movie did not run longer than just over an hour, I felt that there was a chance it might attract a special audience and at least make enough money to defray the limited expenses Leland and Hemingway were hoping to incur in the absence of a realistic budget.

A fortnight before I wrote the final "Fade out," Slim Hayward and Audrey Wilder arrived in Biarritz and moved into the luxurious Hôtel du Palais. Rather than stay alone in Paris while Leland and Billy were out on location shooting *The Spirit of St. Louis*, they had chosen to come to la Côte basque to escape the heat. Slim asked to read my screenplay; after she had finished it, she reported that she had been moved to tears by the ending, proof of the lasting power of Hemingway's prose. Even in the less than graceful format of a movie script, the story with which she was familiar had retained its original emotional impact. I felt reassured.

Although the last few years hadn't been particularly productive, money was not a problem for the time being. But, as is often the case when things seem to be going well, I was in for an unpleasant surprise. I had been telephoning Bettina every night and had always been able to reach her, sometimes as late as one o'clock in the morning. But the night Slim expressed her enthusiasm for my screenplay, I was unable to reach Bettina until three A.M. She explained that she had been to a dinner party and had then gone on to a nightclub, an unusual thing for her to do. But she was as affectionate as ever and complained only of being extremely tired. The next night I was unable to reach her at all. I was slightly alarmed, but as she had told me that she would be coming down to Biarritz that weekend, I dismissed my doubts about what she was up to. On occasion she had stayed in Paris with a friend rather than drive back to Garches, and I reckoned that was what she had decided to do.

We had been getting along better than ever, my guilty feelings about leaving Jigee having subsided somewhat after three years. There was still the mutually unmentioned problem of our getting married, and I assumed that Bettina had decided it would be solved ultimately once more time had passed. When I was unable to reach her at home the next day, I realized that something serious was wrong. I called her half a dozen times without success. I couldn't sleep. Finally I was able to talk to her at Givenchy's, where she was under exclusive contract as a model. She sounded unusually hesitant, upset, but not nearly as upset as I was. I demanded that she tell me the truth if, as I suspected, there was someone else in her life. In a tortured voice she admitted that she had been seeing another man. I asked her who it was, and she refused at first to name him. Then after another bitter exchange she told me that she had fallen in love with Aly Khan.

"Well, *he's* not going to marry you," I said angrily. There was a long silence on the other end of the line. "We've been together for more than three years," I added. "Don't you think you ought at least to come down here and talk things over?" Again there was no reply. "All right, pack my clothes and send them to me," I told her and hung up.

Feeling both hurt and abused, I drove to the Hôtel du Palais where I was to meet Slim and Audrey for lunch and then go on to a bullfight in San Sebastián. I was in no condition to keep my troubles to myself, and as soon as I arrived in Slim's suite I informed her and Audrey of Bettina's defection. Both women stared at me for an instant; then Slim laughed rather drily. As I look back now, her reaction seems more understandable than it did then. I think she was made uncomfortable by the abrupt manner in which I broke the news, especially in light of the harsh circumstances under which I had left Jigee. Audrey was gentler. I asked her why my bad news had moved Slim to laughter. Slim was a friend and a sensitive human being, and her reaction had astonished me. "People like bloodshed," Audrey replied, accurately and succinctly. "Especially that kind."

Other friends had similar reactions. Harry Kurnitz, one of the sweetest human beings I had ever befriended, was widely quoted in our group as saying, "Poor Bettina. Once again she won't be able to eat pork," a funny wisecrack that was not in the least offensive. Arlene Francis, another close friend, grinned mischievously when I saw her in

New York. "And you weren't even having a baby!" she remarked. One of Bettina's closest friends in Paris had said, "Go find her and bring her back." But I realized that even if I had been able to convince her to reconsider, our relationship would never be the same.

John Huston was staying in Paris when I passed through several weeks later on my way to California to begin work on my script with Freddy Zinnemann. He suggested we take a walk and talk things over. I knew his intentions were paternal, as he always had great empathy for the troubles of his younger friends. We took a taxi to St. Germain des Prés and ambled along the streets of his favorite *quartier*. He talked about his own ill-fated love affair with Marietta Fitzgerald and about how unhappy he had been when she had gone back to her husband. I remember that we sat together on the terrace of a sidewalk café and that John was amused when an Arab street vendor dropped a single peanut on our table. "He's trying to get us hooked," he said, grinning. Then after we had purchased a paper bag full of the man's wares, Huston said, "I'm going to tell you something you're not going to like, kid," he warned me. He paused significantly. "Aly Khan is really one swell guy."

"Well, that's good news," I replied ironically. I had heard from some of Bettina's girlfriends that Aly Khan had been seeing a lot of Ricki in Deauville that summer, at the same time as he was courting Bettina, but I made no mention of it to John. I said, "I hope Aly and Bettina will be very happy."

"Sure you do, kid," John said, smiling his most devilish smile.

LELAND THOUGHT it might be a good idea if I went to see Papa in Havana on my way to California, ostensibly to pay him a courtesy call rather than show him my screenplay, as Hemingway was working with the second unit, directing their efforts to catch a big marlin. He had told Hayward that he couldn't perform two functions at the same time and that he preferred not to read the script until Zinnemann and I had completed working on it. Although I was eager to finish my assignment, I agreed to Leland's suggestion. I was also curious to see what progress, if any, was being made in the sighting and catching of a big marlin, knowing from experience that nature seldom cooperates with moviemakers in their efforts to glorify its wonders.

I called the *finca* from the airport in Havana, and Mary informed me that Papa was in better shape both physically and emotionally than he had been during my last visit. He had lost some weight, she said, and was enjoying his job as technical director of the operation. The *Pilar* and another launch, the *Tensi*, were being used as moving camera platforms, each powerboat towing two small replicas of Santiago's open fishing dory so that they could photograph the jumping of a marlin should one take the bait. They had been out every day for a week and had as yet been unable to get a strike. The sea was calm, but the fish were not cooperating.

After leaving my luggage in the guest house, René, the houseman, drove me down to the small harbor of Cojimar, and a motor launch took me out to the *Pilar*. Gregorio helped me aboard and then I climbed up onto the flying bridge and was given a firm *abrazo* by *Pilar*'s "Master next to God." His small fleet was lying nearby while the camera crews and the three doubles for Tracy were having lunch. Knowing that Papa would ask after Bettina, I reported her desertion as the first order of the day. He nodded sympathetically. "Well, I was probably the only son of a bitch in the world that didn't like her," was his first comment, made, I realized, more to comfort me than to express his real opinion. In an odd way it also reflected his loyalty to Jigee.

Then he began to ramble on about his own romantic foibles. He was always getting married, it seemed to him in retrospect—"couldn't help it." "Hell, Pete," he said, "I married three girls from St. Louis, one after the other. It was like I couldn't marry anybody who wasn't from St. Louis. I got to know everybody in St. Louis secondhand, and let me tell you, Pete, it's a dull fucking town!"

I roared with laughter, in which he joined me, and I felt a lot better about life. Gregorio hoisted the anchor, and we put out to sea, followed by the other boats. I noticed that one of the three Santiagos being towed behind the camera ships was a black man, and I queried Papa about it. He grinned sheepishly. The local labor authorities had demanded racial equality in the hiring of Cuban personnel, one of Batista's more liberal dictums. However, Papa had been assured by one of the second unit cameramen that at the distance the small boat was removed from the camera ship the color of the fisherman's skin would not be noticeable. As it turned out, an hour later a big mako shark took the black fisherman's line. The shark didn't jump the way a marlin does when hooked, but the struggle to boat it was nevertheless recorded on film, footage that was viewed with some dismay by Jack Warner in his private projection room in Burbank a few weeks later.

Papa had invited George Brown, an old friend and a well-known

265

boxing coach and trainer, to come to the *finca* for a month to keep him physically fit. Brown, an affable and surprisingly gentle human being, was also an expert at massage, and his daily administrations were meant to relax Hemingway after his strenuous days out on the ocean. While he was absent, Papa thought it a good idea that George should give me boxing lessons, as there was no point in my going out with the camera crews. It was better I reread the script and then box with George, he said, thus keeping us both occupied.

Somewhat reluctantly we obeyed our commander's orders. The tennis court, Brown decided, was the best place for my lessons, and late in the afternoon on the first day of my visit, George and I sparred cautiously in the hot sun. He was attempting to improve my left hook when Papa's Buick entered the gate at the bottom of the garden, and with great haste Brown stripped off our gloves and hurried off to hide them in the guest house—this to ensure that Papa would not be tempted to give me a few pointers in the manly art of self-defense. "He's apt to get carried away when he spars with friends," George remarked.

A daily massage usually took place after Hemingway's return, followed by a shower. "Mind if I piss in your shower?" Papa would ask in mock seriousness, and George would reply, "Not at all, sir. Go right ahead."

"How does he handle himself with the gloves?" Hemingway asked that first evening. "He's got a good right hand," Brown reported, "but needs to work on his left jab and hook."

It would all prove worthwhile when it came time to deal with "the Khan," Papa said with a grin.

The inevitable autumn visitors began arriving in Havana. The first of these was Henry Hyde, who came out to the *finca* for Sunday lunch, which, despite a few tense moments, passed agreeably. Then David Selznick, accompanied by his wife Jennifer Jones flew down from New York, telephoned, and asked me to arrange a dinner or a luncheon with Papa, as they had never met.

Rather hesitantly I asked Hemingway if he could take time off for a meal with David and Jennifer, and he shook his head. People he didn't know or wasn't particularly anxious to meet were always calling when they arrived in town, as visiting the *finca* was now considered to be an "obligatory stop for any VIP on a Caribbean tour," he said. As they were friends of mine, I told him that I would make his excuses and take David and Jennifer out to dinner by myself.

Papa suggested I take them to Chory's, a most unusual nightclub in downtown Havana, where the locals danced to the music of a band equipped with none of the customary musical instruments. The evening turned out to be a great success, and late that night David insisted I bring the Hemingways around for a drink whenever they felt like it, as Jennifer was eager to meet Papa. I passed on the information, but Hemingway said he didn't have time and suggested I take Mary as his "ambassador." After confirming the invitation, Mary and I set out for the Hotel Nacional. Arriving in the Selznicks' suite, we found David in the midst of a gin rummy game with Santiago Reachi, a Mexican film producer. Jennifer, we were told, was "taking a nap." I noticed that our host had a towel around the lower part of his body and that he didn't rise to acknowledge the introduction, saying that he had just come back from the swimming pool. Nor did he and Reachi interrupt their game. They finished their hand and we had a drink and left. Later Mary reported the incident to Papa, who was infuriated by Selznick's bad manners, and from that day on David was often included in Papa's most vicious attacks in his letters to me.

After another week of unsuccessful fishing, the film crews departed, and Slim Hayward arrived for a visit. Papa decided that Slim should stay in the guest house and I should move into town, an arrangement that Slim was most doubtful about, as she was understandably apprehensive about the creature comforts she would find at the *finca*. On the second evening of her stay, I drove out to join them all for dinner, and Slim seemed exceedingly tense when I picked her up at the door of her room. Mary, she told me, had threatened quite calmly to shoot her if she "made a play for Papa," a warning that seemed to have had an alarming effect on her houseguest.

I followed Slim through the garden to the main residence. She was dressed in an emerald-colored strapless evening gown that suited her admirably and was in my opinion, I told her, the perfect attire for a seductress from the big city, a pleasantry she did not appreciate. Papa was waiting for us in the living room. He was naked to the waist, the lower part of his body clothed in a pair of khaki trousers, held in place just below the bulge of his stomach by his favorite Wehrmacht belt. His broad feet were encased in a pair of leather sandals. It was an unusual costume for a dinner party, even in Cuba, but he explained that as it was a warm evening, he had waited to put on his white *guayabera* so as not to "sweat it up." I mixed the inevitable "dry martoonies," which increased Papa's festive mood. Putting his left arm around Slim's small waist, he strolled with her into the library, glass in hand.

They stopped in front of a Spanish still life of a bowl of fruit. "Miss Slim," he said in a ceremonious voice, "if you look long enough at this painting . . . it will mean absolutely nothing to you at all!" Then propelling her in the direction of the living room, his voice changed. "The Narrator," he intoned, evidently inspired by a reading of my script that he said he hadn't read. "And so the couple strode bravely into the sunset." He wriggled his hips. The faded khaki trousers slid a little lower. "Take two," he continued. "We can improve on that shot." He moved Slim back to their "mark" in front of the still life. "Miss Slim," he repeated, "if you look long enough at this painting, it will mean absolutely nothing to you at all." He paused. Then: "The Narrator. And so the couple strode bravely into the sunset." This time he increased the movement of his hips, and the trousers slid to the ground. Naked as the day he was born, he stepped out of them.

Slim stared at him in wide-eyed horror. "Papa, for heaven's sake, what are you doing?" she said, keeping her eyes high enough to avoid looking at her naked suitor.

Hemingway chuckled. "All right for the camera, Pete?" he asked.

"Perfect, Papa," I replied. "Cut and print."

"Please, Papa," Slim pleaded, "put your pants back on!"

He put his drink down on a nearby table and struggled back into his khaki slacks. We were all laughing by that time, although Slim's laughter was anything but relaxed.

Mary entered the room, unaware of the scene that had only just ended. "Papa," she said, in a wifely tone of voice. "Put on your shirt, Lamb. We're about to have dinner."

Hemingway nodded and went off in search of his *guayabera*. Mary crossed to the kitchen, leaving Slim and me alone for a moment. "I've got to get out of here," she whispered to me. "Please, Peter, help me!"

"What can *I* do?" I asked. "I'm just the writer on this picture."

"It's not funny," she said. "I'm scared out of my wits. You've got to do something."

But by the following morning she had devised a plan of escape all by herself. She had told Papa that she had to get back to New York and that she had asked me to take her to the airport in my rented car. A farewell luncheon was scheduled, for which Mary arrived late from Havana with Juan, the Hemingways' driver. Papa and Slim were still down at the pool when they drove up in front of the house. Mary got out and came up the concrete steps where I was waiting. Her hair was a strange reddish color. "What the hell happened to you?" I asked her.

"I've had my hair dyed the color of Slim's," she said, tensely. I made no comment on what I considered to be a disastrous decision and followed her into the house.

During the meal, which was surprisingly friendly, I told Papa that I had probably better be getting back to California to start work with Freddy Zinnemann. "I envy you, Pete," he said, "flying to New York with Miss Slim. You'll probably get to see a few of the World Series games while you're stopping over in the city." I told him that I might just do that, provided I could secure a ticket. Slim's luggage was loaded into my car, and we all said our good-byes. As we started down the drive, my passenger heaved a sigh of relief. "God, I'm glad to be getting out of there," she said. But she wasn't quite ready to fly home, she told me. She needed a few days' rest to recover from her stay at the *finca* and suggested we spend the weekend in Varadero, the Cuban beach resort a hundred kilometers down the coast from Havana. It sounded like a good idea. Outside the front gate I consulted the map that had been provided by the car rental company, and we were on our way. "We must never tell Papa," Slim said, and I agreed, feeling as if I were enacting the part of Robert Cohn going off to Hendaye with Lady Brett.

ONLY HENDAYE, even in its heyday, could never have been as lovely as Varadero. The summer season was over, and the small town was deserted. The hotel where we stayed was right on the beach. The sand was the whitest sand I had ever seen, the water warm and clear, shallow for more than a hundred yards out to sea. In the month of August, the concierge informed me, the wealthy Cuban families anchored their yachts offshore to escape the heat on land during the middle of the day. Now the beach was virtually deserted, as was the hotel dining room where we took our meals. A small band played South American music for the half dozen diners left over from the summer season. The somewhat sad atmosphere of the place amused Slim, gave her a sense of anonymity that she found restful, and she declared that she was pleased that her idea of an escape had worked out so well.

Inevitably we talked a great deal about Papa. She had never been his mistress, she said, as in the early days of their friendship in Sun Valley she had been married to Howard Hawks, whom she described as "a great pillar of nothing." Papa had been married then to Martha Gellhorn, quite a formidable woman in her own right. Slim also told me that the afternoon she had almost shot Papa by accident had been the worst moment in her life; the incident had haunted her for months. Hemingway had never wooed her but had given her to understand that he found her desirable. His was a romantic crush, she said, and quite understandably she had been fascinated by him.

I told her that he had behaved the same way with Jigee, had made her the heroine of his daydreams, but had never made an overt physical advance. Mary had been less jealous at the time, as she and Papa had only recently been married. Mary's decision to have her hair dyed the same color as Slim's was pathetic, we both agreed, and Slim said that she was sad because she realized that she would never be able to visit the Hemingways again, certainly not as a houseguest without Leland.

She was no longer "in love" with her husband, but she adored him and felt an intense loyalty toward him, although with the passage of time their marriage had become a companionate one. Leland was not a well man, she told me; the pressures of the movie business now that he had become a producer were taking its toll on his health. The three children he had had with Margaret Sullavan were another source of worry for him, and Slim was doing her best to be a surrogate mother. She had been annoyed with Papa when he had told her that they must consider the possibility of Leland's dying in the near future, and she had replied that it was a brutal and insensitive thing to say. He had apologized immediately, adding that he contemplated his own death every morning and had done so for quite a few years.

Her life was not an easy one, she told me, which was why she had wanted to relax for a weekend before returning to Manhattan. At her request we ventured out onto the dance floor, although I warned her that dancing was not one of my proudest accomplishments. Nor was it hers, she admitted, as we both did our best to keep time to the complex rhythms of the music. New York seemed thousands of miles away, and so did Havana. We retired to our separate rooms shortly before midnight, until Slim discovered that she had no matches with which to light her last cigarette of the day. And so we became partners in an unplanned betrayal that neither of us regretted, for to the best of my knowledge no one was hurt by our actions.

We flew back to New York, and I stayed on for a couple of days. Hayward had purchased tickets for the World Series games that were to be played at Yankee Stadium, but he was obliged to return to Hollywood before the Series ended, so at his suggestion I escorted Slim to the last game, a dramatic climax that Brooklyn won. I was a Dodger fan, mainly because Brooklyn was the first major league team to employ a black baseball player, and I was delighted that they won. "Papa will be pleased, too," I told Slim as we made our way out of the crowded ballpark that afternoon. "I'm sure he will," she replied, "as long as he never finds out that we went to the game together."

I LEFT FOR CALIFORNIA the next day and moved into my mother's two-room apartment on Veteran Avenue, as she was staying with Jigee in the small house I had helped her buy in the Pacific Palisades. Every morning at ten o'clock, Freddy Zinnemann arrived, and together we cut and edited the screenplay I had written in Biarritz. It was not a difficult job, as he seemed to know exactly what he wanted. No director I had ever worked with had been as well organized and prepared, or as businesslike, and my admiration for Zinnemann increased. In a little less than two weeks we had completed the job.

Freddy suggested we meet for a final reading of the manuscript after it had been retyped, and we were both seated in the living room of my mother's apartment to do so when the doorbell rang. I went to answer it and found myself facing a young man in a gray business suit who asked me to identify myself. Once I had done so, he presented me with a sealed envelope, stating that he was an FBI agent and that the letter, which he demanded I sign a receipt for, was from the headquarters of the U.S. Marine Corps at Camp Pendleton in Oceanside, California. Then he departed.

I was not alarmed until I opened it. U.S. Navy intelligence, I read, was investigating the "loyalty status" of all Marine reserve officers, and in that connection I was being asked to appear in front of a reviewing board in approximately a week. I felt my stomach tightening and returned to my work table opposite Zinnemann. He asked what was wrong and when I told him, he shook his head. "I thought all that was over," he said. "So did I," I replied.

I was well aware of the consequences of an unfavorable verdict of the reviewing board. Any discharge from the reserve short of an honorable one would make it difficult for me to renew my passport. I could also guess how Jack Warner, my present employer, would react to my receiving a "Convenience of the Government Discharge," as he had been one of the most voluble supporters of the committee. I went to see Jigee, and she admitted that for a brief period after the breakup of our marriage she had "gone to a few meetings," but she assured me that she was no longer a member of the Communist Party. She suggested I go to see Martin Gang, a conservative Los Angeles lawyer, who had advised her when she had first been summoned to testify. I knew that Gang was David Selznick's attorney, and since David was a friend, I decided to see him first.

Selznick had always been a staunch Republican, a close friend of Henry and Clare Luce, so a letter from him might well be of some help in establishing my innocence of whatever charges were leveled against me. He agreed to see me that evening and was most sympathetic, but the letter he dictated and that I received the next day was a lukewarm character reference that made no mention of my political past. It was apparent that he didn't want to stick his neck out in anything to do with politics, especially where a branch of the armed services was involved. Fear was still the order of the day in the movie business in 1955, I concluded.

My mother telephoned Larry Beilinson, the Screen Writers Guild lawyer, who was an old personal friend. Although well over draft age, Beilinson, a southerner and a respected member of the community, had served in the U.S. Air Force during the war as an intelligence officer, a record he was justifiably proud of, and he offered at once to accompany me to San Diego for my hearing. "I'll wear my Legion of Merit," he drawled, "and we'll face them together." I thanked him but declined his offer, knowing that an Air Force decoration would not impress the officers at Camp Pendleton.

I then called Henry Hyde in New York. He was a good deal shrewder in his assessment of the situation and said that the presence of a lawyer might well prejudice my case, so it would probably be better for me to face the reviewing board alone. I accepted his advice and on the designated date set out for Camp Pendleton. Jigee came along for moral support. "If we had never met," she remarked with a sad smile, "you would never have gotten into all this trouble."

It was a strange experience driving together through the familiar countryside on a trip we had made so often more than ten years earlier. Much had changed since those early days. Now a freeway bypassed the peaceful towns along the beach. By an unspoken mutual agreement we refrained from talking about the past. We both realized that there was no point in reminiscing and were grateful to have at least remained friends. The only thing that didn't seem to have changed was the Marine Corps. I showed my reserve officer's identification card to the sentry at the gate, was saluted smartly, and was directed to the headquarters building. Jigee wished me luck, and I went inside to face my inquisitors.

Central Casting could not have improved on the appearance of the officers who were to sit in judgment on me. The presiding Marine lieutenant colonel had a chest full of ribbons; I recognized the Silver Star among the rest of the "cabbage" that decorated his green uniform, and I was glad that I had decided not to wear my own greens as Beilinson had suggested I do.

The lieutenant colonel was flanked by a major and a captain, less splendidly decorated. The colonel was a lean, handsome man with closely cropped gray hair, while the two junior officers looked as if they might benefit from a rigorous physical training program. The interrogating officer was a sharp-faced first lieutenant who wore nothing more impressive than his sharpshooter medal and the other tin hardware that was handed out by the Marine Corps' schools at Quantico, my alma mater. In the words of my old buddy and shipmate Gunnery Sergeant Slattery, he was quite obviously a "douche-bag seaman" who had "never heard a shot fired in anger."

Perhaps to make up for his lack of fox hole time, he presented the charges against me in an openly hostile manner that he had presumably only recently learned to adopt in law school. He began by quoting from an article that had appeared in the *Hollywood Reporter* in 1948, prior to the release of *We Were Strangers*, the first movie I had written with John Huston, which I could barely remember at that tense moment. The review stated categorically that the movie was blatant Communist propaganda, that Huston, the director, John Garfield, the male star, and Viertel, the scriptwriter, were all known to be Communist sympathizers, and that the story of the film glamorized the violent overthrow of an established government. I couldn't believe my ears. That an old notice in a trade paper with a doubtful reputation for objectivity could be used as evidence seemed incredible to me.

I said as much. I also explained that the story of the movie was based on the revolt against the Cuban dictator Gerardo Machado, which had been supported by the U.S. State Department, and had certainly not been the result of a Communist conspiracy. Furthermore, I stated that

273

John Huston had never been a Communist and that he had served with great distinction in the U.S. Army Signal Corps in the Aleutians and in Italy. I also denied ever having been a Communist or a Communist sympathizer and stated that I had in actual fact been opposed to any form of totalitarian government since the age of fifteen. The lieutenant then questioned me about Jigee, and I stated that after we were married she had no longer been politically active in any way and that her left-wing sympathies had been motivated by her hatred of fascism, none of which seemed to impress the young man.

He consulted his notes and then asked me about my mother. Was it not true, he inquired, that she had supported a great many left-wing causes and that her home had for years been the meeting place of well-known left-wing dissidents, among them Bertolt Brecht, Hans Eisler, and Charles Chaplin? Realizing that it would be hopeless to explain my mother's political beliefs, which had always been mildly socialistic but had never championed the violent overthrow of any regime, I turned to face the lieutenant colonel. "It seems strange to me, sir," I said in an astonishingly firm voice, "that a Marine officer, with three and a half years of active service in World War II, should be asked to testify against his own mother."

There was a long silence. Then the colonel turned to the first lieutenant and directed him to "desist from that line of questioning." Visibly deflated, the officer collected his notes and sat down. The colonel adjourned the hearing and advised me that I was free to go. On the way out of the room I caught up with him and asked if there would be another hearing. "I hardly think so," he replied. "Anyway, you have nothing to worry about, lieutenant," he added with a smile. The entire proceeding had taken less than an hour.

I STAYED ON in my mother's apartment for another week, waiting for Leland to determine our next move. During the first week of my work with Zinnemann, I had joined Spencer Tracy for dinner a few times, as he had been anxious to know what progress we were making. Then he had gone off rather reluctantly to Colorado to play the part of a mountain guide in a film that was being directed by Edward Dmytryk, so I was astonished when the telephone rang one afternoon and I heard his unmistakable voice asking me if I would like to join him that evening for dinner. I asked him from where he was calling, and he replied: "Colorado." Then he added, "But I'm not going to be here much longer." His words were slurred. He sounded upset. Then abruptly he said, "See you later. At eight o'clock. Chasen's."

"Have you finished the movie?" I asked.

"No, but I'm coming back anyway," he said and hung up.

He sounded as if he had been drinking. He had never been known to walk off a movie set, and as he had not given me a number at which to call him back, I telephoned Bert Allenberg. As usual he was in a meeting. Once he came on the line I told him about Tracy's mysterious telephone call, which I feared might result in big trouble for Spence. He thanked me and assured me that he would call Colorado and if necessary send someone there. He asked me not to mention the matter to Leland Hayward or to Zinnemann, instructions that I followed.

I never found out what Allenberg did, but Tracy stayed in Colorado and completed the film. A few days later Leland called from New York to say he had arranged with Papa to hold a final script conference in Cuba. Hemingway had chartered a large sailing yacht on which we were all to live during the week or ten days of talks, while Papa stayed on board the *Pilar*. It sounded like an impractical locale for a week of work, as living in close quarters on board a medium-sized sailing yacht was difficult enough while on holiday. However, as Leland had agreed to the plan, I realized that it would be useless to cast a negative vote.

To prepare the ground, I was sent ahead to Havana. Leland, Slim, Zinnemann and his wife Renée, as well as Fred's pretty secretary, Pat, were to follow in a few days, all of which I explained to Papa once the usual greetings had been dispensed with. Then he told me of his encounter with the local authorities. Late one afternoon, it seems, two big limousines had pulled up in front of his house and without a word of apology Batista's son had walked into his living room, followed by a couple of bodyguards. "My father says he'll hold up work on the highway until you've finished your movie," the son of the Cuban dictator had informed Hemingway and then had left as abruptly as he had appeared. This was in reference to a new road that threatened to disturb the village location that included Santiago's hut and was, in fact, good news, but Papa was outraged by the unannounced intrusion and bad manners of Batista's son.

He also complained of the many other intrusions on his privacy since his winning the Nobel Prize a year earlier. He was not able to make much headway on the long novel he had asked me to collaborate on years earlier about his part in the early war years in the Caribbean.

Then he asked me about Tracy and whether the actor had lost weight in preparation for his role. A fat Santiago would look ludicrous in the part, he insisted once more.

I told him that I hadn't seen Spence for a while but assumed that he was "in better shape," as he had recently portrayed a mountain guide in a film that had undoubtedly involved considerable physical exertion. In strictest confidence I told him about Tracy's wanting to walk off the set of the movie in Colorado. Papa nodded sympathetically and allowed that anyone who had had a drinking problem in the past could easily be tempted to return to the bottle if he was being forced to do something against his will. He promised not to mention the story to Leland or to Slim and said that he had met Tracy and liked him and, as long as he lost a few pounds, felt that he was the best Santiago the industry had to offer.

Once the main body of our Hollywood contingent had reported for duty, we all were driven down to the Havana Yacht Club and went aboard our assigned craft. Papa, Mary, and Gregorio sailed off in advance on the *Pilar*, and we followed at a somewhat slower pace on the chartered schooner. The Haywards and the Zinnemanns moved into the two main cabins, while Pat, the secretary, and I volunteered to sleep on deck in sleeping bags. Despite our confined quarters, the schooner was comfortable enough, and motoring down the coast to rendezvous with the *Pilar* proved to be a pleasant beginning.

We anchored at sunset in the cove Papa had selected, swam in the refreshingly cool sea, and dined on board the schooner with Papa and Mary. Once Papa and Mary had been rowed back to their powerboat, we all settled down for the night.

I woke up at sunrise, and Slim joined me for a swim before breakfast. We were about to climb up the swimming ladder when we were greeted by a comical sight. A few hundred yards across the placid water, we saw Papa standing in the stern of the *Pilar* urinating over the side, unconscious of our prying eyes. We both laughed, and I explained to Slim that the head on Papa's boat never functioned as well as it should, which was why he was minimizing wear and tear on its pump for more serious needs. We all had breakfast together, and then Freddy, Leland, and I were ferried across to Papa's boat for our first story conference.

Both Leland and Freddy concurred that we should take a united stand in keeping the script to a reasonable length, but once we were seated in the shade of the *Pilar*'s cockpit and refreshments had been served, this resolve appeared to be forgotten. After an hour of discussion it became apparent that Papa wanted to include several passages of his novella that Freddy and I had cut. Taking advantage of my status as favorite son, I argued with him on various points without much success. Freddy supported me in the beginning, but not as firmly as I had hoped he would. Leland abstained from comment, being, I realized later, experienced enough as a producer to know that even if much of the original narration was replaced, it could be deleted later in the cutting room.

Ultimately we arrived at a passage about which Hemingway was even more adamant than he had been earlier. He gritted his teeth and explained that there was "a good deal of poetry" in his original text. I replied rashly that "not being a poet myself, but only the son of a poet," I was well aware of that fact. Papa's blood pressure rose visibly. "Pete," he said, attempting to control his anger, "you don't know what it cost me to use the word *poetry*."

Intimidated by Hemingway's show of bad temper, Freddy and Leland agreed to include the passage that was being discussed, and I apologized for my uncalled-for remark. By the time we concluded the afternoon session, more than twenty pages had been reinstated in the text, even though we were only halfway through the screenplay. While we were being rowed back to our ship, Leland suggested I use a little more "tact" in my arguments with Papa. "You may be right," I replied, "but at this rate we're going to wind up with a movie that's two hours long." I suggested that as Hemingway held Freddy in higher esteem than he did Leland and myself, Zinnemann should carry the ball in all future discussions.

This turned out to be a wise course. In the next morning's session, Zinnemann defended the cuts we had made in California with respectful firmness, Papa was less insistent on including the passages, and by the time we were ready to break for lunch we had gone through the remainder of the screenplay without any further difficulties. Our previous arguments seemed to have been forgotten, and Papa was his old self again, reminiscing about the war in Europe for Slim's benefit.

We were all seated in the stern of the schooner enjoying the late afternoon sun when Slim asked Papa about Capa and mentioned his untimely death. Hemingway repeated the statement he had made to the press at the time, saying that the law of averages had finally caught up with anyone who went repeatedly to war. "I'll tell you about

Capa," he added. "He could never satisfy any of his women, which is why he kept flying from one continent to the other."

I found this to be a needlessly unpleasant remark, all the more so as Capa was dead. "I don't know about his sex life," I said angrily, "but he certainly never left me dissatisfied as a friend."

Hemingway realized that he had said the wrong thing and apologized. Everyone was embarrassed by the tension that had been created, and Papa did his best to smooth things over by telling how Capa's heart had been broken by the death of Gerda Taro during the Spanish Civil War, "the only girl he had probably ever truly loved." I sat in silence while he described how the touring car on whose running board Gerda was riding with Ted Allan, a journalist, was accidentally sideswiped by a Loyalist tank, fatally injuring Gerda. He told how Capa had learned of her death in Paris, where he had gone to sell some of the photographs he and Gerda had taken a few weeks earlier. "They were a couple of idealistic kids," Papa said in conclusion. "They didn't worry too much about getting killed."

I said, "Capa did, that last summer in Biarritz. He knew he couldn't go on risking his life indefinitely."

Hemingway nodded and stared off into the distance. It was quite apparent that he didn't want to go on with the discussion. I realized that Capa's death had upset him more than he wanted to admit. "No talk of casualties in the mess," he said finally, quoting an old British Army saying I had heard him use before. We returned to Havana that evening. The Haywards and the Zinnemanns flew back to New York, while I stayed on at the *finca* until the end of the week. Papa presented me with a copy of a limited edition of *The Old Man and the Sea* before we parted. "For Pete," he wrote on the flyleaf in his clear, methodical hand. "No matter how it will turn out, and it will turn out well."

BUT IT DIDN'T TURN OUT WELL. Zinnemann and Hayward returned to Cuba in the spring of 1956 to begin principal photography, and a few days later Spencer Tracy, accompanied by Katharine Hepburn, arrived. Spence had felt slighted because he had not been asked to join in the final script conferences and, being nervous before taking on a difficult role, he fell briefly off the wagon. Instead of disregarding this lapse of resolve on the part of their star, Papa and Freddy called Spence to task, lecturing him as if he were a truant schoolboy. Kate, who was not in the least bit intimidated by either Hemingway or Zinnemann, sprang to Tracy's defense. It was the first time Spence had started drinking again in more than ten years, she told Hemingway and Zinnemann. Papa then stated that this was far from the truth and, going back on his promise to me, told Kate that he had heard that Tracy had gotten drunk in Colorado on his previous film.

Kate was outraged by what she realized at once had been my indiscretion, so much so that it was almost the end of our long friendship. However, she ultimately forgave me, as did Spence, who toward the end of his life asked her to present me with two of the small watercolors he had painted during his stay in Cuba once she was no longer around to enjoy them, a bequest she informed me of many years later. But at the time her anger was justified, as she felt that I had betrayed Spence.

Many more problems cropped up during the initial weeks of shooting. Hemingway didn't like the boy Leland and Freddy had chosen to play the part of Manolo, who in his opinion looked like "a cross between a tadpole and Anita Loos." Then there was the hand-wrestling sequence, and Zinnemann quite rightly shot it over Tracy's shoulder, as it was a flashback to an incident that had occurred during Santiago's youth. The black man, Santiago's opponent, was photographed in a close-up over the clenched fists of the two contestants, a shot that prompted Jack Warner, after viewing the rushes, to cable Zinnemann that he wasn't paying Tracy a hundred and fifty thousand dollars "just to watch some sweating nigger." He had quite obviously not bothered to read the script or the novel.

It was the straw that broke the camel's back for Zinnemann. He quit the film and flew back to California. John Sturges, who had directed Tracy in *Bad Day at Black Rock*, took over as director of the production, which was soon ordered back to Burbank and finished in a tank with back-projection plates of the Gulf Stream that gave the movie an air of unreality. Hemingway went off to Cabo Blanco in Peru to catch a marlin big enough for use in the sequence in which Santiago's fish jumps after being hooked, but not one of the four marlins that were boated by the expedition weighed over a thousand pounds. So in the end Hayward bought the sixteen-millimeter footage he had seen at an earlier date, and it was included, not very satisfactorily, in the final version.

For the sequence in which Santiago tries to fight off the sharks that ultimately devour his marlin, a rubber fish, baited with meat, was used, having been built by the special effects department in disregard of

Papa's warning that "no movie with a rubber fish ever made a god-damn dime." And in the end he turned out to be right. The film was neither an artistic nor a commercial success. It was not even an honorable defeat, in my opinion, although six months after its release I was notified that I had won the Christopher Award, a gilded disk that arrived in the mail with an accompanying letter stating I had won it for having written a screenplay that had provided that year's "most wholesome entertainment." It is the only award that ever came my way. Ironically, it was stolen from our chalet in Klosters by burglars who were in such a hurry to make off with their booty that they didn't even bother to scratch its surface to make certain it was made of gold.

EDWARD LEGGEWIE, the French college student my mother had hired in the summer of 1935 to teach her older sons "the language of diplomacy," was a serious, pedantic young man who took his duties seriously. Once we had begun to grasp the rudiments of the language, he decided that the best way for us to progress was by introducing us to the wonders of the French classics. It was a subject Hans, my older brother, was not particularly interested in, dedicated as he was at even an early age to the teachings of Marx and Engels. So whenever possible, he skipped our sessions with Edward, and Leggewie and I, forced to spend more time together, established a strong friendship.

Together we read Voltaire's *Candide* as well as Flaubert's *Madame Bovary* and Dumas's *La Dame aux camélias*, the latter of which inspired me with adolescent yearnings for romantic love. Once I went off to college, Edward left my mother's employ and was hired, amazingly enough, by Darryl Zanuck, then vice president in charge of production at 20th Century-Fox. Zanuck was eager to learn French so that he could at least order a meal in the elegant restaurants he frequented on the Côte d'Azur during his summer vacations. Rumor also had it that he had fallen in love with a young French-speaking actress, an even more valid reason for learning the language. Edward was assigned an office near his new boss so that whenever Zanuck had a moment to spare he could converse with his tutor.

Unfortunately, Darryl was fond of practical jokes, with which he occasionally victimized members of his entourage. Inevitably the straight and serious French teacher became the butt of one of these. Leggewie often accompanied Darryl on the morning horseback rides with which he kept himself in shape for polo, a sport that Zanuck had taken up fairly late in life. As a lark, Edward was put on a frisky pony that had already thrown a number of riders and that was well beyond his ability as a horseman. The pony ran away with him and threw him against a tree. He suffered a seriously broken leg that forced him to wear a plaster cast for six months. Zanuck felt contrite at the serious consequences of his prank, and Edward was given a long-term contract with the studio as one of Darryl's assistants. When Zanuck went briefly to the war, he saw to it that his French teacher was commissioned in the Signal Corps, and after VE Day he was made head of the company's production office in Paris, an honorary position more than anything else.

So Edward and I renewed our friendship, initially during the making of *Decision Before Dawn* and later when I continued to use Edward's office as a mailing address. In the meantime Darryl had become something of a Francophile, although his knowledge of the French language was still limited. His mistress, on the other hand, had made better progress with her English. Bayla Wegier was her real name, but to facilitate a possible movie career, Darryl and Virginia, his legal spouse, chose for her the pseudonym Bella Darvi. She was a Polish Jew who had been raised in France, and she was twenty-five years younger than her protector, whose marriage was soon disrupted by the liaison. He decided to move Bella to Paris and thus establish a temporary peace with his wife back in California.

Zanuck had worked hard all of his life, had risen from being a scriptwriter for Rin Tin Tin, a German police dog who was one of the stars of the twenties, to production chief at Warners, after which he formed his own independent company, 20th Century Pictures, which he soon merged with Fox Films. Now having arrived at the dangerous age of fifty and having fallen in love, he wanted to free himself from the demanding duties of running a studio and longed for a bohemian existence sitting in a Paris sidewalk café until it was time to take his pretty mistress to dinner in a fashionable bistro. Let Spyros Skouras, the company's president, run the studio; he, Darryl, felt that he had spent enough of his life in story conferences and projection rooms. He wanted more from the years he had left.

Leggewie became an important factor in this new scheme of things, as he took on the function of private secretary to the ex-tycoon. Edward called me one day in late 1955 to inform me that Darryl was thinking of going to Klosters for the Christmas vacation with Bella. To discuss the available accommodations, Edward suggested that he and I dine with Zanuck. The three of us went to a small bistro on the

Left Bank, and after we had disposed of Zanuck's plans for the holidays, the conversation turned inevitably to the movie business. Zanuck expressed his doubts about the box office potential of *The Old Man and the Sea*, but having produced two other Hemingway films, he was interested in hearing from me if there were any other of Papa's literary properties that could still be purchased.

I made no mention of Papa's sarcastic references to *The Snows of Darryl Zanuck*, his "least favorite movie," but I did suggest that *The Sun Also Rises* could now be brought to the screen, the censorship regulations having relaxed somewhat. Darryl shook his head. "How the hell can you make a story about a guy who can't get it up?" were his exact words. I called his attention to *The Barefoot Contessa*, a recent movie with a similar theme, and Zanuck agreed that perhaps the time had come. He would look into the availability of the rights, he said, and then call me.

He did so two days later. The novel, he told me, had been acquired many years ago by Howard Hawks and Charles Feldman, both of whom "would be difficult to deal with." I informed him that Feldman and Hawks had paid only six thousand dollars for the property, which they had bought from Hadley, as Papa had made a present of the film rights to his first wife at the time of their divorce. Perhaps Feldman, whom I knew to be a close friend of Darryl's, would be content to make a reasonable profit on a book he had not touched for such a long time.

Darryl was doubtful. When it came to business Feldman would not let friendship stand in the way of his venality, he told me, a fact that had been proven often enough in their past dealings. However, as he was about to go to California for a few weeks, he would talk to Feldman and see what could be done.

Not more than ten days later, just as I was preparing to leave for Ireland, Leggewie telephoned to inform me that Darryl had bought the rights to *The Sun Also Rises* and wanted me to report to the studio in Beverly Hills for the initial story conference. Passage on the Air France sleeper flight to New York had been arranged, as well as the connecting flight to Los Angeles. I was amazed at the speed with which Zanuck had acted, and pleased, although slightly concerned about having to work in California. Lazar soon informed me, however, that he had made a deal with 20th Century-Fox for my services and that Darryl would probably have no objections to my writing a treatment and, ultimately, a screenplay in Europe. Recalling Papa's remark that ours was a "transient profession," I packed my bags and set out once again for Orly airport.

The Sun Also Rises, I learned when I reported to the studio, was to be Zanuck's personal project. I was told that the actual writing of the treatment Darryl insisted on as an initial step would not be done in California. He was just as anxious to return to Europe as I was, he confided. I made a halfhearted attempt to avoid writing a treatment by arguing that the book itself could serve as a sufficient guide for a screenplay. It was more a job of cutting and editing than anything else —the dialogue was all there, as was the continuity of events. But Zanuck told me that the studio was insisting that I write a treatment so that "the company" could decide whether they wanted to continue my services on the screenplay. The terms of the deal were generous enough, especially as the money I was to be paid would be earned in Europe, so I agreed to write a treatment.

Although Zanuck had ordered his secretary not to disturb him with any outside calls, Skouras interrupted our discussion several times on the private line that connected him with Zanuck's office. "You can see that it's impossible for us to work here," Darryl told me and wished me a safe journey back to Europe. "I'd like to be going with you, honey," were his parting words as he ushered me out of his office.

Upon my return to the Bel Air Hotel I found a message from David Selznick's office. When I returned the call, his secretary informed me that her boss wanted me to drop by at seven o'clock that evening. I had been in town for only two days, so I found it puzzling that Selznick's office had been able to locate me, but then I realized that Charlie Feldman, undoubtedly privy to Darryl's plans, had kept his other close friend, Selznick, informed.

I packed my one suitcase and set out for Culver City. I hadn't been back to the studio on Washington Boulevard for many years, and arriving in front of the white colonial building brought back many pleasant memories. I stopped to say hello to my old friends, the telephone operators who had never failed to track me down at the Westside Tennis Club whenever I had been summoned, and Cecil Barker, who had been a messenger boy while I had been a filing clerk in the story department. He was now Selznick's personal assistant, and we reminisced briefly while I waited to be admitted to David's inner sanctum.

The same framed photographs were still on the wall, glossy close-ups of Selznick's "stock company": Ingrid Bergman, Gregory Peck,

Joseph Cotten, Alida Valli, and Vivien Leigh. I asked Barker what had prompted his boss to summon me, and he replied: "Beats the shit out of me, lieutenant," one of our favorite wartime phrases. Then Frances, Selznick's loyal executive secretary, informed me that "*he*" was waiting for me and that I should go in.

David was nearly fifty-four years old at the time, I realize now, the same age as Zanuck, and yet he looked tired and world-weary. Like Darryl, success had come early in his life. At the age of thirty-seven he had produced *Gone With the Wind* for his own independent company, the biggest box office hit of all time. To secure the services of Clark Gable for the leading role, he had been forced to cede fifty percent of the profits of the movie to MGM, the company his father-in-law, Louis B. Mayer, had presided over. His share of the profits would have made him a multimillionaire, had he not heeded the advice to sell his percentage of the profits for a million dollars to realize a capital gain. Martin Gang had been his lawyer at the time, and following his advice had probably been the most costly business mistake ever made in the motion picture industry. Had Selznick held on to his "points," as they are called now, he and his company could have flourished for many years.

He had divorced Irene Mayer to marry Jennifer Jones in the late 1940s and had concentrated most of his energies on his young wife's career in the years that followed, a course that had undoubtedly contributed to his decline in the business. But more than his second marriage, his desire to repeat the enormous success of *Gone With the Wind* had crippled his actions. Although he was still thought of as a man with great taste and considerable ability, his reputation as a producer had diminished. All he needed was one more big hit to rehabilitate him, a hope that he was as conscious of as anyone in Hollywood.

"I thought that maybe you'd like to come work for me," he suggested after he had asked after my mother's health and my own well-being. He had several stories he wanted to discuss with me, he said, foremost among them *Tender Is the Night*, the Scott Fitzgerald novel he had been considering for quite a few years, which he still believed would make a good vehicle for Jennifer.

I didn't say anything, but it was clear to me that he was seeking a new beginning for himself, the "second chance" that Scott Fitzgerald had written was never forthcoming. Yet I was flattered by his offer and touched by his affectionate memory.

I replied that I was sorry, but that I had that very afternoon made a deal with Zanuck to write an adaptation of *The Sun Also Rises* and was on my way back to Europe to begin work. He nodded pensively and said that he regretted that he had come too late with his offer. The early Hemingway novel was a good assignment, he stated, and one I certainly should not try to back out of, although he felt Darryl was perhaps not the right producer for the project. "Well, once you've finished with that one we can still get together," he said. "Jennifer is fond of you and so am I, and it would be fun to work together." He told me to be sure to call him the next time I came to California, which I promised to do. It was a brief meeting that was to have serious repercussions a few months later.

ON THAT FRIDAY MORNING, back in Paris, I was told there was only one seat available on the direct flight to Dublin, a service operated by Aer Lingus twice a week. Having arrived a little late at Orly airport I was grateful that the man on the desk had not given my seat away, and I was the last passenger to be led into the narrow forward cabin on the DC3 before takeoff. Relieved not to have missed the flight, I stowed my trench coat into the overhead locker and settled into the aisle seat, only to discover that Aly Khan was to be my companion on the two-hour journey.

He was reading a newspaper, and he looked up and acknowledged my presence with a polite smile. We shook hands. We had met a few times at Judy Garland and Sid Luft's house in Beverly Hills, and Khan asked after them before returning to his study of the racing fixtures in the back of the paper. Then lunch was served, and conversation became unavoidable. He asked me why I was traveling to Ireland, and I told him I was going for a little hunting in Kildare. He agreed that it was a wonderful sport and said he had enjoyed it in the past but had had to give it up because of a back injury incurred while steeplechasing.

He seemed relaxed and friendly, and rather hesitantly I asked him if he would be kind enough to give a message to Bettina. He stiffened visibly, but I continued nevertheless and told him that I still had a small amount of her money that I had deposited for her in a savings account in Switzerland and that I had been unable to reach her to settle the matter. He replied that he was sorry, but he had made it a rule never to interfere in the private affairs of his friends, and we resumed an awkward silence. I felt like a fool for having mentioned Bettina's name, and once we arrived in Dublin he said a hasty good-bye and hurried off down the narrow center aisle of the aircraft. I caught a last glimpse of my onetime rival as I stood waiting to reclaim my luggage. Being a prince, he had none, needless to say, and I watched him somewhat enviously as he got into the back of a green Humber estate car and was driven off by a uniformed chauffeur. I had seen the large country house with its lovely grounds toward which I knew he was being driven, while I would have to wait in the rain for the car rental people to deliver the VW Beetle I had rented for my month's stay at Mount Armstrong.

Our encounter had been nothing like Papa's handwritten, humorous fantasy of "the Khan" and I meeting eyeball to eyeball in no-man's-land somewhere in Israel. It would have cost him very little, it seemed to me, to say, Yes, I'll give Bettina the message. Six months earlier she had sent back the small presents I had given her during the years we had been together, all assembled in a white cardboard shoe box and delivered to the Hotel Montaigne by a dark-skinned servant, an act that had prompted me to write a foolish letter in which I said that I had only now realized how little I had given her in return for all she had given me. But at that moment the wound she had inflicted still smarted, and even burned, as I hadn't realized that her desertion was my own fault, which is the sort of thing you often learn too late.

ISHMAEL WAS WAITING FOR ME, as were the green fields of Kildare and the bogs of Galway. Ricki Huston and the children were in residence at Courtown House, while John was off "filming," the term the locals applied to what they surely considered to be a very strange profession. Betty O'Kelly had by this time taken over as a paid stud groom, a job that also involved her running the big house while Ricki busied herself with furnishing her future residence, the small stone cottage that stood in a corner of the stableyard at St. Clerans.

Knowing that it would be a lonely Christmas, I had invited Liz Taylor and Michael Wilding to spend the holidays with me at Mount Armstrong. A couple of weeks before the holidays were to start, I telephoned Wilding in London to ask if he and Liz were really coming. He sounded subdued but assured me that he would definitely be arriving at midday on the twenty-fourth of December and even gave me his flight number. However, he said he wasn't sure Liz would be able to make it, so I was not surprised when he turned up alone at Dublin airport when I picked him up.

He was not in the best of spirits. Liz had gone off with Victor

Mature, he informed me, adding sadly that he reckoned their marriage was approaching its end. I tried to cheer him up with the usual clichés, among them that being abandoned was not the worst thing that could happen to a man, although I realized that his predicament was much more serious than mine, as he and Liz had two children. However he was amazingly controlled under the circumstances, said that he was still very fond of Liz and felt certain they would remain friends. He added that he was glad to have been given an opportunity to leave London and hoped I had "laid on" a few social events during the holidays so that we would not sit alone together in an Irish country house.

I had been invited to dine that evening by Oona Oranmore and Browne at her small castle, Lugala, in County Wicklow, a reformed shooting lodge her grandfather had built on a lake surrounded by gorse-covered hills. Oona was a Guinness by birth, a slight, blond woman in early middle age that I had met through John Huston. Lord Oranmore and Browne, her Irish husband, had abandoned her some years before, and she now lived most of the year with her young son in the whitewashed castle that stood in almost dreamlike romantic sur-roundings in this remote valley. Her only daughter had drowned in the lake one summer, and Oona had built a small stone pantheon among the reeds at the water's edge, which increased the melancholy atmosphere of her remote hideaway.

Fearing that the dinner party might not turn out to be an altogether cheerful event, I had told Oona that I would let her know if I was coming as soon as my houseguests had arrived, an impolite delaying action that she had accepted quite happily. I now broached the subject with Michael, and he said that by all means we should go, as appar-ently it was "the only game in town."

Not quite certain that I would find my way through the hills of Wicklow, we changed into our dinner jackets as soon as Michael un-packed and set off in my rented VW. I have never had a very good sense of direction, and as I had been to Oona's home on only one previous occasion, we were soon hopelessly lost and did not arrive at our destination until nine o'clock. The moon was out by that time, the night cold and frosty, and our first view of the minute white castle on the edge of the shimmering lake revived our spirits. His first visit to Ireland, Michael assured me, was already more than he could have hoped for.

We were the last of a dozen or so guests to arrive, I realized as we were led into the musty, candle-lit living room by a stern footman. Our hostess, in a flowing, diaphanous evening gown, saw to the introductions that were indeed necessary. Her son, Tara, who was about ten years old, was wearing a pale green jacket with a bright red bow tie that fell generously down his white shirt front. He wore his blond hair in the manner of a young Napoleon Bonaparte, a barber shop apparently not having been on his agenda for quite some time.

I recognized the last member of the party to be introduced as Brendan Behan, the Irish playwright. As our introductions ended with him, I took the opportunity to compliment him on his work, words of praise he barely acknowledged, for he had already fortified himself with several glasses of champagne punch. His round face and bulging stomach reflected a good deal of Christmas cheer, and before dinner was announced he raised his glass in a predinner toast that seemed a little out of place. "Up the rebels!" he intoned, and we were led forthwith into the dining room by our hostess.

The large oval table glittered with all the finery of the house— crystal wineglasses and sterling silver pheasants, as well as gold-rimmed plates. Michael and I were seated on either side of Oona, while Behan took his place opposite her in the chair that normally would have been occupied by her absent husband. I recall the meal as being excellent, a bisque d'hommard followed by pheasant. There was red wine and pink champagne, served generously by a red-faced houseboy wearing white gloves. The toasts offered by the various guests began once the soup had been dispensed with and included the mandatory "Merry Christmas" as well as the by now familiar "Up the rebels," which Brendan Behan repeated at least half a dozen times.

I don't remember much about the subjects of conversation during the lengthy meal; it was mostly small talk about absent friends such as the Hustons, all of it constantly interrupted by Behan's endless toasts, which became less intelligible as his input of alcohol increased. But I remember vividly that after dessert was served, he rose unsteadily to his feet and, swaying slightly, raised his glass in the direction of our hostess. "To her ladyship!" he roared. "God bless her!" and fell forward onto the table, which gave way under his weight with a tinkling of breaking glass and a jingle of antique sterling silver.

Oona said, "Oh, dear," as if someone had spilled a teaspoonful of salt, rose from the debris in front of her, and suggested that it was "time for us to move back into the drawing room." Two of the sturdier gentlemen guests lifted the eminent playwright from where he had fallen and carried him into the adjoining chamber, where they deposited him, breathing heavily, on an ancient sofa. Michael, I noticed, had escorted our hostess to where coffee was being served along with brandy and cigars. They had apparently discovered a mutual liking, based perhaps on the empathy of the discarded, and it was two o'clock in the morning before I could persuade him that we had better be on our way across the icy roads.

Far from sober, he mumbled that Oona had suggested we spend the night, an invitation I firmly vetoed, feeling like a spoilsport. It was nearly four o'clock in the morning when we arrived back at Mount Armstrong. Michael had slept soundly during the long drive, and before we wished each other good night, he confided in me that he had found Lady Oranmore and Browne to be "a most attractive woman in a sort of beaten-up way." I realized then that his broken heart was on the mend and that the onetime lover of Marlene Dietrich and Elizabeth Taylor was ready for more.

The telephone woke me out of a sound sleep a scant four hours later. Betty O'Kelly was on the line from Courtown House, sounding desperate. We must come over to the Hustons' at once, she said; it was an emergency. I asked her if she realized that it was Christmas morning, but she was in no mood for pleasantries. I told her that the soonest my houseguest and I could arrive was in forty-five minutes and staggered into Michael's bedroom to inform him that he must get ready for another social function in a matter of minutes. Then I got dressed and, with my dazed friend beside me, drove the four miles that separated the two farms. It was a bright morning. The sun was melting the frosty dew on the green fields on both sides of the narrow road. Perfect weather for an Irish Christmas.

Betty came bounding down the concrete steps as we pulled up in front of the big gray house. All hell had broken loose, she informed me in a guarded voice. John and Ricki had had a "monumental row" brought on by his discovery that Aly Khan had given her an expensive piece of jewelry for Christmas. He had beaten her with his malacca cane, Betty informed me, which I took to be an Irish exaggeration. Michael and I followed her into the library where the Christmas tree had been set up some days ago. There we encountered Sy Bartlett, a screenwriter friend of John's, along with Nan Sunderland, Walter Huston's widow.

The Huston children, Tony and Anjelica, were busy opening their presents. Tony had had a bad fall from his pony a fortnight earlier, and his head was still heavily bandaged. This did not seem to bother him too much, as he was at that moment playing with a miniature helicopter Sy Bartlett had brought along from California as a Christmas present. The thing made a loud noise as its new owner put it through its paces. After a few minutes a gangling thirteen-year-old boy came into the room and was introduced as David, the son of Ann Woodward, of shotgun fame, who had been invited for the Yule weekend. We were served Tom and Jerrys, hardly the drink I would have chosen to take the place of my customary, early morning orange juice, but I did feel in need of sustenance.

Then John appeared, dressed in pajamas and a robe. He mumbled a tense "Good morning." His right eye was partly closed by what can only be described as a fantastic shiner. I said, "Merry Christmas, John," and he replied, "Yeah, Merry Christmas, kid," with marked sarcasm. "What the hell happened to you?" I asked him. "Did you run into a doorknob?" He glared at me, unhappy with my attempt at humor. "No, my wife" was his curt answer. Then, as if on cue in a Feydeau farce, Ricki made her entrance. She was dressed in beige jodhpurs and a yellow hunting shirt, and although her face was unusually pale, there were no other telltale marks on her except a slightly swollen right hand that she showed me discreetly once we had moved into a quiet corner of the large room.

John lowered himself into his favorite armchair and sat holding his right eye with his right hand while the toy helicopter swooped around the Christmas tree. Huston observed its flight with a dazed expression but, conscious of his role as father on this important day, did not ask his son to desist from playing with his new toy. Betty put on a record, thinking that the music of Christmas carols might counteract the jarring noise of the small aircraft. After a short while John got up, excused himself, and went upstairs to his bedroom, leaving the happy sounds of family life behind him.

Michael Wilding grasped my elbow and asked if there was any chance "of our signing up Mrs. Huston to face the present welterweight champion of the world." "With a right hand like that she could make us both rich," he said. I was about to reply when Creagh the butler came over to inform me that "Mr. Hooston would like to see you upstairs."

I found my old friend stretched out on his bed. A maid had supplied him with an icebag, which he held to his injured eye. "What can I do for you?" I asked him. "Nothing, really," he replied. "Just get her out

290

of here. Right now, this minute." "You can't do that, John," I told him. "It's Christmas, for God's sake." He looked up at me with a crooked grin. "You're right, I guess, kid," he said. Then abruptly his sense of humor returned. "You know, I've always wanted to do a movie about a Christmas like this . . . when everything goes wrong, and finally the house catches fire, and the grandmother leaps out of a second-story window to avoid the flames. A total disaster like this one." He started to laugh, but it hurt his wounded eye, so he stopped.

"Just rest for a while," I advised him. "By lunchtime you'll be feeling a lot better." He nodded. "Okay," he said, "I'll see you in a couple of hours."

I drew the curtains to shut out the bright sunlight. Then I crossed back to his bed. Not without malice, I suppose, but also to sustain his improved mood, I said: "John, you're not going to like what I'm about to say . . . but Aly is really one swell guy."

He grunted, then closed his eyes. To this day I don't know if he had heard me.

THE NEXT DAY I started to work on the treatment of *The Sun Also Rises*, and the problems inherent in the material immediately became apparent. The first half of the novel is about Jake, the storyteller's infatuation with Lady Brett Ashley, and the fact that he is physically unable to be her lover. I recalled Robert Sherwood's maxim, contained in a memorandum to David Selznick while Sherwood was working on the screenplay of *Gone With the Wind*, that the prerequisite for a great love story is that both parties be equally in love with each other and be kept apart by an insurmountable obstacle, a requirement that was met in Book I of Hemingway's novel.

But in Book II, once Jake and his friends have arrived in Pamplona, he seems to have gotten over his infatuation. Brett has had an affair with Robert Cohn, a man Jake has come to despise, and he sees her now in her true light, a lost soul who is unable to deal with her sexual appetite. The love story, the reader is told, has ended. "Say," Bill Gorton asks Jake, "what about this Brett business?"

"What about it?"

"Were you ever in love with her?"

"Sure."

"For how long?"

"Off and on for a hell of a long time."

"Oh, hell," Bill says. "I'm sorry, fella."

"It's all right," Jake says. "I don't give a damn anymore." And he becomes an observer for the rest of the story, no longer deeply involved with the promiscuous heroine, but rather her friend in need, not even tormented by his physical inability to consummate their relationship. This change in the hero's attitude greatly complicated the film treatment I was attempting to write. Not until the very end of the novel is there a romantic scene between Jake and Brett, and even then his acquired cynicism shows him to be a detached storyteller.

"Oh, Jake," Brett says, as they ride down the Gran Via of Madrid in a taxi, "we could have had such a damned good time together."

"Yes," Jake replies. "Isn't it pretty to think so?"

It seemed doubtful to me that this ending would satisfy a movie audience, but there was a sharp reality about those words that was moving as well as apt as an adult conclusion that I, for one, was not inclined to tamper with. All this was not a concern I felt I could share with Zanuck when we met in Klosters in the first week of January, as it might prompt him to ask me to change the entire structure of the novel, the end result of which would again offend Papa.

Darryl had decided to spend Christmas with his wife in California and now he was due to arrive in Klosters for a week of skiing with Bella Darvi. I had traveled there from Ireland to meet with him about the treatment, which I had already sent him. I called him at the hotel where he was staying as soon as he arrived from Paris, and he told me that he needed to rest for a day before starting our story conferences. He wanted to get acclimatized and would spend the afternoon shopping with Bella for the clothes she would need for her stay in the mountains. He called again later in the day and asked me to join him for a walk. Bella was taking a nap, he informed me before launching himself into a brief critique of my treatment, which he had found satisfactory enough for us to proceed to the next step, the writing of the screenplay.

Then he went on to tell me that the day after my departure from California he had received a call from David Selznick that had astonished him considerably: 20th Century-Fox had been negotiating with Selznick for the services of Gregory Peck, who was under exclusive contract to David, because Skouras wanted Peck for the lead in *The Man in the Gray Flannel Suit*.

David, who had been reluctant to release Peck, had then suggested that he would agree to loan out his star provided Zanuck promised to cast Jennifer Jones as Lady Brett in *The Sun Also Rises*. "He had me over a barrel," Darryl said, "so I agreed."

I was outraged by David's double-dealing. "She's wrong for the part," I said. "Lady Brett should be played by an English actress. Jennifer is a nervous, sensitive woman, the opposite of Lady Brett, who is debonair, sophisticated, and amoral."

Zanuck listened to my objections and shrugged. "Well, I'm afraid we're stuck with her," he said. "Anyway, she's a competent actress."

"I know all that," I replied. "And she's a friend of mine as well. But she's still wrong for the part."

"Let's not worry about all that," Darryl said. "The main thing right now is for us to get a good script. We won't be making this thing for at least six months. A lot can happen in that time."

I was not reassured, but we made plans for skiing together the next day, and I walked him back to his hotel. It amazed me that after having acquired the novel for a hundred and fifty thousand dollars, Zanuck would allow Selznick to maneuver him into giving away a most desirable role that many actresses would undoubtedly be eager to play.

I called him in the morning at the agreed-upon time and was told by the concierge that Mr. Zanuck had left the hotel and would return in half an hour. When he finally called me two hours later, he sounded agitated and upset. He and Bella had had a violent quarrel, and he had just taken her to the railroad station and put her on the train for Zurich and the airport, as she was returning to Paris. We lunched together, and throughout the meal he talked only about his personal problems with his mistress. Their relationship, he confided, was hopeless, but he was still very much in love and therefore victimized by Bella's moods and tantrums.

"I'm like Jake in our story," he said. "I can turn this thing every way but loose."

"Fortunately your problem is a little different," I told him.

"It amounts to the same thing," he replied gloomily.

Despite his being thoroughly upset, he insisted we go skiing. His car and chauffeur had arrived from Paris, and we were driven in style to Davos, where we took a cable car to the top of one of the local mountains. With a fresh cigar clenched in his teeth, he tried to join me on a T-bar lift, but in his unhappy frame of mind, he put one of his skis across mine and I fell—and then lay watching him get dragged fifty yards up the slope. The steel edge of one of his skis had cut my hand, and after the necessary bandages had been applied, we finally got on the lift. The rest of the afternoon turned out to be as disastrous as our start. Darryl took at least half a dozen serious falls, and after he survived our first long run he decided that his skiing days were over.

Ostensibly to continue our work, he stayed on in Klosters for the remainder of the week, although I knew that his real reason for not returning to Paris was his not wanting to follow Bella and thereby admit his dependence on her. He reread my treatment and took long, lonely walks through the village and the snowy countryside, after which we would discuss "our story."

The main problem was to clarify why the hero was unable to make love to Lady Brett. I told Zanuck that Papa had told me on several occasions that Jake's impotence had been caused by "his cock being shot off," a difficult plot point to make under the existing censorship restrictions. The scene in the novel when Jake looks at his naked body in a mirror and muses on his wound would obviously not pass the Breen Office, so Darryl suggested we use a flashback to a hospital in Milan, which I ultimately agreed to, although it was not in the original text. If the audience was led to believe that his impotence was not physical but psychological, it would suggest that he could recover, which was an even more serious violation of the original material. As it turned out, we were never really able to solve this problem, as the scene in the hospital proved not to be specific enough.

In *The Barefoot Contessa* Joe Mankiewicz had his protagonist say, "I can love you only with my heart," a line of dialogue that was usually greeted with howls of laughter by the audience, so verbalizing Jake's condition was out of the question. I suggested that it would be best to leave the reason for Jake's impotence as vague as Hemingway had left it in the book, and Darryl agreed that for the time being we might as well follow that course. "We have plenty of time to decide what to do," he said and, as preoccupied with his personal problems as he had been from the start, he departed for Paris. I was to join him there in a couple of weeks, by which time the studio would have exercised the option on my services.

Curiously enough, not long after he left Klosters David Selznick and Jennifer Jones arrived for a brief stay. I was seated next to Jennifer at dinner the first night, and at the beginning of the meal she turned to me and said: "You don't think I'm right for the part of Lady Brett, do you?" It was an awkward moment. I mumbled that she had acccptcd to play the role, had she not, and she didn't reply. However I sensed a certain coolness on her part toward me, which I regretted.

When I arrived in Paris Darryl suggested I move into the Hotel Raphaël, where he was staying, and assured me that the company would take care of my expenses while I was working on the script. One afternoon we were seated in the living room of Darryl's suite when Charlie Feldman dropped in. He asked how the script was going and whcn Darryl was planning to start the movie. Suddenly Zanuck turned to him and said: "Peter doesn't feel Jennifer Jones is the right girl for the part." Feldman said that he knew all about that and had already discussed the matter with Selznick. "You can probably get out of the commitment," he told Zanuck, who excused himself at that moment to take a call from California.

"Why the hell did you make me the heavy?" I asked Charlie when we were alone. "I'm only the writer."

"Well, I do a lot of business with Darryl and David, and I don't do any business with you, pal," Fcldman replied with a false smile.

IN THOSE DAYS the Raphaël was a rather staid establishment, more discreet than the George V or the Plaza-Athénée, the hotels usually chosen by "picture people." Darryl informed me that he preferred to live there so as not to be constantly accosted by "characters looking for a deal." Its bar was a small, unglamorous place at the rear of the lobby, rarely used by the residents, who were mostly wealthy old ladies and serious French businessmen. The manager was an elderly Milanese with a club foot, as courteous in his manner as was the rest of the staff, Dominique, the Italian barman, and the wonderfully efficient Alsatian concierge.

The chestnut trees were in full bloom, and the last few scenes of my screenplay were in the hands of the typist. A difficulty I had not anticipated was the dialogue. Highly stylized, it was compelling to read but would, it seemed to me, sound affected coming out of the mouths of actors. Many of Jake's lines had a British sound, as if the character in the novel was being influenced by the speech patterns of his English friends. Very carefully I altered them, attempting not to disturb the economic use of words of the original text.

Darryl had come to a parting of the ways once again with Bella, and his personal crisis seemed to occupy all of his thoughts. During our working hours he was distracted and less adamant about the changes he required, although I was forced to give in on several important points. Yet the final result seemed like a reasonable adaptation of Papa's novel. The only words in the text that caused Darryl to be unreasonably angry were used to describe the prostitute Jake picks up and takes to the "dancing" in Montmartre. In the novel Jake describes the girl as having bad teeth, a line I incorporated in the directions. To my amazement, Darryl found it to be objectionable. I deleted the phrase with a stroke of my pencil, but Darryl raged on for at least ten minutes. Later Leggewie informed me that any reference to bad teeth always "made the boss's blood boil," an idiosyncrasy that Zanuck was prone to, as his own dentures were far from perfect.

Ultimately Darryl was forced to return to California, as things at the studio were "in turmoil," now that Skouras was in charge, and Edward and I drove him to the airport in Edward's small car. He appeared to be in an aggressive mood. "When will you be back?" I asked him, and he replied that he wasn't sure but that I should stay on at the Raphaël until further notice at the studio's expense.

"What about Miss Darvi?" Leggewie asked.

"I told you, it's all over!" Darryl shouted. "I'm a free man."

"Until she does like this," Leggewie said, crooking his forefinger, the only time I ever heard him make light of his boss's personal problems.

"I am no longer carrying a torch, and that's final," Darryl said angrily, but he had the good grace to laugh.

PARIS WITHOUT BETTINA and without work was dispiriting, even though I was living in unaccustomed comfort. The weeks passed slowly and there was no word from Zanuck. The *feria* of San Fermín in Pamplona was only six weeks away, and as far as I knew no plans had been made to start filming. Then Darryl returned. A lot had happened in California, he explained: he had abdicated his post as vice president in charge of production and was now forced to obey the orders of Spyros Skouras. This would have a drastic effect on his plan for the production of *The Sun Also Rises*. Jean Negulesco had recently completed *Boy on a Dolphin*, which had been filmed on location in Greece and had exceeded its budget, so Skouras had decreed that the company would never again shoot a movie in Europe. *The Sun Also Rises* would be shot in Mexico.

I pointed out to Darryl that Mexico was nothing like the north of Spain—the architecture and the people were totally different—and that much of the originality and impact of the Hemingway novel depended on its locale. But he brushed my objections aside. A second unit, he informed me, would be arriving in Pamplona at the end of June to shoot background footage at the *feria*, and principal photography would take place in Morelia, Michoacán, next spring. The art department would see to it that the Mexican locales matched the footage shot in Pamplona, and he was confident they would do a good job.

In the meantime, he declared, we would concentrate on finding a director and casting the right actors for the principal roles. I suggested Fred Zinnemann, Darryl agreed, and a copy of the screenplay was sent to him in California. A few weeks later Zinnemann agreed to direct, depending on the casting of the role of Lady Brett. As Jennifer Jones had decided to withdraw from the cast, Freddy wanted Audrey Hepburn for the part, which was a bold and interesting suggestion as it would be a great change of pace for this young actress, just as his casting of Deborah Kerr for the lead in *From Here to Eternity* had been an original choice. But unfortunately Audrey turned down the role, which she felt would be bad for her image. Zinnemann forthwith declined to take over the direction of the story, and Zanuck was forced to look elsewhere.

I had good reason to believe that Freddy was worried about working with Zanuck, for he said as much to me on the telephone prior to Audrey's turning down the part. His apprehension was probably why he would not consider another actress for the role. His agent informed Darryl that Zinnemann's decision was final, so Darryl turned his attention to the casting of Lady Brett. To my amazement he suggested Marilyn Monroe, who was under contract to Fox. I thought he was joking at first, but I soon realized that he was serious. I argued that Marilyn was the very antithesis of the character in the Hemingway novel, that even Ava Gardner would be more believable, although she too was anything but an upper-class Englishwoman.

Darryl liked the idea of casting Ava, and a copy of the screenplay was sent to her in Madrid. He then decided that to placate Skouras, we should take a director who was under contract to the studio; although he was not a great admirer of his work, he suggested Henry King. Knowing that King had directed *The Snows of Kilimanjaro*, I voiced concern, but Zanuck was firm in his decision. King would do a more than adequate job, he told me, adding, "You and I will be there, too, honey, and at least Henry is not a difficult fellow to get along with. He'll listen to what we have to say."

Fairly discouraged about his choice of a director, I realized that there was very little I could do to change Darryl's mind. The next issue to be decided was the casting of Jake, and I suggested Henry Fonda. "Fonda has no sex appeal," Zanuck stated didactically. "The women will stay away in droves if we take him." I pointed out that they hadn't stayed away in droves from *The Grapes of Wrath*, one of the best movies Darryl had ever made, but my words fell on deaf ears. "Ty Power can play the hell out of it," he said. "He's a damn good actor. And he owes us a couple more movies." I tried to point out that Ty, in his mid-forties, was too old for the part. "He's eight years younger than Fonda," I was told.

The following morning Darryl summoned me to his suite and told me that he had had a brilliant idea during the night; he wanted to cast Errol Flynn for the part of Mike Campbell. Flynn's career as a leading man had come to an end, and Zanuck felt certain he would accept a feature role. In the same age category, Zanuck decided to offer the role of Bill Gordon to Eddie Albert, less of a departure for an actor who was often used to portray the sympathetic pal of the leading man. The group would be made up of men who were all middle-aged, a far cry from the characters in the novel, who were recent survivors of the First World War. Only Ava's age would correspond exactly with the age of the heroine in the novel. To complete the cast, Darryl said he was going to ask Mel Ferrer to play Robert Cohn. In Zanuck's opinion Ferrer had just the right quality of injured innocence that the role required as well as the ability to project a slightly smug superiority. Mel would be fairly expensive, but Darryl declared he was ready to pay his price to get him.

The casting having been dispensed with for the moment, we prepared to set out for Biarritz, and from there to Pamplona. Dickie Zanuck, Darryl's only son, would be joining us, which in his father's opinion was certain to be a profitable experience, as Dick was planning to follow in Darryl's footsteps. I had met the son and heir briefly in California and had found him to be an exuberant young man full of enthusiasm for tennis and surfing, as well as passionately interested in making movies. I was delighted he would be along.

While still in California I had told Dickie that the waves in Biarritz looked to me to be ideally suited for surfing, a sport that he had become an expert at, and now that he was to be included in the second unit he informed me on the telephone that he would try to smuggle a surfboard into the equipment that was being sent over for the shoot. When he arrived in Paris he confided in me that he had accomplished his secret mission. He promised that on our way back from the location he would introduce me to a sport that "would keep me away from the typewriter" for much of my spare time, a prophecy that turned out to be alarmingly accurate.

While his father was busy telephoning Paris and London, Dick and I visited the beaches of Biarritz on our way to Spain, and he confirmed my opinion that the waves were perfect for the secret plan we had in mind. We arrived in Pamplona on the fourth of July and spent the next two days looking over possible sites for the filming of background material. The town was still calm before the *feria*, and we visited the old quarter with its narrow streets that had not changed very much since Hemingway's first visit. I tried once again to convince Darryl of the folly of trying to create its atmosphere in Mexico, but he was confident that our story would not suffer.

Pamplona exploded like a time bomb as it does annually on the seventh of July. The crowds, the bands, the thousands of celebrants were as impressive as they had been on my previous visits, and both Darryl and Dickie succumbed to the wild atmosphere. The local government was most cooperative in allowing the camera crews to film the events of that week. A wooden platform was constructed over the entrance of the bullring, and the unit was able to get excellent footage of the *encierro*, the running of the bulls, which took place every morning, and to photograph the bullfights that followed in the late afternoon. Darryl departed for Paris after the second day of the *feria*, while Dick and I stayed on until the end.

For once the weather collaborated with the moviemakers; rain did not arrive until the last day. The only disruption of our plans came with a telegram that arrived for Dick from his father, ordering him home via Madrid, so we were forced to cancel our surfing holiday. However, before leaving he saw to it that his surfboard was dropped off in Biarritz by the unit manager, for me to use during what remained of the summer. This bit of bad news helped provide the crash that was inevitable after the high of the *feria*, and, like Jake and his group, we said our sad good-byes, and I returned to Paris.

THE FOUR PRINCIPAL ACTORS Darryl had chosen—Tyrone Power, Errol Flynn, Eddie Albert, and Mel Ferrer—were soon signed and given a starting date. Ava Gardner was still hesitating, but she ultimately decided to accept the role of Lady Brett. The only part still to be cast was that of Pedro Romero, the young matador Brett goes off with at the end of the *feria*. I urged Darryl to look for a profes-sional torero to play this crucial role, as it involved only one short dialogue scene in English. A dialogue coach, I felt confident, would be able to make the performance of a nonactor convincing, and this would avoid our having to find a double for the bullfight sequence. (Luis Miguel spoke enough English to play the one scene in the script, but he was too old for the part and lacked the naive quality that was essential to make his performance convincing.)

Zanuck listened patiently to my arguments but remained dubious. There was still plenty of time to choose the right man, he said, and in his experience he had always found it better to use professional actors than rely on the doubtful ability of amateurs. For the time being he was satisfied that we had an excellent cast and that the script was as "nearly right" as we could make it. "I want you to keep yourself free for a few months next spring," he said, "because I'll need you in Mexico. On salary, of course," he added.

I agreed, and we shook hands. He seemed nervous, distracted, not as friendly as he had been at our partings in the past. Leggewie joined us. He, too, seemed more serious than usual. "Everything all right with you, Darryl?" I asked.

He nodded and lit a fresh cigar. He was dressed in his pajama top and a dressing gown, although it was well past midday. The telephone rang, and he went into his bedroom to answer it. I asked Leggewie what was troubling "the boss."

"He's getting a lot of static from California. From the family in Palm Springs."

"And Bella?"

"They're back together for the moment. But it won't last. The company will take care of your hotel bill until the end of the week," he added.

"Say good-bye for me," I told him, "in case I don't get a chance to," and went back to my room.

I experienced the usual letdown that comes after a job has been completed. I had made no plans for the summer, and although I knew that I should go to Klosters, I didn't feel much like it. I had three days to pack up my belongings and make a decision, so I postponed think-ing about it. Then the telephone rang. It was Dominguín, calling from Madrid. He told me that he had decided to come out of retirement but was planning to fight only twenty times during the current season in Spain and then go to South America for three *corridas*, as he had

had an offer from Colombia that he felt he could not refuse. "And you?" he asked. "*¿Qué tal tu vida?*"

I told him that I had just finished a job, and was trying to make up my mind what to do next.

"You come with me," he said in English.

"I have to work," I told him.

"You never work," he said. "You have a little black man to do all of your writing. Don't try to fool me. Anyway your *negrito* needs a vacation."

His first fight would be in Toulouse the following week, and he suggested we meet in Biarritz on Saturday and then go on from there. Nobody works in August, he said, and spending the month traveling around Spain with him would be a better holiday for me than wasting a lot of money doing nothing.

In a way he was right—and of course I wanted to see him perform. "All right," I said. "I'll meet you in Biarritz on Saturday."

"*Muy bien*," he said. "At the Hôtel du Palais."

"Will you really be there?"

"*Claro que sí*," he said. "*¡Imbécil!*" He sounded exuberant, as if he were starting a new life, and I was influenced by his enthusiasm, felt better about everything, even the movie, the outlook for which had looked less than hopeful half an hour earlier.

Afición means passion, Hemingway had written in *The Sun Also Rises*. "An *aficionado* is one who is passionate about bullfighting," which was not my case. But witnessing Luis Miguel's personal adventure at close quarters was too tempting to turn down on the spur of the moment. I would go along for a week or two, I told myself after I hung up the telephone.

M. del Guidice obligingly consented to store most of my belongings in the *réserve* of the hotel, and with only one suitcase in the back of my Porsche I set off for the *pays basque*. There was a message waiting for me at the Palais when I arrived. Señor Dominguín had been detained in Madrid, the concierge informed me, but would be arriving the next afternoon. I was not surprised. Although I didn't know Spain as well as I do now, Papa had often mentioned the Spaniards' disregard for time and their lack of punctuality. Even during the Civil War both sides had been incapable of arriving at the phase line of an attack on schedule; only the bullfights began at the announced hour, and this was usually accomplished by setting the clocks in the plazas back a few minutes.

I moved into a small room on the fourth floor of the hotel and collected the surfboard that had been dropped off for me as promised by Dick Zanuck. Although the waves were not very big the next morning, I soon discovered that surfing was a sport that would require some expert instruction, and after losing my board on my first few attempts to catch a wave, I was ordered out of the water by the lifeguards who said I was a danger to the other bathers. Somewhat discouraged, I retired to the side of the hotel pool, where a number of my acquaintances had been watching what they considered to be my attempts to drown myself in the Bay of Biscay.

That summer the idle gossip around the swimming pool was more concerned with the bulls than with any other pastime. Luis Miguel's return to the arena had been announced in the press and was considered to be an important event, although Antonio Ordóñez had already established himself as the favorite of the French addicts of the *corrida*. Ordóñez, in the opinion of many knowledgeable aficionados, was the greater artist, even though they admitted that as a *dominador* of the bulls Dominguín had no equal.

Luis Miguel called from San Sebastián that evening and on Sunday morning arrived at the Palais in the company of a young Venezuelan woman, the glamorous mother of two girls. He introduced her as Elena Winkelman. Once we were alone in his suite, he explained that Nena had looked after him in Caracas a few years earlier when he had suffered the worst goring of his entire career and that she had come to Spain to accompany him during a few of his initial fights. It would "look better," he said, if we all traveled together, a ruse that I told him would hardly fool anyone, least of all Lucia. He shrugged and said that he had done his best to keep his word to never fight again, but being "a good husband and father" had not been enough to prevent him from getting bored to distraction.

"I am a son of a bitch," he said in his comical English, "but I can do nothing about *that!*"

I had sensed that all was not well between him and Lucia during my most recent visit to Madrid. She was still in love with him, there was no doubt about that, but she had persisted in her habit of making fun of him and the whole macho world of bullfighting. Hemingway and some of the other foreign intellectuals might well be taken in by the posturing of the "brave young men in their tight trousers," but it didn't impress her all that much, she had told me one night at dinner. It was a dangerous attitude for a young Italian woman to adopt who had chosen to be the wife of Spain's most celebrated torero, albeit retired.

They had been married in Panama by a justice of the peace, but once their first child was born Luis Miguel had given way to the pressure of his family and friends and had agreed to be married by a priest in the small chapel of his ranch near Saelices. The ceremony had been attended by all of the prominent bullfighters of the day as well as many of his Madrid friends. After the religious ceremony a *tienta* had taken place in which all the male members of the Dominguín clan performed. That night the large dinner party in the main patio of the old house was interrupted at midnight by an unusual prank. All of the lights had suddenly gone out, and a small bull calf had been released in the patio, charging the unsuspecting guests, turning over tables and chairs, and causing general bedlam. Once the wild animal had been removed and order restored, a group of flamencos had arrived, and the wedding party had continued until the early hours of the morning—an event full of Spanish folklore that should have served as a warning to Lucia that her husband was still firmly connected to his chosen profession.

Now he had gone back to the "dirty business," as he referred to it sometimes, to "be myself" again; this included adopting his old rules of personal conduct. He would soon be risking his life several times a week, he said, so he felt that he was entitled to do exactly as he pleased, a soldier's mentality with which I was familiar. I asked him about Nena's husband, and he told me that she had been divorced and was wealthy enough in her own right without having to worry about anyone else.

"And Lucia?" I asked him.

He shrugged. "Lucia is my wife," he replied, as if no other explanation was necessary.

WE DROVE TO TOULOUSE for his first *corrida*. The bullfight has always enjoyed a semilegal status in France, and the killing of bulls was permitted with payment of a fine. Like most of the towns near the Spanish border, Toulouse had a considerable Spanish population, many of its residents having moved there at the end of the Civil War. As Luis Miguel was known to be favorably inclined toward the Franco regime, he expected a large part of the audience to be hostile. I asked him why he had chosen to start his comeback there, and he replied that there was more money to be made in France. And whether they approved of him or not was unimportant, he told me, as long as they came to see him. Besides, the only part of the business he had always disliked was the crowd. "The people in the *tendidos* are usually more frightening than the bull," he said. "But you need them . . . you need them to struggle against, to prove to yourself and to them. The crowd is the most dangerous beast in the plaza."

"That's what Blasco Ibañez wrote in *Blood and Sand,*" I told him.

"Did he?" he replied. "Well, I'm glad that it wasn't your friend Hemingway."

The most important ability a bullfighter should possess is to be able to transmit emotion, a sense of danger coupled with grace and knowledge of the behavior of the animal he is facing. Watching a friend, I soon discovered, intensified everything, caused me to be immediately involved in the spectacle to a greater extent than ever before. Luis Miguel's style, which was almost nonchalant, was based on his expertise and his long experience, which had given him the reputation of being cold, partly because he made it all look too easy. As a result the people on the sunny side of the ring were hostile to him, which I found exasperating and which increased the tension I found myself experiencing.

In the end he was successful and cut ears on his two bulls. Elena was seated beside me and was aware of my nervousness. As we got up to leave she remarked that the last two hours of suffering was the price one had to pay for befriending a bullfighter. "That's why their wives stay home," I said. She smiled. Being a torero's wife was the world's worst profession, she told me, adding that it was a job to which she did not aspire. She was a charming and intelligent young woman, aside from her dazzling looks.

After Luis Miguel collected a large package of French francs wrapped in old newspaper, we started on our drive to Palencia, a small agricultural center two hundred kilometers north of Madrid. I soon discovered that he was considered to be even more *antipatico* by his own countrymen than by the French. They disliked him for a variety of reasons; he had been the young challenger on the day Manolete had been fatally wounded in Linares, and all of Spain had been outraged when a few days later Luis Miguel, in the Madrid bullring, had proclaimed himself to be *número uno*. They also disliked him because he was arrogant and proud, because he had the manner of a *hidalgo*, and because he was rich and famous and had been the lover of many beautiful women.

He seemed to relish their animosity. Envy was an important part of the Spanish national character, he informed me; but he didn't care how they felt about him as long as they paid their money and came to see him. He was disdainful of popularity. He had seen the crowd turn on Manolete in Santander three days before his death, and Manolete had been their greatest idol. All he wanted to prove now was that without him the bullrings of Spain and southern France would not be filled to capacity, no matter how great his brother-in-law's artistry was reputed to be.

August is the big *feria* month. A matador at the top of his profession can cram in as many as thirty appearances by including a few night fights in his schedule. Dominguín's intention had been to limit his comeback to no more than twenty *corridas*, but now he was offered many new contracts and even if he accepted only a fraction of them, he would be fighting an average of three times a week. I asked him if having to perform that often was not extremely stressful, to which he replied the opposite was the case. If you fought almost every day, you didn't have time to think about anything else, he said. Killing two bulls on most afternoons became a pattern of your life. Of course it was hard on the body, the constant traveling by car over the bad Spanish roads, never sleeping twice in the same bed. He recalled a time when, after a long season, he had been obliged to ask Gregorio, his chauffeur, to drive him around the countryside on some nights, as he had found it impossible to fall asleep in his own home.

After a few days, Nena declared rather sadly that it was time for her to return to her children and their nanny in Biarritz, so late one night we dropped her off on our way through Madrid. She was planning to drive north early the next morning, and the three of us had a farewell drink. I was sorry that she was leaving us, as she was the only member of our troupe with whom I could carry on an effortless conversation in English. She had also proved to be an engaging companion during the many hours our torero was involved in business meetings with the various impresarios and *ganaderos* who came to see him before each fight.

Domingo, Miguel's oldest brother, now joined us. Their father was managing Ordóñez's campaign, and it was young Domingo's intention to help his brother with the business details of his tour. He was as colorful a character as Luis Miguel and had been a matador for many years himself, although he had not been as successful as his sibling. Early in his life Domingo had belonged to the Falange, the fascist right, but with maturity he had become a leftist with political views in direct opposition to the Franco regime. "My brother is a fascist," he told me soon after we had gotten to know each other, "but I love him just the same."

Domingo made no secret of his political sympathies; he even boasted that Che Guevara had been his friend and that he had hidden the famous guerrilla in his house in Madrid during one of Guevara's visits to Spain. That he was able to exist unmolested by the Spanish secret police was apparently due in large part to Luis Miguel's friendship with Franco. On a partridge shoot some years earlier that El Caudillo had attended along with Dominguín, an aide, to provoke the young bullfighter, had asked, "Which one of your brothers is a Communist?" And without a moment's hesitation Luis Miguel had replied, "We all are," which defiant statement had made Franco double up with laughter, a rare show of hilarity on the part of that dour man.

But for the moment Luis Miguel was solely absorbed in his own struggle to reestablish himself as *número uno*. Nothing else seemed to matter to him. The nervous tics I had noticed when we had first met had become more pronounced now that he was fighting again. Sitting upright in bed prior to the ritual of putting on his suit-of-lights, he would fold and refold the edge of the sheet that covered the lower half of his body, and his habit of turning his head as if he were wearing a tight collar had become more frequent. He smoked cigarette after cigarette, a habit he had acquired at the age of thirteen, which he maintained he couldn't do without. "Look at you," he said. "You're not really happy until you've got a tennis racquet in your hand."

He spoke very little in the hours before a fight but said he preferred not to be alone, so we sat together in silence, and I read the newspaper or a book. Then once we were on the road again, no matter how things had gone in the bullring, he would be relaxed and talkative, would criticize Domingo for his disregard of the value of money, or berate Tamames, his doctor, for his sloppy appearance. As he was the only one who got all the exercise he needed, Luis Miguel was able to curl up in a corner of the backseat and fall asleep soon after our brief stop for dinner, sometimes with his legs across Domingo's knees or his head on his brother's shoulder.

I soon discovered that the position of friend and hanger-on was perhaps less dangerous than that of matador, but it was equally wearing. Nevertheless, it was only rarely that I longed for the cool climate of the *pays basque*, the beach, and the ocean, and I stayed on with Luis

Miguel's troupe for the entire month of August. Papa had once re-marked that it was "a mistake to confuse movement with action," a harsh truth. Not working at my trade was troubling me. Like most writers, I felt guilty when a day passed and I had not written a word.

So one day I called the Hotel Raphaël in Paris to ask for messages, and it turned out that "Monsieur Lazar" had tried to reach me several times in the past week. I called Swifty and after complaining that I had not kept in touch, he told me he had an assignment for me to write a western for Warwick Films, a London-based independent company owned by Cubby Broccoli and Irving Allen. I was to go to London as soon as possible for a job interview.

Luis Miguel shrugged when I told him I would be leaving and gave the reason for my defection. "You don't need money while you're with us," he said. "Wait until the season is over." I explained that I could not be that cavalier in the face of a genuine offer and thanked him for his past generosity. Then I said good-bye to all of my new friends and companions. Luis Miguel accompanied me to the Madrid railroad station, and I boarded the night train for Irún. From there I would take a taxi to Biarritz, collect my car, and proceed to Paris and Lon-don by plane.

ALL WENT ACCORDING to plan, and less than a week later I moved into an apartment on the avenue Montaigne that Jacques Schoeller, Guy's older brother, had turned over to me, as he was off to Tahiti or some other exotic place in the South Seas. Lazar had final-ized a deal with Warwick Films, and all that remained was for me to get back to work and write a screenplay that my new boss was hoping would be a suitable vehicle for Gary Cooper. During our meeting in London I had voiced concern that "the Marshall," as Cooper was known to many of his Hollywood friends, had already played a some-what similar role in *High Noon*, but Allen had assured me that "if the script is good enough, no star minds playing the same part twice."

GETTING BACK TO WORK proved difficult, all the more so as my work on the screenplay was not a labor of love. Like most screen-writers, I had done several westerns in the not too distant past, but I was writing this one solely to make money. "Whoring" proves to be more painful as you get older. Then at the end of the second week in September, the Hemingways arrived in Paris. I knew they were com-ing as Papa had written that he was planning to go to the fall *feria* in

Logroño, where Ordóñez was fighting on two successive days, and then to Madrid before proceeding on to the *feria de Pilar* in Zaragoza, the last important bullfight event of the season. I called him at the Ritz and was summoned to join his party for a drink before lunch. Bertin, the bartender, welcomed me outside the glass doors of *le petit bar* and announced proudly that *"tout le monde est de retour."* Papa and Mary were seated at their favorite corner table with a large group that included Gary Cooper, his daughter Maria, and a pretty dark-haired woman Papa introduced as "La Comtesse." It was evident from Papa's manner that the young woman was his current inamorata and that during their crossing on the *Ile de France* he had once again embarked on one of his imaginary romances.

The Countess, he went on to inform me, was a talented young writer, a statement the young woman disavowed. She was only an enthusiastic dilettante, she whispered in my ear, who had been honored to show some of her "scribbling" to the great author. Mary, at the far end of the table, seemed unconcerned about Papa's courtly manner toward the young woman, having become accustomed to Papa's flirtations, which she realized presented no serious menace to their marriage.

I sat down opposite Cooper and was struck again by his charm. It was not surprising that his smile had seduced a large part of the female population of the world. He had been a friendly witness at the start of the witch-hunt but later had realized his mistake and had done his best to make up for it by insisting that Carl Foreman, one of the accused, be given screen credit on *High Noon*, a film that had won Cooper the Academy Award. Zinnemann and Milestone had sung Coop's praises to me in the past, not only for his talent, but for his generous and modest manner toward his fellow workers.

He was in Paris, he said with a shy grin, to play the part of an international playboy in Billy Wilder's *Love in the Afternoon*, a role for which he felt he was "a little too long in the tooth," especially as his leading lady was to be Audrey Hepburn. But what actor in his right mind could refuse to play opposite her, and in a movie directed by Wilder, he said. I made no mention of the fact that the script I was working on would perhaps be submitted to his agent; I felt too uncertain about how it would finally turn out.

I left after half an hour to have lunch with the Achards. Papa accompanied me to the rue Cambon entrance of the hotel, and we stood chatting for a few minutes while I waited for a taxi. He asked after

Luis Miguel, although he was well informed about Dominguín's comeback, for he still subscribed to *El Ruedo*, the Spanish bullfight weekly. "You must be getting a lot of good material for your book," he said, his eyes narrowing as he studied my face for a reaction.

I told him that I had not yet decided to write anything about the bullfight, and he grunted skeptically. He suggested I join him and Mary in St. Jean de Luz in a week and go on with them to Logroño for Ordóñez's two fights, and without a second thought I told him I would be there.

"I'll reserve a room for you at the Chantaco," he said with a grin—it was his turn to look after the arrangements. "Good to see you again, Pete," he said and waved good-bye as I got into the cab.

Marcel Achard was curious to hear about Papa's health after I told him about the group I had visited at the Ritz. Juliette laughed her most malicious laugh when I mentioned the pretty Countess's name. She was nothing more than an adventuress, she alleged, and had been the mistress of Jean de Beaumont, who had purchased a title for her. All men of a certain age were inclined to be fools whenever they encountered a pretty face, she chirped, a generalization that was surely intended to include her husband, who merely raised his shortsighted eyes in the direction of the ceiling of the small dining room.

Mel Ferrer and Audrey Hepburn were eager to meet Papa, as was Rita Hayworth, who had returned briefly to Paris. After securing Hemingway's agreement, I invited my "movie friends" to lunch a few days later. Papa suggested we go to one of his favorite restaurants on the place du Tertre, although I warned him it had become something of a tourist trap. It was a sunny day and we were able to sit out on the terrace. The party seemed to be going quite well when, as we were having coffee, an elderly man came over to our table and introduced himself as a retired U.S. Army colonel. Rather hesitantly he asked all present for autographs, allegedly for his teenage daughter.

Audrey and Mel complied graciously, as did Rita, but when the man turned to Papa, Hemingway scowled. "Sir," he said slowly and distinctly, "you look to me to be a cocksucker."

The colonel looked dazed and retreated. Mel laughed a hollow laugh, but Audrey was visibly shocked. Rita stared off into the distance. None of us could understand what had prompted Hemingway to use a word that he had often described as the ugliest word in the English language. He soon apologized for his outburst and admitted that he had become cantankerous and intolerant with age.

Once we were back in Hemingway's hired limousine, with the faithful Georges at the wheel, Papa was as agreeable as he had been before lunch. Mary made no mention of the unpleasant incident, and we drove to the Ritz as if nothing had happened. I had written him quite some time ago about the dubious progress that was being made to film *The Sun Also Rises*, but as he had expressed very little interest in the proceedings I didn't bring the matter up. Papa's mercurial changes of mood made us hesitant to speak at all, and so we sat quietly in our assigned places, watching the scenery go by.

Finally Papa said, "Like your town, Pete," which humorous remark confirmed that bygones were indeed bygones, and I decided that now was as good a time as any to remind him that he had agreed to my bringing Françoise Sagan by for a drink that evening. "Maybe you've met enough admirers for today," I added, and Papa chuckled without turning his head from where he was seated next to the driver.

"Be glad to buy a fellow writer a drink," he said, promising to be on his best behavior.

When I arrived at Bertin's small, exclusive chamber, Françoise, accompanied by Annabel Buffet, had already ordered, and before calling the Hemingways' suite to advise Papa that the "troops were assembled," I tried in a subtle way to warn the two young women that Hemingway could at times be difficult. Sagan smiled and said, *"Tiens?"* but neither she nor Annabel appeared to be surprised or alarmed.

Sagan had spent a month during the last couple of winters in Klosters, and I had come to know her well enough to realize that very little short of actual violence ever disturbed her equanimity. She was anything but a celebrity hound and was content to live her own strange life within her own circle of friends and to write about them in her admirable prose. She was an observer, which I sensed was one of the reasons she had expressed an interest in meeting Papa. Yet I noticed that she was smoking even more heavily than usual.

Papa joined us a few minutes later and was on his best behavior from the start. He liked Annabel's dark good looks and complimented Françoise on her early success; he even told her that he looked forward to reading many more of her novels. Sagan smiled bashfully and after forty minutes or so announced that she and her friend must be going. Gazing shyly up at Papa, she told him how pleased she was to have met him and departed.

Bob and Kathy Parrish had decided to join me in St. Jean de Luz

Ava Gardner in Madrid, 1956. (AP/Wide World Photos)

The screenwriter and playwright Harry Kurnitz, having requisitioned a violin from the orchestra at the Hotel Chesa Grishuna in Klosters in 1958, fiddles for his friends.

I had the privilege to count Dominguín as another of my "dangerous friends." Here he and his wife, Lucia Bose, join me as we leave the Hotel Alfonso XIII in Seville to go to the 1960 spring *feria*.

Deborah Kerr and I were married on July 23, 1960. Here we are that
evening, in front of the Hotel Chesa Grishuna in Klosters.

Five men out to break the bank at the Casino Bellevue in Biarritz.
The year is 1961. From left to right: the matador Gitanillo de Triana;
myself; Dominguín; Harry Kurnitz; Dr. Manolo Tamames,
Dominguín's surgeon. Gitanillo fought on the same card as
Dominguín the day the great Manolete was killed in Linares by a
Miura bull in 1947.

Deborah's film *The Innocents,* an outstanding adaptation of Henry
James's classic suspense tale *The Turn of the Screw,* was screened at the
Cannes festival in 1961. Dominguín and Lucia Bose joined us there.

In Biarritz en route to Pamplona, mid-1960s. Left to right: the
novelists William Styron and James Jones; myself; Kathy Parrish;
Gloria Jones; Rose Styron.

At the bullfight in Pamplona: Deborah, Kathy Parrish, and I.

John Huston never gave up his lifelong love of riding. Here he is, with his son Tony, during the filming of *The List of Adrian Messenger* in 1963. (Academy of Motion Picture Arts and Sciences)

Orson Welles, visiting me in Klosters in the 1970s.

Deborah and I with our Pyrenean mountain dog, Guapa,
in a photo taken in Klosters in the 1970s.

from London, where they were living, and had booked seats on the direct flight to Biarritz from Heathrow. Yet as the date approached for me to go to St. Jean, I realized that taking a week off from my western was a luxury I could ill afford because of the approaching deadline. Instead of waiting for Papa to arrive at the Chantaco, I called Bob to say that I would not be coming.

Hemingway was angry that I failed to show up. "If you agree to be somewhere," he told Bob, "the only excuse for not keeping the date is if you're dead." But as long as I had known Papa he had complained of his nonwriter friends' disregard for his work, so I didn't take Bob's report too seriously. Once I had more or less completed my work on the western, I agreed to Zanuck's suggestion to fly to Madrid to meet with Ava Gardner, who had been sent the final draft of the screenplay for *The Sun Also Rises* and was apparently not entirely pleased with what she had read.

Madrid was sweltering in an autumn heat wave, and Ava had abandoned the city for El Escorial, a mountain town that had for centuries been a summer retreat for Spanish kings. She was staying at the Hotel Felipe II, and I soon discovered that Papa and Mary were staying there as well. Knowing that I would have to face him sooner or later, I rented a car and set off for the Sierra de Guadarrama, hoping to kill two birds with one reluctant stone.

The weather was cool in the mountains, as was Ava's reception. She asked after Luis Miguel, a less than affectionate inquiry, and then launched into a brief series of complaints about her role that proved to me that she either had never read the novel or had forgotten its contents. I asked her to detail her objections, but she told me that was impossible, as she had sent her copy of the screenplay to Hemingway, who was probably reading it at that very moment. Then she went on to say that Papa, "the old bastard," had seemed less than pleased that she was to portray Lady Brett, had told her that she "would probably do," as she had "some vestiges of class," a comment that had offended her. She was thinking of bowing out of her agreement with 20th Century-Fox, she said, and I did my best to persuade her that she would be making a mistake, for it was the kind of part that didn't come along every day. I suggested we have dinner that evening after she had retrieved her copy of the script and go over her scenes together. Then I called Papa and he asked me to come and see him later that afternoon.

Surprisingly enough, Papa was less hostile than Ava and accepted my apologies for not having kept our date in Logroño. Instead of going into detail about the faults in my screenplay, he returned Ava's copy to me, marked with his objections. The section that had bothered him most was the sequence in the Milan hospital, which he felt I had plagiarized from one of his short stories. I tried to explain the difficulties I had faced in making Jake's impotence understandable to a movie audience, but he insisted that we go back to the scene in his novel where Jake inspects the results of his wound in a mirror. I told him that this was not even remotely possible because of the censorship regulations, an argument that seemed to placate him somewhat.

His planned trip to Africa was now in jeopardy because of the Suez Crisis, so he would probably be going back to Paris after the *feria* in Zaragoza and then would return to Cuba in December. Everything was "cocked up" for the moment, and my screenplay was only a small part of the general disaster. The industry had screwed up every one of his books, he said, and he should be getting used to having his work distorted, but nevertheless it sent him into one of his "black-ass" moods. Poor Hadley had been gypped by Feldman and Howard Hawks, he continued, and should never have agreed to sell the novel to them.

I promised to do my best to make whatever changes he had suggested in his notes, although I warned him that a screenwriter had little or no control over the final version of a movie. He knew all about that, he said, and only hoped that I would make some money out of the venture. I could do him one last favor, he added, and that was to buy him a tweed cap on my next visit to Ireland, exactly like the one I was wearing, which unfortunately turned out to be too small for him when I offered it to him.

With the passing years I have come to realize more fully the anguish Papa must have suffered at the hands of "the industry." *A Farewell to Arms* had been made twice, with disastrous results. *To Have and Have Not*, too, had been made twice, each version a bastardization of the original work. "My Old Man," "The Snows of Kilimanjaro," and "The Short and Happy Life of Francis Macomber" had not fared much better. *The Old Man and the Sea* was another disaster. *For Whom the Bell Tolls* was only a little less awful because of the performances of Gary Cooper and Ingrid Bergman. Now the prospect of seeing *The Sun Also Rises* suffer a similar fate was just as distressing to him.

After my conversation with Papa I didn't feel much like having dinner with Ava. I thought of resigning from the project, but I knew that the movie would be made in one form or another, and I was still hoping to be able to exert some pressure to keep the screenplay close to the original text of the novel. I also felt that Ava was capable of playing the part, as she had a physical magnetism that was undeniable. Men were inclined to fall in love with her at sight, a quality Lady Brett seemed to possess.

Ava was not all that winning when I went to see her late that afternoon. Rather than go over the script, she suggested we go out for a drink before dinner, and we went to a small bar in the village where she ordered a concoction called *sol y sombra*, sun and shade, a mixture in even parts of sweet and bitter anis. It is not a cocktail that anyone in his right mind would order before dinner, and after the second round she began to express her violent dislike for Zanuck, 20th Century-Fox, and all movie companies in general. The choice of Tyrone Power as her leading man did not distress her all that much, and she voiced her hesitant approval of Errol Flynn for the part of Mike. She had never been to Pamplona, so she was not as worried about shooting the picture in Mexico as I was.

By the time we had finished dinner it was well past midnight, and she suggested we find a place with flamenco music, but fortunately such a place did not exist in El Escorial. I agreed to stay on an extra day so that we could finally discuss the script in detail, but she was not feeling too bright the following morning. Before leaving, I exacted a promise from her not to break her contract, and that promise was the only positive message I was able to bring back with me to Paris.

Darryl informed me that production had been given the green light by Spyros Skouras, and a few days later I departed for Ireland with the screenplay marked by Hemingway. Concurring with John Huston's view of the Emerald Isle, I felt it was a good place to crawl back to and lick my wounds.

MORELIA, MICHOACÁN, had been chosen as a location because of its presumed similarity to Pamplona, and my first view of the small Mexican town came as a shock. The town square of the agrarian community was bordered by low white houses and in no way resembled the Basque city. Its only redeeming feature was a small hotel on the outskirts that was run by an American couple. The place was made up of small bungalows that were comfortable enough for a long stay, and the food was excellent as well as wholesome. Both Ty Power and Eddie Albert had proved to be pleasant companions on our car journey to Morelia, and I was reassured by their enthusiasm for the work that lay ahead.

Henry King, our director, arrived in his own small airplane, and he too, although considerably older than the rest of us, seemed like a congenial man. Ava had rented a small house nearer the town, the only member of the cast who had decided to forgo the comforts of our motel. Mel Ferrer and Audrey Hepburn were already installed in the largest of the bungalows, and Errol Flynn, accompanied by his young male secretary, a fledgling screenwriter who was helping him write his memoirs, had been assigned to another of the many small huts. The assistant director was a young man named Stanley Hough, a former baseball player, a pleasant and competent technician who had worked with Henry King on several movies.

During our first meeting Hough described to me the trouble he had had selecting extras. Knowing that the people in the north of Spain were totally devoid of Indian blood, he had started to choose the least Indian-looking of the many applicants and was immediately accused of racism; a platoon of soldiers had to be called out to avoid a riot. He was slightly unnerved by the experience, as he had been stoned and had narrowly avoided serious injury. In the end he had been forced to pick extras at random and said that now it was up to our cameramen to include the right racial types in the background.

Darryl arrived the day before we were to start shooting and moved in with the rest of us without a complaint about his less than glamorous quarters. I asked him immediately whether he had chosen an actor to play our bullfighter, and he informed me that on a recent visit to a New York nightclub with Bella, they had seen a young man who Bella had stated was one of the most "handsome guys" she had ever laid eyes on, and Darryl had at once signed him up to play Pedro Romero. His name was Robert Evans, and he was a partner with his brother in a successful clothing firm. But as he was "movie-struck," he had abandoned his lucrative business to become an actor. I was amazed at the haphazard way Darryl had come to such an important decision, but he declared that the part was a small one and that he thought Evans would be able to "get away with it," as he had already portrayed Irving Thalberg in a previous film, hardly a recommendation.

The first scene to go before the camera was the fishing sequence with Jake and Bill Gordon that takes place before their arrival in Pamplona. Henry King suggested that he fly Ty, Eddie, and me to a location about thirty-five miles north of Morelia, and we agreed somewhat reluctantly. We made sure Ty was seated next to King in the four-seater aircraft, as he had been a Marine transport pilot during the war, and if King had a heart attack, he would be able to take the controls. We arrived without mishap, the entire sequence was filmed in one day, and we returned to Morelia in time for an early dinner. Darryl decreed that in the future we would travel by car, as he disapproved of the lives of any of the principal actors being put at risk.

Eddie Albert seemed adequate in his role of Jake's amusing friend, but Ty was a little too charming and affable as Jake. He was a competent actor, however, and I mentioned to King that his looks and charm should be played down. King nodded and said he was well aware of the problem. I had the distinct feeling that I was being listened to with polite disinterest and asked Darryl to intervene, which he did at once.

The next scene on the schedule took place in the town square and included all of the principals. Ava appeared on the set in her costume, which looked much too contemporary and was topped off with a bright red beret. Errol Flynn as Mike Campbell wore the same headgear, as did Eddie Albert. I ambled over to where Zanuck was seated in a deck chair behind the camera and commented on my observations. He agreed with me about the contemporary look of Ava's clothes but said that there was nothing we could do about it now. Ava had insisted that her wardrobe be designed by an Italian couturier and had not bothered to show her clothes to anyone in the unit. It was an amazing admission of helplessness from one of the most powerful producers in the business.

I also told him that red berets were worn in Pamplona by only one section of the Spanish military and that navy blue would be a better color if Ava was to wear a beret at all, but Darryl said that it was too late to make any changes in the cast's costumes. "Nobody but you and maybe a few Spaniards will know the difference," he said. The bands in the square were playing, and the Mexican extras were dancing their version of the Basque *jota*, and the red berets stayed on the heads of our four leading actors.

In the first major scene to be shot Flynn was surprisingly effective as Mike Campbell, and Darryl muttered that he would probably win an Oscar in this, his first character part, seemingly pleased with what he considered to be a brilliant bit of casting.

The unit returned to the town square with its swarthy dancers to continue the sequence as well as to shoot out of continuity some of the other café scenes. Henry King, I discovered, had never been to Pam-

plona, and I was dismayed that no one at the studio had thought to
send him there while the second unit was filming. Isabel, the script
girl, who was his constant companion, assured me that Henry had
"picked up the mood of the *feria*" by screening the thousands of feet
of film that had been sent back to the studio by the second unit. That
was like trying to discover what a soldier at the front feels by looking
at the newsreels of a battle, so it was not surprising that the atmosphere of the Hemingway novel eluded him entirely.

I voiced my concern to Darryl, who suggested we talk with King
that evening after dinner. We met in Henry's bungalow, where he was
quite willing to listen to what the boss and the screenwriter had to say.
Darryl indicated that I should speak my piece, and I did so without
hesitation. I suggested that our story was not unlike Sartre's play *No
Exit*, which it turned out Henry had never seen or read. Well, their
existence is a living hell, I went on. Robert Cohn is in love with Brett,
as are Jake and Mike Campbell. Bill Gordon is aware of the tension
between the three men and tries to be a peacemaker. But in the scenes
that were being filmed, I went on, our principals were more like a
group of Hollywood actors in Tijuana for the weekend, harsh words
perhaps, but I was trying desperately to say that the prevailing mood
of the Hemingway novel was being ignored.

King listened politely and nodded without interrupting my discourse. I mentioned that Brett actually verbalizes this aspect of her
and Jake's frustrations when she tells him that their relationship might
well be a punishment for "the hell I've put some chaps through," a
key to her attitude and her actions. He was well aware of all this, King
replied. He had told Ty that he should remember that "every time he
looks at Ava, he should feel tears starting to fill his eyes."

I glanced over at Darryl, but he made no comment. Realizing that
subtlety was pointless, I said that Jake was beyond tears, that he was
cynical and detached as a result of his emasculation, and that if he
merely appeared to be melancholy and lovesick, the audience would
soon lose patience with him.

Henry shrugged, said he felt weary, and the meeting was adjourned.
As we walked back to our bungalows, Darryl appeared to be just as
depressed as I was. He said, "The trouble with Henry is that he's
never met people like these." However, he said it was too late to
change directors and suggested I talk privately to Ava and Ty. But I
felt that might only make matters worse by undermining King's authority. The next evening, while I was having dinner with Mel and

Audrey, Mel volunteered the opinion that the scenes that had already been shot fell far short of the story's potential. The atmosphere of the novel, its undeniable magic, was just not there. "But there isn't much *you* can do, Pete," he added with a wan smile.

Mel continued to give Robert Cohn a diffident aloofness that was too bland and that diminished the resentment of Jake and Mike Campbell and softened the whole premise of the story. He was not altogether to blame for his shortcomings, as Darryl and I had removed all the anti-Semitic remarks from the text, a mistake as it turned out. But at the time anti-Semitism was a theme that Hollywood was inclined to handle with kid gloves, and our decision not to deal with it was in keeping with the industry's policy.

AT THE END of the first week of principal photography Ava declared that she had tired of her self-imposed isolation and suggested I join her for dinner at her rented house. Thinking that this might be a good opportunity to discuss her role, as well as feeling flattered to have been singled out, I accepted her invitation.

Her driver was a husky mustachioed Mexican named Guillermo, who had instantly become intensely loyal to his world-famous employer. He picked me up punctually after work and drove me at breakneck speed to Ava's house, a scant two miles away. The place was modestly furnished but had a big refrigerator and a brand-new gas stove. Ava had brought along her maid, and after letting me in the young woman proudly took me on a tour of the kitchen that had been imported for her use. Her mistress appeared a few minutes later, dressed in a gray gym suit, her face devoid of makeup, which only seemed to enhance her looks. She agreed that her dwelling was comfortable enough for our brief stay, adding that at least she didn't have to see anyone she didn't want to see after work.

She suggested we have a dry martini before dinner, and when I told her that I would prefer a Coca-Cola she shrugged and made some remark about not trusting any man who didn't drink. I realized that it would be a mistake to try to engage her in a serious discussion of our work, and so we chatted cheerfully about the past, her life and mine. She was uninhibited in her criticism of my leaving Jigee, which I made no attempt to explain. Then she began to talk about Luis Miguel and the burden of "his awful family"; after a second martini, went on to describe her marital problems with Sinatra and Artie Shaw. As dinner was delayed, I could do nothing to dissuade her from mixing "a last martini" before our meal.

A bottle of wine was served with the food when it finally arrived, and although she drank only half a glass, her long diatribes against men in the movie business were the main subject of her monologues. It seemed strange to me that the industry that had provided her with a status she must once have desired was finally accountable for her discontent, or perhaps she had never anticipated the burdens of fame. Ava then informed me that she was presently involved with Walter Chiari, the young Italian actor who had been Lucia Bosé's lover for several years, but that too, she said, was an impermanent liaison as far as she was concerned. It was nearly midnight by this time, and as she had dismissed Guillermo, I told her that I was going to call a taxi to take me back to my quarters.

She didn't want me to do that, she told me, she wanted me to stay the night. I pointed out to her that this would look compromising to the others, but she said she didn't care. She seemed to be motivated by an almost panicky loneliness, so I agreed to spend the night in her guest room, thinking I could leave before dawn and walk back to my bungalow. But even this suggestion failed to satisfy her. She wanted me to stay in her room, she said, to be close to her at least until she had fallen asleep.

I told her that life had not equipped me physiologically for the role of teddy bear, a remark she ignored, although it was obvious that she was not remotely interested in my becoming her lover. She got quickly into one of the double beds that stood in the room and shed the bottom half of her gym suit. She was half asleep when I got into the adjoining bed after taking off my shoes and trousers, but she insisted I push my bed against hers. After an affectionate hug she wished me good night and lost consciousness.

I was dog tired, and fell into a troubled sleep from which I awoke at five-thirty in the morning. I dressed in the semidarkness and made my way out of the house. It was a longer walk back to the bungalow than I had reckoned, and it was six-fifteen before I arrived at our compound. As I passed Errol Flynn's bungalow, he stepped out of his hut, dressed only in his pajama bottoms, his face covered with lather for his morning shave.

He smiled lewdly and remarked that I had "obviously been doing some late gardening." I answered that his intimations were inaccurate, sounding just about as foolish as I felt. I made hastily for my quarters, cursing myself for having been weak and stupid: I knew it wouldn't be very long before he had informed most of the others of our encounter. I got into my own bed and slept soundly until a grim-looking Stanley Hough arrived in my bungalow at nine-thirty. Ava had not yet arrived on the set, he informed me. She had been late in makeup, so the company had been forewarned and had managed to get a couple of setups without her. But this was "all bad news," and he wanted me to know it.

Ava made her appearance an hour later, dispensing greetings and apologies to all hands, acting totally unlike the woman she had been just before falling asleep. I was even more astonished by her attitude toward me. Instead of a discreet "good morning," she gave me an overly affectionate hug and kiss that provoked raised eyebrows and secret smiles from Ty and Errol, who were waiting patiently to appear with her in the scene that was scheduled. Fortunately Darryl was still in his bungalow and had not yet heard the gossip. Nor had Henry King been informed of my early morning return to camp, for without a reprimand he went quietly to work and soon had made up for the lost time.

During the lunch break Stanley Hough took me aside and, without mentioning the rumors he had undoubtedly heard, asked me to do everything I could to see to it that our leading lady did not repeat her tardiness. I told him that I could do very little to change her behavior, and he replied: "Well, you have more influence on her than I have," adding, "I know that it's not your job, but I'd appreciate your help anyway."

Mel Ferrer asked me to stop by and see him for a drink that evening, and in a most friendly way he began to lecture me on what a harmful influence a woman like Ava could have on my career and my life. We had often played tennis together in Paris and had a relationship that permitted the giving of unasked-for advice, and so I laughed and thanked him for his brotherly concern. I also told him that I had no ambition to become our leading lady's boyfriend, which was not quite the truth, for her affectionate behavior was provocative and almost made me forget how trying she could be after a couple of drinks. Sober, in the clear light of day, she was both endearing and attractive, and I was not immune to her charms.

That night Darryl dined with the Ferrers and me. After Audrey had retired, he asked for Mel's and my help in the casting of the one speaking part that was still open, that of the prostitute Jake invites to accompany him to the *bal musette*, a sequence that was to be shot in a Mexico City studio. He said quite bluntly that he had a personal interest in finding a girl to play the role. "I woke up with an erection this morning," he announced with a grin, "so I think I'm about through carrying a torch for Miss Darvi."

We both laughed, and after a moment's thought Mel suggested Juliette Greco for the part. I agreed that she would be all right, but as the character had only one scene, I said it was doubtful Greco would fly all the way to Mexico City to be in our movie. Mel volunteered to send a cable to her, adding that there was no harm in our trying to get her.

The next day Ava again asked me to her house for dinner, and during the ensuing weeks the pattern of our first night was repeated. I became her houseguest and eventually convinced her not to drink so much, and from then on she was seldom late for work. Our relationship continued as it had begun and was purely platonic. She wanted to remain faithful to Walter Chiari in deed, if not in her thoughts, she said, and it occurred to me that the role of Lady Brett was influencing her behavior, despite Henry King's inadequate direction.

I didn't see myself as Jake, but I did find that I was taking on the role of detached observer, a little bit in love but gratified to be out of contention. My nightly absences were now being taken for granted, as both Ty and Eddie Albert had taken up with two young Mexican women who were working as extras, and who was sleeping with whom didn't seem to matter anymore. Ava referred to these young women as *"putas"* whenever she had had too much tequila; "whore" and "fag" were her favorite descriptions of people she was suspicious of, evidence of an outmoded morality she had obviously discarded early in her own life.

As she became more at ease in the part of Lady Brett, her insecurity in the role seemed to lessen. She was perhaps not the character Hemingway had created, but she had a luminous quality that was compelling. What was lacking was what Papa had referred to as "remnants of class" as well as a matter-of-fact coolness I had felt was the key to Lady Brett's demeanor. But it soon became apparent that Ava had a thorough understanding of her role. She was quick to make dialogue adjustments in a scene, and had she had a sensitive director like George Cukor, she would certainly have given a more convincing performance.

Talent is a most winning quality, as seductive as beauty in an actress, and my admiration for Ava increased. Even if she was not the Lady Brett that appears on the printed page, she managed to portray a personage that was most desirable—probably more desirable, I was inclined to think, than the heroine of Papa's novel. And in spite of Mel Ferrer's brotherly warning, I began to feel myself falling under her spell. My common sense told me that it was undoubtedly wiser to limit my feelings to mere fantasizing, a resolve it was difficult to keep as we saw each other every day. "Why didn't we get together long ago?" she asked at one point and, paraphrasing Brett instead of Jake, I replied, "Yeah, we could have had such a damn good time together."

Soon Zanuck departed for Los Angeles, and Robert Evans, our Pedro Romero, arrived. He was a nice-looking young man of average height, nervous and eager to make friends. As our matador he would have to wear tight-fitting silk trousers, and this turned out to be a complication, as he was broad in the hips. It was a defect Luis Miguel had often been jeered for, but compared with Evans Dominguín was pencil-thin.

Evans arrived in Morelia a scant two weeks before starting his role, and in that time he would have to learn how to handle a fighting cape and the muleta. A young Mexican *novillero* had been hired to tutor him in this and then play his *mozo de espadas*, his sword handler and valet. Despite the language barrier between the two men, Evans made some progress, but the time allotted was far too short for him to assimilate the mannerisms of a torero, the required bearing as well as a bullfighter's precise movements in the ring, so foreign to an American.

I disclosed my doubts about the young actor's ability to Ava, a move that turned out to be a mistake. Out of empathy for a fellow actor she said that Evans should be given more time. It was like asking a young European to simulate the movements of a professional baseball player, I told her, a statement that only aroused her anger. Darryl was in California, so I decided to go to Stanley Hough with my worries, as he seemed to share them to some extent. He suggested I speak to our director. Doubtful that I would get a sympathetic hearing, I managed to corner King during a lunch break and expressed my concerns: the whole of the third act was dependent on the believability of Romero, I stated flatly. If he failed to come across as the genuine article, the entire story would go out the window. King rubbed his chin and allowed that I was perhaps too aware of what a bullfighter should look like. An American audience would be less perceptive. "American or

French or Spanish," I argued, "you're asking them to believe that a woman who is in love with Ty Power, has had a brief fling with Mel Ferrer, and has been Errol Flynn's mistress is suddenly going to go off with this kid Bella Darvi admired in a nightclub! I have nothing against Evans . . . I just think he's wrong for the part. He'd be fine if you were making a modern Romeo and Juliet set in Brooklyn."

I noticed that King's hands were tightening into two fists. "Peter," he said, "I have always had one rule, and that is that I'm never going to allow one person to spoil any of my movies. So why don't you just forget about this kid and concentrate on shooting the bullfight sequence Darryl put you in charge of?" It was a barely polite way of putting me in my place, and it was certainly not how he would have responded if Hemingway had been there. I sent a strongly worded wire to Darryl at the studio and went off with the unit manager to buy the bulls for the movie's *corrida*.

Juanito Silveti, a Mexican matador, had been hired to double for Robert Evans, as he was about the same height as the actor and had the same coloring. He and his wife, Doreen, had befriended Ava in Spain the previous year, and I found him to be a civilized and intelligent young man when he appeared on the set. As it was not a task I felt I could accomplish on my own, he came along to help choose the bulls he would be fighting. His father, Juan Silveti, was something of a myth in Mexico, famous for his bravura in and out of the bullring. According to Papa he had a peculiar habit when drunk, which was often: he would enter a bar, take out his penis, and, after lining up a dozen silver dollars beside his organ, would challenge all comers to equal this feat. He had as many knife and gunshot scars on his body as scars from the horns of the bulls he had fought.

Juanito was a much less flamboyant character, restrained and thoughtful. "My father's life is perhaps fun to read about," he remarked sadly as we drove through the peaceful Mexican countryside, "but less amusing if you happen to be his son." We arrived at the ranch, and I counted thirteen bulls in the paddock in front of us. "I hope you're not superstitious," I told Juanito, but he merely laughed.

"Buy all thirteen, and I'll fight them all," he replied, words I recalled two days later when the second bull tossed him high into the air. He brushed himself off and, true to his family tradition, insisted on going right on with the filming. His face was bruised, and I instructed the cameraman to shoot him in a couple of close-ups, thinking that if Evans turned out to be hopeless we could always use Silveti in the part, as he spoke enough English to get through the scene. I knew there was only a slim chance of getting King and Darryl to agree to this, but I thought there was no harm in trying.

Zanuck returned to Morelia for the bullfight sequence, which was to be the most costly scene on our schedule, involving hundreds of extras to fill one section of the local bullring. All of our principals were seated in *barreras*, their ringside seats. The band struck up a *paso doble*, and Bob Evans, flanked by two local matadors, began the ceremonial march across the ring. Catcalls and laughter from the Mexican extras greeted them, provoked by Evans's appearance. The way he walked, the way he wore his *montera*, the matador's cap, the way his knee-length trousers fitted him—all took away from the reality of the *paseo* the crowd was accustomed to seeing. Henry King shouted "Cut," and Stanley Hough was sent to cajole the crowd, asking them to refrain from rowdiness and laughter. *"Parece que va matar una rata,"* he looks like he's coming out to kill a rat, Silveti muttered beside me.

The *paseo* was repeated, and Henry King assured Darryl that he could make the whole thing look legitimate by cutting away from Evans's face to Ava and Ty, thus not including the matador's full figure in the establishing shot of the opening parade. However, several other scenes were vital to the story: Pedro Romero dedicating his bull to Brett and, preceding this, his breaking the banderillas in half before placing them, a colorful gesture made for Brett's benefit. When the camera was rolling on the latter scene, the wooden shafts of the barbed sticks refused to break, and again the Mexican extras roared with laughter. The prop man hurried out to saw the shafts in half, and again Stan Hough pleaded with the extras to behave.

I noticed that Zanuck and King were conferring behind the camera and went over to join them. Realizing that they had at last been made aware of the truth of my objections to Darryl's casting, I suggested that it was still not too late to substitute Silveti in the role of Pedro Romero. The company could shoot reaction shots with the principals while Juanito changed into the suit-of-lights he used as a double and then take over from Evans.

Darryl was less than pleased with my intervention and turned to Hough for his opinion. Stan shrugged and agreed that this was a possible solution, but he was careful not to exceed his position of assistant director. "What do you think, Henry?" Zanuck asked, turning to King. "Darryl," Henry said, "I have always had one rule, and that is that I will never allow just one person to spoil any of my movies."

"All right," Darryl said, chewing on his cigar, "then let's get back to work."

I knew that his decision was final and that nothing I could say would alter it. If King had at least agreed to shoot the sequence with both men, the final choice could have been made in the projection room. I was like a lowly company-grade officer objecting to the wisdom of an attack that had been decided on at headquarters by the brass. And, as in a war, the hopeless attack continued.

Many years later I ran into Bob Evans in Hollywood and discovered that he had matured into a good-natured and enthusiastic movie producer. "You were right about my not being cut out to be an actor, Peter," he said, clapping me on the shoulder. He had known all along, it turned out, that I had done my best to have him replaced that spring in Mexico when we were both a lot less philosophical about the movie business. Apparently he had borne me no lasting grudge, proof of a generous nature.

WHY DID I STAY ON? The current joke among members of the crew claimed that I was the "highest paid assistant director in the business," as my only function seemed to be getting Ava to arrive on the set on time. The fact that I was still on salary was certainly not the answer. I knew that I had no contribution to make, as even the meaningless post of acting as Darryl's representative while he was away was no longer a valid excuse once he returned to Morelia. I suggested to him that it might not be a bad idea for me to go back to Europe, but he shook his head and said, "No, I want you to stay until we finish up in Mexico City." I could have insisted on leaving, of course—I was a free agent—but aside from incurring Darryl's wrath (and he had been both generous and loyal), I felt that I would be abandoning ship while the rest of the crew was still at general quarters.

I also felt that I had an obligation to Ava. I had been enamored of her at the beginning, but by the time our work in Morelia was completed my feelings had changed. I was still spending an occasional night at her house, but like an old married couple that had settled for a platonic relationship, we went without a word of explanation each to his own bed, as though we had been doing so for a good many years. She asked me to drive with her to Mexico City when the unit was scheduled to leave the location, and as she was traveling alone, I agreed to accompany her on the three-hour drive.

It turned out to be a much longer journey. We left Morelia at noon with Guillermo at the wheel of the Cadillac, hoping to arrive at our destination before dark. After fifty kilometers we had our first flat tire. While Guillermo changed wheels, we ate the picnic lunch Ava had brought along. She was in a happy mood, not at all disturbed by the delay, and swallowed a couple of small glasses of tequila before distributing chicken sandwiches to the three of us. An hour later the spare tire blew out, and although Guillermo managed to keep the big car from going into a ditch, he was obliged to hitchhike to the nearest filling station to have the inner tube repaired. He returned an hour and a half later. To help reduce the contents of the tequila bottle, I had had several shots myself, and just when we were going to arrive, if ever, didn't seem to matter anymore.

The bright lights and the bustle of the big city had an immediate effect on my traveling companions. We checked into the Bamer, one of the best hotels, and Ava declared that she wanted to go out on the town. It was eight-thirty in the evening and, tired by our journey and the tequila, I suggested we put off celebrating our arrival until the next day. "No," she insisted, "tomorrow is Sunday and we can sleep all day. We're going out tonight! So put on your best suit and pick me up in an hour. If you won't take me to dinner, I'll go by myself." I knew that this was not an empty threat, and after a shower followed by a brief nap, I took the hotel elevator to the penthouse suite that had been reserved for her.

She was dressed in all her finery, and after the weeks of gym suits and face cream, she looked radiantly beautiful. Guillermo had informed himself of the best restaurant in town, and we set off in style in his freshly washed limousine. I had been warned that Mexico City was not an undangerous place late at night and was therefore eager to dine and return to our hotel as quickly as possible.

At first glance the restaurant that had been recommended to Guillermo looked like the Saturday night meeting place of the local demimonde. Its decor was fiercely modern: gray walls and a small black wooden dance floor set in the middle of a burgundy-colored carpet. I felt ill at ease among the black-haired, navy-blue-suited dandies and their gaudy women, all the more so as we were immediately the center of attention. Ava, at the height of her career, had a special status in Latin countries, a Hollywood goddess who was rumored to have feet of clay because of her many overpublicized marriages and liaisons. We ordered drinks and dinner, and after the champagne cocktails had been served she suggested imperiously that we dance, which was the last thing in the world I wanted to do.

We ventured bravely out onto the parquet and were immediately joined by a score of other couples who wanted to get a closer look at my partner. Even had I been less self-conscious, the South American rhythms would have been too much for me, but under the present circumstances I found myself moving more woodenly than ever. Ava laughed and began to pound the staccato beat of the music on my right shoulder, without noticeable success. "My God," she said, "I may finally have to let you make love to me just to get you to relax!" I allowed that even that extreme measure probably wouldn't help, and she giggled and told me to hold her closer. I saw that the vichyssoise had arrived at our table and, feigning extreme hunger, convinced her to give up on her hopeless task.

It was well past midnight by the time I had paid our bill and we had rejoined Guillermo. "Where will we go now?" Ava asked once we were back in her car. When I suggested the hotel, she laughed as if I had made a joke. Guillermo said that the only nightclub he knew was a place called Guadalajara la Noche. His warning that it was a rather rough locale did not seem to discourage Miss Gardner. When I repeated that I was tired, she resorted to the usual drunken insults. I got out of the car at the next traffic light, but Guillermo ran after me and pleaded with me to come back. I agreed on the condition that he would join us for a last drink, and so the three of us entered the garish nightclub and were seated among the prostitutes and *pistoleros* who appeared to be the principal customers. Ava had a couple of tequilas, complete with salt and a lick of lime, and finally at three o'clock in the morning we staggered back to the Hotel Bamer.

I accompanied her to her penthouse suite, and as we entered the sitting room a telephone call came from Walter Chiari in Rome. I waited patiently while she spoke to him in the main bedroom, and when she finally emerged she seemed less than pleased with the outcome of her long conversation. "He's arriving here in a week or ten days," she announced glumly. "Aren't you pleased?" I asked her, trying not to sound like a rejected lover. She shrugged dubiously. "I don't know," she replied, adding that it was always difficult to have an outsider around while she was working, even a boyfriend. She undressed, ordered a glass of cold milk from room service, and got into her bed. I kissed her good night after the milk had been delivered and started for the door.

"Where the hell are *you* going?" she demanded.

"To my room," I told her, for once firm in my resolve to get a good night's rest. I felt relieved that my days of playing the part of Jake were about to come to an end.

THERE IS A SCENE early in *The Sun Also Rises* in which Brett comes to Jake's apartment late at night because she finds herself longing for him and then invites a Greek count who has been her escort to join them. Count Mippipopolous has offered to take her to Biarritz and Cannes, a proposition she has rejected humorously. It is one of the most touching and delightful scenes in the novel, and I had included it in the screenplay because it is charming while it demonstrates Brett's disregard for money. Like Isherwood's heroine Sally Bowles, Brett is promiscuous, but venality is not a part of her character, as it was not for the women who moved in the bohemian societies of Berlin and Paris after World War I. It was an important point to make about Brett's character.

Once again I was appalled by Darryl's casting, for he chose Gregory Ratoff to play the role. Ratoff was an old crony of his, the butt of many of his practical jokes, a strikingly homely man and not at all the sophisticated character described by Hemingway. Knowing that I had already irritated Darryl with my repeated objections to the casting of Pedro Romero, I was careful to voice my doubts about Ratoff in a hesitant manner. Zanuck brushed them aside impatiently. "Greg will be wonderful," he declared. The only problem he foresaw was that the high altitude of Mexico City might be injurious to Ratoff's health, as he had already suffered a mild heart attack. But it was up to Ratoff and his doctors whether Greg should accept the role.

Tyrone Power had installed an oxygen cylinder in his dressing room that he used whenever he felt short of breath after a long scene, and Darryl told Ratoff that he would make the same arrangement for him once he arrived. This decided the issue; in less than a week the elderly Russian-Jewish actor checked into the Hotel Bamer. So as not to prolong his stay, the scene was scheduled to be shot within a few days.

Watching it turned out to be sheer torture. Not only were Ratoff's looks a violation of what the part required, but his broad accent made most of what he said barely understandable. Darryl realized that something was going wrong, and he seemed as disturbed by the way the scene was being played as I was. He blamed Henry King for the lack of subtlety and was even more dismayed by Ratoff's inability to remember the dialogue. Ava, too, appeared to be unsure of herself, obviously put off by Ratoff's accent and his appearance, which made his offer to take her to Biarritz or Cannes sound like the proposition of a dirty old man. With Darryl standing beside me nervously chewing on his cigar, Ratoff sweating under the lights, and King doing his best to deal with the sound man's objections that he couldn't understand the dialogue, I knew that it was not the best time for me to give Ava even the most subtle words of guidance, although she asked for my opinion after each take.

On the drive back to the hotel in her car, she was in a sullen mood. I sensed that she was dissatisfied with the day's work and that she expected words of reassurance, but I was too depressed by Ratoff's performance to make any comment. Once we were back in her suite and she had made herself a dry martini, she asked me point-blank for my reaction. I said that I wasn't happy about the scene but that there was nothing either of us could do about it. "You didn't like the way I played it, did you?" she persisted. I shrugged and said that perhaps she had been a little too "tarty," an ill-considered comment that set her off in a rage.

"I played it like a whore, is that what you're saying?" she replied.

I tried to retract my statement, but to no avail. Her anger increased. She kicked at the drinks table, sending glasses and ice bucket flying. When she finished her tantrum the sitting room of her suite looked as if it had been hit by a minor hurricane. She went into her bedroom and locked the door, and I retired to my own quarters.

Although the realization had come too late, it was apparent to me that she had an inexplicable hatred of prostitutes, a deep-seated fear of being identified as one that was absurd. Although she had recovered her equilibrium an hour later and asked me to join her for a late supper, a milder outbreak was provoked by my telling her that Juliette Greco had arrived from Paris to join the cast. "All these French dames are whores," Ava raged. And Greco was no exception. "You'll see, she'll go to bed with Zanuck because she wants to make it in the movies." I told her that she was mistaken, that Greco had already made a name for herself as a singer, but Ava was not to be pacified. If she was that famous, why had she agreed to play such a small role? she asked. "She wants to be an actress," I replied. "Sure she does," Ava said, sarcastically, "and she knows just how to go about it."

The damage to the living room of her suite was repaired, and Ava decided to give a cocktail party for the crew and cast as her contribution to the end-of-picture party. Mel and Audrey brought Juliette Greco along, and Ava greeted her frostily. Greco spoke only a little English and appeared to be intimidated by her surroundings, so along with Mel I engaged her in conversation in French and told her how much I had admired her the many times I had heard her sing at Maurice Carrère's nightclub in Paris. While we were talking I heard my name being called commandingly by our hostess, and Juliette looked concerned. "You'd better obey," she said. She didn't want to have any trouble with Miss Gardner, she told me, who was obviously possessive of "her writer." Mel and I laughed and told her not to worry, that Ava's bark was worse than her bite. Mel suggested that the four of us, he, Audrey, Juliette, and I, dine together the next evening, and I accepted his invitation, glad for a change of routine.

The cocktail party dragged on, and once the last guest had departed I stayed with Ava for a late supper in her suite. She had had quite a few drinks, and her mood had not improved as a result. Walter Chiari was arriving from Rome the next day, she informed me, and, aware of her less than happy frame of mind, I did my best to reassure her that all would be well. She shook her head. She was not in love with Chiari, she said. She liked him, but that was all, and she hated the publicity that his coming to visit her would provoke, a notoriety she intimated that Walter enjoyed.

I sympathized with her, but I urged her to be kind to a man who was apparently very much in love with her and who was coming a long way to be with her. "You sound like you're glad to be getting rid of me," she said, perhaps an accurate reading of my mind that I tried to deny. "Nothing is going to change as far as you and I are concerned," I told her. "No matter what you decide to do with your life once he's here. Anyway, the most important thing right now is for you to finish the movie." "Yes, the movie, that's all you care about," she said and poured herself another drink.

She insisted that I spend the night with her, and as she was well beyond any rational argument I agreed. She was suddenly more affectionate than she had ever been, and once she had fallen into a deep sleep on her side of the bed I got up and dressed and returned to my room, more mystified by her complex nature than ever before.

. . . .

CHIARI turned out to be a pleasant young man, not the fiercely jealous Italian I had expected him to be. He had a good sense of humor about himself, and he asked good-naturedly who in the company he should be suspicious of in regard to Ava's affections. "It's probably you," he added and sighed resignedly. "She's still your girl," I assured him. "For the time being," he replied. He needed exercise to cure his jet lag, and Ava suggested a game of tennis before lunch. I warned Walter that he would be affected by the high altitude, but he said that didn't worry him, as his heart was in excellent condition, in spite of the life he had lived.

We went to the local tennis club, and I rallied for half an hour with Ava while he bought a pair of sneakers and rented a racquet. When Ava was thoroughly out of breath, Chiari and I faced each other for a set of singles and we all lunched afterward on the terrace of the club. Walter and Ava returned to the hotel, and I went to a bullfight with Juanito Silveti and his wife. For the first time in many weeks I felt free to do exactly as I pleased, and I enjoyed myself thoroughly in the company of people who had nothing to do with movies. That evening, as I was getting dressed to go to dinner with the Ferrers and Juliette Greco, my telephone rang. It was Ava. She said she wanted to see me for a few minutes and asked me to come up to her suite right away.

"Where's Walter?" I asked apprehensively. "He's down in the bar," she replied. "I told him I'd meet him there as soon as I was dressed." I voiced my doubts about the wisdom of my coming to her apartment, but she insisted, saying that she had to talk with me. She left the hallway door unlatched and, after entering cautiously, I found her in the dressing room of the suite, putting the final touches to her makeup. She had not yet put on her dress and was wearing a brassiere and a slip, which under different circumstances wouldn't have mattered, as I had often sat with her in her dressing room while her hair was being prepared for a scene. She looked well and admitted that the brief exercise she had taken had done her a world of good. "I haven't had a drink all day," she said, "and I've decided to go on the wagon."

"Never a bad idea," I said. "What's on your mind?"

"I just wanted to talk," she said. "I missed you this afternoon. I also want you to know," she added after a pause, "that I don't want to lose your friendship now that the picture is almost finished."

"Not to worry," I replied, using one of her favorite phrases.

She complained about the light in the dressing room and asked me to follow her to the small bathroom connected to the second bedroom in her suite, which was up a short flight of stairs. "Why don't you put on a robe?" I suggested.

"I can't be bothered," she said. "I'm late. Anyway, you've seen me like this dozens of times." We crossed the sitting room and went into the small guest bathroom. She was leaning across the sink, putting mascara on her eyelashes, when the front door buzzer sounded. "My God, that's probably Walter," she whispered. "You stay in here, lock the door, and whatever happens, don't open it."

By this time we could hear someone pounding on the door. It was Chiari, there was no doubt about that, and he was shouting angrily for Ava to let him in. It was a ridiculous situation. I whispered to Ava that it would be much better if he found me sitting in the living room, rather than my trying to hide from him. "Don't be so stupid! He's jealous of you," she said and shut the door in my face. It was like a Feydeau farce, I thought to myself as I locked the bathroom door, turned out the light, and sat on the edge of the bathtub to wait.

For a while I could hear angry voices coming from the sitting room, and a few minutes later Chiari tried the door of the bathroom and challenged me to come out of hiding. I knew that if I did there would be an unpleasant scene, although I could easily have explained my presence by telling the truth. I also knew that Ava would be the one to look the most ridiculous. I lit a cigarette and waited. After twenty minutes I heard the front door slam, and I ventured out into the empty suite. Once I had returned to my own room I found a message from Juliette asking me not to pick her up but instead to join her in the restaurant where we were to dine with Mel and Audrey.

I have forgotten the name of the place, but I recall a large patio surrounded by bougainville bushes. Ty Power and his Mexican girlfriend, the Ferrers and Juliette, Zanuck, Eddie Albert, and Ava, accompanied by Walter Chiari, were all seated at a long table. Mel explained that Darryl had insisted on being the host for the entire group, and so they had all joined forces. There was an empty chair opposite Walter, where I had no choice but to take my place. Everyone appeared to be in a festive mood as margaritas had already been served and the meal ordered. Chiari looked over at me with a hurt expression on his face. "I know you were hiding in the bathroom," he mumbled in a low voice, and I answered that I had no idea what he was talking about, a lie that he chose disdainfully to disregard.

Early the next morning, Ava called me and with gales of laughter informed me that when she and Walter had returned to her suite later in the evening, he had gone immediately to the guest bathroom and had discovered that the door was still locked. Obviously I had shut it behind me without removing the safety latch.

We wound up that night, I remember, in a large, rather elegant nightclub, a dimly lit place with a band and the usual dance floor. Ava had forgotten about her decision to go on the wagon, and although she was far from inebriated she was no longer her genial sober self. At a nearby table sat a large group of Mexican men who stared rudely across at us, which annoyed Ava. "Don't pay any attention to them," I told her, but she was well beyond taking reasonable advice. In a loud voice she complained about the rudeness of our neighbors, using her favorite Spanish insult to describe them. "*Son maricones, todos,*" she said; they were faggots all.

Chiari leaned over in my direction. "In five minutes," he said, "we will be fighting like cowboys and Indians."

"Not me," I replied. "I'm a devout coward." Ava got up from the table and excused herself. We all sat in silence, watching her move off in the direction of the toilets. She failed to return and after a quarter of an hour Silveti and I went to find her. The female attendant informed us that she had left, and we hurried out into the street and were informed by the doorman that Miss Gardner had set off on foot at least ten minutes earlier. "Things are not all bad," Silveti remarked comically. "She's heading north."

Chiari and I paid the bill and, with Guillermo at the wheel of his ancient Cadillac, we toured the bars and nightclubs of the district without success. Chiari was less concerned than I expected him to be, undoubtedly having experienced similar incidents in Rome. At midnight we abandoned the search and returned to the hotel. At four o'clock in the morning the telephone next to my bed aroused me out of a deep sleep. It was Ava. She was in a bar and had no money, she informed me in a husky voice. I took down the address and set out to find her. I thought it strange that she hadn't called Chiari, but there had been no time to ask her anything before she hung up. Nor did she make any attempt to explain her actions once I had paid the bill and we were on our way back to our hotel in a taxi. She had sobered up by that time, was briefly apologetic for the trouble she had caused, and before she returned to her penthouse suite gave me her solemn promise that she would go on the wagon for the remainder of our stay in Mexico City.

This time she kept her promise, and the last ten days of filming were concluded without any further complications. Chiari flew back to Rome not long after our disastrous evening out on the town. They had quarreled and made up several times before his departure and finally, according to Ava, had resolved not to decide anything about their future until she returned to Europe. Then Beatrice, Ava's older sister, arrived. Her nickname was "Bapie," and I found her to be a good-natured, rather plump dyed blonde with glasses, who it soon became evident was a stabilizing influence on her younger sister. If Ava had inherited the greater share of beauty, Bapie had come away with the common sense. She also had a good sense of humor, which was embellished by her southern accent.

I was seated on the edge of Ava's bed late one Sunday morning, having been asked to come and discuss some problem that had plagued Ava during the night, when Beatrice appeared briefly in the doorway. "Come out of there, you two," she proclaimed loudly. "A bedroom is for sleeping and a little clean screwing and that's about all." This and various other semivulgar sisterly remarks delighted Ava, as did the fact that her predictions about Juliette Greco had turned out to be accurate, for it was now apparent to all hands that the dark-haired French singer had become Zanuck's paramour. "I told you that was exactly what would happen," Ava crowed. "These French dames are all alike."

As a result of his newly found inamorata, Darryl appeared to be a changed man. He was genuinely in love this time, he confessed to one and all. Whereas the hold Bella had had on him had been mostly physical, his feelings for Juliette went far beyond mere sexual attraction. For Juliette, Darryl obviously represented a possible fulfillment of her ambition to become an actress, a familiar aphrodisiac in the movie business. It was much more surprising to me that Zanuck was still capable, at the age of fifty-five, of such intense feelings. Not that the mid-fifties, even then, seemed to me to herald the beginning of senility, yet his falling so desperately in love was unusual. Of all the moguls in the industry, only he and David Selznick had lost their heads to their hearts so late in life.

And like Selznick, Zanuck's love life was finally to contribute to his ruin. During the next few years he cast Greco in several important roles in films that failed to return their costs. Ultimately, when she left him, he found another aspiring French actress to take her place, which led to a confrontation with his son, who was by this time running the studio. I remember seeing him before his final disagreement with

Dick, walking his new mistress's poodle down a side street off the avenue Montaigne, his steps faltering slightly as the small dog pulled at its leash. He greeted me pleasantly enough, although he didn't stop to chat as he would have done in the past. It occurred to me that his story would make an interesting novel, a mixture of *Blue Angel* and *Dodsworth* in which a middle-aged man sacrifices everything he has worked for, money and power and fame, for the dangerous pitfalls of romantic love.

But during those final days of our stay in Mexico City he was his old self, the energetic producer, unhesitant to use his authority. He insisted again that I stay on until Ava had completed her dubbing sessions and then admitted that he had written a few scenes to embellish Greco's part in the film. I stared at him with disbelief. "But her part has no function in the story other than to illustrate one of Jake's moods," I said. "He picks the prostitute and takes her to the 'dancing' merely to shock his friends and to lampoon his own unfortunate condition." He was well aware of all that, Darryl replied; the few scenes he had written would do nothing to violate the spirit of the movie. There was no use arguing with him until I had read what he had written or had seen the rough cut, when in either event it would be too late.

As a conciliatory gesture, before he left Mexico City Darryl told me that he was thinking of producing Romain Gary's novel *The Roots of Heaven*, which 20th Century-Fox had acquired, and asked if I would be interested in working on the screenplay. John Huston had signed to direct the movie, which was to be filmed in the Chad. I told Darryl that for the good of all concerned he would be well advised to look for another writer. Africa and Huston would provide enough worries without my added presence to complicate matters, and Zanuck agreed. We parted amicably. Despite our many disagreements and the disappointing result of our work, I retained a sincere liking for him.

An absurd, final incident took place three days before I left Mexico City. The last scene had been completed, and to celebrate Ava suggested that she, Doreen Silveti, and I have an early dinner on the way home from the studio. Doreen knew of a picturesque place that was open early, and it was still daylight when we arrived at the restaurant, which had been built to resemble a Spanish country tavern, complete with a patio built around a stone fountain. We were the only diners at that hour and enjoyed a tranquil meal during which Ava kept her promise not to drink any hard liquor. When we were on the point of leaving, a group of mariachis appeared and began to play. Ava begged to be permitted to have just one farewell tequila, and I relented and called for the check. Doreen had gone to the ladies' room, and Ava got to her feet and moved off in the direction of the patio, dancing a fandango.

Suddenly, as she neared the stone fountain, I saw her fall. I rushed forward to help her, and out of the corner of my eye I saw a waiter running toward her as well. As I reached her, I stepped into an open manhole and found myself up to my armpits in icy water. The shock was numbing, and I fought to get my breath. Ava had managed to get to her feet and, grabbing me by the arms, tried to drag me back up onto the tiled floor. Seeing that I was not hurt, she began to laugh, and when at last I was back on dry land, she hugged me, laughing even harder as I stood there in my gray flannel suit, wet to the skin. At this point someone turned on the lights in the darkened patio, and there we were for all to see, two apparently drunken American tourists.

Ava had tripped over the manhole cover, I realized later, and had fallen clear, while I had stepped into the open hole like a character in a Mack Sennett comedy. Guillermo drove us back to the Bamer, and as we got out of the car we were confronted by the movie crew, who were all assembled on the sidewalk waiting for the bus that was to drive them to the airport. Stanley Hough looked at me with raised eyebrows. "I hope you make it back to L.A., Pete," he said quietly. There was no use trying to explain; I just went to my room and took a hot bath. It was a fitting ending to the saga of my last Hemingway movie. Ava finished her dubbing sessions in two days, and we caught the first available flight to Los Angeles.

IT WAS NOT a very happy homecoming—far from it. Humphrey Bogart's death early in 1957 had cast a pall over the lives of his friends. John Huston, Sinatra, Lazar, Judy Garland, and Sid Luft were all deeply affected by the courageous manner in which Bogey had faced the end. His home had been the center of their lives, ruled by an irreplaceable friend whose quiet common sense had furnished them with a refuge from the unreal atmosphere of the town. Betty Bacall was thrust into the tragic widowhood that she had known for some months would be her lot, but the knowledge that Bogey's ordeal was finally over brought her no relief.

We lunched together at the Bel Air Hotel and talked for a long time about alternatives facing her. She had decided to sell the house at 232

Mapleton Drive and move back to New York, although she was involved with Sinatra in a relationship that troubled her, as she sensed it would probably not last very long. For the time being his friendship was a consolation that kept her from feeling utterly lost, and she said as much. I pointed out the obvious—that she was a young woman and that a whole lifetime still lay ahead of her. She nodded, accepting the trite truth of my words, which at this moment she did not quite believe.

Knowing that Sinatra was still emotionally involved with his ex-wife, she asked me about Ava, and I assured her that there was no chance of their getting back together. Ava would be returning to Spain as soon as she had been to see her dentist, her doctor, and her business manager, all necessary chores for an expatriate on a visit home. Betty nodded and sighed, and I felt I had done very little to relieve her anxieties and her sadness. I also told her that I would be returning to Paris in a few days, and she replied wistfully that she envied me, as Paris was a city she felt she could live in quite happily.

It was an illusion we had all shared, I told her, but it wasn't the place that mattered, it was the people who were a part of your life, a fact she was well aware of at that moment, she said. Yet I agreed with her that it was probably time for her to leave California now that Bogey was gone. It seemed like the end of an epoch to both of us, and the aura of melancholy it evoked was undeniable.

On the evening before my departure I took my mother to dinner. She had recovered from the trauma of selling her house on Mabery Road and seemed quite content to be living in the small apartment on Veteran Avenue where I had worked with Freddy Zinnemann on the script of *The Old Man and the Sea*. She was giving dramatic lessons to a couple of young actresses and actors to make ends meet, but the main interest in her life was her granddaughter Christine, whom she visited regularly at Jigee's house in Pacific Palisades. She was worried about Jigee's health, her smoking and drinking, and was doing her best to influence her to change her habits. Knowing that my decision to return to Europe was irrevocable, she asked me not to stay away too long. "Someday I won't be here when you come back," she warned me, words that saddened me but that I didn't quite believe.

To escape once again was my only desire, and it was without regret that I was driven to the airport in a studio car, a last generous gesture of my former employer. But when I arrived in Paris I was less certain that I had done the right thing, for returning to an even temporary base provoked a summing up that was somewhat depressing. It was almost ten years ago that I had come here to join Jigee and the Hemingways at the Ritz, and I was pointedly aware of my lack of accomplishment. As a screenwriter I had gone from one unsatisfactory assignment to another, and although my brief stint as a script doctor in Africa had resulted in my writing a fairly successful novel, my two more recent jobs had left me thoroughly disenchanted with the movie business.

Yet I had enjoyed being a member of a production team, even in an unproductive capacity, for living in a group, it seemed in retrospect, was better than being completely on my own again. I found myself missing Ava's company despite all of the problems it had involved. The day we parted in Beverly Hills I had a suspicion that I would miss her, a feeling I managed to suppress. So I had promised I would go to see her in Spain, which was a gentler way of saying good-bye, for her and for me.

Inevitably the streets of Paris made me think of Papa. I hadn't heard from him since my departure for Mexico. In Los Angeles Freddy Zinnemann had reported that he had made a courtesy call to the Finca Vigía and that Hemingway's appearance had disturbed him, as his health seemed to have deteriorated in the last two years. "How you doing?" Freddy had asked him, and Hemingway had replied grimly: "All right . . . Black Dog and I are trying to outlive each other."

I went to Leggewie's office and collected the mail that had accumulated there, as I had thought it unwise to have it forwarded to Morelia. Strangely enough, there were two letters from Hemingway that he had written after returning to El Escorial from the *feria* at Zaragoza. He reiterated his admiration for Ordóñez, who had triumphed on two successive afternoons. They were still planning to go to Africa together the next year. "He is a wonderful boy," Papa wrote, "pure where Miguel [Dominguín] has been corrupted." He added that apart from his personal feelings, Ordóñez was maybe the best bullfighter he had ever seen. Juanito Quintana and all the old-timers agreed with him. Quintana had said that there were only four great bullfighters in this century—Joselito, Belmonte, Manolete, and Dominguín—and that Ordóñez was better than any one of them.

The letter ended with three brief paragraphs that confirmed Zinnemann's report. He had put a certain amount of strain on his heart holding those fish so close for "Honest Leland *et ce brave Spence,*" he had written in a large scrawl. He had beaten a few tougher raps, he added, but intimated that if he were to die he would be leaving the field clear for "Irving Shaw, Irving Marie Alcott, Irving O'Hara and other promising practitioners." The next paragraph was in a humorous vein. He also sent his best to "anyone he knew," but added that he was conserving his strength for Africa. He had booked passage from Venice to Mombasa on the second of January 1957 and would wear a sandwich board for his return to Italy, "stating simply: Have No Fear Daughters of the Doges. Hemingstein Is Now Positively Not Fucking No One." At the bottom of the letter he had written: "Love, Papa."

There was a second handwritten note dated the thirtieth of October 1956, the day after Israeli troops invaded the Sinai peninsula at the height of the Suez crisis. The first few sentences were dedicated to his and Mary's health and a request to leave the binoculars and the tweed cap I had bought for him in Ireland with Georges at the Ritz bar, which I had already done. The letter ended with a discussion of the Suez crisis. He ridiculed Irwin Shaw and Ben Hecht for their support of Israel and expressed a wish to join the Arabs in their fight, except that the Arabs were too wealthy and he had never learned Arabic.

He was a man who never forgot his grudges, it seemed, but as the letters were seven months old I saw no point in answering them. The Suez invasion had outraged many other intellectuals, who had condemned Britain, France, and Israel, but Papa's hatred of Irwin Shaw and Ben Hecht seemed unjustified, although Hecht had made several outrageous statements in the past, such as that he rejoiced every time a British soldier was killed in Palestine.

I felt lonely and depressed. My small room at the Raphaël suddenly had the aura of a prison cell, and feeling the need to escape it I called on an old girlfriend. She answered the telephone after the first ring and began to remonstrate with me for not having called or written. I made some weak excuses, and she informed me that she was getting married in a few days, news I accepted with a sense of relief, as our relationship had never been satisfactory. I congratulated her and wished her luck. It was one of the few times in my life that an emotional problem had solved itself, and when she suggested we meet that evening for a farewell drink, I agreed without hesitation.

I took a long nap to get over the time change and set out for my farewell drink with the young woman. It was a strange encounter that I have never forgotten. Elegantly dressed and newly coiffed, she seemed more nervous than I had expected her to be. She informed me that she had met her fiancé only a month ago, that he was a handsome, young French businessman of a good family, and that she had decided to accept his offer of marriage a fortnight later. Independently wealthy and an orphan, she had always had the tendency to be impetuous, which had been the source of most of our quarrels.

I made some sort of fatuous remark such as "All's well that ends well," and suddenly she burst into tears. It was upsetting to say the least, all the more so as her emotional outburst was totally unexpected. "You shouldn't be the one who's crying," I told her. She nodded, blew her nose, and wiped away her tears. "Anyway, if you're not sure you're doing the right thing, wait a while, live in sin with your beau, and see if you still feel like marrying him in a few months' time," I counseled her.

It was too late to change her plans, she replied; she was going through with it. I realized that she had always suspected that she was being courted for her money, doubts she had been free of while we were together, as I had made it clear from the first that matrimony was the furthest thing from my mind and had quoted a witticism Louise de Vilmorin had uttered at a dinner party, that "only priests and homosexuals were anxious to marry nowadays." Trying to reassure her I remarked that marriage was a lottery at best, but my words did little to improve her state of mind. She asked me what my plans were, and I told her that I was thinking of going to Biarritz for a few weeks, or perhaps even St. Tropez, "to mend my broken heart." Ignoring my feeble attempt at humor, she suggested that in case I decided on the latter I should make use of her apartment there, a generous offer I declined.

She was more cheerful at the moment of final parting, and after seeing her to her car I walked slowly back to my hotel, relieved to be free of all entanglements. My euphoria was short-lived. An old back injury recurred, a pinched nerve I had acquired on the tennis court that had a crippling effect on my body. For four days I was confined to my expensive prison cell, and just as I was getting better Lazar called from London and invited me to join him in Beaulieu, his first stop on his annual summer vacation. I had never been fond of the French Riviera, but as I knew surfing was out of the question for the time being, joining my energetic friend for a fortnight of luxurious living seemed like a good solution.

SWIFTY was his usual frenetic and amusing self, a mine of show business gossip, given to boasting about the many deals he had made recently, which made me feel slightly regretful about deserting California and yet reassured me, as I knew that had I stayed on I would have even less chance of ever writing anything but screenplays. The making of money was one of his favorite arias, but in that he was no different from most of my Hollywood friends.

At my suggestion we went to visit Garbo, who was staying in a villa owned by George Schlee overlooking the Mediterranean, a social call that pleased Lazar, who was as eager as anyone else to meet the famous retired actress. Greta was charming and friendly, and we talked about diets and the state of my mother's health, pointedly avoiding any mention of the movies. Her favorite director, George Cukor, was also a friend and client of Swifty's, and so they had at least one mutual interest.

Never patient with idle chatter, Swifty asked the question that was uppermost in his agile mind: "Have you ever thought about going back to work, Greta? George has a story he'd like you to do."

Bathed in the golden afternoon sun, Garbo's face showed no change of expression. "Oh, I don't know," she said slowly. "Oh, I don't know." The words, uttered in her deep voice, hung listlessly in the warm Mediterranean air.

Hastily I changed the subject. On the way down the driveway of the villa Lazar inquired, "Did I ask the wrong question?"

"No, not really," I told him. "Anyway, you got the right answer, didn't you?"

Swifty informed me that we had been invited to a cocktail party by one of his socially prominent friends, a group that had become important to him now that he had "arrived." "You mean, *you've* been invited," I said. "No, we've both been invited," he insisted. "Anyway, you're coming along!"

Knowing from experience what sort of gathering it was certain to be, I suggested that I meet him somewhere for dinner later, but he was adamant. "We'll only stay half an hour," he promised. "Then I'll take you anywhere you like for a good meal."

The cocktail party turned out to be precisely the sort of social gathering I had envisioned—gray-haired men in blazers with golden buttons and perfectly coiffed ladies in cocktail gowns, nearly all of them twenty years my senior. After an hour of small talk I not too discreetly glanced at my watch to remind Lazar of his promise, and we made our apologies to the host and hostess and departed in Lazar's rented automobile.

Swifty was staying on in Beaulieu for a few more days, as he was awaiting the arrival of Janet Thomas, a witty and good-natured young woman who occasionally accompanied him on his summer vacations. Together they intended to travel to Provence and attend the bullfights in Arles and Nîmes, where Luis Miguel was scheduled to appear. It was my intention to meet them in Avignon, where we had reserved rooms at a four-star hotel, and from there to drive to the neighboring towns for two additional *corridas*. Lazar had become an aficionado as a result of his befriending Dominguín, and he was looking forward to seeing his new friend in action.

Our daily routine of rich meals and lack of exercise was making me restless, and after my monastic three months playing the off-screen role of Jake Barnes in Mexico, it occurred to me that St. Tropez would provide the cure for which it had become almost as famous as Lourdes, so I rented a car and set off for that less formal part of the French Riviera. Among the St. Tropez regulars I ran into Roger Vadim, a skiing companion from the previous winter in Klosters with whom I had vaguely discussed various movie projects. Vadim had brought prominence to the resort, as he had made his first picture there with Brigitte Bardot, who later became his wife. His close friend and business associate Raoul Levy was a freelance producer, an amusing, if not considered too reliable, upstart in the French world of *le cinéma* who had served as a nose gunner in a Belgian bomber crew attached to the RAF. His adventurous war service seemed to have prepared him for the almost equally hazardous existence of an independent producer, which he was pursuing with the same reckless abandon.

Levy and Vadim were about to make a movie in Spain based on a French novel; Bardot, now Vadim's ex-wife, was to play the leading role. The handsome young director had helped Brigitte achieve stardom, and she had agreed to appear in this movie, partly to repay him for his earlier sponsorship. Vadim, in his gentle, hesitant way, suggested I come to Madrid for a few weeks to rewrite the English dialogue, which he was planning to shoot at the same time as the original French version. It was a simple task, he assured me, that would not take up very much of my time. Because of the extreme heat of Castile in August, the crew and actors working on the film would be based at El Escorial, and it was in these by now familiar surroundings that Vadim suggested I stay for the fortnight that would be needed to do the job.

It sounded like a painless way to pick up some extra cash, all the more so as I was intending to join Luis Miguel later in the month and accompany him on the last leg of his summer tour. Because of my back injury I had left my car in Paris, and knowing that I would need it while in El Escorial, I decided to leave St. Tropez after a few more idle days, return to Paris, and then drive down to Spain.

A week later I arrived at the Hotel Felipe II and, after a brief rest, began my task of translating and adapting the sparse dialogue of the existing script—simple words that *La Bardot* might be willing to learn and say. Vadim, whose English was hesitant but fairly comprehensive, seemed satisfied with the first scenes I completed, but when it came time to make his leading lady say the words I had written, she refused categorically. BB, as she was known to her friends and the French public, had outgrown and outshone her Svengali-like ex-husband, and there was nothing either he or Raoul Levy could do to make her change her mind.

There was a certain logic to the stand she took. It was too late for her to learn English, and to act in a language of which she had learned to say only a few words would make her look ridiculous. I wasn't too concerned. I had agreed to do the job to make a little money and because I was planning to go to Spain anyway. Nor were Levy and Vadim particularly perturbed. Most Italian movies were postsynchronized, and both of my young friends were accustomed to using all the tricks of the trade. However, to facilitate the dubbing sessions for which a less reluctant actress would be hired, I continued with my translation, at the same time simplifying the French dialogue.

When I had completed all the words required of me, I said farewell to one and all, was paid in cash for my trouble, loaded up my Porsche, and joined Luis Miguel for a brief tour of Andalucía, after which I returned via Biarritz to Klosters and the bracing air of the Alps, which I had learned finally to appreciate after my stay in warmer climes.

Autumn in Graubünden, provided the weather cooperates, can be a season of magic. As the area is well below the tree line, the colors are impressive even on rainy days, and although Klosters becomes something of a ghost town for six weeks, the solitude is bearable and almost a welcome change. If the snow comes early, as it used to in those days, the transition to winter is painless, and the landscape is transformed overnight into paradise. All this transpired according to plan in 1957, and by early December the winter season was in full swing. I was happy to be reunited with all my old friends and to be able to make the first tracks down many of the long runs that make the Parsenn an unrivaled skiing area.

Not long after Christmas Tola Litvak called from Vienna to ask if I would consider joining him for a couple of weeks to do some work on a screenplay for a movie he was about to put into production. It was another repair job that I was not particularly eager to do, but as I had not yet started to write the bullfight novel I had in mind, I agreed to come and help him fix a few scenes.

IT HAS LONG BEEN MY VIEW that reminiscences are in order when they recall a part of the past that is over and done with, so that whatever indiscretions may result from looking back can do little harm to the people who have survived. When they touch upon the lives of those who share the author's present, he is obliged to act as his own censor. We inflict enough pain on the human beings we love without revealing secrets that might cause them embarrassment. That is the reason for my brief preamble—an explanation for my limiting the account of the most important turning point in my life to a synopsis of events rather than a detailed narrative.

Snow was falling on the ancient city of Vienna the day I arrived. It covered the parks and the monuments and was turning to slush on the streets my father had loved as a boy and had enjoyed during the last years of his life. Tola was there to welcome me, as was Noel Howard, who had been elevated to the job of second unit director. The same atmosphere of nervous apprehension that is always in evidence prior to the beginning of principal photography was noticeable.

George Tabori, a Hungarian novelist and playwright who had been a frequent guest at our house in Santa Monica, had written the screenplay. It was based on Guy de Maupassant's classic short story "Boule de Suif," which had inspired John Ford's *Stagecoach* as well. I read it the evening of my arrival in the comfortable room Tola had taken for me in the Hotel Imperial. At his request I also read the treatment Tabori had written that had convinced Litvak to buy Tabori's original story. The arena of the drama was the Austro-Hungarian frontier that a group of travelers were attempting to cross shortly after the end of World War II, among them a scientist who was wanted by the Russians and whose escape an English gentlewoman, his mistress, was trying desperately to arrange.

In the de Maupassant story, a chubby prostitute seduces the Prussian officer who is detaining the group, so that those with whom she is traveling can make their getaway, and she is looked down upon by her companions for accepting the German's advances. This slender plot had been transposed to fit the postwar situation on the iron curtain border. Yul Brynner was to play the menacing colonel, now a Russian, and Deborah Kerr the lady who sacrifices herself for the welfare of the group. Jason Robards had been cast as the scientist. It was all tantalizingly romantic. The Russian colonel turns out to have a heart of gold, and the English lady is attracted by him, so that sacrificing her honor becomes more acceptable. The story seemed to work pretty well, and I was puzzled about just what Litvak wanted me to improve.

As a rule, a screenwriter hired to rewrite a script finds something to complain about in his predecessor's work to justify the money he is being paid. I do not pretend to have been more virtuous than my peers, but in this instance making changes for the sake of change seemed not only unnecessary but foolhardy. Litvak was scheduled to begin shooting in a little more than a week; the sets had been built and the casting completed. Except for the ending, which I thought might be improved with a few lines of additional dialogue, there seemed little I could do to earn my wages. I had been summoned to Vienna, it was my impression, to act as a spare tire in case of an unforeseen blowout, a most unlikely event, and I told Litvak so. He shook his head and said we would discuss the script later, after Deborah Kerr and Jason Robards had arrived.

Yul Brynner was already in residence at the Hotel Imperial, being outfitted in a Russian uniform, jackboots and all. De Maupassant's Prussian officer was a nebulous character. Not so his Soviet counterpart in Tabori's story, or else Brynner would certainly not have accepted the part, nor would the entire project have been justified. And despite the authoritarian and bullying nature of the Russian colonel in the script, both he and the English lady had to be brushed by a physical attraction that bordered on true love.

Considering the tensions of the cold war in 1958, the movie was a somewhat bold undertaking. The Russian colonel was a forerunner of the Soviet submarine captain who has recently crossed the screen in *The Hunt for Red October*. But in the winter of 1957–58, *glasnost* was a word no one outside the Soviet Union had ever heard of, and to show a Russian officer in a sympathetic light was an innovation very much in the Litvak mold. He had been the first producer-director to make a hero out of a German soldier less than five years after World War II in *Decision Before Dawn*.

He had chosen Yul Brynner to play the part of the "hero heavy" because he was the right type, a mixture of Slavic and Oriental, and also because Yul's manner was imperious and menacing. Brynner spoke fluent Russian and had at one time even held a Soviet passport. My first meeting with our leading man took place on the street outside the Vienna studio where I had accompanied Tola to inspect a set. We were about to get into the car to return to the Hotel Imperial when Yul suddenly appeared. He got in beside the driver, a place he declared imperiously he always occupied. I commented on his not wearing an overcoat, and he replied that he never wore one, words that were followed by violent coughing. I ventured to say that the cough went well with the line, which provoked general laughter and a quick puzzled backward glance from Yul. But he decided not to take offense at this lese majesty, although his behavior suggested he was still playing the part of the King of Siam, to which he owed his stardom.

His regal manner and his dictatorial utterances I soon learned were more show than anything else; they concealed an astonishingly civilized nature, although being a star and a king were profoundly allied in his concept of what his behavior was to be. A few days later, while we were all having lunch—Tola, Noel Howard, Brynner, and I—Litvak brought up the subject of Yul's riding lessons, as at one point in the story he was to appear on horseback. Yul said that he "hated horses" and looked upon them as dumb, dangerous beasts. I begged to differ, and Tola suggested I take over Yul's introduction to equitation, a proposition Brynner accepted reluctantly.

So I joined him in his initial outing on a bay gelding the studio had hired. The animal had a better disposition than the actor and soon became one of his favorite possessions. He bought it, declaring that when the movie was finished he would ship it to the United States, where he feared his blossoming career might ultimately have him playing in a western. I realize now that managing to convince Yul that a horse could be one of his best friends was my major contribution to the making of *The Journey*, as the film was finally called; the three or four lines of dialogue I wrote were of less importance.

There were so many more preproduction chores for Tola to take care of in the days that followed that he and I did not go over the script for a fortnight. In the meantime our leading lady arrived, as did Jason Robards, Eli Wallach and his wife Anne Jackson, Robert Morley, Gérard Oury, Marie Daems, and the less well known actors who were to play subsidiary roles. But Deborah Kerr, with her beauty, her simple and direct manner, stood out above all the others. Tola had told me that she was an exceptional woman, and I soon realized that his glowing description had not been an exaggeration.

Our press conference was surprisingly well attended by Austrian and British reporters, for the arrival of a Hollywood movie company was quite an event in the Austrian capital. There followed a dinner for the crew and actors hosted by Litvak. I was seated on Deborah's left, while Tola sat on her right. Gérard Oury and Marie Daems had been cast as the French passengers on the bus, and as neither of them spoke English, they were assigned places on the far side of the table. Yul, in the company of a pretty, young Austrian girl, sat facing us. She was to play a small role in the film, but a more important part in his life, as she ultimately had a child with him.

Needless to say, I was delighted with the seating arrangement. Men all over the world had fallen in love with my dinner partner merely after seeing her on the screen. To share her company for an hour or two was even a more telling experience, as she was equally charming in real life. Unlike any of the other celebrated actresses I had met, she was modest and almost self-effacing, intelligent, and, needless to say, beautiful in a very special way, with her pale skin and reddish blond hair. Oscar Wilde is credited with the aphorism that an actress is more than a woman, and an actor less than a man, which I found to be accurate.

We talked with complete disregard for any of the other people present, and we even danced a waltz, the obligatory Viennese music supplied by the orchestra. Champagne was served, and there was a toast or two, and before the evening had ended I had fallen in love with her. She was married and had two daughters, she told me, who were at that moment residing in California with her husband, a fact not to be disregarded, but it did nothing to change my immediate adoration of her. Before we parted late that night, she ventured to say that she hoped that wherever we happened to be in the distant future, we should never lose touch with each other.

Litvak, the shrewd romantic that he was, had taken notice of our mutual attraction and the next day, when I confessed my feelings to him, stated that "no one worth having was ever unattached," dangerous friendly advice, but in all probability an accurate assessment. My duties involving the Tabori script were less than taxing, so I spent a good deal of my time roaming Vienna and its many antique shops, purchasing presents for our leading lady. In one of them, a small silver box with an ornate heart on its lid, I left a note that was discovered by Deborah's husband when he arrived in Vienna on a short visit, precipitating events neither Deborah nor I had planned.

There were unpleasant scenes and confrontations that now, more than thirty years later, it is unnecessary to mention. It had not been Deborah's intent to change her life, but she was overtaken by events and before the movie had been completed late in the spring of 1958, we were a couple, happy and plagued by problems at the same time.

The burden of the legal proceedings that followed that year fell mainly on Deborah's shoulders. She is not, and was not then, a person who can bear to inflict pain on others, yet somehow she survived, as did her children and her first husband. Happiness, my mother wrote in her memoirs, is almost always built on the unhappiness of others, a sad truth that had become apparent to us but that caused Deborah great anguish. Yet despite the legal complications and her pangs of conscience, she continued to play her role in *The Journey* to perfection. Tola's moral support and Yul Brynner's friendship helped her through that most trying period.

FEARING that a Hollywood divorce, for that was what we were now involved in even though we were thousands of miles removed from California, would have a disastrous effect on her children, her main concern was for their welfare. Tony Bartley, her husband, was equally conscious of this and brought their two daughters, Melanie and Francesca, to England and had them made wards of court. One of the conditions imposed by his lawyers was that I should have no contact with them. As the schools the two small girls were attending near London had not yet let out for the summer holidays, we rented a house in Guéthary, a few miles north of St. Jean de Luz, for the month of June, for Deborah was desperately in need of a vacation. Then in July it was her intention to spend the rest of the summer with her daughters.

Henry Hyde, my old wartime friend, had agreed to act as Deborah's attorney, and he urged us to invite a third party to share our temporary domicile. We asked Marie Daems, the young French actress who had appeared in *The Journey*, to join us, and she agreed. Marie's actor husband had gone off with her best friend, so she was not particularly anxious to return to Paris, and the three of us moved into the dilapidated villa I had rented sight unseen.

Despite her own troubles, Marie was a cheerful companion, and we spent a more or less relaxed fortnight together, until Marie decided that it was time for her to face her own disaster. Then toward the end of our stay I learned that Luis Miguel was fighting in Toulouse, and as I was eager for Deborah to meet him, we drove to the nearby French city. Deborah had never been to a bullfight, and she had mixed emotions about witnessing what she knew to be a cruel spectacle.

An hour before the start of the *corrida*, we visited Miguel at his hotel, and Deborah was instantly charmed by him. This lessened the shock of what went on in the ring, particularly as the young matador appearing with Dominguín that afternoon was almost fatally gored while placing a pair of banderillas on his first bull. The danger confronting a man she had just met made Deborah less aware of the fate of the bulls, although I noticed that she covered her eyes while the bulls were being pic-ed, a gesture that Luis Miguel saw and later imitated as he passed in front of us on his first triumphant tour of the plaza. That he had noticed this while he fought won him an even greater place in her esteem.

Before starting on our drive back to Guéthary, we went to visit him. He had even seen the tears that had come to Deborah's eyes at the prolonged death of one of the animals that had been fought by another bullfighter. "You don't have to come and see me again," he told her consolingly. "But I want to," Deborah replied bravely, but then said she was leaving for England in a few days.

Miguel glanced quickly in my direction. When I explained that I would not be accompanying Deborah, he looked puzzled, and, as perceptive as ever to the problems of the heart, he realized I would be somewhat at a loss without Deborah. "Then you must come with me," he said. "It will make you feel a little better for a while." I told him that it was high time for me to go to work, and he shook his head, saying that he doubted I would be able to get back to the typewriter in my present state of mind. After another month on the road with him, he remarked lightheartedly, I would have learned all I needed to know about "this crazy life" and be better prepared to write the novel he knew I was planning. Very few writers, Hemingway included, he said, had ever had the opportunity to share an active torero's campaign for several seasons, so I would not be wasting my time.

Another month of research seemed like a small investment; I also knew that going back to Switzerland without Deborah would probably turn out to be unproductive, focused solely on waiting for news of her.

So I told him not to be surprised if I turned up somewhere in Spain in a week or so. He said, "I'll save a seat in the car for you."

It turned out to be a seat on a small aircraft, "the only one in Spain that is still flying," Dominguín informed me with a mischievous smile. It was a biplane and reminded me of the Rapide I had flown in with Huston in the Belgian Congo, only it was slightly larger, with room for eight passengers. Teodoro, Miguel's driver, took us to the Madrid airport and then set out for Barcelona to meet us on the following afternoon in San Feliu de Guixols, a Catalan summer resort. Domingo, Miguel's oldest brother, was with us; Pepe, the middle sibling, was traveling with the "competition," acting as Ordóñez's manager. A quarter of an hour before takeoff we were joined by Jaime Ostos, a young Sevillan matador who was fighting on the same card with the maestro at Luis Miguel's suggestion.

I recall feeling a slight nervousness as we walked to the aircraft. I had flown all over the world—in the South Pacific during the early years of the war, to Europe later, and on all civilian airlines—and I had had only one uncomfortable experience: a Navy transport pilot had mistakenly taken off downwind on a small South Pacific island called Efate, and as he had climbed steeply to avoid the oncoming palm trees, the luggage straps inside the DC3 had given way, and a fellow Marine and I had struggled valiantly to keep the piles of mail-bags from engulfing us. We were both on our way back to the States to be enrolled in Officer Candidate School at Quantico, Virginia, and it had seemed ironic to us that we were about to crash on the first leg of our journey home.

Having at last found the right partner in life, it occurred to me that it might be equally ironic to be killed now. But my nervousness was short-lived. Ostos and Luis Miguel, accustomed to risking their lives in the bullring, were on their feet as soon as we were airborne, with Miguel giving advice to his young *compadre* on how to improve his passes with the muleta. They chattered away in incomprehensible Spanish, arguing and needling each other, while we flew over the dry plains of Castille. We landed in Barcelona and were met by a taxi that drove us to San Feliu.

There was no room for me in the hotel, so Miguel ordered a cot set up in the living room of his suite. While we were having dinner, Walter Chiari appeared. He was making a movie in Barcelona and had driven to San Feliu to see the fight that Sunday. Chiari had apparently forgiven Luis Miguel for stealing his girlfriend, Lucia Bosé, and Miguel told him that instead of sleeping in the lobby he could move in with us as well. During the night our host's snoring became unbearable, and Chiari and I moved our mattresses out on the terrace. We all breakfasted there together, Miguel eating sparingly as always on the day of a *corrida*, although the fight was a minor one. But even if the bulls were small, there was always the chance of a goring.

Chiari returned to his film unit that evening, and Ostos, Domingo, Miguel, and I were driven to the Barcelona airport and were flown by our two friendly Spanish pilots to a small airfield near Nîmes. Flying was a less tiring way to travel, Luis Miguel admitted after we arrived in that small Mediterranean city, but he wondered out loud if the old way of traveling wasn't better. Seated in the cramped quarters of an ancient car or bus with his *cuadrilla*, a matador's only thoughts were of the bulls. By air he arrived too quickly, which gave him too much time to think, "and the less a bullfighter thinks, the better," he added.

Before the fight in Nîmes, Picasso burst into Miguel's suite without being announced, accompanied by his son and several hangers-on. They were all *rojos*, Miguel said in an aside, Spaniards who had fled Spain after the Civil War, which didn't seem to bother him. Picasso was a friend, and that put him above all political differences; Miguel also respected Picasso's resolve not to return to the country of his birth while Franco was in power. Dominguín had attempted to persuade the painter to return to Spain for a visit, as he believed that the government, with its new attitude toward America and France, would welcome him. Miguel had mentioned the possibility to El Caudillo recently during a partridge hunt, and Franco, as usual, had made no reply. One of his aides had said, "He did the Guernica," to which Luis Miguel had reportedly replied, "No, you did that."

But during Picasso's visit that afternoon, the talk was mostly concerned with the bulls. Having introduced me, Miguel mentioned that I was a friend of Hemingway's, and Picasso briefly related how Papa had come to visit him during the liberation of Paris and had offered him a hand grenade for his protection. "What do I want a grenade for?" Picasso said he told Papa. "I'm a painter!" He laughed, amused in retrospect by Hemingway's bellicose attitude.

A blond Argentinian newspaperwoman, her curvaceous body wrapped in tight blue silk, costume jewelry dangling from her wrists, was let into the room by Laguna, Miguel's valet, who always guarded the door on such occasions. Her eyes lit up when she saw Picasso. "Ah, Maestro!" she gushed, planting a kiss on Picasso's tanned cheek, which he wiped away with the back of his hand. He was visibly annoyed. His eyes narrowed. Unperturbed, the woman snatched a piece of paper from a nearby writing table and held it out to him. "Draw anything, Maestro, anything at all!" she demanded. Picasso took the lipstick she handed him, as on the spur of the moment she had been unable to find a pen or pencil, and wrote *"Olé"* with one quick flourish. Then after a hurried good-bye, he led his coterie out of the room, like a Roman emperor hurrying to get to the Colosseum.

Luis Miguel dedicated his first bull to him, and to my amazement Picasso put the *montera*, the black cap Miguel had tossed to him, on his bald head for an instant, provoking laughter from the spectators around him. It was not the sort of clowning that would have endeared him to the public in his hometown Málaga, but in Nîmes it did not seem to matter.

THAT NIGHT we drove across the base of France, to Mont de Marsan in the region that is called Les Landes, where we arrived at three o'clock in the morning. The last few hours of the drive were worrying, as Teodoro was getting sleepy. He had already driven the Mercedes from Madrid to Barcelona, to San Feliu and then to Nîmes. I offered to take the wheel, but he wouldn't admit to fatigue, so I kept up a muffled conversation, not wanting to disturb Miguel, who was sound asleep in the back of the car.

Miguel had made the customary telephone calls after the fight, first to Lucia and then to his mother, who had informed him that his father's health had suddenly deteriorated. For several years the old man had complained of pains in the rectum but had refused to see a doctor. Now there was talk of surgical intervention, which alarmed the entire family. A noticeable change in the generally easygoing manner of my friend was evident. He had been totally absorbed in his tour up to that moment, constant striving to convince the somewhat hostile fans that he was still *número uno*.

A bullfighter who has remained at the top of his profession always faces the same challenge. The public tires of his success in part because his performances become repetitious. Although each bull presents a new challenge, the three phases of the spectacle remain the same; unlike an accomplished actor who can change roles as he matures, a bullfighter is forced to follow the same script every time he appears. The fans soon grow tired of his artistry and even of his survival. They want a challenge to his supremacy by a new star, a contest between a young and an old matador. That was why Spain was already divided into two camps, the Dominguistas and the Ordoñistas, and it was growing more and more apparent that if these two men could be convinced to fight on the same card it would be good for the fiesta and, of course, the box office.

Yet Luis Miguel continued to be emphatic in his refusal to appear with his brother-in-law. He repeated his assertion that there wasn't enough money in the world to make him change his mind. He loved Carmina, his favorite sister, and he knew how upsetting the intrafamily rivalry would be for her. He was willing to fight on alternate days with Antonio in any *feria*, but never on the same afternoon. Now his father's critical illness, as well as the repeated offers of a series of *mano a manos* with Ordóñez, was troubling him more than he would admit. He began to revert to a quiet seriousness, a manner that in his youth had caused Manolo Tamames to refer to him as "Hamlet," a "young man without joy" who had been deprived of a normal childhood.

Miguel had always had a sharp tongue, a sarcastic wit that was often unkind and that had prompted an acquaintance to remark that "if he ever bites his tongue, he'll die of blood poisoning." Now that he was beset with new problems, this aspect of his nature began to come to the fore, and even his closest friends were victims of his caustic remarks. Yet friendship was one of the few things he believed in, as was loyalty, a quality he suspected did not exist among most bullfighters outside the ring. That was the main reason for his antagonism toward Ordóñez, who had been his and his father's protégé at the beginning of Antonio's career. He was unable to forget Antonio's statements to the press that the old man had cheated him, which, even if true, should not have been aired in public.

He was in a hurry to get back to Madrid that evening to see his father. We stopped for an early dinner in Carcassonne, and I telephoned Deborah. Then we continued our drive south. Teodoro switched on the radio for the bullfight news, which was postponed as Franco was making a long speech to the nation. For the most part, the old general's voice was monotone, without emotion, while he detailed the accomplishments of his regime. Only as he began to approach the end of his address was there any overtone of real feeling.

"He's going to weep now," Teodoro muttered to me, his eyes on the road ahead. "He always does at this point." And sure enough, Franco's final phrases brought on a carefully rehearsed amount of bathos, as he sang his country's praises, the eternal leader in the Western world's struggle against bolshevism. The *vivas* and the shouts of *"¡Arriba España!"* gave way to the national anthem, and Luis Miguel sat up slowly in the bed he had made for himself on the backseat.

The news of the troubled world followed, and then came the usual summary of what had gone on in the various bullrings of Spain and France. Teodoro turned up the volume and we listened in silence. Near the end of the newscast the announcer stated that Ordóñez had been gored while fighting in a town near Madrid. The horn wound, in the upper thigh, was described as *grave* and the medical prognosis of the attending doctors was *reservado*, although Ordóñez's life was said not to be in danger.

Dominguín made no comment. His jaw tightened. I noticed that he had leaned back in his seat and that he stared out the window for a long while before reaching for a cigarette. Teodoro shook his head. Accidents of this kind were a part of every bullfighter's life, he informed me; you could expect them to happen at least once in every season. "What time is it?" Luis Miguel asked. He had pulled his black eyeshade back down over his eyes. Teodoro informed him that it was ten-thirty. "We should be in Madrid by four o'clock in the morning," Dominguín replied. "Wake me when we get to Alcobendes," a town about fifteen kilometers outside Madrid. I glanced back at him. He was rearranging the two pillows he always kept with him on his travels; then he stretched out again. I noticed that his right hand was folding and refolding the edge of the woolen blanket he had pulled up over his body.

ORDÓÑEZ'S DARK EYES, set in his pale, unshaven face, beheld his brother-in-law with the glazed look of a man who was still in shock. No, we hadn't disturbed him, he said, the pain from his wound made sleep impossible. Luis Miguel's decision to visit his wounded colleague at that hour seemed quite extraordinary to me. Certainly no hospital in the United States would ever have allowed such an intrusion, even by a member of the family. The night porter on duty had been hesitant to divulge the patient's room number, but at Luis Miguel's insistence he had supplied the information.

Teodoro and I had waited in the dark corridor while Miguel had put his head through the half-open door. Then he had gestured for us to join him inside the hospital room. Ordóñez nodded feebly in our direction and managed a muttered greeting. An intravenous needle was in his left arm, and Miguel glanced at the bottle hanging from a white metal stand to see if there was still sufficient liquid in it. Then with Antonio's acquiescence, he pulled back the sheet covering the lower part of Ordóñez's body to inspect the wound in the upper part of his thigh.

An alarmed-looking nurse came into the room and stated her disapproval of our presence, but her patient assured her that it was all right. She stayed on nevertheless, standing at the head of the bed while Antonio explained in labored detail how the bull had caught him. He felt confident that he would be able to fight again in a month's time, he told us, and we said our good-byes. Our visit lasted less than half an hour. There had been no expressions of sympathy. Miguel had patted Antonio's shoulder, Teodoro and I had muttered the customary *lo sientos*, and then we walked slowly down the dark hallway and out of the main entrance of the Clínica Ruber.

I remember that we spent the remaining few hours of the night in Luis Miguel's small house on the Calle Nervion, and as he drank his customary glass of cold milk before going to bed he recalled the wounds the bulls had inflicted on him during his many years as a matador. Not counting the bruises and the tossings, he had been seriously gored a dozen times. On many of these occasions he had been operated on without an anesthetic to cut short the recovery period that would keep him inactive. He had photographs, horrendous pictures that showed his face distorted by pain while the surgeon did his work.

Was it worth it? I asked him as the early morning light of a new summer day was becoming visible behind the curtained windows—all the suffering of the animals and the people whose trade it was to kill them in twenty minutes with a sword. It was an art, a part of the folklore of his country, but was that justification enough?

He smiled good-naturedly. If the bullfight were to be abolished in Spain, the breed of brave bulls would soon become extinct, he replied, an argument I had heard from him before. Besides, it was the only way a poor boy could get rich, own a piece of land big enough to feed his family, and ride and hunt like a member of the upper classes. But there was more to it than that, he added. A torero, if he turned out to be a good one, became a part of the legend of the Iberian peninsula, could take pride in the fact that he would be remembered for a while, which was worth more than money. "That's why you write, isn't it?

¡Coño! It's not just for dollars and cents! *Y que las chavalas te hacen caso* —and that the girls take notice of you!"

"There's very little blood spilled when I write," I told him.

"Maybe that's what's wrong," he replied, pinched my neck affectionately, and went off to his room.

He was gone when I came down for a late breakfast, had driven off to see his father at La Companza, the ranch near Toledo that he had bought for his parents with the first big money he had made. Looking disheveled and tired, he came back in the late afternoon. Things were worse than he had thought, he told me. He had been planning to drive north that night, hoping to join me in Biarritz for a week's vacation, as he had several engagements to fight near there, one in Bayonne and two more during the *feria* in Vitoria, a two-hour drive south of the French border. But all of his plans were in doubt now; he couldn't possibly leave Madrid before a decision had been made about his father's operation.

I told him that I would go to St. Jean de Luz by train and wait for him there. I too felt in need of a rest, from what I wasn't quite sure.

He nodded. "I'll see you in a week's time," he said.

The familiar comfort of the Hotel Chantaco was a welcome respite from my days on the road, and I had time to take notes for my bullfight novel, the protagonist of which I had decided to model on Luis Miguel, who was as compelling a hero as Huston had been and was therefore worth writing about. Franco's Spain was also an arena that had not been shown in a work of fiction—all to be seen through the eyes of an American journalist with my own political viewpoint. Our early lives had been so different. Dominguín had been raised with only one objective: to make a name for himself in the bullring. The prospect that he might die young must have crossed his mind from the age of eleven on, while I had grown up in the safe environment of a small southern California town. The rise of Hitler in Germany and the war that came along when I was eighteen years old had brought on my first serious thoughts of death. And even during those early years, the possibility of my becoming a casualty of war had never been a realistic concern. Miguel had become a full-fledged matador at the age of seventeen, in charge of his own *cuadrilla*, as well as the principal provider for his large family. He had gone to war at an earlier age than I had, which made him seem older to me than his years, my senior in a strange way who treated me as if I were his younger brother.

Many of my friends were spending the summer in nearby Biarritz.

Tola Litvak was staying at the Hôtel du Palais with Sophie, now his wife. Swifty Lazar and Harry Kurnitz were there, too, and Irwin and Marian had returned to their villa near St. Jean. Orson Welles arrived for a long weekend, and we renewed our acquaintance from our early days at RKO, where I had adapted three Faulkner short stories while Orson was shooting *Citizen Kane*, his masterpiece. Although he professed to remember our meeting on the lot, I felt fairly certain that he was only being friendly and polite.

Welles was a fervent Ordoñista, and in his booming voice he extolled the superior artistic qualities of his favorite matador over Luis Miguel's mastery. Orson had become an aficionado in his youth while visiting Spain before the Civil War, had even tried his hand with the cape and the muleta. His relationship with Hemingway was less than cordial, and I joked with him about the love and admiration he shared with Papa for the young matador from Ronda.

He confided in me that he was writing a screenplay about an old man's obsessive admiration for a young torero; the protagonist of his story was an aging movie director intent on recapturing the magic of his youth by following a young bullfighter around Spain. Didn't he feel any sympathy for the older man who was defending his position against the young challenger? I asked him teasingly. "Certainly not," he replied. "Your boy is a sophisticated man of the world, while my idol is a poor, frightened gypsy boy trying to make the grade." He roared with laughter at his own exaggeration. "Anyway, my story is about an old man's love affair with youth," he went on to say. "It's not a treatise on the *corrida*."

"Are you writing about yourself or Papa?" I asked him.

"About both of us," he bellowed before succumbing once again to uproarious laughter.

Litvak, who was dining with us that night, was amused by our prolonged, half-serious argument. The two of us were in love, he remarked, proof of our retarded manhood. Orson, who as a rule did not take kindly to personal criticism, didn't bother to deny Tola's accusations. "Not retarded manhood," he corrected Litvak, "but premature senility in my case." His voice boomed out across the restaurant. "It's like an old man falling for a ballerina by merely watching her on the stage. Without the sexual overtones, of course," he added. Bullfighters had the same unusual quality that could provoke adulation in men and women alike, he went on to say. Manolete had been the first Spanish national hero since El Cid, Campeador, "a fact that your other friend,

Papa, seems not to be aware of, else he would never have made the slighting remarks he has been accused of making."

He was referring to an interview in which Hemingway had described the "cheap tricks" that Manolete had employed in the ring, a statement that had caused a furor in the Spanish press. "Poor Antonio," Orson said, shaking his head. "His most famous admirer can wind up doing him some serious damage . . . which needless to say he'll overcome."

We were lunching alone by the side of the hotel pool, and I told him that I was thinking of writing a novel about Miguel, as I had found him and his world to be fascinating subjects.

"Not a novel," Orson said didactically. "A novel is an outdated art form. Write a screenplay. You've done it all your life . . ."

"Without much pleasure or success," I replied.

"Listen . . . if you manage to write just one thing you're *fairly* pleased with, you're way ahead. But use any form you like. A modern novel is not so different from a screenplay. And whichever one is best, we'll make into a film." His relaxed attitude toward work was inspiring. "Do it . . . don't just talk about it," he said. "Or maybe wait a month or so until that great prima donna, your friend, agrees to tread the same golden sand as my poor, dear Antonio. Because ultimately he will! As sure as we're sitting here in the sun wasting our time!"

Welles was not the only person to predict that a confrontation between the brothers-in-law was inevitable. The handful of Spaniards staying in the Palais were equally adamant in their predictions. A contest between two outstanding toreros had always enlivened the fiesta—Joselito and Belmonte, Manolete and Dominguín, as well as half a dozen similar examples reaching back into the nineteenth century. The wealthy Spaniards vacationing on the Côte basque were somewhat more reserved in their admiration for bullfighters. Toreros, despite the notoriety accorded them in the press, were a product of the lower classes, mere entertainers, some of them artists excelling in an impermanent art form. They were not considered acceptable in society, were not admitted to the Ritz Hotel in Madrid, even those like Manolete and Luis Miguel who had become the darlings of a small group of aristocrats.

Dominguín, my companions informed me, had attempted to jump the class barrier by wooing the daughter of a Spanish grandee. To overcome the objections of his prospective father-in-law, Luis Miguel had attempted to elope with the nobleman's daughter, but at the last minute she had lost heart and had failed to appear at their rendezvous. It had been a blow to the young bullfighter's ego, as well as his heart, although he had recovered rapidly. I was introduced to the woman many years later, and when she was told that I was a close friend of Luis Miguel's she smiled nostalgically, but I had the impression that she did not regret having obeyed her father's wishes.

There were a good many other young women of her class whose heart beat faster when Luis Miguel appeared in the ring, and one of them is now his wife. But in 1958 the ladies who were swayed by his charms were mostly foreigners, not hindered by the taboos of class. Yet his rival Ordóñez was making inroads on his place as *número uno*, and most of the young women around the swimming pool at the Hôtel du Palais were crazy about Antonio, both as a bullfighter and as a man.

There is a strange syndrome connected to the *corrida* that manifests itself most strongly among foreigners who are neophytes about the fiesta. Pretended expertise is expressed didactically. If you really *knew* about the bulls, your preference for a certain torero was proof not only of your taste, but of your profound knowledge that made you a superior aficionado. Ordóñez was the new messiah now. Luis Miguel was a master craftsman, but Antonio was a young genius, a Mozart in his shining suit-of-lights.

The Shaws and Harry Kurnitz shared my view that it was absurd to express one's preference when it came to judging the work of two artists. Both men had their individual styles, both men were masters in their profession. It was a little like arguing who was the better writer, Tolstoy or Dostoyevsky, Irwin said with a smile. We went as a group to watch Luis Miguel fight in nearby Bayonne, where he cut ears on both of his bulls. But even this minor triumph did not improve his mood; yet he insisted on going to the casino after a late dinner. Gitanillo de Triana, the renowned gypsy bullfighter who had been an intimate friend of Manolete's and had appeared with him and Luis Miguel on that tragic day in Linares, operated a flamenco locale in one wing of the casino, and he came along into the gaming room, as did Harry Kurnitz.

It was a gala evening—many of the players around the chemin de fer table were in dinner jackets—and Dominguín, after exchanging a thick stack of French francs for chips and plaques of all colors, took his place alongside the other players. He bancoed Kurnitz's large stake and then as he raked in the chips, Harry leaned across the table and said, "You treat me as if I were a bull," a remark that produced a brief moment of hilarity in that deadly serious establishment.

But before the evening was over Harry had won it all back and Miguel had lost everything he had started with and more, "the equivalent of one bull and a half," he commented nonchalantly on the way to the small seedy bar opposite the casino where losers often retired for a last round of drinks. He was being plagued by a *mala racha*, he said, a spell of bad luck, with the cards and in his private life. Teodoro was asleep in the Mercedes in front of the casino, and Miguel woke him up, having decided to drive to Madrid, even though it was almost four o'clock in the morning. I knew that he would be fighting in Vitoria in two days, which meant he would have to travel north again in less than forty-eight hours, and I tried to dissuade him, but he said he had important problems to take care of at home. The bulls he was to face in Vitoria were Miuras, the most infamous breed in Spain, the breed that had killed Manolete as well as a score of other toreros, but that did not deter him, and he drove off through the warm summer night.

WE SET OUT for Vitoria on the morning of the fight, Lazar and I, with Janet Thomas on the uncomfortable backseat of my small car. There was very little traffic once we crossed the border, and we arrived at the small hotel where we were to meet Dominguín and collected the tickets he had left for us. The Maestro was asleep and was not to be disturbed, we were told by the concierge, so we ate a late Spanish midday meal in the crowded dining room. The town was in a festive mood. A brass band was playing in the street outside, and rockets were exploding in the cloudless sky. After a brief walk around the picturesque town, we returned to the hotel, and Swifty and I went up to Luis Miguel's suite. Instead of the usual half dozen friends and well-wishers, he was alone in his room, with Laguna, his valet, in attendance.

I noticed that he was tense and somber. Then to my surprise Lucia came into the room, followed by Manolo Tamames. She was still as beautiful as when I had first met her, her alabaster skin setting off the deep glow of her dark hair. She smiled her faint Giaconda smile, and I told her that I was surprised to see her there, knowing that her summers were as a rule spent in exile. She nodded; she was there only out of necessity. Then taking me aside she explained that Luis Miguel's father had been diagnosed as suffering from a malignancy in the rectum and had been taken to Germany for an operation by a specialist.

Little hope was being held out for the old man's survival; the malignancy had already spread to other parts of his body. As soon as Miguel had completed the scheduled two fights in Vitoria, they were to join the other members of the family at the clinic in Düsseldorf. Tamames confirmed the gravity of the situation. Fear of the knife had caused the old man to postpone an operation, and now it was too late to save his life.

It turned out to be a disastrous afternoon. From the moment Luis Miguel stepped into the bright sunlight to begin the *paseo* it was apparent that he was not himself. His face was unusually pale, and there was not a trace of a smile as he acknowledged the applause of the people seated in the shade. I had always known him to be coldly rational, without superstitions or mystical beliefs. The postcards of the saints that his valet never failed to put on display in his room were there, he told me, because it was a tradition. He never prayed in the chapels of any of the bullrings and never crossed himself before opening his cape. But that afternoon the menacing prospect of his father's death seemed to increase his feeling that the fates had turned against him. Old Domingo had been his manager, his counselor, and his best friend, and he knew that soon the old man would be gone forever. The Miuras, too, were obviously on his mind.

Jaime Ostos was once again on the card that afternoon. Dressed in a black and gold suit-of-lights, his lithe figure expressed youthful confidence as he stepped quite jauntily across the brown sand. And as is often the case in that strange business, one man's misfortunes seemed to benefit his less well known rival. Luis Miguel's first bull was a difficult animal that under ordinary circumstances he could easily have dealt with. But he appeared uncertain, even frightened. He decided not to place the banderillas because of the bull's hesitant, defensive charges. The crowd, thinking that it was being deprived of an essential part of his performance, grew dissatisfied. By the time he had taken the muleta in hand, they were shouting abuse. He killed badly after two tries and was booed for his efforts as well as insulted by the more rowdy elements in the stands.

When it was Jaime Ostos's turn, he performed with a wild bravery that was undeniably inspired by Miguel's failure. The audience cheered the young Sevillan, prompting Ostos to take even greater risks. Lazar and I sat watching the spectacle with growing apprehension. Luis Miguel's second bull looked to be an even more dangerous animal than the first and, in a moment of hesitance on Miguel's part, caught him and sent him flying into the air. He landed face downward and appeared to have broken his nose. The crowd jeered him mercilessly, and he tried desperately to regain his poise, but to no avail. He killed finally and retired to the *callejón* amid a storm of whistles and boos.

Ostos's second bull was another triumph for the young sevillano. He seemed inspired, oblivious to danger, and was carried out of the ring on the shoulders of a small group of his supporters to deafening cheers and applause. Thoroughly depressed, Lazar, Janet, and I hurried back to the hotel and made our way upstairs to our friend's suite. He was lying on his bed, and Tamames was bending over him, examining his bruised face. His nose, it turned out, was not broken, nor had he sustained any other injuries, surprisingly enough, as the bull had tossed him at least six feet into the air.

He was alive, and that was what counted. His earlier deep gloom had given way to his customary laconic cynicism. Lazar invited him to dinner, but Miguel declined. If he went into the dining room, he explained, some drunk or mentally deranged Basque might spit in his face, or otherwise insult him. It was bad enough that he would be facing the same crowd the following afternoon; it was better that he dine quietly with his wife upstairs in their suite.

Swifty did not insist. However, when I suggested we start on our long drive back to Biarritz, he declared that he was too worn out by emotion to face the three-hour journey. Inquiring about rooms for the night, we were informed by the hefty Basque proprietress that there was only one room available, which unfortunately did not have a connecting bath. Lazar looked incredulous when I had interpreted this news. "Let me get this straight," he said, "there's no john or place for us to shower if we stay the night?"

I explained that as in most small European hotels there was a bathroom on each floor that was available to the guests and was cleaned after each person had used it. "Can I have a look at it?" he asked, and the by now amused proprietress led us upstairs for an inspection tour of the facilities. Lazar and Janet exchanged a long meaningful glance. I perceived that she nodded discreetly, and Lazar declared that he would take the double room that was being offered them. He followed me down to my car to collect the small overnight bag he had been wise enough to take along, and I set out on the road back to France, where I knew I would be able to telephone Deborah in England.

When I arrived back the next day, I was met by the Basque proprietress, who was all smiles. "If you have any more friends like Señor Lazar," she said, beaming, "I hope you will bring them to my house." Then she explained that Janet and Swifty, once they had dined, had given the hallway bathroom the most thorough cleaning it had had in years. Amazingly, Janet had even produced a can of Ajax with which she had come equipped and after putting it to good use had left it behind as a present.

The anecdote even brought a smile to Luis Miguel's face when I relayed it to him, although he was obviously preoccupied. His *banderillero de confianza* had returned from the midday *sorteo*, the drawing of lots for the bulls that were to be fought that afternoon, and after wishing Miguel luck, Lazar and I left for the arena.

That he had made up his mind to wipe out the memory of his failure of the previous afternoon was apparent as he faced his first bull of the day. Instead of the masterful distain that was his usual trademark, he fought like a *novillero*, a young apprentice who is anxious to make an impression. He threw caution to the wind, was risking his life over and over again, not only for the benefit of the hostile fans, but for his self-respect. Domingo Ortega, one of the masters of the art of bullfighting, had written a treatise on the craft many years earlier in which he stated that a bullfighter needed to have three qualities, *Valor*, *valor y valor*, courage, courage, and more courage, and Luis Miguel was obviously out to prove the truth of that statement. He cut ears on both of his bulls and won back the respect and admiration of the crowd.

The *feria* in Vitoria has never ranked with the *ferias* of Seville or Madrid or Bilbao in importance, but for Luis Miguel that day it was one of the most crucial moments in his life. He was proving to himself that he could put death in its place.

STRANGELY ENOUGH, in the opening chapters of *The Dangerous Summer*, Hemingway mentions that disastrous day in Vitoria but fails to mention the bullfight that took place the following afternoon. His informant, he wrote, was Juanito Quintana, his old friend from his early days in Pamplona. Knowing Juanito to have been an eminently fair-minded man, I can only suppose that he didn't stay on in Vitoria for the second *corrida*, although he most certainly must have read about it in the Pamplona newspapers the following day. What is even more curious is that Hemingway in his articles for *Life* magazine makes no mention of Dominguín's family crisis, either because he didn't know about it or because it didn't fit with the plot of the story he was telling. Hemingway would certainly have been sympathetic to the trauma of the approaching death of a father, and Quintana undoubtedly knew about old Domingo Dominguín's fatal illness by the time he informed Papa of what had transpired in Vitoria.

Hemingway insinuates that Dominguín's inability to deal with the Miuras that day was due to the fact that the famous breeder of these celebrated bulls did not permit shaving the animals' horns. Shaving the horns was one of the malpractices that outraged Papa, just as it did Juanito Quintana. They both chose to ignore that Dominguín subsequently fought bulls from the ranch of Pablo Romero, who also did not allow the shaving of horns. Papa does state, however, that in the past three decades matadors had been fighting in much more dangerous terrains, closer to the bull, and that the increase in danger had resulted in what he chose to call the breeding of "half-bulls," as breeders were obliged to comply with the dictates of matadors who were able to choose the animals they were to fight.

These "half-bulls" have degenerated since that dangerous summer and are barely "quarter-bulls" today; yet the casualties have not abated, a grim reminder that death is still an integral part of the fiesta. Papa's preoccupation with the size of the bulls and their horns was not shared by most aficionados, as their frame of reference did not date back to the 1920s.

At the end of his introduction to *The Dangerous Summer* Hemingway wrote: "I had made the reservation that if the bullfights were fixed or phony I would leave and go back to Cuba explaining to Antonio why I could not stay. I would not say anything to anyone else about it and I knew he would understand. That way it turned out I would not have missed the spring, summer and fall for anything else that you could do. It would have been tragic to miss it and it was tragic to watch. But it was not a thing you could miss."

IN THE AUTUMN of 1958 Deborah made her last movie for MGM, thus completing her contract with the studio that had brought her to California two years after the end of the war. The screenplay was based on a delightful novel by Nancy Mitford called *The Blessing* but, as usual, it had lost much of its original quality in the adaptation, partly owing to the censorship regulations that were still being enforced. Directed by Jean Negulesco, with Rossano Brazzi in the male lead and Maurice Chevalier playing a secondary role, the movie was filmed in Paris and the wine country of Bordeaux. It was somewhat of a disappointment for Deborah, although the atmosphere on the set was congenial, and beset as she was by her personal problems, it was good for her to be working.

It was a difficult period for both of us, with repeated separations and the legal complications we were involved in. Yet we were able to spend a month in Ireland in the late autumn and a few weeks in Switzerland, where her daughters joined her for a short winter holiday. Although she found the people in Ireland amusing, she preferred Switzerland. She declared almost immediately that she was never going to be a skier, but all of my friends adored her, and once the snow started to melt she fell in love with the countryside, the clean mountain air, the friendly atmosphere of Klosters, where we spent a fortnight in my small chalet, as well as the fact that everything functioned—the telephone, the clean trains that ran on time.

It was a country in which she felt she could make her home, and we bought a large piece of land where we planned to build a house large enough for her children as soon as they would be allowed to join us there. It was, and still is, one of the most beautiful places in the Alps. Two small ponds and an ancient barn built in 1693 stand on four acres of undulating meadow, and we chose the site for our house on the high ground overlooking the surrounding forest. Three deer were nibbling the new grass on the day in March 1959 when we first saw the property, and I sold my former chalet without a moment of regret a few days later. For once I was sure of what I was doing.

Jigee and I had agreed on a friendly divorce, but it was Deborah's pending divorce that caused us to be separated again during her daughters' Easter holidays, so I flew to Madrid to join Luis Miguel for the beginning of that year's campaign. I had started writing my bullfight novel, *Love Lies Bleeding,* and felt it would be beneficial to spend another month in Spain. Miguel had fought successfully in Toledo and had signed to fight during the Corpus Christi *feria* in Granada, so we set off together in his car for Andalucía.

Ordóñez was scheduled to fight the following afternoon, and Hemingway, we were told, would be arriving in Granada with a small group of supporters for that fight. By coincidence Betty Bacall was in Granada making a movie and I was looking forward to seeing her again now that she had recovered somewhat from the trauma of Bogie's death.

The drive south was complicated by a rainstorm that had filled the potholes with water and had made the road treacherously slippery. We arrived at midnight, and despite the late hour I called Betty's room on the chance that she was still awake. She joined us for a nightcap in Miguel's suite, the terrace of which had a view of the ancient city. Betty had first met Domínguín on the set of *The Barefoot Contessa* where he was visiting Ava, and they had renewed their slight acquaintance during his brief stay in California a year later.

Granada was in *feria,* and the three of us stood on the balcony looking down on the city from which rose the distant wail of flamenco music and the perfume of spring flowers. Miguel suggested we go down into the town for a drink, and I ventured to remind him that he was fighting the next day. I may even have said, *"Mas cornadas dan las mujeres,"* the cliché that infers that women can wound you more often than the bulls. He replied with his favorite good-natured insult that accused me of being a "fockin' Jewish homosexual," which, when I translated it for Betty's benefit, made her growl and say, "Well, that's nice," with her customary sarcasm. Yet he and Betty went off quite happily together, and I crawled into bed, worn out by hanging on to the hand grips supplied by the Mercedes-Benz company. The return of my friend woke me out of a sound sleep at four in the morning. He was in an excellent mood, declared that *"el pato Donald,"* his name for Betty because of her sharp voice, was a very nice woman and that they had had an agreeable evening "without getting drunk or misbehaving."

I took Betty to the bullfight that afternoon, and her previously declared preference for Ordóñez vanished into thin air. Miguel's charm had not been wasted on her despite the language barrier. He was at his best because he knew his rival was to appear in the same ring the next afternoon, and perhaps also because Betty was there to admire him. He cut ears on both of his bulls and was rewarded with a standing ovation by the rather serious-looking crowd that had filled the plaza.

"¡Todo el mundo contento!" Everybody is happy . . . those were invariably the first words with which Laguna would greet us once he had unlocked the Maestro's door after a successful fight. He was a thin, lively Andalucian in his late thirties, rather impressed with the importance of his position as sword handler for the leading matador in Spain. He had placed all the usual calls to Madrid and Saelices hours before and had given a generous tip to the hotel telephone operators so that there would be no delay. The calls had not yet started to come in, and Luis Miguel was resting on his bed before taking a shower. He

smiled at me and asked how *el pato Donald* had enjoyed the afternoon. Then the telephone rang and his manner changed abruptly. Ordóñez had been gored by his second bull while fighting in Aranjuez, forty-five minutes south of Madrid. Luis Miguel telephoned the Clínica Ruber, the same hospital Ordóñez had been taken to the previous summer. After a long wait Manolo Tamames came on the line and informed Miguel that the wound, although serious, was not a dangerous one. Not more than five minutes later the impresario of the Granada bullring called to ask Luis Miguel if he would consent to take his brother-in-law's place the following afternoon. Miguel told him to come to the hotel to discuss the terms.

As a rule a successful matador is reluctant to appear as a substitute. There is an element of tempting fate for a bullfighter to fight on a date that had not been arranged long in advance, another of the absurd superstitions Miguel chose to ignore that evening. "We're here," he declared, "so we might as well fight again tomorrow."

I asked him why it was that Ordóñez was being caught by the bulls so often, and he shrugged and said it was a matter of luck. Antonio was a bullfighter who stood his ground, and it was inevitable that he would collect a number of serious gorings. Domingo, Luis Miguel's brother, called later with an explanation of the bad news; an *espontáneo*, an aspiring amateur, had jumped into the ring and had made several passes with the bull, an unwelcome incident that might have influenced the animal's behavior. But it was bad luck more than anything else, Domingo concluded.

I went sightseeing the next morning and had just returned from visiting the Alhambra when an ancient Madrid taxi pulled up in front of the hotel and discharged a weary Slim Hayward along with her traveling companion, John Crosby, a television columnist with the Paris *Herald Tribune*. We went to the bar for the drink Slim required to recuperate from her "ghastly trip," and she told me that Papa, "her tour guide," had been so upset by Ordóñez's misfortune that he had loaded her and Crosby into a taxi early in the morning and had paid the driver handsomely just to get them both out of the way, proof that he "cared more for his bullfighter than his middle-aged Lady Brett," she added with a sarcastic laugh. Her Spanish vacation was turning into a nightmare, a not untypical exaggeration, but once she was reunited with Betty Becall, her onetime protégée, she recovered sufficiently to join us at the bullfight with Crosby.

Luis Miguel's performance was even more impressive than on the previous afternoon, and as soon as he had showered and changed we were on the road once again without saying good-bye to his newly acquired fans. He seemed pressed for time, like a soldier who has won an engagement and is eager for the next battle to begin, and when we stopped at the side of the road a few hours later to stretch our legs, he turned to Teodoro and said, "From now on I'm going to plant my feet in the sand and not move." It was a remark, Teodoro hinted with a grin, that was tinged with *mala leche*—"ill will," I suppose, is the polite translation. Had he changed his mind and decided to fight on the same card as his brother-in-law once Antonio had recovered? I asked him. *"Vamos a ver,"* he replied, we'll see. Yet I began to suspect that he was about to abandon his firm decision of the last few years.

HIS MOMENT of *mala leche* was soon forgotten, and we lunched in a restaurant in Aranjuez that was famous for fresh asparagus, which were now in season. We talked about Papa and his fatherly concern for Antonio. "He enjoys disasters," Miguel remarked. I told him that I would certainly have stayed with him if he had been injured, and he was forced to agree. But Hemingway had never made an effort to see him fight, Miguel added, and I realized that Papa's preference for Ordóñez bothered him despite his statements to the contrary. "Well, you'll soon have a chance to see your friend," he said, telling Teodoro to stop at the Clínica Ruber when we reached Madrid.

But Papa had abandoned his patient, we discovered when we were ushered into Ordóñez's hospital room. He had gone to the Prado to relax, Antonio informed us, and would be back in the evening. The pain from his wound had subsided somewhat, and when Tamames came into the room he told us that with any luck Antonio would be able to fight again in a month. I was eager to see Papa, but Miguel was in a hurry to leave for Villa Paz, where Lucia was waiting with the children. Tamames told me that Hemingway was traveling with Bill Davis, an American expatriate who had a villa near Málaga, and that the two were planning to drive south the next day. As soon as Antonio had recovered sufficiently, he would be joining them there for a long rest. Miguel was due to fight in Algeciras the following week, and he assured me that we would all get together at Davis's villa on the way to Algeciras. "Give Papa my best regards," I told Ordóñez, and he smiled and said he would. "Mine, too," Miguel said rather curtly, and we were on our way.

Throughout our travels I had always heaved a sigh of relief when we were on our way to the country. Staying in Madrid inevitably involved long periods of waiting, while Miguel conferred with Don Servando, his secretary, or negotiated with representatives of the bullrings. And now, after his father's recent death, he was his own manager and, with the occasional advice of his older brothers, took care of his personal business interests, some of which had nothing to do with the bullfight. In that one regard the world of the bulls resembled the movie business: endless meetings, many of them fruitless, with people arriving late, the more so in bullfighting given the Spanish disregard for time.

So I was grateful that Monday afternoon that Miguel's office was closed and we drove directly to his ranch. We arrived in the early evening. The windows of the big house were still shuttered against the heat, and the dark living room with its many dusty glass boxes full of stuffed animals had a musty, unused smell. The heavy leather furniture he had bought during his bachelor days gave the place the look of a provincial hotel lobby that had been closed for repairs. It was still the hour of the siesta, and no one was around. Then Lucia, dressed in a robe, appeared on the stairs that led into the main hallway. She came slowly toward us and was kissed dutifully on both cheeks by her husband, her summer widowhood interrupted for what she knew would be only a short while.

She led us into the dining room with its long wooden table and brought us each a cold drink. After a moment I excused myself and went to my room to unpack my small suitcase and to take a shower before stretching out on the narrow bed. I opened the shutters, and the smell of sage and rosemary came drifting in from dry fields. Our welcome had not been an enthusiastic one. Lucia was obviously still struggling to adapt herself to her husband's broken promise to give up his profession. I had a suspicion that she still felt herself to be a stranger in her adopted country and was homesick for the north of Italy, where being confined to a country house would have been a less lonely existence.

The melancholy atmosphere was somewhat relieved at dinnertime, when the house began to come to life. Little Miguel, Lucia's firstborn, appeared with his nurse, Remy, and was fussed over by his adoring father. Lucia was expecting a second child in a matter of months, which explained the robe she was still wearing at dinner. Tamames had arrived from Madrid, his patient being well on the road to recovery. Maridi, Miguel's cousin, was there, still a young girl but mature beyond her years. There was little talk of the bulls during the meal, undoubtedly out of respect for Lucia, although she must have known that financial necessity was one of the reasons her husband was fighting again.

The evening ended early by Spanish standards. Luis Miguel went up to bed before the rest of us, and I sat for a while with Tamames in one of the cool patios discussing the changes that had come to Spain in recent years. On my way up to my room I passed the main courtyard, and there was Teodoro washing the Mercedes in preparation for the next day's journey. We would probably be returning to Madrid after lunch, he told me. There was a lot of business to attend to, and his boss had told him to be ready to start early in the afternoon. That Miguel was restless was quite evident; the quiet *finca* was difficult for him to adapt to. He still had said nothing about appearing with Ordóñez, but I sensed from Teodoro's comments that it was now a foregone conclusion.

The next day after a hurried lunch, we said good-bye. Lucia received the embrace of her husband stoically, without asking when she would see him again. She would be leaving for Madrid in a week or two, she told me, so she might at least catch a glimpse of her husband whenever he happened to pass through the city. She would be nearer her doctor, as well, she added. She stood with her son at her side as we drove down the dusty road on our way to the main highway, a sad figure in her long white robe, waving to us until we were out of sight.

ALGECIRAS is anything but a typical Andalusian town. Like Málaga, it is an important seaport, but unlike Málaga, even the old quarter is functional and ugly: flat-roofed buildings crowd narrow streets, and only the broad avenue that borders the waterfront has a certain mercantile grandeur. What the bustling town does have is a surprisingly gracious hotel, the Reina Cristina. Built in 1902, it has the appearance of a Norman inn, with dark green shutters against its pale pink walls. It stands in a large park overlooking the bay at the western end of the waterfront.

In Dominguín's time the bullring was on the other end of the town, but now, decades later, it has been replaced by a modern structure double in size, and beyond it is a new *barrio* of high-rise tenements as ungainly as those that have sprung up all over Spain. On the bare hillside between the main road and the bullring, town planners left space for fairgrounds, so to attend a bullfight today one has to navigate past rows of temporary stalls that sell inedible candy, barbecued sausages, Spanish donuts, and a variety of other offerings meant only for the most robust stomachs. During the June *feria* the grounds are cluttered with a Ferris wheel, dodge 'em cars, and all the other worn mechanical paraphernalia that moves from town to town during the summer season, following the same itinerary as the toreros, who offer a more expensive diversion.

Nowadays I try to pass as quickly as possible through Algeciras on my way to the Atlantic beaches that lie beyond Tarifa and that provide a welcome change from the Mediterranean coast, for I have lost much of my *afición*, my passion for the *corrida* that was fostered by my friendship with Luis Miguel. But that summer of 1959 I was still personally involved in his struggle to remain at the top of his profession, and my involvement was also linked to my relationship with Papa, who was already less a hero than an elderly friend.

As always we had arrived at the Hotel Reina Cristina late at night, and as Miguel was still asleep, I sat alone on the terrace reading the Spanish newspapers. I heard footsteps, and when I looked up I recognized Papa's unmistakable figure standing in the rear doorway of the hotel. He was accompanied by Bill Davis. They came over to where I was sitting and I rose to shake hands. Papa said that they had driven down from Málaga for the fight and asked after Luis Miguel, adding that he had heard Miguel was having a good season and that he was sorry we had missed each other in Granada. He was friendly, a little more formal than usual, and he said Mary would be pleased to see me. He suggested I join them for lunch.

I made some excuse, as I never liked to eat a big meal in the middle of the day, and asked Papa about Antonio. He said that Ordóñez had remained behind at La Consula, Davis's villa but that he had recovered almost completely from his Aranjuez wound and would be active again soon. He and Antonio were equal partners, he told me, and were going to split "fifty-fifty" the "monies" they both were going to earn —Papa's fee from *Life* magazine and Antonio's earnings as a matador —a statement I was inclined to doubt. Davis smiled and said nothing, obviously embarrassed by Papa's boast, probably knowing it to be something Antonio had agreed to in jest.

Luis Miguel looked surprised when I told him that Papa had come from Málaga to see him fight. "He said he promised you that he would," I added, and Miguel shrugged, saying that Hemingway was jealous of our friendship, a view I didn't share. I asked him what had finally decided him to fight on the same card as Antonio, as I had learned from the newspapers that they were to fight several *mano a manos*, which meant they would be the only matadors appearing on some days.

He shrugged. It was the money, of course, he replied, "the same old thing." The offers they had received from more than half a dozen bullrings had been impossible to refuse. He admitted that it would be hard on his sister, Carmina, although having been raised in that world she had undoubtedly expected it to happen. Anyway, there was no use worrying about all that now, he said. You had to live one day at a time. Then to change the subject he asked about Deborah, wanting to know if she would be coming to Spain soon. I told him that she was going to work in a movie in California at the end of the summer and that I would probably join her there. He said that she obviously needed my support but that if I didn't go to the States there would always be a place for me in his car.

In "The Dangerous Summer," Hemingway's bullfight reportage for *Life*, later published in book form under the same title with an admiring foreword by James Michener, Hemingway described the fight in Algeciras that afternoon and wrote that Luis Miguel dedicated the second bull to Mary and himself. It was reported to the Hemingways that in his *brindis*, or dedication, Miguel said: "Mary and Ernesto: I dedicate the death of this bull to our friendship that will last forever," words that sound as if some journalist had invented them. Miguel vehemently denies that he ever dedicated a bull to Papa, which is understandable, as more than thirty years have passed since that day, and his bitterness toward Papa has increased with time. For my part, I seem to remember feeling gratified that Papa had made an effort to see Miguel fight, hoping that this might tone down the bitterness of the rivalry between Domingup and his brother-in-law. I don't remember the *brindis*, but it might have occurred the way Papa recorded it.

After praising Dominguín for his work that day, Papa wrote: "Seeing what a great and versatile matador Luis Miguel was and the perfect condition he was in I knew what Antonio was up against when they would begin to fight on the same program. Luis Miguel had his place to maintain. He claimed to be the number one bullfighter and he was rich. That was weight to carry in the ring but he really loved to fight bulls and he forgot about being rich when he was in the ring. But he wanted the odds to be in his favor and the odds were tampering with the horns. He also wanted to be paid more money than Antonio per fight and that was where the deadlines came in. Antonio had the pride of the devil. He was convinced that he was a greater bullfighter than Luis Miguel and that he had been for a long time. He knew that he could be great no matter how the horns were!"

Papa and Mary went to pay their respects to Miguel after the *corrida*, and, as always, his presence caused a stir. He stayed only a short while, knowing that as soon as Luis Miguel had "cooled out" he would want to bathe and dress and get back on the road. The Hemingways, too, were anxious to be on their way, as they were meeting Ordóñez at his ranch near Medina-Sidonia. We met briefly at the bar, and I told Papa that I was probably returning to California for two months, as Deborah was scheduled to make a film for 20th Century-Fox based on a book by Sheilah Graham called *Beloved Infidel*.

Hemingway expressed astonishment that I was prepared to miss the major part of the bullfight season, especially as it was now certain that Ordóñez and Dominguín would be fighting on the same card within a week. Luis Miguel, I added with a smile, would be able to "soldier on" without me. "Yeah, I guess he will," Papa replied with a grin. "But we'll miss you." Both he and Mary said that they were anxious to meet my "new girl," as they had only heard good things about her.

THE SCREENPLAY of *Beloved Infidel* was far from perfect, but as Deborah was still under contract to 20th Century-Fox, she had been advised by her agent that it was better for her to make the film than to face suspension. Gregory Peck had been chosen by the producer, my old friend Jerry Wald, to play the part of Scott Fitzgerald, while Deborah was to portray Sheilah Graham, a British gossip columnist who had been Fitzgerald's mistress during the last years of his troubled life. Both Deborah and Peck represented highly idealized versions of the characters portrayed in Graham's romantic memoir, as in appearance Peck was a far cry from the ailing writer at that last, tragic stage of his existence, and Deborah was too beautiful and ladylike to faithfully represent his rather plump and blowsy mistress. I knew I was back in Hollywood again.

Henry King, who had directed Peck in two of his best movies, *Twelve O'Clock High* and *The Gunfighter*, had been chosen by the studio as director. Although that was reason enough for me to stay away from the set, King, when we ultimately met in Deborah's dressing room, was surprisingly cordial, obviously having forgotten our differences during the filming of *The Sun Also Rises*. Sy Bartlett, a veteran screenwriter who had written *Twelve O'Clock High*, was called in as a screenplay doctor, and the production proceeded on its troubled way, with Deborah gritting her teeth and doggedly doing her job.

Now that she was back in her old house in the Pacific Palisades, one of Deborah's minor concerns was how I would be received by her friends. Foremost among these was David Niven, whose close friendship she valued, dating back to the early days of her career and her marriage to Tony Bartley. I had met Niven during the halcyon days of the Bogart household and had come to admire his wit and his talent as a raconteur, but I had never known him well. So finally a meeting was arranged, and David came to lunch on a bright Saturday afternoon. At the time, for propriety, I was staying in Brentwood in a spare room at the home of Deborah's secretary, a nervous, pleasant woman named Myrtle Tully, the widow of writer Jim Tully.

Not one to take sides in a friend's marital problems, Niven put Deborah at her ease by avoiding the subject of her divorce and by treating me as an "old chum" rather than a vague acquaintance. His nickname for Deborah was Hilda, as she had often enjoyed playing the part of a cockney char lady in their off-screen moments. The conversation at lunch mainly concerned the future, as Niven too had grown tired of living in Hollywood and seemed eager to return to Europe. I held forth on the advantages of living in Switzerland, adding that the one side benefit Deborah would gain by marrying me would be her automatically becoming a Swiss resident.

Saying that she had to "study her words," Deborah excused herself after lunch and, to my surprise, David suggested I join him in a drive to Malibu in his open car. I was expecting a stern lecture on my responsibilities to his dearest friend, but instead David began to talk about his own private problems. Yordis, his wife, he explained, had recently asked him for a trial separation, and he appeared to be deeply troubled by her unexpected demand. Relieved not to be told once again what a lucky fellow I was, I listened to the details of his intimate travails and then asked the obvious question: did he want her back?

He said he did in a most emphatic manner. He was desperate about the possible breakup of his household and the effect it would have on his two sons from his first marriage, which had ended with the accidental death of his wife. He was planning, he said, to take his boys on a long fishing trip in the Canadian Rockies, hoping that while he was away Yordis would change her mind. I told him that I wasn't particularly good at giving advice but that it seemed to me the fishing trip was a mistake. He would be sitting by a campfire every night listening to the tall tales of his Canadian guide while putting himself into a holding pattern that would provide his wife with a feeling of blissful security. Why didn't he take his sons to Hawaii instead, I suggested, where the presence of all those pretty girls would take his mind off his aching heart and might influence Yordis's security about her husband's affections.

Niven seemed delighted with my suggestion, and we headed back at once toward Santa Monica. The next day he telephoned to say that Frank Sinatra had offered the use of his villa near Honolulu and that the male members of the Niven family would be winging west before the end of the week. He said that he was also going to look into the possibility of moving to Switzerland, all of this a result of our conversation. Less than a fortnight later I read in one of the gossip columns that Mrs. Niven had joined her husband on Waikiki beach and that all was well again for the time being. Then a year later the Nivens moved to Switzerland.

To use David's words, I had made a new chum; it was a friendship that lasted for more than twenty years, until he was stricken with an incurable disease that led to his death in 1983. Two years before he died he called our house in Klosters to tell Deborah and me that he was flying to the Mayo Clinic to determine what was wrong with him, as he suspected it was some kind of nervous disorder. I offered to accompany him, but he said that he was quite capable of making the trip by himself. I told him that I would find out who was the leading neurologist in Switzerland, so that upon his return he could get a second opinion. Both doctors, it turned out, gave the same diagnosis, and he knew that he was in for the gradual loss of his muscular responses to the commands given by his brain.

As one goes through life and manages to survive the passing years, more and more of the stories concerning one's friends tend to end in tragedy. Yet David's fate was the most heartbreaking of anyone I have known. He, who had enjoyed words both as a raconteur and as a writer, whose playful mind perceived life to be more comical and absurd than anything else, was finally stricken by a disease that seemed to have come along for no reason and that locked him into a solitary confinement that his courageous spirit battled against hopelessly. In the end he was unable to speak or eat, and a few months before he was released from the torture chamber his body had become, he scrawled a final note to Deborah, his "Hilda," that gave proof that he was still there, struggling to send a last message to his friend. Through her tears she managed to decipher the words and went off to her bedroom to weep. And I felt as if a heavy stone had fallen on my heart.

THAT SUMMER I began to work in earnest on my bullfight novel. After I had driven Deborah to the studio every morning at six o'clock, I found that I could work undisturbed in my room at Myrtle Tully's house, the same room in which her late husband had written his novels. Occasionally my mind would wander across the six thousand miles that separated me from the arena of my story, but as I had had no news from Luis Miguel, I could only assume that all was going well with him.

I went to visit Jigee and made a belated reacquaintance with my seven-year-old daughter, Christine. She was a bright, lively child, an enthusiastic swimmer who seemed happier to be moving along under the surface of Deborah's swimming pool than anywhere else. With Jigee's permission, I had introduced her to her stepmother-to-be, and Christine was charmed immediately by Deborah's gentle nature. Unfortunately, I found Jigee to have deteriorated greatly since I had seen her two years earlier. Although she assured me that she was not an alcoholic, she seemed to need the two dry martinis she mixed for herself before lunch to get through the day. She was living with a man named Beryl Firestone, a polite, unprepossessing fellow quite a few years younger than her. My mother expressed the opinion that Beryl was not an ideal companion for Jigee, adding, however, that perhaps he was better than no companion at all. In any event, she concluded that it was useless to try to interfere in the affairs of others.

But she was worried about Christine and spoiled her hopelessly to compensate for the child's troubled home life. She was delighted with Deborah, however, and formed a friendship with her that lasted throughout their long acquaintance. She admired her as an actress and as a person and was relieved that I had finally found a woman to share my life whom she approved of in every way. Deborah was intrigued and amused by her future mother-in-law, and the evenings the three of us spent together were relaxed and satisfying. If only Jigee could be cured of her dependence on alcohol, we all agreed, she might yet be able to reconstruct her life. But Jigee was adamant about not needing psychiatric help and she refused to go to a clinic to cure her of her drinking, which she insisted she herself could control.

We saw each other frequently, mostly on weekends when I came to pick up Christine. There were no recriminations on Jigee's part. Occasionally she would ask after some of our friends in Klosters or express nostalgia for Paris. She did say that she was astonished that Papa had never written her during the years following our separation, but she did not feel bitter toward him. He probably wanted to avoid taking sides, she said, as well as being reluctant to provoke an unnecessary scene with Mary. Nor did she seem to bear Bettina any ill will. Mostly we talked about Christine. Christine and my mother were all that really mattered to her, she told me, and when I urged her to stop drinking for her daughter's sake, she laughed ironically, as if to say I had no right to challenge her on that issue. It was not an argument I could pursue.

She also said that everything she had heard about Deborah had been complimentary, and she was pleased that Christine liked her future stepmother as much as she obviously did. She admitted to a slight feeling of jealousy whenever Christine returned from her visits to "the house with a pool." But she assured me that she could control her feelings as long as her daughter was happy and finally "spending some time with her father." I urged her to attempt to find a job, but although she had finally appeared as a friendly witness before the committee, she suspected that her left-wing past still stood in the way of her getting work in the movie industry or even in publishing.

We had decided on a fixed sum of money that she was to receive each month, we had begun divorce proceedings, and she was now more relaxed when we were together. The change in her physical appearance saddened me and revived my feelings of guilt. She was only forty-four years old, and I still found myself hoping that somehow she would be able to make a new start, as she was still quite attractive. Vicky, her daughter with Budd Schulberg, the shy creature who had shared our life in Zuma Canyon, had gotten involved with an older man of doubtful character whom she had ultimately married, a disastrous first try that she nevertheless survived, but Vicky's situation weighed heavily on Jigee's mind. She said she had the feeling that everything was forever going wrong for her, a reason for her drinking that she herself admitted. When we had first met she had been self-sufficient and independent, and now it was obvious that she was incapable of finding a way to regain her confidence and to find an interest. Each time we parted that summer it was as if I were abandoning her all over again. I reproached myself and read the reproach in her eyes. Even though we were striving to be friends, the past was there like an unsurmountable barrier. That I had found a solution to my own life did not help.

The summer wore on. I managed to work, but I was counting the days that remained before Deborah would finish her movie. Then one evening I read in a late edition of the local paper that Luis Miguel had been seriously gored while fighting in Valencia. I put in a long-distance call to the Clínica Ruber in Madrid, where I surmised he would have been operated on. To my amazement, when I asked to be connected to his room he answered the telephone. Speaking in a faint voice, he thanked me for calling him from so far away and then admitted that the wound he had received was a serious one. I tried to cut short the conversation and asked him how long he would be staying in the hospital so that I could call him again once he was feeling stronger. "I won't be here for more than a couple of days," he replied. He had agreed to fight in Bilbao in less than a fortnight, he added, and he intended to honor his contract.

It sounded like pure insanity to me. The August *feria* in Bilbao, the largest of the Basque cities, was well known for the size and strength of the bulls, and for Miguel to fight there before he had fully recuperated seemed suicidal. I said as much. "I gave my word that I'd be there," he replied. Knowing that other friends would try to dissuade him, I didn't argue. He asked again how long it would be before Deborah and I would return to Spain, and I told him we would probably be back in less than a month. "Don't stay away too long," he said and hung up.

Two days later I read in the *Los Angeles Times* that Antonio Ordóñez had been gored while fighting in Palma de Mallorca, and I felt somewhat relieved, thinking that their bitter contest would now be postponed for at least a month. But obviously Ordóñez's wound had not been serious, for ten days later the morning news broadcast devoted a more extensive account of their rivalry. Both men had recovered sufficiently to fight, and on the second day of the *feria* Dominguín had been gored again. Although his life was not in danger, the wound was serious enough to put him out of action for the remainder of the season. Ernest Hemingway, the newscaster added, had been present at the bullfight, as the Nobel Prize winner was covering the event for *Life* magazine.

There was no doubt in my mind as to why this near-fatal accident had occurred. Throughout his career Luis Miguel had depended on his reflexes and his physical fitness. That he should have agreed to fight in Bilbao only eleven days after major surgery seemed incredible. Obviously he had abandoned his normally sound judgment and had allowed himself to be carried away by his pride and the pressures of the fierce rivalry with Ordóñez. He told me later that he had felt so weakened during the first *corrida* that he had had to sit down in a chair inside the *callejón* whenever he was not in action in the ring. In *The Dangerous Summer* Hemingway wrote: "If Luis Miguel had been managed by his father, who was wise and cynical and knew the odds, instead of by his two nice brothers, who needed the ten percent from him and Antonio each time they fought, he would never have gone to Bilbao to be destroyed."

The sentence is typical of much of the duplicity that is contained in Papa's reportage. How nice can brothers be who allow ten percent of the action to influence a decision that could cost their younger brother his life? Having known Domingo and knowing Pepe intimately, I am certain that they did not persuade Luis Miguel to fight. Miguel had made all the decisions about his own career for many years, and, if anything, Pepe and Domingo probably were against his honoring his contractual obligations, which could have been legally annulled by a doctor, Tamames or any other. Miguel apparently felt that despite his weakened condition he would be able to perform adequately. That Ordóñez was recovering from a less serious goring that had occurred only two days later and was lying in a room two floors down must have affected Dominguín's reasoning, made him forget that Antonio was six years his junior. Together they decided to go to Bilbao, both of them abandoning their customary common sense.

Luis Miguel paid the price. While trying to lure the second bull he was fighting that afternoon away from the picador's horse, he was not able to move out of the way quickly enough when the bull charged him. The horn went into Miguel's abdomen and reopened the wound he had received in Valencia, but it did not perforate his intestines. Had it gone a few inches higher it would probably have cost him his life. It was the most serious goring he had ever received.

MANY YEARS LATER, after his final return to the ring at the age of forty-six had ended in another wounding, this time in Bayonne, France, I went to see him in the penthouse apartment he shared with his cousin Maridi. A doctor was removing the stiches from his testicular sack, which had been sliced open by the bull's horn. Lying naked on his bed, his eyes closed, he was doing his best to endure the pain he was suffering. Two or three of his friends were standing by to give him moral support. Knowing that his sense of humor never left him at the worst of times, I thought a rough joke was in order to relieve the tension. "All I want to know," I asked in Spanish, "is if it still works." He recognized my voice and my accent and opened his eyes. *"Dame un besito, y vas a ver,"* he said—give me a little kiss and you'll soon see.

Later that day, during lunch on the terrace of his apartment, he was given to philosophizing about his career. All the outstanding bullfighters of the second half of the century had represented a political and cultural epoch of Spain with their style in the ring and their personalities. Manolete had been typical of the strict, authoritarian aura of the early Franco era. He, Luis Miguel, personalized the *apertura*, the opening of Spain to foreign influences, and Manuel Benitez, El Cordobés, represented the modern Spain of rock and tourism, the aura of the Beatles, which he had brought to the bullfight.

"And Antonio Ordóñez?"

Miguel said, "I don't know. He's a friend of yours, so why don't you ask him."

The bitterness of their rivalry had subsided long ago, but Miguel was still unwilling to discuss his brother-in-law's standing in the profession, although he was well aware that in the opinion of some aficionados Ordóñez was held to be the outstanding matador of the postwar period. The common wisdom was that Ordóñez had no peer when faced with a good bull but that with a difficult animal Dominguín had always maintained his place as a more versatile and accomplished torero, although not as pure and deeply moving with the cape and the muleta.

Orson Welles agreed with that evaluation of the two as artists. I asked him about Manolete, whom he had seen near the end of his career, and Orson verified everything I had heard. "He had personality!" Welles said, his eyes narrowing as if to help him remember the picture of the famous Cordoban in the ring. "What your boy has, only he wasn't a man of the world, a lover of beautiful women, Picasso's friend, and all that. Manolete had a purity about him and courage and a nobility—his long melancholy face was tragic even when he smiled, which he did rarely. He reminded you of our Lord."

"Your Lord," I said.

"Yes, of course, my dear boy," he said with a chuckle. "I forgot. Anyway, maybe Luis Miguel better represents the Spain of today, the falling away of all the old shackles. He's as close to an upper-class torero as you'll ever find, although he wasn't born to the purple."

DEBORAH AND I were married on the twenty-third of July 1960 in the Gemeindehaus in Klosters by the town clerk. Her divorce had become final on the previous day. My marriage to Jigee had ended with her tragic death in January of that year while our final divorce papers were still pending. She had gone to the bathroom in the early hours of the morning and, probably somewhat under the influence of the sleeping pills she took every night, had attempted to light a ciga-rette. The match had exploded and had set fire to the nylon night-gown she was wearing. She died three weeks later as a result of the burns, a horribly painful end.

While in the hospital she had told her sister, Ann Frank, that she didn't want me to visit her, a message Ann delivered to me via tele-phone. Money for the medical expenses and ultimately Jigee's funeral was all that was required of me, Ann informed me. We had never had a very friendly relationship. She had her sister's sharp wit, without Jigee's charm and prettiness, one of life's injustices to which she was unable to adjust.

Inevitably thoughts of the tragedy filled my mind when I was asked to sign the town register above the German word for "widower," which was now my legal status. There was no escaping the past. I remember glancing around the room at the familiar faces of Marian and Irwin and Harry Kurnitz, who I felt certain shared my unhappy thoughts for a moment or two.

We came out of the town hall into the bright Alpine sunlight of what had started out as a cloudy day. It had snowed during the night, and the peaks of the surrounding mountains were a dazzling white above the deep green of the meadows below. A Swiss friend, Walter Haensli, was waiting at the foot of the concrete steps in a jaunting cart pulled by a pony, and Deborah and I, accompanied by eight-year-old Christine, were driven off in style to the Shaws' chalet, where a wed-ding lunch was served. Yul Brynner and his wife Doris were among the guests, as were Tola and Sophie Litvak and many of our other friends. My mother was moved to tears by the simple words of the ceremony, although she later objected to the Swiss male-chauvinist rules laid down for the married couple.

There are days that are engraved in one's memory and that remain there almost as a warning that nothing lasts forever. Irwin was at his best that July afternoon. He had insisted that Deborah should come to his house in the morning before going to the town hall, declaring that it was unbecoming for the bride to depart for her wedding from the same residence as the groom, a surprising show of propriety. He was still in excellent shape, a middle-aged *bulvan*, which was how Oscar Levant had described him years before. Marian, self-contained and pretty as ever, was the hostess of the festivities. She laughed when I reminded her that when I told her I was in love with Deborah, she had said, "I think your mother should send you on a trip around the world to forget," a quip no doubt prompted by my less than conventional bachelor existence. Harry Kurnitz gave us his wistful blessings and presented us with an antique brass tub that still stands beside our fireplace in Klosters. His only venture into matrimony had not been successful, he reminisced, for once his wife had had her teeth fixed by an expensive Beverly Hills dentist, she had left him. Lazar telephoned from California to wish us well, regretful because he wasn't with us. It was one of those rare occasions that are unmarred by doubt; for an hour or two we were able to forget the difficulties that had preceded this day and to put aside any worry about what the future might bring.

We left the next day for Biarritz on a brief honeymoon, as Deborah was due in England in less than a week to spend time with her daughters. Our luggage failed to arrive with us, having been misplaced in transit in Paris, but that minor mishap caused only a moment of irritation. I pointed out to Deborah that she had been spared the chore of unpacking. We both purchased a change of clothes and went to the bullfight in Bayonne where Ordóñez and Luis Miguel were appearing together.

As a member of his entourage Dominguín had often taken along a middle-aged dwarf named Don Marcelino, a renowned aficionado, and as soon as the opening parade had ended, one of Luis Miguel's *cuadrilla* lifted Don Marcelino up from the *callejón* and squeezed him in between Deborah and me in our front row seats. A quarter of an hour later Luis Miguel crossed the ring to dedicate his first bull to us. "So recently married and already such a big son," he said with a grin.

Both he and Antonio did well that afternoon, the bitterness of their rivalry apparently forgotten, or at least deferred. Even the Basque weather was willing to cooperate, and it did not start to rain until the day after Deborah departed. I decided to stay on in Biarritz to work on my novel.

. . . .

THE *APERTURA*, the breaking down of national barriers, was much in evidence as the nineteen sixties began. I recall a luncheon party Deborah and I attended at the house of Ricardo Sicré late in the summer of our marriage, after Deborah had returned from England. Sicré was a Catalan businessman who had acquired U.S. citizenship and had served in the O.S.S. during the war at a time when his sympathies were influenced by the Spanish left. He had done well in business with Frank Ryan, an American financier based in Spain, and his social life no longer reflected his old left-wing sympathies. That day at his villa in the Moreleja, one of the newly elegant suburbs of Madrid, the guest list included Prince and Princess Rainier of Monaco, Hemingway, Audrey Hepburn and Mel Ferrer, members of the Spanish aristocracy, Irving Lazar, Deborah and me, and various others. We were being served an aperitif in front of the pool house at the bottom of his garden, and I stood with Papa surveying the scene. He was discussing Castro's Cuba, from which he had not yet retreated, speaking in a low voice to inform me that Fidel was "not as bad as the press painted him," when Lazar arrived on the scene in the company of Harry Kurnitz.

As these last two guests made their way slowly toward us, I identified my two Hollywood friends for Hemingway's benefit. "Kurnitz," Papa mumbled sourly. "He's supposed to be Slim's new lover." I laughed but didn't bother to deny that ludicrous statement. Then as Harry came over to greet me, I introduced him to Papa. "This is Harry Kurnitz," I said with a grin, "Slim's new lover."

"It must be a lonely job," Papa said sarcastically, starting to turn away.

"Oh, I have my books and music," Harry replied. Strangely enough, Papa didn't laugh. He seemed subdued. Nor was he particularly impressed with any of the other guests. He exchanged a few words with Lazar, whose reputation as literary agent he was acquainted with, and then we all trooped up to the house and the luncheon table. Deborah was seated next to Papa, and although he treated her like an old friend, it was apparent that he had taken an instant, inexplicable dislike to Rainier, evidence of his generally "black-ass mood."

He hadn't wanted to return to Spain at all, he told me when the meal had ended. He had finished his articles for *Life* magazine but was worried about the contents. He said that he hoped Luis Miguel would not be offended by what he had written, but as I had not yet read the reportage I merely shrugged and said that I was looking forward to reading it. "We tried to be objective," he said, which sounded like an apology to me, the sort of thing he often said when he knew he had been mistaken. Antonio had urged him to come back for a month or so, he added, as he was still going to fight on the same card as Luis Miguel, although not *mano a mano*. "I'm pretty tired of the whole business" were Papa's last words to me that afternoon.

Deborah flew back to London to be with her children the next day, and I drove my Porsche back to Biarritz, knowing that Luis Miguel and Ordóñez would be fighting in Mont de Marsan in two weeks. Papa's reportage had already been published in *Life* when I arrived at the Hôtel du Palais. Orson Welles, who was staying in San Sebastián for the Semana Grande, had been sent the three copies of the magazine which he had left behind at his house at Aravaca, outside Madrid. He remarked that he thought the articles were "very one-sided," especially all the accusations of Luis Miguel fighting bulls with shaved horns, "when you and I, dear boy, know that they've all been doing it and that there's been the smell of Aqua Velva around the fiesta for years." Islero, the bull that had killed Manolete, had had shaved horns, a fact Papa had failed to mention, Orson went on. And to make matters worse, Hemingway had repeated his slighting comments about Manolete's "cheap tricks in the ring," not a phrase to that would endear Papa to his Spanish readers if the pieces were ever to be published in Spain.

I was just as glad that I hadn't read the articles, as I didn't relish the prospect of informing Luis Miguel of Papa's duplicity. But I needn't have worried; he had already been fully briefed as to the contents of the reportage. He was not surprised, he told me. Hemingway had behaved "like a vulture, waiting for a disaster to happen." What angered Dominguín more than Papa's preference for Ordóñez was his pretend friendship and his solicitude after Luis Miguel's gorings. I expressed the opinion that Papa already regretted many of his comments, but Luis Miguel brushed aside all my excuses for Papa's behavior. He was going to seek the advice of a lawyer and perhaps sue both Hemingway and *Life* magazine. I told him that I saw little point in bringing a legal action. The bullfight critic on the staff of *ABC*, then the most influential Madrid daily, had already done enough to discount Hemingway's articles.

"As usual, I can count more on my enemies than my friends," Luis Miguel replied. The allegation that he had for years fought "fixed bulls" infuriated him even more. "Just look at Papa's face," Dominguín said bitterly. "It's as if Picasso had painted him with one mean eye that tells the whole story." He was pointing to a photograph of Hemingway in a recent issue of *Paris-Match*.

"We all have Picasso faces," I told him. "And as we get older the mean eye gets to be more noticeable."

We drove north to Mont de Marsan a day or two later, arriving as always late at night. The small bullring in the French town had been sold out weeks ahead. No ticket was available, so Luis Miguel arranged for me to stand in the *callejón*. He was fighting the next afternoon in Puerto Santa María and had requested permission to leave after killing his second bull, the fourth of the afternoon, which the local authorities had granted. We drove to the plaza together, and after wishing him luck I made my way along the narrow passageway to one of the *burladeros* reserved for managers and hangers-on.

Near where the percale fighting capes were being draped over the *barrera*, I encountered Papa. His face looked gaunt, his arms and chest those of a very old man. He gave me a bear hug and said, "Good to see you, boy!" Then after a pause he added, "I notice all the bullfighters have writers now." I replied that only his torero had a writer with the Nobel Prize, and he chuckled appreciatively.

The town band struck up a *paso doble*, and from across the ring the *paseo*, the ceremonial parade, began. I hurried on to the *burladero* that had been indicated to me as my place, and I watched Ordóñez, Luis Miguel, and a third bullfighter cross the ring. There was the usual practice swinging of the capes, and Luis Miguel took up his place inside the circle of sand, waiting for his first bull to come out.

He fought that day with his usual mastery, although he declined to place banderillas, which disappointed the public. But with the muleta he excelled himself and cut two ears. I moved over to where he was toweling off his face before taking a tour of the ring, and he glanced at me with a grim smile. "You have strange friends," he said drily. "Be ready to leave after the fourth bull," he added. "I've got a long drive ahead of me."

Forty-five minutes later, having cut another ear, he gestured for me to follow him, and I made my way toward one of the exits. Papa intercepted me. "Congratulate Miguel for me," he mumbled. I told him that I would and hurried on my way.

Teodoro had parked the Mercedes outside the service entrance so that we would be able to make a speedy getaway. I got into the back of the car and delivered Papa's message. "He nodded to me," Miguel replied, "but I looked the other way. I'm not even going to be polite anymore." Nothing more was said during the drive back to Biarritz.

In September I drove to Madrid, and Papa and I met for the last time at the Hotel Suecia, where he was staying. He invited me to lunch, and when I arrived in the dining room of the hotel, he and a large group were already at the table. The only person I recognized in Hemingway's entourage was Aaron Hotchner. The others were all strangers. I remember that a pleasant-looking French woman called Monique Lange was present, along with her young daughter, and that Papa recommended a novel she had written recently called *Les Plantanes*, which I later adapted to an ill-fated screenplay that was to be directed by Roger Vadim.

At the beginning of the meal Papa was a little distant. Then I realized that he seemed generally disconnected, removed from the scene around him, already buried in a private despair. The only person he favored with his attention was Monique Lange's daughter, a pretty child who seemed to intrigue the old man. *"Te amo,"* he said to her, raising his glass as if only her infantile innocence could move him. I left at the end of the meal feeling thoroughly depressed. Our friendship of so many years seemed to have ended, perhaps, I thought, because of the bitterness that had erupted between him and Luis Miguel. I regretted not being able to bridge the gulf that now appeared to exist between us.

LESS THAN A YEAR later I was back in Biarritz, staying in one of the least expensive rooms on the third floor of the Palais. The weather during the first two days of July was anything but summery. Heavy rain clouds had arrived from the north, with dark clouds hanging over the horizon of the Bay of Biscay. The air seeping in through the partially closed windows was cold, more like late autumn than midsummer. In less than a week the *feria* of San Fermín was scheduled to begin. Although I knew that the weather on the southern side of the Pyrenees was apt to be milder, it looked as if that year's festivities were certain to be menaced by intermittent rainstorms.

Deborah was due to join me in a few weeks, and in the meantime I spent most of the day at the typewriter. In midafternoon the telephone rang. It was Art Buchwald, calling from Paris. He said Irwin had told him where to reach me. His voice sounded unusually serious. A news flash had come into the office of the Paris *Herald Tribune* saying that Hemingway had been killed in a hunting accident in Ketchum, Idaho.

I was stunned. I knew that the partridge season in Idaho didn't open until September, and I told Art that the report was quite obviously false. But Buchwald insisted that Papa had been shot, killed by a blast from his own shotgun. Knowing how careful Hemingway had always been with weapons, I still refused to believe the news. Art said he would call me back within the hour, as soon as more news had come in on the wire.

Papa had been reported dead so often in the past that I thought there was a good chance the report was false. Then Art called a second time; Hemingway's death had been confirmed, and it was believed he had committed suicide. It seemed incredible, and yet he had spoken so often of his father's suicide that the fact that he had chosen the same fate had a frightening logic. I rose from the bed where I had been sitting with a heavy heart. Knowing that Ordóñez was staying in Biarritz prior to traveling to Pamplona, I called his hotel, but there was no answer in his room. Not wanting to remain alone, I set off into town to find him. In the middle of the shopping district was a bar called Le Royalty that was popular in those days before the season got into full swing. As I approached it I saw that Antonio was seated at a sidewalk table with two or three of his Spanish friends. He rose as I approached and embraced me. He had heard the news and was as grief-stricken as I was.

"He's gone," he said. "It's better for him," he added, slowly and thoughtfully, "even if it's bad for us." We walked down the crowded street together for a block or two without being able to find the right words to express our feelings. Then we turned back and said good-bye at the bar where I had found him. "I'll see you in Pamplona," he said and squeezed my shoulder.

In the days that followed the details of Papa's last few months were reported in the press. I called Bill Walton, a close friend of Papa's and mine, and he confirmed the facts of Papa's illness. He had been unable to write or read, Walton told me. The shock treatments he had been submitted to at the Mayo Clinic to cure him of his deep depressions had left him a shadow of his former self. Once he had returned to his home in Idaho it had been impossible to keep him away from the many guns he owned. So ultimately he had had his way and ended his own inner torment. Juan Belmonte, the legendary bullfighter, now in his late sixties, was quoted as saying *"Ha hecho bien, Don Ernesto"*—

Ernest did the right thing. A year later, after a last ride around his ranch, Belmonte chose the same method to exit from his life.

Papa's violent end was as deeply upsetting as Capa's mortal wounding. The horror and finally the sadness were repeated, and what I felt that dark day in July was a sense of bereavement that went back over the years, a realization that Papa's judgments, his advice, his humor were all things of which those of us who knew him well were now forever deprived. There were, of course, people whose reaction was different—the many Papa had antagonized. Irwin was shocked upon hearing the news, but his bitterness did not follow Papa to his grave— Irwin was much too kind a man for that. James Jones, whom Papa had attacked inexplicably when *From Here to Eternity* was published, could not forget Papa's unjustified attacks decrying Jones's talent as well as accusing him of cowardice. Jim's remarks, expressed in the crudest terms, shocked Irwin, who loved Jimmy as I did. The vulgarity of his remarks bothered us both, even though we well understood his vindictiveness.

But other mutual friends who, like me, had known Hemingway for many years were deeply affected by a permanent sense of loss. We all knew that Papa had been capable of moments of malice, yet despite these occasional "black-ass moods," we had all come to appreciate his humor and his wisdom and the shy, affectionate side of his nature that was little known to the outside world. His friendship had been a major influence on all of our lives.

Today, rereading the pages of the published version of *The Dangerous Summer*, I am struck again by Hemingway's talent. His descriptions of the Spanish countryside and his ability to involve the reader in the events he describes still give evidence of his old magic. But I can't help feeling that much of what he might have written is missing. The book compares unfavorably with *Death in the Afternoon*, especially because one expects a great deal more of a mature writer who has returned to one of the passions of his youth, which by his own admission he had come to have grave doubts about. And much of it reads as if he were "throwing instead of pitching," words that he used with accuracy in a criticism of some of the passages in my second novel.

In this, his last reportage, he became too personally involved in the rivalry between Dominguín and Ordóñez because of his love and admiration for one of the contestants. His feelings for Antonio made him abandon his objectivity, and as a result he occasionally sounds mean-spirited, which is uncharacteristic of his later work. He admitted to me that he regretted some of the things he had written, but unfortunately he was not given enough time to apologize for the injustice of his supposedly objective report. He left behind him a man whose irreconcilable bitterness exists to this day. "Hemingway's Nobel Prize was merely the Marshall Plan working in reverse," Luis Miguel still proclaims whenever Papa's name is mentioned, hardly an accurate literary judgment, but proof that unlike the wounds the bulls had inflicted on his body, the wounds Hemingway had opened with his pen will never heal.

I WAS IN NO MOOD to return to Pamplona that year. However, I did continue going to the bullfight. One result of my occasional crossings of the Spanish border was my increasing friendship with Orson Welles. Like Hemingway's, Welles's *afición* was slackening, although his admiration for Ordóñez never faltered. His planned movie about an older man's obsession with a brilliant young matador was never realized. As was often the case, he became involved in other projects. He made a film based on Kafka's *The Trial*, and before he had finished editing it Lazar made a deal with *Life* magazine for me to write a profile on Orson. "Don't make it all a bouquet of roses," Swifty warned me at the outset. "Show his negative side as well."

It was undoubtedly sound advice, but as I explained to Lazar, I was not about to denigrate such a talented and loyal friend. Welles and I spent a week in Biarritz and San Sebastián together, and he was pleased to give a full account of his long, volcanic career. Then I joined him in Paris to have a look at a rough cut of the film. It was a dazzling masterpiece, faulty in many ways, but overpowering. I wrote an admiring article. The movie was released, but it failed despite mostly positive reviews. My article was never published, but our friendship flourished. Orson had won the confidence of a Spanish producer named José Vicuña, who, despite his misgivings, decided to finance a movie for Orson to write and direct. I suggested he read *The Survivors*, the play Irwin and I had written many years earlier. Welles did so and was enthusiastic about its possibilities.

I accepted a small fee and moved to Madrid so that Orson and I could work together on a first-draft script I had previously written. For three stormy weeks we worked together at his house in Aravaca. We quarreled so violently about some of the changes he suggested that Paula, his wife, would often come running down the stairs to the ground-floor studio where we stood facing each other, thinking she must make peace before we came to blows. But our differences of opinion were never personal and never for one instant affected our friendship. Most of the time he had his way about small changes of dialogue, and in the end we finished a shooting script with which we were both satisfied.

Then, faced with a budget that exceeded their expectations, José Vicuña and his brother Teddy lost heart. A month before Orson was to begin principal photography, the movie was canceled. As we were all friends, and as the play was returned to Irwin's and my ownership, I gave up the fee that had been promised me. It was a sad day, but the experience of working with Welles made up for my disappointment. "They're afraid I won't finish the movie on schedule and within the budget," Orson scoffed. "If they would only look at my record, they would realize that I never failed to fulfill my obligations," a perhaps not altogether accurate statement.

Orson was surprisingly philosophical in defeat. Other producers had failed him in the past, and he appeared to be resigned with his lot, although he was amazed that the money had "chickened out," as the budget was modest even by European standards. He went back to editing his own unfinished version of Don Quixote, which he had financed himself. He had a cutting room in the basement of his villa, complete with two moviolas, and almost as if to soothe his injured ego, he ran large sections of his film for me on the small screens of the expensive equipment. It was another of the many projects into which he put his own money but which never saw the light of day.

To finance his expensive madness (for he seemed to know that he would never be able to complete the film), he accepted acting roles in movies that he wasn't particularly interested in, such as one scene in Zinnemann's *A Man for All Seasons*, in which he portrayed the dying Cardinal Wolseley. Knowing that I was on good terms with Orson, Zinnemann questioned me about him prior to offering Welles the part. "He'll do it, and he'll be brilliant," I reassured Freddy. "But will he be difficult?" Freddy asked. "Sure, he'll be impossible, but it will be one of the highlights of your picture," a prophecy that turned out to be accurate.

When Akim Tamiroff died and deprived Welles of his Sancho Panza, he started a film about a movie director for which he prevailed upon John Huston to play the leading role. The story had had its beginning in his complex mind while following Antonio Ordóñez on one of his tours. Orson had always scoffed a little at Huston's personage, probably because he recognized a rival act when he saw one, but before they had finished the first week of working together he fell under the spell of John's charm and larger-than-life personality, feelings that were mutual. John told me that he had enjoyed the experience, one of his last acting assignments, because the movie was "such a desperate venture." Halfway through many of the scenes a bailiff would arrive to confiscate Orson's camera or the lighting equipment, which made work the kind of perilous undertaking John enjoyed, an adventure shared by desperate men that finally came to nothing.

Throughout these, Orson's last years, we often met, went to bullfights together, and enjoyed long and costly meals.

Unpredictable in his opinions, Orson was a most rewarding companion, although his disregard for money was alarming. Paula, his pretty Italian wife, became a close friend of Maridi, now Luis Miguel's mistress, and as a result Orson developed a great personal liking for the now retired Dominguín. I learned from Miguel that Paula was having an affair with a young Italian, a navigator with Al Italia. As Paula was constantly concerned about her lover's safety, she would come to Luis Miguel's apartment in Madrid to secretly telephone her lover at whatever airport his plane had landed. Luis Miguel complained good-naturedly about these repeated long-distance calls, saying that he might well be forced to return to the bullring to pay Mrs. Welles's telephone bill.

As Christmas approached, Orson informed me that he was planning to come to Klosters for the holidays so that his daughter Beatrice could enjoy a white Christmas. Paula and the child arrived in our village a few days before Orson, and Paula asked to have a word with me in private. She confessed that she was being unfaithful, adding that Orson knew her so well, was so keenly aware of all her moods, that he would guess the truth at once, and the prospect terrified her. They hadn't seen each other for many months, she explained. I suggested she remain calm and above all not volunteer the news of her adultery, as that might spoil the Yule festivities for all of us, advice that she agreed was sensible and that she was relieved to hear.

Orson arrived and seemed to enjoy being in Switzerland for the first time in his life. He was wined and dined by Irwin and Marian and spent many long hours talking to my mother about the theater, their mutual passion. Then one afternoon he took me aside to talk about Paula. "She seems so terribly nervous," he told me, "and she's so thin. I'm worried about her. I think what she needs is a good love affair."

He added, "It's a cure that's always done wonders for me," and roared with laughter. I didn't know what to say.

One night not long after his arrival, Deborah, Paula, Orson, and I went to dinner in the bar of the Chesa Grishuna, the charming small hotel that was still one of our favorite places. As we were led to our table, Orson suddenly bristled and stopped. Opposite us, sitting quietly tête-à-tête, I perceived Dee Hawks, Howard's most recent ex-wife, accompanied by a man I didn't know. "My God, is that that shit Jim Aubry sitting there?" Orson thundered. "Don't tell me I've come all this way just to run into that shit again!" I said, "Sssh, Orson," but there was no stopping him. "Don't sssh me, Peter," he said in a loud voice. "The man's a shit, and everyone knows it." He never explained his anger at Aubry, but needless to say the evening began under strained circumstances, until finally Dee and Aubry finished their dinner and left the restaurant with a polite nod in our direction.

On occasions like these—and this was not his only public outburst that I witnessed—Orson reminded me of my father. He too had had a volatile temper and had felt no restraint about making a scene in public when confronted with a person he considered to be a sworn enemy. He was also drawn to fly-by-night producers, partly I suppose because, like Orson, he had already antagonized the more legitimate ones somewhere along the way. Hollywood producers avoided Orson, although to a man they praised his great talent. He was considered by many people to be a *monstre sacré*, but in my dealings with him there was nothing monstrous about him. He was always most generous with his time and talent, and most rewarding as a companion.

He was plagued by bad luck but managed to rise above all of his disasters. A fire inside his house at Aravaca destroyed his files as well as most of the negatives of his "Quixote." He abandoned Europe and moved his family to Sidonia, Arizona, a hamlet that was a stop on the Union Pacific railway line and was thus easy to reach by train, so he could board a Pullman car from Union Station in downtown Los Angeles to return home. Later the Welleses went to live in Las Vegas to avoid state taxes. Orson's main source of income was from voice-overs on television commercials. Finally he bought a small house on North Stanley Drive in Hollywood that had the look of a miniature southern mansion, where he lived with Oya, a Yugoslav sculptor who had appeared briefly in a brilliant documentary he had made called *Fake*.

North Stanley Drive is in one of the districts that have fallen out of fashion with the years, a short street that runs north from Hollywood Boulevard and ends in the Hollywood Hills. It is a tidy but run-down lower-middle-class neighborhood, hardly the area you would expect a personality of his magnitude to select for living out his last years. From this miniature Tara he would venture forth each day to lunch at Ma Maison, a restaurant that was briefly in fashion and was run by the nephew of Claude Terrail, a well-known Paris restaurateur. Young Terrail was pleased and honored to have Welles as his daily customer and always kept the small table near the restrooms for his illustrious guest, allowing him to sign for his frequent meals.

Whenever I was in California I lunched with Orson at his favorite bistro. He was still lionized by many young actors and directors, among them Peter Bogdanovitch and Al Pacino; he admired talent in the young without a trace of bitterness. But he kept away from the big Hollywood parties to which he was occasionally invited and went only once to one of Irving Lazar's lavish soirees, where he enjoyed himself immensely but did not return. He muttered repeatedly to me that he was involved with "some middle-European hustlers and crooks" who were going to finance his next venture, but nothing ever resulted from these complex and mysterious dealings. He wrote several screenplays that have remained unproduced.

I saw him for the last time at the Hôtel de la Trémoille in Paris. I had asked him to read a play I had written, and as always he was brilliantly helpful, a source of wise and practical suggestions. He was immensely fat and wore a huge robe that covered him like a gray, wrinkled tent. He seemed incapable of movement. He had a small poodle that from time to time jumped up into his nonexistent lap to be fondled. He complained of being a prisoner in his hotel room. He, who had faithfully frequented Le Grand Véfours and many other expensive restaurants in the not too distant past, was now reduced to room service, meals on a tray, always accompanied by too much white wine.

It was anguishing to see him like that, and I knew he was rapidly approaching the end. However, his mind was as sharp and bright as it had always been, which I suppose was some sort of blessing. He said, "Dear Peter, it's wonderful to see you. You always manage to make me feel better, even now."

I started to leave, and he seemed incapable of rising from his armchair, which had been placed near the door so that he did not have to get up to admit the waiter. I couldn't imagine how he was capable of going to an airport and getting on a plane, but he did manage to return to California, where he died not too many months later. Beatrice, his daughter, came to Europe on her honeymoon, bringing her father's ashes with her. She was complying, I was told, with one of his last wishes: to have his ashes buried at Antonio Ordóñez's *finca* in Ronda. Ordóñez invited me to the brief ceremony that was to take place in his garden, but somehow I couldn't make myself go. Beatrice was also bearing her mother's ashes. Paula Welles had been killed in an automobile accident in Nevada not long after Orson's death, and she had wanted her remains to be buried in Italy, the country of her birth. It was a strangely macabre mission for a young woman to undertake while on her honeymoon.

I remembered her as a child, her pretty face expressionless while she danced flamenco at her parents' bidding, delighting an already overweight Orson with the graceful movements of a *sevillana*, so similar in bearing and facial features to the way he looked as a young man. Her performance, I remember, took place in a deserted patio of the Hotel Alfonso XIII in Seville at *feria* time and was delightful. It brought tears to her father's eyes, although he managed to continue puffing on a huge cigar.

IN A LONG LIFE I have always been lucky to have a great many friends. The friendship that lasted the longest and that never wavered was that of Irwin Shaw. For fifty years we never exchanged a cross word and were never estranged, not even for one day. Yet his appearance in these reminiscenses is fragmentary. The reasons I have avoided a more detailed account of our friendship are twofold: first, it would take another volume to tell the story and, second, I never thought of his friendship as being in the least way dangerous. As we first met when I was nineteen years old, he knew me well enough not to have any false illusions about my character. Unlike Huston and Hemingway, he was well aware that I was never tempted to prove my manhood by seeking out a more perilous existence than being a writer (which had always seemed perilous enough to both of us), knew I wanted merely to live a full life by enjoying my work and my leisure, aims that he also seemed to share. Irwin's main criticism of my lifestyle was my inability to spend as many hours seated in front of the typewriter as he did, a justified censure. Yet he was always loyal and supportive and generous to a fault in every possible way.

I realized with alarm as we grew older that there was a self-destructive strain in his character, which ultimately brought on his premature end, and once he was no longer there my life changed radically. I found that Klosters, where we had both made our headquarters for more than thirty years, was no longer a place I wanted to spend most of my time. The village and the surrounding mountains we had both loved began to remind me too insistently of the lifelong friendship we had shared. A few of our old cronies were still around, but that did nothing to ease the feeling of melancholy that I found oppressive in spite of the beauty and comfort of the home I shared with Deborah.

Not only is Irwin no longer there, but many other familiar faces are absent from the streets of the village and the ski runs that lead down into that lovely valley. Capa has gone to his grave long ago, and Tola Litvak and Sophie are dead, as are many of my other skiing friends. My mother lies buried in the small cemetery behind the Protestant church, and Garbo, who outlived her for more than a decade, no longer takes her solitary walks through the summer meadows and stops at our chalet for lunch. Bob and Kathy Parrish, although happily still very much alive, have sold their house and come back only once in a while for a nostalgic visit. Nor do Irving and Mary Lazar come to Klosters anymore.

Periodically I have been tempted to move, but Deborah, like most women, resists all change. Then, too, I often recall one of Papa's last words of advice: "As you grow old, it is better to defend what you have." And so I spend most of my time in the south of Spain, in a small house near Marbella that Deborah and I purchased twenty years ago as a summer residence. Marbella is a town that changes so rapidly day by day that nostalgia is out of the question. The climate is almost as good as advertised: not quite Mediterranean, which makes for a wilder sea. I have a large variety of undangerous friends who, with the exception of Luis Miguel, are not connected to my past and are most willing to help me enjoy the present. With its atmosphere of accelerated growth, it seems at times an odd place to have landed, but the natives are friendly, and the air is as yet unpolluted. In contrast to the higher altitude of Klosters, I find that my bones and muscles do not yet remind me too often of the many years I have depended on them for the variety of sports I have always enjoyed that have never failed to provide me with a sense of well-being.

So I am not inclined to berate the rapid change that has transformed what was once a pleasant fishing village into a noisy town that for many of its citizens has outgrown its original charm. And when I look up at the peaks and foothills of the Sierra Blanca, which are not unlike the Santa Monica mountains of my childhood but are sufficiently different just the same, the frivolous thought occasionally occurs to me that someday a rich Arab might come along, buy them, and take them away. It is not an altogether alarming notion. It provides me with a false feeling of comfort to offset the growing realization of my own impermanence.

Index